SAMUEL PEPYS

The Man in the Making

By the Same Author

KING CHARLES II

THE ENGLAND OF CHARLES II

THE YEARS OF ENDURANCE 1793–1802

YEARS OF VICTORY 1802–1812

ENGLISH SAGA 1840–1940

SAMUEL PEPYS:

THE YEARS OF PERIL

THE SAVIOUR OF THE NAVY

ETC., ETC.

SAMUEL PEPYS

aet. 34

SAMUEL PEPYS

The Man in the Making

ARTHUR BRYANT

'Mens cujusque is est quisque'

COLLINS
FOURTEEN ST. JAMES'S PLACE LONDON

First edition 1933
New edition 1947
Reprinted January 1948
Reprinted October 1948
Reprinted July 1949
Reprinted October 1954
Reprinted September 1959

PRINTED IN GREAT BRITAIN
COLLINS CLEAR-TYPE PRESS : LONDON AND GLASGOW

TO

THE CAST OF

THE GREENWICH PAGEANT

IN AFFECTION AND

GRATITUDE

CONTENTS

ILLUSTRATIONS

MAPS

PREFACE

It is fourteen years since this volume was published for the tercentenary of Pepys' birth and in the year of Hitler's rise to power. That power has since been destroyed with the aid of the instrument of force which Pepys spent his life in fashioning. But for the Royal Navy we could not have survived in 1940. Nor could we and our allies have liberated Europe.

For Samuel Pepys was the creator of three remarkable, and still surviving, things. The first, in the order of their making, was his Diary. The second was the civil administration of the Admiralty—the rule and order that still give permanence to the material form, fighting traditions and transmitted knowledge of the Royal Navy. A century after Pepys' death, at a time when his achievement as a diarist was unknown and his name almost forgotten, Lord Barham—the man who shares with him the honour of being England's greatest naval administrator—testified that there was not a department of the Admiralty that was not governed by the rules he had laid down in the seventeenth century. It was Pepys who made the scabbard for the sword that Nelson, and the heirs of Nelson, used.

Pepys' third creative achievement sprang from the second. He has been described as the father of the Civil Service. Here, too, his orders hold. The rules he laid down and the administrative principles he elucidated have become part of the continuing life of his country. His family may have grown somewhat large of late, but it is still governed by the moral standards, integrity and tradition of inflexible service on which in his lifetime he insisted. It has become in the course of generations what he strove to make it: a permanent watchdog against corruption.

Yet the work for which Pepys is best remembered and loved remains his Diary. It extends to over a million and a quarter words: the length of a dozen fair-size novels. After three centuries, there is not a page in it that does not arrest the reader and quicken his perception of humanity. It is probably the most searching and honest record of a man's daily doings ever penned. It is also one of the most vivid. As historical material I know of nothing with such power to recreate the thought and daily *minutiae* of a vanished age. It is strange to reflect that this wonderful achievement should have been wrought at the end of crowded days of labour—the record of which is to be found not in the Diary but in Pepys' vast collection of naval and administrative papers.

In this volume, covering the first thirty-six years of his life and the whole span of the Diary, I have tried to blend these two sources into a composite picture of a great Englishman's development. It is a story complete in itself and independent of what follows in the volumes I have written on Pepys' later life—"The Years of Peril" and "The Saviour of the Navy". It records a European War, a Fire of London, an Economic Crisis and a Revolution. Since I wrote it we have experienced two of these and are passing through the others. It may help to set our ordeal in perspective to read with what courage Pepys faced these shadows.

ARTHUR BRYANT

Rapsgate
May 1947

SHORTENED PEDIGREE OF SAMUEL PEPYS

to illustrate the relationships referred to in this volume.

(A full pedigree will be included in the second volume.)

The Pepyses of Cottenham from whom also descended the Pepyses of Norfolk, John Pepys of Ashtead, Thomas Pepys of Hatcham, Mrs Norton, Mrs Jane Turner, etc.

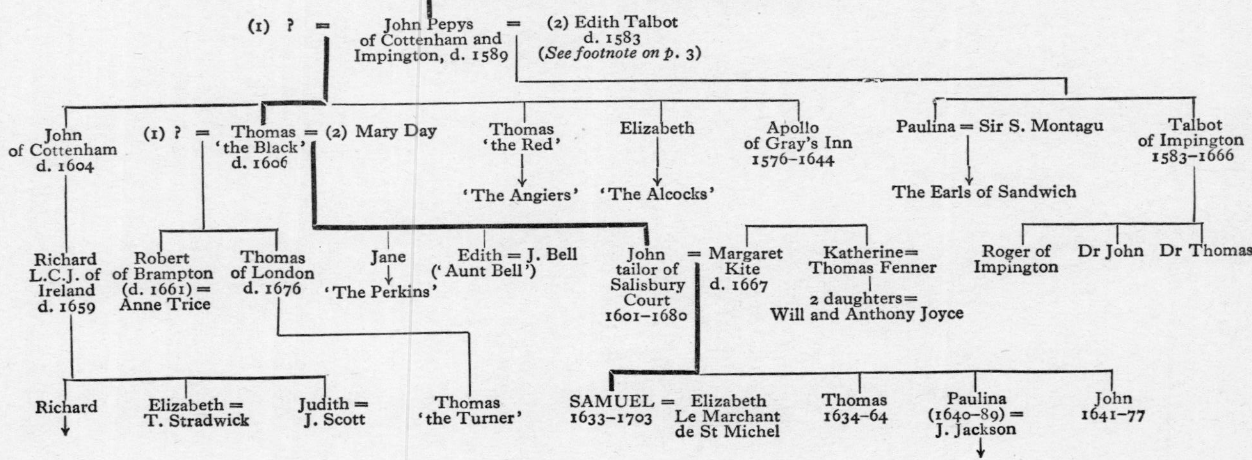

Chapter I

The Infant Samuel

"... Walked over the fields to Kingsland, and back again; a walk, I think, I have not taken these twenty years; but puts me in mind of my boy's time, when I boarded at Kingsland, and used to shoot with my bow and arrows in these fields. A very pretty place it is; and little did any of my friends think I should come to walk in these fields in this condition and state that I am."
Diary, May 12th, 1667.

North of Cambridge lie the Fens. The sea from which they arose laps at their northern boundaries and north and east great rivers lazily wind across them, drawing black cattle to drink among the sedges at their brink. This land would be one of silence, were it not for the innumerable company of larks, of bittern, coot and moorhen, of sedge warblers and reed sparrows, which ever provides it with a faint and not discordant music. In summer it is still, as the monk William of Huntingdon remembered it, a land of clouds and orchards and golden corn. Yet it is so only by right of battle waged ceaselessly by its inhabitants against the invading armies of water. Whenever civilisation has receded—when Roman legion fell back or monastery bell was silenced—the waters have taken back their own. Salt tides have swept in with the winter gales through forsaken walls, and the rivers have flowed out, cold and remorseless, over the fields and houses of man.

Winter mist and the horizons of summer have left their age-long impress on the fenman's mind. He is imaginative, quick to dream and quick to fear; on the confines of life for him hover ever the legions of the unknown—fiends and apparitions that arise out of the "hideous fen" and beckon him on through bramble and briar to the dark waters. Therefore he holds hard to life, dreading to lose even for a moment his grip on material things. Fog, damp, cold and ague have given him a fine zest for food and drink, and the hot summer's sun warming his fertile land inclines him to be amorous. Fighting against the slow and relentless ways of water, he is patient and untiring in labour: and from these things, for all his fears, his great heart is formed. For he holds his fruitful fields by right of work and courage.

Out of this land came the Pepyses. For centuries they had grazed and ploughed, haggled at markets over country wares and peered at the fen skies. Villeins as they were in breed and tenure, they had yet contrived to raise themselves from the black mud beneath them. For though the Pepyses were no great folk themselves, they were quick to recognise those who were. To the monasteries whose towers rose on the horizon they had clung, climbing thereby inch by inch out of the marshes. For two hundred and fifty years the Abbey of Crowland was served in all its clerical and agricultural needs by "Pepizes". Reeves, rent-collectors, haywards, granators, a long line of office holders slowly learnt to forget the servile taint in their blood and to despise the ways of manual labour.* Administration grew to be their hereditary craft.

By the fifteenth century the race had become of definite importance in the fen villages north of Cambridge. Three

* I owe this commentary on the early descent of the Pepyses to the learned researches of Miss F. M. Page, whose study of the Estates of Crowland Abbey is being published as Volume II of the "Cambridge Studies in Economic History".

Pepyses in turn were bailiffs to the Abbots of Crowland, hard-headed men wringing the fruits of the soil from the rustics for their masters and dying in an odour of appropriate sanctity, leaving silver pieces for dirges to be chanted in the high choirs for their souls. One of these rural bureaucrats settled at Cottenham, where a tiny eminence marks the higher level of south Cambridgeshire from the limitless sea of fen. Here, in substantial ownership of rental, tithing and granary, the Pepyses survived when the monasteries by which they had risen went down in the cataclysm of 1539. The new era of free competition was not unfavourable to the race, for they had already learnt to use their elbows. Half a century later John Pepys of Cottenham bought with his second wife's* dowry the Manor of Impington and settled it on the infant offspring of the match. Then in 1589 he died, leaving the six-year-old squire, Talbot Pepys, to the guardianship of his elder sons, John of Cottenham, Thomas the Red, Apollo and Thomas the Black. The last-named, who married Mary Day of Wisbech, had three daughters and three sons. Of these the youngest, John, who was born at Impington in 1601, finding Cottenham a little overstocked with Pepyses, went to

* It is difficult to believe that Edith Talbot was anything but John Pepys' second wife. The lady was, in a modest way, an heiress and was left by her father, Edmund Talbot of Cambridge, £40, "with my sovereign of gold and chalis of silver, and six silver spoons and a covering to a satte of silver double gilt, with all my messuages, lands etc. in the Fen and in Wisbeache and else where in the Isle of Ely, with my messuage at Impington which I lately bought". The evidence in favour of her being John's second wife is twofold; that the youngest son, Talbot, was left the manor of Impington and a squirearchal rank never attained by his elder brothers, and that this child was christened with the name of Talbot. The inference is that John Pepys of Cottenham, like his grandson Samuel, waxed rich with passing years, and that his second marriage was consequently a much grander affair than his first. Hence the Pepysian squires of Impington.

London at the age of fourteen as a tailor's apprentice. After serving his time he set up on his own as one of a little group of "foreign" tailors who, not being London born and of the privileged Guild of Merchant Tailors, traded under certain rather dubious rights in the neighbourhood of Blackfriars and Salisbury Court. Here he took a long lease of a house, abutting westward into St Bride's Churchyard and eastward into Salisbury Court, and peaceably practised his craft. A meek, mild, pious man, he married at the age of twenty-four Margaret Kite, the sister of a Whitechapel butcher—a young woman of humble stock who before marriage had been a washmaid. Poor John might well have made a happier choice, for though like him she was pious, she was neither meek nor mild. But she bore him eleven children and thereby did the world some service. For the fifth of these, and the third to survive infancy, was Samuel, who was born above his father's shop on February 23rd, 1633. Thence eight days later he was carried to the font of St Bride's Church across the way and baptised into the Anglican Communion.[1]

Such events, during Samuel's earliest years, were not uncommon in the Pepys family, and the subsequent burials of little brothers and sisters in the green plot without, which was at once their playground and their resting-place, almost as frequent. Besides his elders Mary and John, there was a new brother, Tom, in the summer of 1634, a sister Sarah a year later, a brother Jacob (who died in the same year) in 1637, and another, Robert, in 1638. To support so constant a succession of mouths, the family had to live frugally, and life at first must have seemed rather a scramble to little Samuel.[2]

Yet in the seventeenth century even the younger son of a humble London tailor was born into a cheerful and lively heritage. At the end of the courtyard into which his father's front door looked were the cobbles of Fleet Street, with the wooden water conduit and its little doors to beckon one on. Beyond, a whole world of colour, movement and noise was calling. Here on the cobbles was stirring drumming, as carts and coaches rumbled down narrow posted streets and apprentices bawled their wares at the passers by. Overhead painted wooden houses leant together till young Jessica could whisper to Lorenzo from the attic casement, and gilded signs —flower pots, grasshoppers, silver luces—creaked and swung on iron frames. And from every alley and courtyard came smells of wine and tobacco from taverns where Falstaff's cronies still drank and sang—the "Black Spread Eagle" in Bride's Lane or the little alehouse in Popinjay Alley—of rich fats cooking in gossips' kitchens and the hot rank odour of crowded humanity. For when Samuel peered out of his father's window it was Shakespeare's London he looked upon.[3]

Along the skyline ran the spires and bell towers of a hundred and nine churches, crowded together within the liberties of a medieval city and chiming, as the hours passed, their litany of prayer and praise. But beneath these lay another city, given over to merchandise and the fierce, fibre-bracing competition for wealth of a new world. The men who thronged the churches on Sundays struggled furiously for the wages of mammon all the week: the wharves piling along the river, the pent-houses that huddled against every open wall, the shops that projected far out into the ever-narrowing roadways, all bore witness to the intensity of this service. Even in the nave of St Paul's itself, far beneath the great roof, the money-changers and vendors did their business. Notices of servants for hire were posted on the pillars; sharks, gulls and courtesans pressed together; and the noise was as that of bees, a strange humming or buzz, mixed of walking tongues and feet, "a kind of still roar or loud whisper". Only in the evening the clamour of the merchants and the rumble of wheels ceased; then lights shone in latticed windows and lanterns swung in the wind as the moon came up above the tall white chimneys and song floated from tavern doors; and, when all was dark, the chimes broke the silence, and the watchman's call:

> Take heed to your clock; beware your lock,
> Your fire and your light, and God give you good-night,
> One o'clock!

Beyond the city lay England. It was still a land of great open fields and few hedges, of little farms and sheepcotes and poor pelting villages. Throughout that green and smiling countryside were scattered jewelled manor-houses, guarding and ruling, clusters of brick or stone barn and granary, bake-house and brewery, panelled hall and courtyard, and wide low upper chambers and gallery. Into this land old Izaak, the hosier, would slip away from Fleet Street with rod and angle and

> With his Bryan and a book
> Loiter long days by Shawford Brook,

to see the rosy milkmaids bring home the milk with song, and to land immortal fish. Here a squire and his friends could course a hare all day on open down, and, far away among the Devonshire orchards, the rector of Dean Prior could scorn the lure of the town and sing of

> ...blossoms, birds and bowers,
> Of April, May, of June and July flowers,
> Of Maypoles, hock-carts, wassails, wakes,
> Of bridegrooms, brides and of their bridal cakes.

Here men and their ways were unchanging, and the old cycle of the year, with its work and play, was unbroken, from the New Year, when the village boys came round with the wassail bowl to bless beast and barn and tool, through bleak Lent days and February-fill-the-dyke to the green joys of Easter; from summer wakes and Harvest Home and the hock-cart, with its bacon, beer and steaming frumenty, through November haze and the mystic rites of All Hallow Tide to the carols and the mumming players and the sweet wintry festival of Christ's birth:

> Thy nut-brown mirth, thy russet wit,
> And no man pays too dear for it.

To all this world of eager, passionate life a seventeenth-century child was born heir. Yet it was a heritage none the less which Samuel's parents did their best to keep from him. For the outlook and habits of that middle class of citizen to which they belonged had already been revolutionised by the translation of the Bible into the vernacular. In the course of two generations the hot ferment of Hebrew fervours, Hebrew taboos and Hebrew jealousies working on the literal and somewhat childlike English mind had given rise to that mighty force which we call Puritanism and to a new breed of Englishmen nursed in its principles—ordered, self-righteous and conscious of a divine mission. The process had been so swift that the educated rulers of England were almost entirely blind to it; Charles I and Laud never realised its existence till it overwhelmed them. The infant Samuel who was born in 1633 when that process was in its midst inherited the zest for life of the older England to which his forbears had belonged; but the training of his childhood formed him against nature as a pioneer of the new—industrious, respectable and jealously watchful of his own integrity.

Therefore the kindly, careful, Bible-reading tailor and his shrewish, ill-lettered wife taught Samuel and his brethren to beware of the world which called to them so boisterously—the fine courtiers and ladies who glittered from the coaches outside the shop, the open doors of the lit taverns where ancient Pistol still fought and toyed with Doll Tearsheet, the beckoning sluts across the way in Fleet Alley. They made it plain to their little ones that the joys that London offered at such easy terms must lead to poverty in this world and hell-fire in the next; it was evil to dance, to play at cards, to bedeck the body for love, to visit an alehouse. Instead they taught them the psalms of David, crowded them on Sabbath mornings and afternoons into the family pew at St Bride's (varying the goodly fare sometimes by waiting in the crush outside some popular place of worship till the doors opened to admit them to the glories of Puritan eloquence within), and impressed on them the importance of tidiness, punctuality and keeping out of debt. For the most part the seed fell upon barren ground, for of Samuel's brothers and sisters, most died and the survivors proved but stony places. But some fell upon good ground and in due time and after many set-backs brought forth fruit.[4]

Most of the grown-ups who surrounded Samuel in his early years were of the same careful and pious strain. There was his uncle Thomas Pepys, a close cunning fellow who brought up his own children in the strictest school of fanaticism; his father's half-brother, sober, substantial Mr Wight, the fishmonger; his mother's beggarly relations, Kite the butcher and Fenner the blacksmith, with their sober wives; and Aunt James, "a poor, religious, well meaning, good, humble soul, talking of nothing but God Almighty". This slightly forbidding band, in sombre-coloured cloak and high hat, was mostly encountered on the Sabbath, when they gathered to gossip over dinner before the afternoon service or round the supper table afterwards.[5]

Yet Puritanism could not take all the colour and savour of life from the ken of an eager and loving little boy. One could always slip away into the noisy streets, dive among the carts and coaches on the house-crowned bridge or take boat to Southwark where amid a rocking, shouting crowd one might watch yelping curs tossed roof-high by bulls in the Bear-Garden or sit, breathless and entranced, listening to Shakespeare's magic ranted from the high boards of the Bankside playhouses. From the first the theatre had a remarkable fascination for little Samuel; whenever he could he would squeeze into the "Red Bull" in Clerkenwell to hear some blood and thunder melodrama; and once, being a pretty child, he was all but beguiled into playing the girl Arethusa's part at a performance of *Philaster* at the house of the magnate, Sir Robert Cooke. (In after years it amused him to think that he should have been chosen to represent a beautiful woman.) It was pleasant in summer to run down the steep alleys to the riverside and, splashing through the mud, bathe one's legs in the cool water while one shouted time-honoured gibes at the passing watermen, or to accompany one's parents on Sunday afternoons through the fields to Islington where one could blow oneself out on old Pitt's cakes and ales at the "King's Head" and throw stones at the ducks in the pond outside. And when the round of winter games in the churchyard or Bride's Lane with one's brothers and sisters flagged, there was always a wealth of free sights—the constable carrying some malefactor to the stocks with all the boys and girls of the parish running after, or a fire, or a street brawl, as the churned-up muck from the kennel flew to left and right; or sometimes one might stand on the wheel of a cart to see a hanging, while the prisoner lengthened the thrilling suspense by long prayers and orations in the hope of a reprieve. Nor was there any lack of festivals and ceremonies to break the monotony of the days; Shrove Tuesday with its fritters or Holy Thursday when Sam with other little boys walked the parish bounds in procession with a broom-staff in his hand, and the great annual Fair of St Bartholomew where all London forgot for once to be Puritan as it gaped with delight before apes that danced on ropes, girls in tights, nimble fellows who walked on their hands with their feet tied to their posteriors, and appraised such rarities as horses with hoofs like ram's horns, geese with four feet and cocks with three.[6]

For the rest, Pepys' early infancy revolved round the family hearth in that little square of ground between Salisbury Court and St Bride's Churchyard, where now the wares of Messrs Watney, Combe and Reid are sold to the patrons of the "White Swan"—the shop below where his father and his men would sit at their work cutting and stitching, the kitchen where on weekdays they all ate and drank, the little room where important family consultations were held, the attics, three stories high under the gables, where the children slept. It was, in its sober, frugal way a good home of the middle sort, entailing on its members at least an outward respect, if no great constancy of practice, for things godly: thirty years later, after the Restoration, one of them was still signing himself—"I take leave as ever to be, Your truly loving brother till death". Outside work, religion, and domestic economy, its chief pursuit was music; for in this universal English pastime even the Puritans delighted. It was a particular pleasure of tailor John's when the day's labour was done, to take his old bass viol and play; at such moments the good, easy man grew quite lively. And in this, his favourite recreation, he found his son Samuel a wonderfully apt pupil.[7]

Though the John Pepys *ménage* was a humble one, it had its affinity to more important households. The soil of Cottenham had proved prolific, and not all of the race were the younger sons of younger sons. A few yards down Salisbury Court was the house of another John Pepys, a Templar,* who had an estate in the country and kept his own coach. He was descended, however, through four generations of Norfolk gentlemen, from the same stock as his humble neighbours and namesakes—one of the old bailiffs of Crowland—and, having a kind, merry daughter who loved children, acknowledged the kinship and showed his young cousins much friendship. One of Samuel's greatest treats was to be asked to stay at old John Pepys' country house at Ashtead on the Epsom Downs—a grand place it seemed to him then, though in after years he found it not quite so imposing. Here he and his brothers and sisters would gorge themselves with mulberries in the garden, play with Peter, their host's man, who would let them blindfold him in their games, or lose themselves among the hazels and bushes of the little wood behind the house, and on Sundays giggle at the pompous sermons of the poor dull country parson in Epsom Church. In after years, "Ashsted, my old place of pleasure", was a very dear memory to Samuel Pepys.[8]

Another early recollection of the country centred in the village of Kingsland, a mile or two to the north of the City. Here, when he was still a child, Samuel, with his brother Tom —a year younger than himself—was boarded for a time at

* He had actually risen in the law by his adherence to rough old Lord Chief Justice Coke, whose Marshal he had been and for whom he had devilled many years before in the examination of the Gunpowder Plot conspirators. But this Samuel did not know till many years later; at the time when he first set eyes on him, John Pepys was nearly sixty and a man of great dignity. *C.S.P.D.* Oct. 9th, 1612; *Diary*, Jan. 30th, 1668.

the house of an old nurse, Goody Lawrence. It was a pleasant spot, where a little boy could roam over the fields towards Islington shooting with his bow and arrows. "A very pretty place it is", he commented twenty years later, "and little did any of my friends think I should come to walk in these fields in this condition and state that I am". They may be pardoned for their lack of foresight, for at Kingsland Sam was very small fry indeed; his aunt, Ellen Kite, was a servant at Mrs Herbert's, the local chatelaine's, at Newington Green. His stay at Kingsland was probably due to his health. Every summer he became exceedingly hot and broke out in pricklings and itchings all over his arms, breast, thighs and legs; in the winter, on the other hand, upon the least taking of cold, his nose swelled, his water stopped and he suffered from an agony of suppressed wind. And at all times he was subject to a constant pain in the kidneys, accompanied every now and then by the most distressing manifestations.* 9

When Samuel was seven, he lost his eight-year-old brother and playfellow John. In the same December the eldest of the family, thirteen-year-old Mary, followed her brother to the grave in St Bride's Churchyard, the little cortège of mourners marching down Salisbury Court to Fleet Street and thence into the church. Samuel was now left his father's eldest child. A year later two more deaths took place in the house —those of Sarah Pepys, aged five, and Barbara Williams, the family servant. The years that saw these domestic revolutions witnessed upheavals of a larger kind. In November, 1640, the Long Parliament met and all London turned out to watch its ear-cropped martyr, Prynne, ride in from West-

* "I remember not my life without the pain of the stone in the kidneys (even to the making of bloody water upon any extraordinary motion) till I was about twenty years of age." *Rawlinson MSS. A.* 185, ff. 206–13.

minster amid a concourse of shouting thousands with sprigs of bay and rosemary in every hat. It was the herald of revolution. All that winter the City was in a ferment, the cry of "Reformation!" going up ceaselessly against King, Court and Prelate, and the rabble surging into Westminster Hall, hooting the King's officers, affronting the Lords and thrusting leeks under Archbishop Laud's very nose. In the spring of 1641 blood was let, a vast crowd standing in tense thousands on Tower Hill to watch Strafford's head fall. But the nation's fever still continued, and before Pepys was nine the King strode down with armed men to Westminster to arrest the five members, and his proud, independent capital opened its gates to shelter them. The autumn of 1642 saw the London apprentices barring Prince Rupert's path with a hedge of 20,000 pikes on Turnham Green, while John Milton pinned a sonnet to his doorpost to bid Cavalier Captain, Colonel or Knight-at-arms spare the Muse's bower. Barricades sprang up along the Chelsea Road, suburban Hyde Park Corner became a fort, trenches were dug on Constitution Hill. Englishman sprang to arms to slay Englishman.[10]

How much of these events little Samuel witnessed we do not know. Somewhere about his tenth year he left London for his native country. There were still Pepyses in "Cottenhamshire", and at Impington Sam's great-uncle, Talbot Pepys, the old Elizabethan, ruled the manor. Though a great man in his own little world—he was a Bencher of the Temple, Recorder of Cambridge and had represented that borough in Parliament—Talbot had not forgotten the half-brothers who had cared for him during his minority and was always ready to befriend their grandchildren. Two hours' ride to the west were other Pepyses. One of Talbot's sisters had married a Huntingdonshire squire, Sir Sidney Montagu, who in 1627 had bought the Priory house of Hinchingbrooke from the ruined spendthrift, Sir Oliver Cromwell. Lady Montagu had been accompanied on her migration from Impington to Huntingdon by her brother, Apollo Pepys, who seems to have attached himself to his brother-in-law and settled with him at Hinchingbrooke. Apollo was a man of some distinction, a lawyer like his half-brother, a Pensioner of Gray's Inn and at one time a Recorder of Cambridge. He was of a neat person, with a trim Elizabethan beard as befitted the far period from which he hailed, and at the time of his great-nephew's departure from London, rising seventy years of age. It was possibly through his agency that little Samuel was placed for a while at the Free School at Huntingdon—one of England's fine old provincial grammar schools and one which thirty years before had nursed the boisterous youth of Oliver Cromwell.[11]

At Huntingdon Sam was among friends. Besides old Apollo and the Montagus at Hinchingbrooke, his father's elder brother, Robert Pepys, was settled a mile away at Brampton, where he possessed a small landed property and the widow of one Trice, who had brought him several children by her former husband. Nor did Samuel's Huntingdon relations end there, for by a curious chance his mother's sister, Elizabeth Kite, had married a local fellmonger and Alderman of the town, one John Barton. Another cousin, Tom Alcock, was his schoolfellow.[12]

Samuel's stay at Huntingdon was not a long one—enough to make him count among his acquaintances in later years such local worthies as Lewis Phillips, the lawyer, Robert Barnwell, the steward at Hinchingbrooke, and Tom, the tapster at the "Crown". Beyond the little town there was nothing to impress a lad used to the clatter of Fleet Street: the slow melancholy Ouse and the watery fields of Portholme, the woods towards Grafham and the corn on the

Huntingdonshire uplands. He remembered better the places passed through on his occasional journeys to town—always exciting events—the badness of the Baldock lanes, old Brecock, best of hosts, at Stevenage and Lord Salisbury's noble gardens at Hatfield. Yet even Huntingdon had its occasional excitements in those days. In the summer of 1642, Captain Walton raised the Trained Bands of the county for the Parliament, abetted by Lewis Phillips, who refused the Sheriff's orders to proclaim the King's Commission of Array, while Henry Cromwell, bearing the royal sign-manual in his pocket, rode through the town with fifty armed men. A year later, Captain Oliver Cromwell was in Huntingdon recruiting that "lovely company" "of honest sober Christians", who, as the nucleus of his Ironsides, were to cast the kingdoms into a new mould. The Pepys clan was as divided as the Cromwells. Of the sentiments of Sam's Puritan father and mother there could be little doubt, and Uncle Robert of Brampton was transmogrified through the Parliamentary militia into a Captain, but old Uncle Apollo, being an Elizabethan, had been accustomed to honour the King's majesty and deplored the wars. In this he was at one with his brother-in-law, Sir Sidney, who, for refusing to take the oath to live and die with the Parliamentary Captain-General, Essex, was lodged for a while in the Tower. In 1644, when the war was at its height, the two old friends died within a few weeks of each other, Apollo lamenting his ruined estate, scattered in the hands of other men and the calamitous times in which his last days were cast. Yet Sir Sidney's heir, Edward Montagu, like most of the younger generation, was passionate for the cause of Reform and, with eager hero-worship, followed his neighbour, Oliver Cromwell, into the field. In such an atmosphere Samuel could scarcely fail to grow up a Roundhead.[13]

Before the triumph of Parliament was complete, the boy was back in London. Five minutes' walk from his father's house, where the booksellers' shops crowded up to the walls of the cathedral, lay the school of St Paul's, which Dean Colet had founded as a seminary for the New Learning five generations back. Here in a world of bells, books and switches, with the roar of the City just beyond the schoolroom, Pepys spent the last years of his boyhood. Here, as a little lad, he came to say his Catechism and write his name, paying 4*d.* to the poor scholar who swept the room, and took his place thereafter in the Vestibulum where the children of the lower forms were instructed in the elements of the Latin tongue, the Catechism and Christian manners. All round him on the walls were those long Latin inscriptions which good Dr Colet had delighted to set up, intimations of his mind and intentions, even on the very windows where teacher and taught could read their duty: "*Aut doce, aut disce, aut discede*". Accidence and Grammar, Livy, Virgil and Cicero and thence to Aristotle and Thucydides; Aeschylus, Sophocles and Aristophanes, Samuel followed the well-trodden path by which Paul's scholars climbed to the Eighth Form, becoming thereby "perfect grammarians, good Orators and Poets, well instructed in Latin, Greek and Hebrew". Samuel was never perhaps all these things, but he acquired enough learning at least to pass for a learned man and to love good, worthy books of all kinds. In after years he could read for pleasure Cicero's Oration against Catiline, correct (a little falteringly) his younger brother's Greek orations and entertain a Dutch Admiral, who had no English or French, in Latin. It was certainly more than most public men of to-day inherit from their schooling. Here also Pepys made some friends and many acquaintances—his favourite, Jack Cole, ingenious, witty, erratic; John Powel; good, honest Dick Cumberland, the tailor's son, to whom in later years he would gladly have given his sister and who rose from such humble beginnings to be a philosopher, a mathematician and a bishop; Jonathan Radcliffe; William Brownlow; learned Richard Meggott—he also rose to some eminence; Henry Yelverton; Tom Davies; Christmas the mimic; Bernard Skelton; and silly, importunate, impertinent Robert Elborough, who was the butt of everyone's sport and afterwards became a curate and preached "in as right a parson-like manner...as I have heard anybody". Over all these Grecian lads presided the Puritan antiquary, Dr Langley, whose awful presence and speech "struck mighty respect and fear into his scholars", which however—it is pleasant to know—"wore off a little after they were used to him". He composed for his charges (for which perhaps they did not thank him) a short Rhetoric and a compendious Prosodia, and was a friend of the learned Selden, whose long, spare figure, crooked nose and popping eye were often seen in the school—a circumstance which explains the young Clerk of the Acts' subsequent boast that he was acquainted with him.* He was assisted in his labours by Samuel Cromleholme, the Sur-master, a lover of books, antiquities and rarities, and a very worthy and imposing, if somewhat dogmatic, pedagogue.

In this atmosphere, Sam learnt to scan a mental horizon wider than was offered by the crowded household in Salisbury Court or the rustic world of Huntingdon. He spoke with learned fluency on Apposition Day of the seven Liberal Sciences, stood the cross-examination of the examiners in Latin, Greek and Hebrew before the assembled Governors of

* *D.* Nov. 29th, 1661: "I told Mr Coventry that I had heard Mr Selden often say that he could prove that in Henry VII's time he did give commissions to his captains to make the King of Denmark's ships to strike to him in the Baltic." This was, as Pepys admits, a lie.

the Mercers' Company and composed classical orations on the far from academic events which were moving the world of England without. But Pepys, as befitted a pupil of the most Puritan of English schools, was not in the least shocked by these tremendous changes; his young mind was by now far too liberal for that. A tailor's son with the learning of the ancient republican world at his finger tips could see nothing incongruous in the spectacle of stern and inspired graziers, attorneys and cobblers sitting in judgment on an anointed King. On January 30th, 1649, he stood in the street at Charing Cross and watched Charles I's dripping head held high above the block, and afterwards, as the snow fell on a saddened and bewildered England, confidently informed his fellows that, were he to preach a sermon on the event, his text would be: "The memory of the wicked shall rot". Pepys' politics were soon to undergo a drastic revision, but a clever lad of fifteen may be pardoned for being more radical and daring than his fellows. For the moment he was happy to mimic the flight of the eagles and train his unfledged wings to follow Cromwell and Milton and Harry Vane.[14]

Chapter II

First Manhood

"I by having but 3*d.* in my pocket made shift to spend no more, whereas if I had had more I had spent more as the rest did, so that I see it is an advantage to a man to carry little in his pocket." *Diary*. Feb. 16th, 1660.

A year later, in February, 1650, Samuel Pepys, now nearly seventeen, stood before the Master and Wardens of the Mercers' Company in their great hall as a petitioner for one of the Exhibitions for Paul's scholars, which lay within their grant. It was a momentous occasion in the boy's life, for on his success or failure his future career might depend. Trade was bad and the execution of kings and banishment of courts, however pleasing to the young republican mind, do not assist the tailoring business; and in the previous autumn the Merchant Tailors, finding business growing ever more restricted and taxes ever higher, had petitioned the Lord Mayor and Court of Aldermen to suppress their humble rivals the "foreign" tailors of Whitefriars and Salisbury Court. When John Pepys, good citizen, had gone as had been his wont for the past thirty years to St Sepulchre's to record his vote for the public officers of the coming year, his franchise had been denied him on the ground that he was no freeman, and in January, 1650, he had learnt that the Merchant Tailors were proposing to prosecute all "foreign" tailors within the City and Liberties. A week before his son's great ordeal before the Governors of St Paul's, the poor man had hastily and tearfully petitioned the proud Company for admission, offering to pay any sum within reason to obtain his freedom and so "avoid trouble and molestation". Under these circumstances there was little hope of Samuel's being able to continue his education without a scholarship. The Mercers sat with the scales of his future before them: on one side lay the paternal scissors and on the other the pen. The scales inclined, and Samuel Pepys, possessor of a Robinson Exhibition tenable at the University, resumed the pen.[1]

In June that summer Pepys was admitted as a Sizar on the boards of Trinity Hall, Cambridge, where his cousin, Dr John Pepys, the second son of his great-uncle Talbot of Impington, was a Fellow. The University, in keeping with the rest of England, was undergoing a strenuous purge from the nation's new rulers; a republican test had been tendered to the holders of all offices and fellowships, and those honest enough not to take it had been expelled. In the nearby college of Magdalene, where a particularly drastic purge had been applied, a hot Puritan was appointed as Master. John Sadler was thirty-six at the time, had a taste for administration and prophesying conveniently in keeping with the times and, as republican Town Clerk of London, stood in high favour with the government. It so happened that he was a neighbour of Pepys' father and had a house in Salisbury Court. A fortnight after Sadler's appointment by Parliament as Master, Samuel was admitted a Sizar of Magdalene. In the following spring, while Cromwell in the far north was preparing to drive the young King of the Scots from his last refuge, he was transferred from the books of Trinity Hall to those of Magdalene, going into residence and donning his gown for the first time on March 5th. Four weeks later he was elected a Scholar on the Spendluffe Foundation. The winds of change, that had blown so chill for many Englishmen, had brought good luck to young Pepys.[2]

He was eighteen now—not many inches over five feet in height, dark, round in the face, with large, enquiring eyes. His clothes, which were those of a young man of modest station, were inclined to be untidy, and early poverty and strict training had left their marks on him: a certain caution and preciseness of utterance showed the son of the Puritan tailor and the thrifty housewife. But, once off his guard, the natural impetuousness of his temperament revealed itself; he was quick to feel, eager for pleasure could he but sample it, and irresistibly good-humoured. He liked company of all sorts, loved to talk and be talked to, and was greedy to sample every novelty. Above all he was curious—"with child", as he himself put it, to see every strange thing—avid for knowledge and ready to seek for it anywhere, for his was a liberal genius. All this did not reveal itself at first; to his tutors he seemed a sober youth, prudently yielding the wall to those bigger and rougher than himself, a scorner (as befitted his station and the times) of swearing, drunkenness, dancing and all light pleasures, and a great respecter of virtue. Perhaps he seemed so to himself, but he was mistaken.[3]

In a free University, such a one finds his natural element. And for all the sombre harness in which it was now dressed, there was still freedom at Cambridge. The young dons of Magdalene with their biblical names, Joseph and Samuel and Hezekiah, might talk with all the nasal preciseness of a saintly age, but human nature remained much the same as before. Services in College chapel might be read with unusual fervour, and without such sinful enticements of the flesh as surplices or organs, but to the ordinary undergraduate—and in essentials our Samuel was one—they remained what they have always been, daily fences to be taken with lectures, disputations and visits to one's tutor without enthusiasm or any other concern but to get them over safely and punctually, lest fine or gating should follow. A fasting night was merely an opportunity of supping pleasantly out of hall in a tavern—"a shadow of religion without any substance". And the godly young dons themselves proved on closer acquaintance to be remarkably like other young men—Joseph Hill of Yorkshire, so full of words, Northamptonshire Hezekiah Burton, John Peachell who relished his glass like any other honest fellow, and Pepys' own tutor, the ingenious and voluble Mr Morland, whom his pupil never ceased to regard, for all his latter fame and inventiveness, as a fool. As for the undergraduates themselves, they were the same cheerful, loquacious creatures that they have been in all ages. There were Pepys' chamber-fellows, Bob Sawyer, one day to become Attorney-General but now humble enough, and Kit Anderson, studying for medicine and by no means averse to a wench, when he could find "an exceeding pretty lass, right for the sport"; Thomas Fossan, the Londoner, and Hoole, Castle and Nicholson his fellow pupils; Clem Zanchy, a year older, Jack Hollins, the Yorkshireman and, dearest of all, his old friend of St Paul's, Dick Cumberland, a lad of reading and parts after his own heart.* Others there were more remote, whom Pepys encountered in later years but with whom at that time he was on no more than bowing terms—John Skeffington, the baronet's son, "one with whom I had no great acquaintance, he being then (God knows) much above me", Stillingfleet, the Gospel preacher and Dryden, the poet. The friends of after-life were mostly encountered later, for socially Pepys outsoared nearly

* In 1686 Bishop Cumberland dedicated his work on Jewish Measures to Samuel Pepys, Secretary to the Admiralty, "for that good affection begun in your youth thirty years ago in Magdalene College Cambridge".

all his Cambridge contemporaries. "We had much talk", he once recorded after a chance meeting with one of them, "of all our old acquaintance of the College concerning their various fortunes, wherein to my joy I met not with any that have sped better than myself". But for the moment these rough lads were the bread and staff of Pepys' life—the boon companions with whom he talked all night of mysteries divine and terrestrial in bare, boarded chambers; bought stewed prunes from Goody Mulliner across the way, and walked the fields towards Madingley or the river meadows by Chesterton, whence a boatful of boys might ferry across to stand for a moment, silenced as the magic of a summer's evening caught up their spirits, among the ruins of Barnwell Abbey.[4]

It was on one of these walks that Samuel Pepys was first made aware of what was to remain for ever the haunting fear of his life. It was a hot summer's day in the year 1653 and he and a number of his friends walked out from Cambridge to Aristotle's well, where they slaked their thirst with great draughts of cold water from the conduit. When he got back to College he was seized with a violent pain and lay for some days in agony, after which the hereditary stone,* hitherto lodged in his kidneys, was carried into the bladder—a transference which Pepys himself attributed to the weight of the water he had drunk that day and which was attended by alarming and bloody symptoms. Henceforward he was subject to constant and growing fits of pain.[5]

* The disease was apparently entailed on his family. On Nov. 4th, 1660, he found his mother in "greater and greater pain of the stone"—she ultimately voided a large stone which to Pepys' disappointment she threw into the fire—and on Jan. 27th, 1663, he notes that his brother John at Cambridge "hath the pain of the stone and makes bloody water with great pain, it beginning just as mine did".

It was shortly after this event, in the Michaelmas Term of 1653, that the first record occurs of over-drastic action on Pepys' part to moisten another "mighty drought" to which he was "subject after intent speaking". There were many pleasant taverns in Cambridge—the "Falcon" in Petty Cury, the "Three Tuns" on Peas Hill, the "Rose" (where many years later the diarist was once kept awake all night by the noise of drunken scholars)—and humbler alehouses where a poor student might be merry at his ease. On October 21st, Sam, with his acquaintance Hind, was solemnly admonished by his tutor Morland and Mr Hill in the presence of all the Fellows of the College for having been scandalously overseen in drink the night before.[6]

Indeed, behind its imposing façade of Godliness republican Cambridge was built of coarse and human enough material, and was probably none the worse for it. Pepys' cousin, Barnardiston of Cottenham, introduced him to Mrs Aynsworth, the jolly bawd who kept an inn for all the good fellows of the county and taught him to sing *Full forty times over*, "a very lewd song". It perhaps did him no great harm, for his Puritan home and schooling, acting on a frame not naturally given to chastity, had tended to make him a prude. Even in manhood, when the veneer of purity had long been lost, this most outspoken of men in other things could never quite bring himself to call a spade a spade.[7]

But in all else young Pepys was healthy enough. He loved music and good talk and enjoyed the company of his fellow creatures, and he worked hard because learning was joy to him. He read widely, admired Roman virtues and Greek dialectics, and thought himself a philosopher because he could name the qualities of the elements from Aristotle and quote with feeling Epictetus' axiom—"τὰ ἐφ' ἡμῖν καὶ τὰ οὐκ ἐφ' ἡμῖν".* And he had good friends: the kindly, restrained, humorous face of his comrade, Cumberland, still looks down from his portrait to reassure us, and his Cambridge cousins, the Angiers, descendants of his great-uncle, Thomas Pepys the Red, watched over him and befriended him. So his days at the University were prosperous, and in after years pleasant to look back upon. In October, 1653—it was a week or two before the bacchanalian evening with Hind already mentioned—he was preferred to a scholarship on the Smith Foundation and given his degree.[8]

Exactly when Pepys left Cambridge and by what means he earned his livelihood when he did, we do not know and perhaps never shall. His own statement, made in the House of Commons, in after years implies that he went straight from the University into the service of his cousin, Edward Montagu, but as the same statement adds that it was in the honourable capacity of Montagu's secretary (which we know to be a lie, though a very natural one in a highly-placed public man, anxious to hide the lowness of his beginnings), it is hard to attach much importance to it. It seems probable that the Bachelor of Arts returned at any rate for a time to his father's home and even served in the shop. He certainly carried clothes to his father's customers—a fact which filled him with shame when he re-encountered them.[9]

Poverty did not prevent him from falling in love. Even at Cambridge, the divine discontent which makes fools and poets of us all had touched him, and he long honoured fair Betty Archer's memory. Perhaps it was her obduracy which made him first try his prentice hand at literature, for while still at the University he wrote a play called *Love-a-Cheat*, which subsequently, when turning over old papers, he

* "Some things are in our power, others are not." See *Diary*, Sept. 9th, 1662.

burnt in the heartless manner of manhood. Perhaps even earlier the gentle passion had touched the boy's sensitive heart: he had written an anagram on the name of sweet Elizabeth Whittle, who lived in his father's alley (and became in due course the grandmother of Charles James Fox); and once, revisiting the scenes of his youthful sojourns at his cousin's house at Ashtead, he recorded with what great pleasure he viewed his old walks, "where Mrs Hely and I did use to walk and talk, with whom I had the first sentiments of love and pleasure in woman's company, discourse and taking her by the hand, she being a pretty woman".[10]

He had not long left Cambridge when he met his match. She was the daughter of a French Huguenot who had come over to England with Queen Henrietta Maria, lost his place at Court (we do not know how, but he said it was on account of his religion), and married the daughter of an Anglo-Irish gentleman, Sir Francis Kingsmill. She was very beautiful, with a little round face of an almost unearthly pallor set in curls. He was twenty-two and she fifteen. And he loved her ecstatically, passionately, so that the very intensity of his emotion made him physically sick and he could not rest till he had her. It was all utterly illogical and unreasonable: she was penniless, a mere child, not even his countrywoman, and he himself was without money or prospects. The Pepyses had generally married so prudently, haggled for the very last penny of dowry which their fortunes could justify, and got themselves such careful, competent and (since something must be sacrificed to obtain so much) ugly wives. And here was Samuel quite mad to secure himself, not a livelihood, not a decent settlement of land, not a frugal, honest mate of his own class and country, but a little pale chit of a foreign beauty who could bring him nothing but trouble. For one who pretended to be a philosopher and to govern his life by the wise rules of Epictetus, it was a sad fall.[11]

Yet when your true fenman sets his heart on anything he generally succeeds, and Samuel was of Cottenham stock. Perhaps it was not very difficult to wheedle the consent of Elizabeth's father, a poor, good-natured, ingenious man, with the high-sounding name of Alexander le Marchant de St Michel and a pocket as empty of cash as his mind was full of whimsies and propositions of perpetual motion and such like uneconomic absurdities. Indeed the good man was brought so low that even a penniless, but industrious, young student like Pepys might seem a desirable son-in-law, and the match was certainly enhanced in his eyes by the fact that Samuel was a good Protestant. So, as soon as he was used to the situation, he accepted his child's impetuous lover cheerfully and told her that he was happy that she had matched with one who was not only, for his years, learned and wise, but who would, he hoped, with Christ's aid quite blow out of her those foolish thoughts which she had had of popery. On which she kissed his eyes (a thing she loved to do) and whispered that she had taken to her heart a man too wise, and one too religious in the Protestant faith to suffer her thoughts to bend that way any more.*[12]

So Samuel had his little bride, taking her at the altar on October 10th, 1655, as she stood at his side in her laced petticoat. "Saw a wedding in the Church", he wrote many years later, "and the young people so merry one with another, and strange to see what delight we married people have to see these poor fools decoyed into our condition, every man and woman gazing and smiling at them." As yet it was his turn.

* See, for a detailed account of this conversation between father and daughter, a most interesting letter from Balthasar St Michel to Pepys dated Feb. 8th, 1673, and printed in *Howarth*, pp. 44–7.

The ring he had bought for her with his scanty shillings at the goldsmith's near the New Exchange enfolded her finger, and afterwards they ate their wedding dinner in a tavern on the steep slope of Fish Street hill where the carts rumbled down the cobbles to the bridge. At that wedding dinner there was much kindness and loving respect between bridegroom and bride, for theirs was no marriage of convenience. And perhaps, than what was theirs at that moment, life offers nothing better.[13]

Yet, for better or for worse, Pepys had taken Elizabeth le Marchant de St Michel to wife, with her impecunious father and mother and her shifty, feckless, dashing young rogue of a brother, Balthasar. The formalities were completed a few weeks later, when the banns were duly proclaimed in St Margaret's Church, Westminster, and the civic ceremony (required by the new republican law of England but so strangely unwelcome to the church-bred, conservative-hearted people of that land) performed before a Westminster magistrate on December 1st. After that he began to learn a little about her.[14]

He loved her and was intensely proud of her beauty, yet there were things to which he could not shut his eyes. She was careless and untidy—a child who could not even keep her own clothes tidy, let alone make a poor man's home. And though he read to her continually, in the evenings and on long Sabbath afternoons, and tried to make her as learned and universally curious as himself, the plain fact remained that she was somewhat of a fool. Her favourite books were long meandering French romances, whose tedious narratives she would even repeat in company in the most uncalled-for and irritating manner. Moreover she had a will of her own and, though she loved and admired her clever husband, liked to follow the bent of her own imperious little ways. In the end Samuel, who had almost as strong a will as his kinsman's kinsman, the great Protector, tamed her, but not without friction.[15]

Very early in their married life they quarrelled seriously. It did not last long, for their affection for each other, despite all their incompatibility, was too deep, but for a time they appear to have been separated, Elizabeth going into lodgings with friends at Charing Cross.* These early differences were a very bitter memory to Pepys, who could scarcely bear his wife to remind him of them,† and at his father's house were long preserved the tell-tale papers of that warfare. What caused it we do not know; but it seems probable that it arose from Mrs Pepys' over-free display of her charms, and her husband's frenzied resentment. A certain Captain Robin Holmes, a fine-coated swashbuckler of a fellow, cast eyes on her and appears to have received encouragement. There were probably others. At any rate Pepys grew desperately jealous —a circumstance of which his wife did not fail to take advantage. She could always in after years shame her husband by speaking to him of his "old disease of jealousy"; once when she suspected a recurrence of the malady, she industriously and maliciously inveigled him into reading aloud Sir Philip Sidney's strictures on this uncourtly complaint.[16]

The beginnings of married life between young folk of different training and temperament can never be easy. The passions of a young man of strong feeling who is deeply in love are not unlikely to embarrass a girl of fifteen, and

* On Aug. 15th, 1663, Pepys records going to Deptford with Mr Palmer "one whom I knew and his wife when I was first married, being an acquaintance of my wife's and her friends lodging at Charing Cross during our differences".

† *D.* July 4th, 1664: "Very high and very foul words from her to me... and reflecting upon our old differences, which I hate to have remembered". And see *D.* Aug. 13th, 1661.

Mrs Pepys was no more. Her husband's sexual life was robust and eager; hers, at any rate at this time, was not. She suffered in a delicate part of her body from a recurrence of painful humours and swellings, of which, poor child, she was naturally very sensitive; and every month she was prostrated for some days with acute pain. Of all this Samuel at first can have had little understanding. He wanted her with all his being and he may well have set down her inability to want him in the same way* to fickle-heartedness. After all, immunity from the vice of snoring (and this was among Mrs Pepys' virtues) is not the only requisite of a bride. And Samuel was of an age when all things are desired and expected.[17]

Yet though heart's desire attained proved only disillusionment, and those interpreters of married life, children, did not come to the Pepyses, the young people for all their quarrels were generally happy enough. When Samuel was cross and Elizabeth wished to be forgiven she would come to his bedside and do all things to please him till he could hold out no longer; or when it was her turn to sulk, he would coy with her till she ceased crying and they were friends once more as they always were. Then they would sit together of an evening playing backgammon, or Elizabeth in her old morning gown, which Samuel called her "kingdom" from the ease and content she used to have in wearing it, would recite French poems for his delight.[18]

But the first of Pepys', the married man's, problems, must have been purely economic. He had wedded at twenty-two and he had to find bread for himself and his wife. Happily

* On Nov. 14th, 1668, after the great crisis about Deb, Pepys records how he had slept more with his wife as a husband in the past few days than in twelve months before, "and with more pleasure to her than I think in all the time of our married life". And see *D.* Aug. 2nd, 1660.

for him, fortune smiled. The rise of the Republican army had levelled the proud Presbyterian merchants of London as low as the Royalist squires over whom they had triumphed beneath the might of a little hierarchy of fanatic enthusiasts, artisan colonels and pagan philosophers—the most curious government England has yet seen. This levelling process had raised the comparative status of a poor "foreign" tailor in the order of things, and Pepys' father in 1653—one suspects some gentle pressure from without—had been admitted to the charmed circle of the London Merchant Tailors. In the same year the seizure of supreme power by the fenman, Cromwell, materially advanced Samuel's prospects. For Cromwell loved, and was loved in return by, young Edward Montagu, whose capacity and fidelity he recognised. In July, 1653, when he was only twenty-eight, Montagu was called to the Protector's Council of State and in November of the same year made a Commissioner of the Treasury. Nor was he the only one of Pepys' kin to benefit by these changes. In 1654, his father's first cousin, a Pepys of the elder line, Richard of the Temple, with whose children Samuel was intimate, was appointed to the great office of Lord Chief Justice of Ireland. The rise of a Huntingdonshire squire to the mightiest position ever held by an Englishman was thus not without significance to the house of Pepys.[19]

From the first of these Samuel received preferment. The same month that witnessed his own marriage saw his cousin Montagu called to the Admiralty Commission. In January, 1656, Montagu received a greater call, being appointed Joint-Commander with Robert Blake of the English battle fleet, now under orders to sail for Spain on active service. The new Admiral, who was neither then nor later very happy in the management of his own private affairs, was in need of someone to look after his lodgings in Whitehall and attend to his financial transactions in London. Samuel was selected,* and in February duly attended his new master across the river to Lambeth to see him take coach for Portsmouth where the Fleet was lying. A month later when Montagu wrote a letter from the *Naseby*, then on the point of departure in St Helens Roads, he addressed it to his servant Samuel Pepys at his lodgings in Whitehall. For there in a little turret overlooking the Gateway, in the very midst of the old rambling royal palace of Whitehall, now the seat of the Protector's government, was established Samuel Pepys, the tailor's son, and his wife Elizabeth.[20]

From his window he could see the whole palace, an anarchy of buildings of every date and type, crowded between the river and the park. Beneath his gaze, and almost through the very centre of Whitehall, ran the public road which linked the city of Westminster to Charing Cross village and London. To the east the eye travelled across the palaces of the nobility, which still lined the Strand and whose gardens of fruits and flowers ran down to the Thames, to the vanes and spires of London with old St Paul's towering above all. Westward, beyond the park, were fields with the Kingston and Exeter roads running across them, the suburban pleasance of Hyde Park with its horse-ring, the Westbourne stream lazily seeking Thames through meadows of cowslip and buttercup, and the villages of Kensington and Chelsea.

The Whitehall in which Pepys lived had changed much since he had first seen it as a child during his family's Sunday rambles. The throng of gallants who long ago stood at the entrance gate there to ravish themselves with the sight of the ladies' handsome legs as they took coach, the saucy liverymen

* It is possible that he was already installed in Montagu's household before his marriage; the fact that the marriage, both civic and ecclesiastical, occurred at Westminster, is significant.

LONDON IN THE SEVENTEENTH CENTURY

who jeered at the honest gaping Londoners passing down the lane, the red and golden beefeaters lazing over the great black jacks in the Hall, were now but ghosts. Yet the silence and cobwebs of the past twelve years were also vanished. For in the very palace of the vanished kings, there had sprung suddenly into being a greater king, and Whitehall, like England without, felt for the first time since the death of Elizabeth the beat of a mighty and single pulse—"one management of affairs, quick, sudden and with expedition". And all around were the ministers of that imperial dominion, men with coats of buff and red, steel-breasted and capped, bearing pike and musket as the sign of their commander's empery.[21]

Here Pepys did business for Montagu—his honoured master, as he called him on the inscriptions of his letters—banking his money, protecting his official perquisites from self-seeking magnates and making such payments as he received orders to make. "Sam Pepys", wrote his employer, "you are upon sight hereof to pay unto Captain Hare or his assignes the sum of £104", and Sam, leaving Elizabeth at her housework, would duly make his way through the waiting soldiers and hurrying scullions to the river steps, there to take boat for London to seek his lord's client in the covered walks of the Exchange or stand, cap in hand, at the parlour door of a Lombard Street goldsmith-banker. All this he did with methodical care and dispatch, and found it a pleasure to see his master's affairs in proper order. For the blood of the Crowland bailiffs was in his veins, and Samuel at twenty-three was an administrator.[22]

Not that Samuel's functions at this time were all administrative. When his master wanted swords and belts, black and modish for his own wearing, caps for his little daughters, or cushions and fine hangings to be sent to Hinchingbrooke, it was Pepys who bought them. In these domestic commissions, he was much aided and commanded by Montagu's elder sister, Lady Pickering. The wife of a powerful and thriving republican,* this lady was the cream of Cromwellian fashion and had a pretty taste in fine clothes and the due arrangement of books, looking-glasses, and silver bedsteads. In all these she gave Samuel, to whom she must have seemed a very grand person, constant advice. Her direction became of particular importance in the autumn of 1656 when Montagu returned to England with the holds of his ships laden with Peruvian treasure, captured from a home-coming Spanish galleon off Cadiz. "This singular providence of God", as Montagu in a letter to Cromwell termed it, brought Pepys a great deal of work. His master shortly after his arrival went down to Hinchingbrooke to recuperate, leaving him to pilot through the shoals and rapids of the Prize Office the silver furniture and fine hangings, the boxes of doubloons and the chests of sugar, the drugs and rare roots, which he claimed as his share of the booty. The most troublesome prize of all was the young Marquis de Baides, son of the fallen Viceroy of Peru. During the fight off Cadiz, his father, mother and sister had all been slain and his entire fortune captured, and Montagu's kindly and sympathetic heart had been touched by his plight. Till the boy could be ransomed, he left him in the charge of the Pickerings and his servant Pepys, bidding them apply some of the captured furniture to provide him a suitable bedchamber. It was possibly in the discharge of these charitable duties that Pepys first acquired that acquaintance

* According to the Anglican, Walker, Sir Gilbert Pickering was "first a Presbyterian, then an Independent, then a Brownist and afterwards an Anabaptist, for he was a most furious, fiery, implacable man and was the principal agent in casting out most of the learned clergy". Walker, *Sufferings of the Clergy*, p. 91.

with Spanish which he was later to find so useful both in the formation of his library and the recording of his amours. Montagu had been content to converse with the young marquis in Latin: it is in keeping with what we know of Pepys' eager love for learning that he should have wished to improve the occasion by making himself master of a new language.[23]

Pepys' duties at Whitehall were also of a domestic kind. He was the head of Montagu's little London household. It is true that this only consisted of the footboy, Tom, old East the messenger, and a couple of maids, but it was enough to get Pepys into serious trouble with his master in the winter of 1657. In Montagu's long absences with the Fleet and at Hinchingbrooke, there was little for his London servants to do and they were put on board-wages and left to obtain their meals at one or other of the numerous cook-houses around the palace and in the streets of Westminster. At these the maids appear to have made the acquaintance of certain amorous and, to their employer's mind, undesirable fellows, with the result that one of them eloped, accompanied, it appears, by some of Montagu's goods. A subsequent enquiry, over which Samuel's cousin, Roger Pepys, the lawyer and son of old Talbot Pepys of Impington, presided, ended in his being accused of being privy to the marriage and guilty of anything but discreet behaviour.[24]

At these charges, Pepys was in despair and all of a tremor to prove his innocence. "It troubles me", he wrote to his employer, "to hear what your Lordship's apprehensions are concerning me. The loss of your Honour's good word I am too sure will prove as much my undoing as hitherto it hath been my best friend". The whole trouble, he explained, was due to the lack of proper employment for the young women and the ill company they thus met at the cook-houses:

he, for his part, so soon as he perceived it, had done his best to prevent ill-consequences by giving the maid a plentiful allowance to provide for his diet. As for the suggestion that he himself had been keeping disorderly hours, there was not a word of truth in it; he had never been forth at night on week-days and, in future, would not even do so on Sundays, "though this", he added, referring to some specific charge against him, "was not past seven o'clock, as my she-cosen Alcock knows, who supt with us at my father's".[25]

Yet though these letters of this twenty-four-year-old upper domestic resemble closely, in their clarity, their marshalled evidence, their insistence on the writer's unassailable integrity, the treasured epistles of the later Clerk of the Acts and Secretary to the Admiralty, it is impossible to escape a suspicion that Pepys was not as innocent as he pretended. Judging by references to her in the Diary, he was accustomed to treat the erring maid's colleague, Sarah, in a manner scarcely compatible with the duties of the chief officer of a household and highly indecorous in a young graduate of sober antecedents and scholarly tastes. To salute a cookmaid with a sociable and cheerful kiss was, in the seventeenth century, one thing: to take her on one's knee and employ one's hands about her person quite another. Yet this, a few years later, is what Pepys admits to doing with Sarah.[26]

But nothing was proved. "I see little cause", he assured Montagu, "to doubt of giving your honour a good account of the goods in the house and my care in keeping them so". As for the future, he would see to it that the next maid should diet on four shillings a week with himself and his wife and by that means, he added, "the disrepute of a maid's going to a victualling house in neglect of your Honour's own doors will be prevented". And he busied himself with the help of

Montagu's sister-in-law, Mistress Ann Crewe, in finding another domestic. She, at any rate, should have plenty to do —making fires, cleaning the rooms and washing the clothes, scouring the silver and pewter and the like. Satan, Samuel was convinced, found mischief for idle hands to do.[27]

Though Montagu's household in London was small enough, Pepys as its head was a member of a far vaster and more important organisation. Down at Hinchingbrooke were the officers of a great rural magnate's establishment—Robert Barnwell, the agent, a personage of some dignity and substance* and a former friend of Pepys' uncle Apollo, and honest, jovial, old Edward Shepley, the steward. Both these dignitaries were very kind to young Samuel, particularly Shepley† who sent him turkeys and news of his relations from the country and was always ready to drink a glass with him when he came to town. At a very early stage of his career, Pepys had learnt the art of making himself agreeable to his superiors. Yet he was on equally good terms with the lesser lights of Montagu's country household—"my friends his servants" as he later called them—turbulent, boasting, pot-swilling Ferrers, the led captain, Archibald the butler, John Goods the messenger, and Betty and Susan the maids.[28]

More important in the Montagu *ménage* than any of these was John Creed, my Lord's secretary, a pushing, cunning, and highly competent man, far nearer to Pepys in age than the other household chiefs, and his equal in wit and intelligence. Though far from a Puritan by nature, Creed was wise enough to conform closely to the moral fashions of the time;

* In December, 1661, he was a candidate for the post of Clerk of the Peace at Huntingdon. *Carte MSS.* 73, f. 641.

† On July 5th, 1666, after lending Shepley £30 on excellent security, Pepys added in some shame for his anxiety for the latter: "But to see how apt everybody is to neglect old kindnesses".

spoke with the nice precision of the virtuous and would as soon hang as enter an ale-house on the Sabbath. But his real weakness was money (for the acquisition of which he possessed gifts approaching to genius). Pepys regarded him as a crafty rogue and was jealous of him, yet never failed to find his companionship a pleasure, for Creed had humour, learning and judgment. At the moment, this man had Montagu's ear and with it real power, for the latter, as was then the practice, took his private secretary with him on his official occasions, and Creed at such times was for all practical purposes secretary and treasurer of the English fleet. Of infinitely less importance, but like Creed the constant attendant of Montagu, was the boy, Will Howe. Quick, high-spirited and intensely musical, he was a great delight to the admiral, as also to Samuel, who loved to sing or jest with him.[29]

Pepys' early service for Montagu, humble as it was, brought him into contact with important folk and events. When Montagu was at sea—as he was again during the attack on Mardyke in the autumn of 1657—Pepys made it his business to keep him posted in the great events passing before those quick and watchful eyes of his as he slipped through the crowd at Whitehall. He saw the Lord Protector go down in state to meet his Parliament, heard the rumours of his approaching Kingship and witnessed the arrest of a fanatic preacher who declared that the spirit within him which bade him speak was greater than the government which bade him be silent. He saw the growth of new and almost regal ceremonies in the palace, of ushers with wands who stopped the people who for nearly a generation had been wont to wander at will through Whitehall, and of the transformation of his chief's radical brother-in-law, Sir Gilbert Pickering, into a self-important and officious Lord

Chamberlain.* Sometimes, too, he caught glimpses of the mighty in their undress; of Cromwell shaking his sides with laughter as he made his gentlemen dress themselves up in captured Popish copes and vestments.[30]

With some of these great personages Pepys was even, in a humble way, on speaking terms. He spoke to Colonel Ingoldsby about his master's timber and often dined at the table of Montagu's father-in-law, the Presbyterian magnate, John Crewe, at his fine new house in Lincoln's Inn Fields. Here he was always welcome: the Crewes, for all their greatness, were simple-hearted folk, and with the young members of the family, Lady Montagu and her brothers, Thomas and John, Pepys was almost on terms of equality. As for old John Crewe himself, he was always ready to discuss business or politics with this intelligent, respectful, prudent young man, his son-in-law's servant and kinsman, as he waited at his bedside or coach door. Only his wife was somewhat of a trial: "the same, weak, silly lady as ever", Pepys found her long after, "asking such saintly questions".[31]

Yet Samuel was still a very humble sort of person and exceedingly poor. In their little room in the turret, Elizabeth used to make coal fires and wash his foul clothes with her own hand, for which he added in the days of his pride, "I ought for ever to love and admire her, and do". Once he was so hard up that it seems he was forced to pawn his lute for forty shillings, and his daily companions numbered such lowly folk as coachmen, cookmaids, carpenters. None the less he

* "As for news", wrote Pepys to Montagu with a quiet humour which often creeps into his rather stilted letters, "hee that sees the strictness used for stopping that free passage of strangers through Whitehall, and the ceremony used in passing the presence chamber, will say Sir Gilbert Pickering is a perfect Lord Chamberlain, and who meets Colonel Jones with a white staff in his hand will acknowledge him as perfect a Controller." *Carte MSS.* 73, f. 187; Dec. 22nd, 1657. Printed *Howarth* 9.

stored away what shillings he could spare against a better day and sealed his letters with his own arms.[32]

Poor though he was, it must not be thought that Pepys was without pleasures: for such he had a true genius. Though Commonwealth London was shorn of nearly all its old pageantry and merriment and one could scarcely see a man of quality in its streets, it was still full of delight for Samuel: a new ingenuity in Mr Greatorex the instrument-maker's shop, a chance drink with some stranger in a tavern, or a traveller's tale could alike give him exquisite pleasure. He had his treasured possessions; his books, the fine pair of buckskin gloves he once bought himself in an expansive moment, his noble fur cap. And though it was not for many years that he first knew the grandeur of a sirloin of beef of his very own, he could relish acutely what good things came his way—cream and brown bread, a hog's harslet or that excellent dish of tripes covered with mustard which he once tasted at Mr Crewe's.[33]

But dearest of all his early pleasures was music. He still possessed his father's old bass viol, and on this it was his joy to accompany himself as he sang—

> My mind to me a kingdom is,
> Such perfect joy therein I find,

or *Orpheus' Hymn*, or *Fly boy, Fly boy*; and, better still, to join in companionly music with others. He could pipe a flageolet as he journeyed down the river or sat for an hour in the sun in St James's Park. And he was always ready to raise his voice in harmony with friends: a bed-time psalm or a bawdy tavern chorus came alike to him, so long as the singing was true.[34]

Men of music Pepys never lacked for friends. In the valley of humiliation the pilgrims found the shepherd boy singing.

In those days of poverty, London was full of musicians who had flourished in the royal court and were now penniless tavern-fiddlers. Such Samuel sought out and made his companions, Matthew Lock the composer, Henry Purcell harmonious father of a greater son, Hill the instrument-maker and forerunner of a long musical line, and poor, modest, friendly Mr Spong. In such society he would sometimes enjoy the best of treats life held for him—a concert. Once in a music practice in Mr Hingston's chamber he heard a song written by Payne Fisher, the poor mendicant poet, and set by Hingston (who had served Charles I and now served Cromwell, and was in due time to serve Charles II) for six voices with symphonies between each stanza of which the refrain ran:

Funde flores, thura crema,
Omne sit laetitiae thema,
  Facessat quicquid est amari.
Tuba sonet et tormentum
Grande fiat argumentum
  Invicti virtus Olivari!

Music, like good wine, was indeed of no party.[35]

Yet behind all Pepys' work and pleasure lay a shadow—the shadow of death. Ever since his twentieth year he had suffered under a constant succession of attacks of stone in the bladder. In the winter of 1657–8, when he was busy defending himself against the charges concerning the runaway maid, the trouble grew rapidly worse: sometimes the pain was so insupportable that he was forced to cry out in his torment. It was bitterly cold that winter, so that, as Evelyn records, the very feet of the birds froze to their prey. Cold at any time was apt to bring suffering to Pepys, and the extremity of January and February brought matters to a head. By March an operation could no longer be averted. And in the seventeenth century, when chloroform was unknown and medical science innocent of the knowledge of septic germs, a major operation as likely as not meant death.[36]

At such a moment Pepys naturally turned to the familiar faces and scenes of childhood. Among his father's neighbours was Thomas Hollier, the lithotomist and surgeon to the great hospital of St Thomas. To him the good old man anxiously directed his son's steps, and under his charge and that of Dr Joyliffe, a brilliant young physician who practised at Garlick Hill and whose own career was soon to be cut tragically short, Pepys underwent the first great ordeal of his life. Since his father's house was too small, it was decided that the operation should take place in the neighbouring home of his cousin Jane Turner, the daughter of John Pepys of Ashtead, who had been so kind to him as a child. She had inherited her father's house in Salisbury Court, where she lived with her husband (a wealthy Yorkshire lawyer), and a brood of merry children of whom the eldest, Theophila, was now almost a woman. Mrs Turner had lost nothing of her youthful taste for larks and escapades or of her kindliness, though the latter had taken a slightly devotional turn; she was a great pillar of St Bride's Church. She and her daughter, The, and their cousin, Joyce Norton, who lived with them, did their best to make poor Samuel comfortable.[37]

With these kind people to tend him, he prepared himself for certain pain and perhaps death. To ease his suffering Hollier called into consultation his old master, Dr James Moleyns of St Bartholomew's,* who prescribed a soothing draught of liquorice, marsh mallow, cinnamon milk, rose water, and the white of eggs. March 26th dawned; then,

* He was a great royalist, and once attended Cromwell whom he treated successfully for gravel in the bladder. Eucardio Momigliano, *Cromwell*.

in the presence of his nearest relations and of Mrs Turner and her company, Samuel made himself ready for the knife and swift, burning pain. Somewhere without, his good Aunt James, much supported by those poor, frenzied fanatics among whom she had her being, was praying hard.[38]

The operation was a complete success. Hollier (though human enough in his love for a jovial evening and his insensate fear of the Church of Rome) was a master of his craft. In that year he cut thirty for the stone and all lived, though soon after four others whom he also operated upon perished: such seemed a miracle in those days: we can now guess that his instruments had become septic and that, had Pepys' turn come a little later, we should have had no diary.* From the patient there was taken a stone the size of a tennis ball—in technical language, about two ounces of uric acid of renal origin. Then a cooling and demulcent drink was prescribed of lemon juice and the syrup of radishes.[39]

His delivery was a turning-point in Samuel's life and left a deep impression on his mind.† In after years, when March 26th came round, he gave a dinner to those who had stood by him on that momentous day—"my solemn feast for the cutting of

* In December, 1659, Pepys attended the Jewish Synagogue and there heard "many lamentations made by Portugall Jewes for the death of Ferdinando the merchant, who was lately cutt (by the same hand with myselfe) of the stone". *Carte MSS.* 73, f. 325. Printed in *Howarth*, p. 14.

† It left him also with an intense interest in the disease of the stone, even when it appeared in the animal world. So, on May 25th, 1665, he made a particular note of what Mr Alsopp, the brewer, told him of "a horse of his that lately, after four days' pain, voided at his fundament four stones, very heavy, and in the middle of each of them a piece of iron or wood". As for his own stone, this Pepys carefully preserved in a case which he had made for that purpose and duly produced it whenever any of his friends needed encouragement to undergo a similar operation. *Diary*, Aug. 27th, 1664; and *Evelyn's Diary*, June 10th, 1669.

the stone" he called it. In 1664 he wrote with still vivid feeling of "how it hath pleased the Lord in six years' time to raise me from a condition of constant and dangerous and most painful sickness and low condition and poverty to a state of constant health almost, great honour and plenty, for which the Lord God of Heaven make me truly thankful". He had been through the valley of the shadow and, when the mists dispersed, his star was shining brightly in the sky. Now he was "like to live", and, though he knew it not, to get an estate.[40]

Chapter III

A Mean Clerk

"So by water to the Exchequer, and there up and down through all the offices to strike my tallys for £17,500, which, methinks is so great a testimony of the goodness of God to me, that I, from a mean clerk there, should come to strike tallys myself for that sum, and in the authority that I do now, is a very stupendous mercy to me." *Diary*, May 12th, 1665.

By May 1st, 1658, Pepys' recovery was complete,* and he began life again. It seems probable that he never returned to live at Montagu's lodgings, though part of his service for him still continued. We know for certain that on August 26th of that year he was settled in a house of his own with his own maid to wait on him. His move to the Exchequer can therefore be dated with some assurance to the summer of 1658.[1]

Through all the changes and revolutions of the past generation, the administrative clerks of Westminster who kept the wheels of state moving continued to work. Most vital of all the offices of government was the Court of Exchequer. Its judicial functions were carried out in state by learned barons sitting in square caps before a vast chequer-covered table in Westminster Hall, but its most important business was performed unseen in the Exchequer Office in Old Palace Yard. Here sat the receivers and tellers of the national revenue. In the Tellers' Office, as each department of state paid in its dues, the teller entered the payment into a book, whence

* *D.* May 1st, 1660: "This day I do count myself to have had full two years of perfect cure for the stone, for which God of Heaven be blessed".

his clerks at once transcribed it on to a slip of parchment which, thrown into an adjacent pipe or funnel, slid swiftly down into the Tally Court where two wooden tallies were struck for the amount paid and one of them given to the payer as a receipt. It was in the business of this great state department that Pepys now became engaged.[2]

How exactly he got his new appointment we do not know. Doubtless Montagu, who was again at sea that summer and had since Blake's death commanded the English fleet, was able to do a good deal for his humble kinsman if he chose. Moreover one of the four Tellers of the Exchequer, Leonard Pinckney, was a friend of Samuel's old benefactor, Shepley the steward of Hinchingbrooke. It was perhaps through Shepley's good offices that Pepys was appointed as clerk to Pinckney's colleague and the most important of the tellers, George Downing (later to become famous as the godfather of the street that bears his name). It was not exactly an official post,* for Downing himself paid his salary of £50 p.a. —equivalent to perhaps five times that sum in our present money—yet for all practical purposes it made Pepys a civil servant, since in the seventeenth century the senior officials of government were responsible for providing their own clerks to carry out the subordinate work of their departments.[3]

Pepys' second employer was not an amiable man. A rough, pushing, young careerist, George Downing had been bred in Massachusetts and had taken to the régime of pious aggression now established in the mother-country like a duck to water. After a short period as a preacher in Colonel Okey's regiment, he had become Scoutmaster General in the Commonwealth army—a post for which his peering habits and

* *D.* Jan. 31st, 1660: "I could discern that Hawly had a mind that I would get to be Clerk of the Council, I suppose that he might have the greater salary, but I think it not safe yet to change this for a public employment".

quick, decisive, categorical mind admirably fitted him. He had since then been a member of Parliament and English Resident at the Hague. He was a great hand, as befitted one who moved in a world of secrets and intrigue, at cyphers or "characters" as they were called in that age, and Pepys under his direction became a master of the same curious art. He held his post at the Exchequer as a minor employment, more for its emoluments than its importance, and performed it chiefly by deputy.[4]

Pepys was decidedly frightened of his new employer, whom he regarded as a stingy and perfidious rogue but whom he served with trembling and expedition. He was entirely at his beck and call when he was in England (fortunately, Downing spent much of his time in Holland), running messages for him, rising in the midst of his dinner to answer his summonses and even distributing his invitations when he gave a party. When he was remiss, he was soundly chidden by his master, who, as a good Commonwealth man, was not nice about minor courtesies and saw no harm in giving those about him the rough side of his tongue. Pepys shared his subjection with his fellow clerk, Hawley,* who had been in Downing's service before him and knew the ropes.[5]

For the rest, the new clerk's duties were not particularly arduous. Sometimes he carried money for Downing; more often he was employed in receiving cash from one or other of the state departments—the Excise or the Probate of Wills—telling it over till the last bag was counted, or paying it out to the soldiers and other state creditors. The work had some perils; one might lose a score or so pounds from one of the bags, as poor Hawley once did, and have to account for it afterwards; and it was temptingly easy to borrow the money for private purposes in the hopes that one would be able to

* For Hawley's relations with Downing, see *Thurloe*, VII, 9, 360.

refund it without inconvenience when the day of reckoning came. Pepys himself was somewhat prone to fall into this free and easy habit.[6]

His labours were lightened by the companionship of his fellow-workers, for the clerks of the Exchequer formed a large and spirited band. Though the old institutional ceremonies and celebrations of pre-Commonwealth times, such as the annual dinner on St Thomas' Day, had lapsed, the young clerks made up for it by a constant round of sly entertainments of their own. They had their weekly club at Wood's in suburban Pall Mall, and could be found any time of the day, when they could escape from their professional duties, at Will's, Harper's or the "Dog" or any other of the drinking houses of Westminster and Whitehall. Into this sociable life Pepys entered joyfully and unrestrainedly, and was always ready of an evening to eat pot venison and drink ale to abundance and sing a round of song with his fellows till Westminster chimes struck midnight.[7]

Of these companions, the brothers Dick and George Vines, the tally-joiners, who lived in Palace Yard and so loved music, Jack Spicer who sometimes deputised for Pepys and Hawley but was more often to be found playing cards at Will's, and William Bowyer were the favourites. The latter was nine years older than Pepys, but wonderfully youthful in mind and appearance, not very clever—so that in later years his old friend thought him simple—but of an excellent good humour. His father, a ruddy-faced old man who came of a good Buckinghamshire family, was the doyen of the office* and seems to have acted as a kind of mentor to the

* The old gentleman ultimately perished in February, 1664, riding through the river at night. "He was taken with his stick in his hand and cloak over his shoulder, as ruddy as before he died. His horse was taken over-night in the water, hampered in the bridle." *D.* Feb. 1st, 1664.

young clerks: "my father Bowyer", as Pepys always termed him. He and his wife and their four daughters who all resided in the Exchequer were regarded by Samuel almost as a second family—perhaps too much so for Elizabeth who once, during a quarrel, tearfully begged her husband to put her away and take one of the Bowyers if he disliked her. Their country home at Huntsmore in South Bucks was always at the Pepyses' disposal when they wanted a retreat; even the needy Balty de St Michel, presuming on his brother-in-law's popularity, left his horse at grass there.[8]

Between the junior members of the government departments a close alliance existed. Beneath the Council Chamber in Whitehall was the great room in which the clerks of the Council wrote. With these, their brothers of Exchequer were on convivial terms. Their usual meeting-place was Marsh's, and here Pepys could generally be certain of meeting those congenial souls, Will Symons and little Peter Luellin. Mighty impertinent Samuel found the conversation of the former in later years, but for the present he seemed a brave fellow enough and honest. As for Luellin, he was at once a delight and a caution, always drinking and merry, full—far too full—of bawdy talk and song, and quite irresistible in his disreputable pranks: once at an alehouse in Poyns-like fashion he held out his companion to a too-trusting landlady as an eminent physician so that the good woman poured out the tale of her infirmities into their delighted ears. Like Pepys himself both these young gentlemen were married, but one gathers, by the lateness of their evenings, not too seriously: six years later, when Symons was deprived of that solace, the diarist in one of his inimitable sketches drew the mourning husband thus: "But Lord! to hear how W. Symons do commend and look sadly and then talk bawdily and merrily, though his wife was dead but the other day, would make a dogg laugh".[9]

There were others: Chetwind so pale, sallow and ingenious—the Crœsus among the clerks, for he was a man of property; Tom Doling, Parry and Thomas; Dick Scobell, who came of secretarial stock, and Gregory of the Exchequer; Mount at whose chamber in the Cockpit at Whitehall Luellin lay; and Sam Hartlib, son of that curious philosophical, discoursive old German Pole whom Milton so praised. All these were members of the clerks' social club, where they drank, chewed tobacco and canvassed such congenial topics as how to tell by a trick whether a woman be a maid or no, and all by day engaged in the business of administering the state affairs of England, writing in their offices or standing bareheaded while their masters sat in council or committee. Later they appeared to Pepys in the light "of the old crew", of whom as the years passed he became increasingly, though modestly and secretly, ashamed: at the moment he was quite proud to mingle in such fine, jovial company.*[10]

But Pepys in 1658 had a source of pride, greater even than that of his office and new friends. For the first time in his life he had a home of his own. Some time in the summer of that year he took the lease from one Vanly of a house in Axe Yard on the west side of King Street, just where the

* *D.* Jan. 29th, 1664: "Comes Mr Hartlibb and his wife, and... Messrs Langley and Bostocke (old acquaintances of mine at Westminster, clerks),... Here was other sorry company and the discourse poor, so that we had no pleasure there at all, but only to see and bless God to find the difference that is now between our condition and heretofore, when we were not only much below Hartlibb in all respects, but even these two fellows above named, of whom I am now quite ashamed that ever my education should lead me to such low company. But it is God's goodness only, for which let him be praised".

dense congeries of alleys and lanes that lay between the Palace and Westminster shaded away into that corner of the Park which is to-day the Horse Guards Parade. It was not much of a house—"my poor little house", he once called it—but it was a great advance on the chamber in Montagu's lodgings. It had a dining room, a study or closet where Pepys could make up his accounts and lock up papers, a garret at the top and (in addition to the connubial bedroom) a dressing chamber below of his very own; to say nothing of a yard behind where one could fatten turkeys, stock pigeons and throw one's refuse. Around were other little houses, and some larger, where such more important folk as Samuel Hartlib and Richard Bradshaw, the Dantzig Resident, lived; other people's yards and gardens with fruit trees in the spring; and at the end of the lane, winking across King Street at them in the evening, the lights of Harper's.[11]

It was all inconceivably grand. Even the disadvantages of having one's cellar flooded when the Thames rose, the endless barking of the neighbours' yard-dogs at night or the noise of the billeted soldiers and their horses across the way at Hilton's could not detract from the joy and satisfaction of it. Here was a proper setting for one's belongings—they were growing too. Samuel could even put by a little money, now that he was master of £50 a year; within two years of his appointment he had managed to save £40 and invest it with his Uncle Robert of Brampton. As for his clothes, on great occasions he could really make quite a show—a suit with great skirts, a silver lace coat and a fine cloak, which unfortunately met with an unmentionable accident on the very day that he first put it on in the spring of 1659. More ordinarily, however, his wearing was a suit of black stuff clothes, such as that which in grander days he was to pass on to his brother Tom.[12]

Perhaps to Elizabeth the most valued of these accessions to the family's possessions was the maid, Jane Wayneman, who took up her duties on August 26th, 1658, and for three years formed a comfortable background to the household. She was a gentle, whimsical sort of a girl, who could not bring herself even to kill a turkey, though, as she grew older, her objection to force was so far conquered by her sense of mischief as to allow her to cut off a carpenter's mustachios —an outrage which reduced the poor man to tears and caused his wife to deny him her company in the belief that he had been fooling about with his wenches. Like Mrs Pepys, Jane was inclined to be untidy so that at times Samuel took a broom and basted her with it, but the meek humility with which she bore this outrage always caused him to regret it. Her duties were of that universal domestic kind familiar to the handmaidens of young married couples of the middle-class, and ranged from rising at two to start the day's washing to lighting her master through the streets on a dark night. This paragon was remunerated at the rate of three pounds a year. After the manner of the seventeenth century, she lived with the family, shared their more humble visits and amusements and when occasion demanded it their bedroom, combed her master's hair and put him to bed. One sees her in Pepys' pages sitting by his bedside, innocently mending his breeches, as he reads himself to sleep.[13]

Axe Yard was full of neighbours, who after the manner of their kind were both friends and rivals—Major Greenlife and his wife, with whom Hawley boarded, old Mrs Crisp with her harpsichord, her pretty grandson Laud and her prettier daughter Diana, and Mr Hill who, like the apprentice of the song, once provided a wedding in the alley. But Pepys' favourite neighbours were the Hunts, perhaps because they came from his native Cambridgeshire. Mrs Hunt was a good understanding sort of woman: her husband an official in the Excise, a worthy man of Puritan persuasion. It was to them that Elizabeth went for company when Samuel was making a musical night of it at the Vines' or drinking late (under the pretence of sealing letters for the country) at Will's or Marsh's. When he called for his lady, he generally found them all playing a social round of cards.[14]

Yet Pepys' friends were not limited to folk of his own trade and neighbourhood. Critical as he often was, it was yet almost impossible for him to meet a fellow creature without becoming interested in him. The idiosyncrasies of mankind, to ordinary folk so puzzling and irritating, were to him a perpetual source of delight—once in after days going into a playhouse he presented the doorkeeper with six shillings, one of which the rogue by a sleight of hand spirited away, pretending that he had not received it. "I was prettily served", recorded Pepys; "the fellow...with so much grace faced me down that I did give him but five, that, that though I knew the contrary...I could not deny him". Those who find the foibles of their fellow mortals so entertaining have friends everywhere.[15]

The acquaintanceship of Pepys, even at this period, had a wonderful catholicity. It ranged from Wootton the gossiping city shoemaker, with whom he drank and talked of the far-away days of the old stage while he waited for his purchases, to one who in his deep learning, humility and spiritual grandeur was almost a saint. Before the Restoration, William Fuller, one of the finest scholars of his age, and deprived of all his clerical preferments on account of his loyalty, was earning a pittance by keeping a school at Twickenham. Here Montagu sent his sons, and here, Pepys, who was sometimes left in charge of them while his patron was at sea, probably first met him.* With his sure feeling for genuine goodness, Pepys took the older man to his heart, drank in his learning, consoled him in his poverty and honoured his goodness.[16]

A friend of a more ordinary kind was Henry Moore, the lawyer. He appears to have been at this time a member of Mr Crewe's household, for whom, as also for Montagu, he acted in various capacities. He and Pepys, who were socially much on a par, often met, shared the same dinner of bread, ale and cheese at Clare Market, discoursed religion, classical tragedy and law notions with much solemnity and pleasure, and saw each other home of an evening: indeed such was their love for one another's conversation that their talk was apt to be interminable, "as he and I", wrote Pepys, "cannot easily part".[17]

Lesser friends were young Butler—"Monsieur l'Impertinent" as Pepys christened the gay chatterbox of an Irishman —son of an ancient but ruined royalist house; the learned Thomas Fuller, lecturer at St Bride's Church and perhaps the most distinguished antiquarian of his age; naval acquaintances (made through his service to Montagu) such as Robert Blackburne, the rigid, honest Commonwealth Secretary to the Admiralty; Roger Cuttance, captain of Montagu's flagship, the *Naseby*; Pierce the purser and his namesake Pierce the surgeon, both of the same ship, the latter with a very beautiful and rather fashionable wife whom Pepys much admired—"the best complexion that ever I saw on any woman". At the other end of the scale were more intimate but very humble friends, the results of casual contacts made while strolling for news and small wares among the busy

* *D.* July 18th, 1666: "Dr Fuller, now Bishop of Limerick in Ireland, whom I knew in his low condition at Twickenham".

trading population of Westminster Hall—poor Will* that used to sell ale at the hall door; Mrs Howlett and her pretty daughter Betty, whom Pepys called his little sweetheart and second wife because she so resembled Elizabeth; Mrs Michell the bookseller, at whose stall friends were wont to enquire for him and where he used to get his parcels tied up or stand for hours reading, and her gossip, old Mrs Murford. But perhaps of the inhabitants of the Hall, Samuel was at his happiest among the "maids"—the euphemistic name by which were known the pretty linen vendors, who once sold their wares where to-day American visitors, parties of school children, and constituents seeking their representatives pass gaping by. A particular favourite was Betty Lane, a free-hearted buxom lass whom one could always inveigle to the "Trumpet" across the way. For Samuel's liking for a wench showed no sign of diminishing: Catan Sterpin; the pretty woman who sold children's coats at the corner of Cheapside; † the fine lady that walked, so pretty and sprightly, across Gray's Inn Walks on Sunday afternoon and whom he sometimes contrived to speak to, all touched in turn his admiring heart. Provided one did not go too far and was true in the last resort to one's wife, there could be no great harm in it. Yet Mrs Pepys was not so assured; once after Catan had dined in Axe Yard, she insisted on following her indignant husband round the streets all afternoon as he went about his lawful occasions.[18]

Such were the companions of Samuel the clerk, treading

* The proprietor, presumably, of "Will's", the house at which Pepys so often drank.

† Poor woman, she met a sad end. For Madam Bennett, the famous bawd, "by counterfeiting to fall into a swoon...became acquainted with her and at last got her ends of her to lie with a gallant that had hired her to procure this poor soul for him". *D.* Sept. 22nd, 1660.

the daily round of Whitehall and Westminster. He would rise as soon as it was light (though seldom earlier) and, while his wife still abed read to him, make himself ready, write a letter or practise on his flageolet. Breakfast, as we know it to-day, he did not take: a morning draught of ale or purl at "Will's" or the "Harp and Ball", or, on grander occasions, of pickled oysters, anchovies and wine would suffice to set him up for his morning's work. Thence to the office (while Elizabeth cleaned the house or trudged to market), where sometimes, if Downing was at home and Exchequer payments were heavy, he would be busy enough but where more often there was little to do; in the latter case he almost invariably found himself before the morning was over sitting in Harper's over a drink and a yarn, or taking a midday walk round St James's Park or Westminster Hall. Dinner, the day's principal meal, followed about half-past twelve or one. Judged by modern standards, this, for a man who normally took only one full meal a day, was no great affair: a piece of beef from Wilkinson's the King Street cook-shop, or even, when the larder was empty and the domestic finances very low, a dish of "pease porridge and nothing else" was the only kind of fare he could expect at home. A pleasant alternative was to walk in Lincoln's Inn Fields and dine with the Crewe household, where even if the dining room was full of guests, there would always be a dish of buttered salmon or some such appetising rarity with the servants below. On holidays or great occasions, Sam might go further afield: to dine with his cousin, Thomas Pepys, the turner, in Paul's Churchyard, who, being a shop-keeper, could afford rather better viands than a salaried clerk—"only the venison pasty was palpable beef which was not handsome"—or feast with his fellow clerks on the "ordinary" at the "Chequers".[19]

The afternoon was not normally a busy time for Pepys.

Unless there were soldiers to be paid and the office claimed him, he could spend it as he pleased—fiddling with his friends the Vines' across the way or going down the river in a sculler to do business in London, perhaps taking Elizabeth with him to visit the fine shops in Paternoster Row and buy—but this did not often happen—some paragon for a petticoat. With the evening, when small boys with lanthorn and flaming link waited in the lampless streets to light wayfarers along the alleyways of houses, came a return to the office, a letter to write and seal at Marsh's or Harper's, and fiddling, singing and ale till it was time to sally out and, making the cobbles ring with footsteps, seek the latch of the little house where Elizabeth and Jane Wayneman were waiting.[20]

Sundays, according to the wont of the times, were given over to divine service and relations. On such days, Samuel would seldom fail to spend the evening and sup at his father's house, where his mother, now growing old and querulous, his brother Tom who helped in the shop, Pall, his junior by eight years and John, still a schoolboy at Paul's, completed the family. Here he could generally, not always to his pleasure, count on meeting his mother's brother-in-law, the blacksmith Uncle Fenner and all his crew—to wit his two daughters Mary and Katherine and the very disagreeable brothers, Will and Anthony Joyce, whom they had married. They were a queer, inharmonious family—"sometimes all honey one with another, and then all turd, and a strange rude life there is among them", commented their disgusted cousin. Will Joyce and his wife Mary in particular were always quarrelling—a cunning, crafty fellow, Will, with a bragging, impertinent tongue that spared nobody and yet so maliciously witty, in a rude and uneducated way, that even Samuel who disliked him could not help laughing. On the whole

Pepys preferred his brother Anthony, who was in the tallow trade and, though a troublesome fellow and a fool, was less of a ranter and built on a quieter model. Moreover his wife, Kate, was a young, pretty and comely woman for whom her cousin had always a weak spot in his heart. On the whole, however, Samuel was bored by them and decidedly ashamed of their kinship.[21]

Far more pleasing were the more occasional visits to his father's house of the children of Lord Chief Justice Pepys of Ireland. Both the latter's daughters had married good, substantial folk—Judith, John Scott, and her sister Elizabeth, Thomas Stradwick the confectioner. The latter, a wealthy and kindly man, as befitted his calling, generally entertained the whole family over a great cake on Twelfth Night—occasions on which Samuel, warmed by the good fare and the thought of owning such fine relations, was always particularly merry. For the same reason the kinship of the Turners was a source of gratification; and he seldom missed, on his Sunday afternoon visits to his father, making a brief excursion down the court to call on his kind benefactress and her daughter, The.[22]

If Sunday was the day for relations it was also the day for Church. Morning and afternoon our Protestant ancestors crowded to the parish churches to praise and worship. Of their services the sermon was by far the most important part, and a seventeenth-century sermon was no light thing: an hour was the accepted minimum, and the more famous divines were accustomed to preach for several hours at a stretch to packed and breathless congregations. So popular was this feature that quite ordinary citizens of no exceptional piety would often drop into half a dozen churches of a morning to sample the oratory: Pepys was particularly given to this recreation.

Yet, though he had been bred in a Puritan school, there was little trace as he grew up of any religious fervour about Samuel. In this he was a typical product of his generation. For nothing, so history teaches, is more inevitable than that the excessive enthusiasms of one age produce in the next weariness and repulsion. That which was sweet in the mouth of the fathers will be bitterness in that of their children. For the errors, frailties and injustices of man are so many that the thing which he seeks is in the end inevitably rendered shameful by the manner in which he seeks it. So the follies of one generation are redressed by the opposing follies of the next.

It was so with Pepys and those born in his day. The spiritual ecstasies that had been so real to their parents ceased to have any meaning for them. For as they grew up, they saw on every side witnesses of the lamentable failure that attends the efforts of those who seek to rule the terrestrial earth according to the laws, not of men, but of angels. The righteous war to exterminate the malignant, the idolater, the enemy of God, for which their fathers had taken up the sword so joyfully, was seen to have ended, not in the rule of the saints, but (where it always ends) in that of the profiteers. Reformation had proved but ruin, freedom of conscience but fiercer oppression—for new Presbyter was but old Priest writ large—and the universal use of pious language had led to the unedifying practice of money-grabbers, plunderers and fornicators justifying or concealing their sins by the words of God. As Roger North, himself the child of a Puritan father, put it, "when the experiment of reformation had proved a deformation of all that was good, and religion so furious as was before held out found to be mere hypocrisy to serve as an engine of power and tyranny, and all the pretensions of public advantage found to be nothing but private wealth", the youth of the nation resolved to have no more of these things and set to work to undo all that their fathers had done.[23]

To Pepys, for all his acquaintance with its outward forms,* the old personal religion of a generation before was a closed door and closed for ever. The trumpet of inspired oratory that had sounded for his father's contemporaries was in his prosaic ears only the droning of "a dull fellow in his talk and all in the Presbyterian manner, a great deal of noise and a kind of religious tone, but very dull", and Pepys could no more bear to be bored by religion than by anything else. When such a one preached, he would open his Bible and read over the story of Tobit. What he liked most was a reasoned, ready and learned sermon without any affectation or nonsense. And being sickened by the effrontery and vulgar impertinence of so many of the services and extemporary prayers of Commonwealth divines, he began to turn naturally enough to the discarded forms and rules of the Church of his youth. For Mr Pepys was already beginning to feel a very marked leaning towards order: he had seen enough of anarchy to know the advantages of its great opposite. Therefore he now transferred his faith to the traditions of that Church in which he was born, and, in the safety of his own family circle, began to talk very high in its support, much to the horror of his good mother to whom all this was idolatry. Not that he knew much about the ways of that Church; save once or twice at Cambridge he had never taken the Anglican sacrament nor had he even seen a surpliced choir or heard the sound of organs. But a reasonable and orderly uniformity in Church and State now secretly became his ideal, as it did that of many another young man.[24]

As a result, a certain vagary crept into his churchgoing. In

* "I wonder that there should be a tune in the psalms that I never heard of." *D.* Aug. 9th, 1663.

one or two obscure corners of London there were still cellars and upper rooms—dens and caves of the earth, the loyal Evelyn called them—where the ministers of the banished Church defied the law and read the old Prayer Book to Anglican congregations. These Pepys now began to patronise, setting out on a Sunday morning from Westminster to hear Mr Gunning at Cary House by Exeter 'Change (where Evelyn and his fellow communicants had been seized one Christmas morning by armed soldiers) read his Church's glorious, forbidden liturgy and preach on such subjects as the blessed widowhood of Anne, the mother of the Virgin. And in the afternoon, if he could escape from the rather formidable task of listening to Mr Herring, the Presbyterian incumbent of St Bride's, he would slip away to hear the eloquent Robert Mossum (in more happy years Bishop of Derry and as yet a poor sequestered clergyman) thrill his auditory at the little chapel of St Peter's by Paul's Wharf. Occasionally he would even attend Mr Gunning's Friday fasts.[25]

Indeed his own feelings and the course of outside events were slowly conspiring to make Pepys a royalist. In September 1658 the great Protector died and the rule which his genius and courage had given to an anarchical England died with him. It was difficult for any man who loved order and decency in public affairs to view with anything but disgust the procession of corrupt politicians and pious but lawless generals who fought one another for power and plunder in the next eighteen months. And Pepys, it is clear, was horrified; in 1660 he admitted that he had read with great satisfaction an account of their trials and deaths. In April, 1659, an unpaid army, at the dictation of the military chiefs at Wallingford House, dissolved Richard Cromwell's parliament and shortly afterwards prevailed on that peaceable and unheroic gentleman to "dispose himself as his private occasions should require". A month later it restored the Rump, the fifty-odd survivors of what had been once, nineteen years before, a national parliament of over five hundred, but of which all but this corrupt remnant had long ago been expelled. These proceeded to make short work of those who had supported Oliver's strong and kingly government, which, since it had outraged at once the republican principles of their best members and the plundering proclivities of their worst, had been highly unpopular with them.[26]

Though never anxious to follow him to perilous extremes, Edward Montagu had been a steady and loyal adherent of Cromwell. Apart from his natural devotion to his great cousin, he had every reason as a landowner to respect whatever made for order in the state and to abhor anarchy. Now he found the solid earth quaking under his feet. A few weeks before Richard Cromwell's fall he had been ordered to sail in command of the Fleet to the Sound to negotiate a peace between Sweden and Denmark, and more particularly to keep a watchful eye on the Dutch fleet which, with motives not altogether disinterested, was engaged in the same task. Here in May he had received the shattering news of the new Protector's downfall. It was, moreover, only too plain that his own would shortly follow.[27]

It was at this juncture that Samuel Pepys made his first appearance on the stage of history, though the exact reason for his entry is not quite clear. His service to Montagu had not stopped with his appointment to a government office, though he no longer lived in his lodgings. In the month of Oliver's death he was still taking charge of his cousin's plate, storing it under his own eye in the great chest in the Exchequer. Now, eight months later, he was called upon to serve his patron in a far more important matter.[28]

On Thursday, May 26th, there anchored within gunshot of Montagu's flagship in the Sound the ketch *Hind*, hot with news from revolutionary England and bearing with it a packet for the Admiral from the Committee of Public Safety. The ship also carried, as Montagu carefully noted in his journal, Mr Pepys. Next day in the evening the *Hind* weighed anchor and sailed for England, Pepys once more accompanying her. It was his first acquaintance with the sea. It was moreover a happy one, for two years later the Clerk of the Acts of the Navy remembered with great affection "my little Captain"—his name was Country—"who carried me to the Sound". It is not difficult to guess that the voyage was also fraught with significance for Montagu and that the young clerk who made it bore news for his private ear of no idle kind.[29]

One thing is certain: that within a few weeks of Pepys' visit to the Fleet, Montagu was in secret correspondence with the King. Not that Pepys knew anything of it, for the Admiral was the most secretive man in the world. But Montagu must have known that if he decided to throw in his lot with poor exiled Charles II, there was one humble member of his entourage and family whom he could trust.* For his cousin Sam Pepys was now definitely a King's man.[30]

Many a secret health in those troubled days when Rump and army fought over the prostrate body of England did Pepys and his fellow clerks drink to the King over the water. Hatred of the ruling fanatics, longing for order, care for his cousin's interests all added to his loyalty. That summer the republicans did all in their power to slight Montagu—sent commissioners from England to override his authority at

* On Sept. 22nd, 1665, Montagu, then Lord Sandwich, bore witness, so Pepys tells us, to his loyalty, saying "that whatever he was, I did always love the King".

the Sound, deprived him of his regiment of horse, and threatened to take his Whitehall lodgings—"as if resolved" as one delighted royalist reported to another, "to decline all the precepts and examples of policy in the Christian world by aggravating a malcontent in supreme command so far out of reach". So goaded, the cautious Montagu was driven to act, even to the extent of disobeying orders and sailing in August with his whole fleet for England, trusting to his influence with the seamen to effect a *coup d'état* for the King. But before he arrived, he learnt that the royalist rising which had been planned had collapsed. His appearance at Hosely Bay on September 6th was, therefore, something of an anti-climax. That evening three republican commissioners, Colonels Thompson, Kelsey and Walton—the latter an old enemy and one who had just removed Pepys' uncle, Robert of Brampton, from his captaincy in the Huntingdon militia—boarded the *Naseby*. Three days later Montagu was in London. Thence, after making a careful and non-committal statement to a suspicious Council of State, he retired, as was his wont in times of trouble, to Hinchingbrooke.[31]

All this helped to enhance in Montagu's eyes the value of his humble cousin, whose secret political longings corresponded so closely with his own. When he needed someone to make a copy of the confidential narrative,—"recollected for my own guidance"—which he had written on board the *Naseby* after the news of the royalist rising's failure, it was Pepys whom he employed to copy it out. And when he reached Hinchingbrooke, there to remain obscure and out of action till the clouds had blown over, it was to Pepys, watching the great world from his office in the Exchequer and from Whitehall and Westminster taverns, that he turned for news of all that was passing.[32]

It was a strange England that Samuel drew for his cousin in the letters which he sent to him from London during the early months of that winter. The soldiers had taken possession of the land. "But the eyes of Englishmen," as one old parliamentarian wrote to the leaders of these new tyrants, "are not so easily put out. An arbitrary sword may tyrannise over men's persons and estates for a time, but it doth never conquer spirits." Across Pepys' pages pass in procession the chief actors of that terrible time—Vane, Fleetwood, Lambert, Desborough,—tales of things "hatched at the Admiralty Chamber where the army officers sit", rumours of new confusions and tyrannies in every part of the country. On December 5th the angry London apprentices presented to their equally angry elders assembled in Common Council at the Guildhall a petition demanding the restoration of the City's ancient liberties. Alarmed, the Committee of Public Safety packed the town with troops. The scene which followed is best described in the words which Pepys wrote next day to Montagu:

> The souldiers as they marcht were hooted at all along the streets, and where any stragled from the whole body, the boys flung stones, tiles, turnups, etc., at, with all the affronts they could give them; some they disarmed, and kickt, others abused the horse with stones and rubbish they flung at them; and when Col: Huson came in the head of his Regiment they shouted all along a Cobler a Cobler; in some places the apprentices would gett a football (it being a hard frost) and drive it among the souldiers on purpose, and they either darst not (or prudently would not) interrupt them; in fine, many souldiers were hurt with stones, and one I see was very neere having his braines knockt out with a brick batt flung from the top of an house at him.

This spirited affair was one of many similar, enacted throughout the length and breadth of England. At Portsmouth,

Plymouth and Colchester the townsmen rose against the soldiers, demanding a free parliament. Coroners sat in inquest on slain apprentices, hand grenades were piled ready by waiting pikesmen in St Paul's, and poor folk everywhere expected fire and massacre. "Never was there, my Lord," wrote Pepys, "so universal a fear and despair as now."[33]

Yet in England, however cold the wind blows, there is always some garden in which the heart of its people can find comfort. Montagu had six children, and amid the thunders of revolution Samuel Pepys continued to execute errands and do small pleasant services for his little cousins. The eldest was the girl Jemimah, then aged thirteen. A clever, merry, affectionate child—though like all her race sensitive, and, constitutionally, a little fearful—she was Samuel's favourite. For her, Mistress Jem as he called her, he was always ready to put himself out, to buy toys to send to her in the country and to romp with her when she was in town. Her sister Paulina, three years her junior, never appealed to him in the same way: he recorded her end ten years later with a certain heartlessness: "being mighty religious in her life-time and hath left many good notes of sermons and religion... which nobody ever knew of.... But she was always a peevish lady". As for the elder boys, Edward and Sydney, these Pepys saw frequently: escorting them by coach to good Mr Fuller's school at Twickenham and visiting them at Mr Crewe's, where they sometimes lodged during the holidays, to test them in their Latin and play a post-prandial game at battledore and shuttlecock.[34]

Poor Jem suffered from some malformation in her neck which prevented her from holding her head erect, and in the October of 1659 Pepys was busying himself among other matters in finding her a medical specialist. With his usual enthusiasm he produced one, Mr Scott—possibly some relation of his she-cousin of that name, whose father, the Lord Chief Justice of Ireland, had died early in the year. Montagu was anxious to know a little more about him before entrusting his daughter to his charge and stipulated that he should be interviewed by Mrs Crewe, and Pepys wrote describing how he had, "not without much importunity" (thus enhancing both his own industry and his protégé's importance) prevailed upon Scott to visit that lady. The doctor demanded a hundred pounds—a great sum in our present money—for his skill and pains, hoped to effect the cure within three months and flatly refused to attend the girl anywhere but in his own house (there was some suggestion that she might lie at Pepys'), "his practise being so great as that he never stirs abroad to any". These terms appear to have been accepted, for by December the child was installed with her maid, Mistress Anne—a somewhat shrewish party with whom Pepys had many an angry bout—at Mr Scott's. An instrument was fixed to her neck and, from a medical standpoint, the doctor was as good as his word. But in certain other particulars Pepys' recommendation did not altogether justify his early enthusiasm, for Scott not only drank himself, but allowed his youthful patient to do so also. All this proved an additional source of work and worry to Pepys, who, during the time of Jem's sojourn at the doctor's house, was constantly visiting her and supplying her with necessities.[35]

So the troubled year of 1659 drew to a close, with the government clerks of Westminster and Whitehall clinging to posts which grew ever more precarious* and Pepys picking his way amid widening chasms to do small errands for his absent patron. He collects Montagu's small debts, consults

* In that year Pepys' companion, William Symons, "made shift to keep in, in good esteem and employment, with eight governments". *D.* Jan. 8th, 1664.

with the republican magnates about his lodgings and advises him from day to day on the course of events. And all the while the world of London and Westminster tumbles about his ears: the soldiers are everywhere in mutiny, regiments of opposing janizaries face each other in the streets, the printing presses have gone mad, flooding every tavern with wild libel and rumour, and no man's life, property or liberty is his own. And as the new year dawns on a snow-covered England, and far away on the Scottish border Monk starts to march, the London apprentices, passionate for the blood of their slain companions, make a white effigy of Roundhead Colonel Hewson—"with one eye in the head and a halter and rope about his neck, a horn on his head, and a writing on his breast,—'This is old Hewson the Cobbler'".[36]

Chapter IV

The Curtain Rises

But Samuel Pepys was otherwise engaged. For before him lay a virgin quire of paper and a great task. What rare freak of thought or circumstance prompted him at such a moment to start to keep a diary no man will ever know. Perhaps the very uncertainty of the times contributed: in days of revolution an alibi has its uses.* More probably that strong feeling for history which always characterised him was the motive. Even as a child he had loved to read old chronicles—the sad history of Queen Elizabeth's youth had haunted him almost in his cradle and throughout his life he could never light on an historical relation or forgotten document without a thrill.

* Two hundred miles away a humble Cheshire squire was also keeping a diary—and for this reason. Four years before he had been arrested on a false charge of being present at a treasonable assembly a hundred miles from his home. After a year of imprisonment he had proved his innocence by means of a notebook which contained a list of all the guests he had entertained and the meals for which he had been out, and which he had kept to square accounts between himself and the tenant farmer with whom he boarded, calling the neighbours therein mentioned to swear to his presence in Cheshire at the time when he was accused of being elsewhere. Henceforward squire Oldfield kept a diary, noting carefully the names of all those he met and the exact spot at which he met them. This diary stopped short on May 8th, 1660, the day on which Charles II was proclaimed King and the old rule of law, securing Englishmen from arbitrary arrest, was restored (*Shakerley MSS.*, Oldfield Diary 1656–60.)

And now in the winter of 1659–60, history was being made all round him: the dramatic descriptions of passing events in his letters to Montagu show how conscious he was of this. Perhaps it was to store up material for these that he began to compile it. The Diary in its opening pages gives a daily record of the affairs of the great world: it is only later, when the concerns of his own life demand more and more space, that he notes with surprise that he has recorded scarce a single item of news, so busy has he been. As Pepys' Diary proceeded, the picture ceased to be that of 1660 with himself in the foreground and became that of himself with 1660 in the background.[1]

For its performance he was already well equipped. Either at Cambridge, where the subject was beginning to be studied, or on his first entry into clerical employment, he had made himself master of Thomas Shelton's *Tachygraphy*, a new system of shorthand or "characterie", as our forefathers called it, which had come into use about the time of Samuel's birth.* It was not a good system, judged by modern standards, for many of the signs were arbitrary in the extreme,† and on at least one occasion Pepys improved on them by an innovation of his own. But in its own day it was regarded as wonderful enough,—a heaven-sent medium for preserving sermons, making copies of important letters and, as one inspired Cambridge graduate, commenting on its author's proud title-page claim, put it, something of a miracle:

* Thomas Shelton's *Short Writing* was first entered in the Stationer's Register in 1626. His *Tachygraphy* followed in 1638. The earliest printed English work on shorthand, Timothy Bright's *Characterie, or The Art of Short, Swift and Secret Writing by Character*, appeared in 1588. The use of the word "secret" is worth noting.

† Though none perhaps so strange as the wavy line surmounted by a dot, which in William Addy's Bible (1687) symbolised the phrase "the Spirit of God hovered over the face of the waters".

What! write as fast as speak? what man can do it?
What! hand as swift as tongue? persuade me to it.
Unlikely tale! Tush, tush, it cannot be,
May some man say that hath not heard of thee.[2]

Written in Pepys' neat, slightly sloping hand, with the names of people and places and occasional words inserted in longhand, Shelton's system was the vehicle for giving to the world as great a masterpiece in its own way as *Don Quixote* or the *Iliad*. For at heart this young clerk who had learnt to use it so deftly was an artist. His were the artist's two gifts of selection and sincerity; instinctively he knew what incident or mental process to include to give his canvas the image of life, and he loved his art so intensely that no consideration of weariness or shame could ever prevail with him to omit an iota of what he deemed essential. The shorthand was thus doubly precious; it enabled a busy man to write swiftly, and it hid what he wrote from prying eyes.* When Pepys talked to his Diary, he told it nothing but the truth, and herein lies the alpha and omega of all great art. For nearly ten years he drew in unwearied detail a man as God made him and that man himself. It is this catholic inclusiveness in material and this unerring artistry in selection that places this clerk's journal among the imperishable books of the world.

Not that Pepys knew that he was an artist. Of his other assets—his industry, integrity, high administrative ability, his "liberal genius", as he once called it—he was fully aware. He was that rare being, a man with the dual capacity for reflection and affairs: and of the two his gift for the former was

* As Mr W. Matthews points out, Protestant travellers in countries where the Inquisition flourished sometimes carried shorthand Bibles. The distinction between shorthand and cipher was not yet fully established, and probably one of Pepys' motives in using it was its comparative secrecy: it could not, for instance, be read by Elizabeth. The last entry in the Diary appears to support this view.

greater even than his splendid talents for the latter. But in his day the outlet for a literary artist without private means was almost negligible and the few who, like Bunyan, found it did so by mere chance; and thus Pepys naturally devoted himself to that administrative career for which he was so admirably equipped. Yet it happened that at the very outset of that career he resolved, as many others have done, to keep a journal. And into its keeping, as his tired eyes peered through the candle light, he gave, not the perfunctory record which other diarists give, but that which even the most generous struggle to hide from the world, his whole soul. From the crowded and eager life which he, as man, lived so fully, the secret artist in him turned as each day ended to draw again its image by that rarer, intenser light which blinds all eyes but a few:

> The light that never was on sea or land;
> The consecration and the poet's dream.

So on January 1st, 1660, the curtain rises to reveal Pepys' life, as no other man's life has ever been revealed, and even in its rising the full genius of the artist is made plain as the stage is set:

> Blessed be God, at the end of the last year I was in very good health, without any sense of my old pain, but upon taking of cold. I lived in Axe Yard, having my wife and servant Jane and no more in family than us three. My wife after the absence of her terms for 7 weeks gave me hopes of her being with child but on the last day of the year she had them again.

In three sentences Pepys has introduced himself, his home and his family to the world. Then he briefly surveys the political situation—the Rump sitting again, Admiral Lawson with the Fleet in the river, Monk with his army in Scotland and the City clamorous for a free parliament. As for his own private condition—"very handsome, and esteemed rich, but indeed very poor; beside my goods of my house and my office, which at present is somewhat uncertain, Mr Downing master of my office". Now we know all that is needful, and the drama can begin. And in no uncertain manner it does:

Jan. 1st (Lord's Day). This morning (we lying lately in the garret) I rose and put on my suit with great skirts having not lately worn any other clothes but them. Went to Mr Gunning's chapel at Exeter House....

As though to mark the writer's unconsciousness of what he was setting out to do, the first few pages of the Diary are confined to the record of bare events—the quiet and rather frugal fare at home (finishing up that long-lived cold turkey which his wife had redressed), the payment of his half year's rent to landlord Vanly's man, and the wind and cold which disturbed his partner's slumbers. It is not till after some weeks that he first ventures on one of those characteristic and rather naïve reflections that in sheer unconscious truthfulness outdistance all the deliberate confessions of our modern world, appending to the description of a convivial evening with his fellow clerks at the "Sun" tavern the odd remark: "I by having but 3d in my pocket made shift to spend no more, whereas if I had had more I had spent more as the rest did, so that I see it is an advantage to a man to carry little in his pocket". Yet the artist in him, selecting and arranging the incidents of his day like jewels, is there from the opening line: lover of the plastic moment, he stands revealed to our delighted gaze in that January entry:

up till the bell-man came by with his bell just under my window as I was writing of this very line, and cried, "Past one of the clock, and a cold, frosty, windy morning". I then went to bed, and left my wife and the maid a-washing still.

The very years vanish into nothingness in the alchemy of his art, and we stand by the side of this living being, long dead, as he tells us of the guttering candle, "which makes me write thus slobberingly", the discovery of his wife's dressing of the maid's head, "by which she was made to look very pretty" or the joy he felt in his first shave:

> This morning I began a practise which I find by the ease I do it with I shall continue, it saving me money and time; that is to trim myself with a razor, which pleases me mightily.

And what a bond of human sympathy goes out to join him to us and all married men in the resigned entry: "Home and being washing day dined upon cold meat".

But the secret Pepys, who sat over his diary at night and was made one with the ages, was only the shadow of that other Pepys whose doings he recorded and who, that January, 1660, seemed to the outward world much the same ordinary young fellow as he was before. He made his way of a morning to the Exchequer where generally there was "nothing to do" with the national coffers nearly empty, carried out the usual errands for Montagu—seeking out Calthorpe the banker to demand his money, persuading the great Sir Anthony Cooper not to claim his Whitehall lodgings and writing him letters full of news and rumours culled in Westminster Hall—and played cribbage of an afternoon with Jem. The latter alarmed her relations by coming out suddenly in spots: Pepys hastened to her bedside and reported the divergence in diagnosis that followed: the lady presented her humble duty, he wrote; "she hath some pimples rise in her body which my Lady Wright and her maid say is the small pox". The doctor, on the other hand, had pronounced otherwise, declaring that the much discussed eruptions were nothing but heat bumps. "But, my Lord," Pepys added, "if it be that, she hath none in the face at all; for her health she was last night as well and merry as ever I knew her." A week later he was playing cards with her again.[3]

For the rest life was humble enough: a slice cut by his wife from the brawn Lady Montagu had given them, the morning draught drunk at a tavern with Mr Shepley and a sailor, the cold Sunday when there was not a single coal in the house and he and Elizabeth had to seek warmth and shelter at the paternal home in Salisbury Court. Money difficulties were causing him much anxiety: the little nest-egg of £40 or so which he had so carefully saved was in the hands of his Uncle Robert of Brampton, from whom he had expectations and who had lent it out at interest to his cousin Eleanour Becke, who could by no means be prevailed upon to part with it for another four months; and Samuel needed cash badly to balance his accounts at the office. On the evening of Monday, January 9th, there was a crisis; after a day of loafing in coffee-houses and taverns, he returned home to find his colleague Hawley calling to tell him that he had been missed at the office and that to-morrow he must balance his cash accounts. That night he went to bed in great trouble, but in the morning bethought him of his kind friend Mr Andrews, John Crewe's steward, and hastened out early to wheedle another £10 from him. But the measure of the man is shown by his entry for the day, for even in this crisis he could not resist the opportunity of a chance encounter with Greatorex, the instrument-maker, to loiter in an ale-house while that ingenious craftsman displayed the wonders of a new sphere of wire which he had invented: "very pleasant", recorded Pepys and then, resuming his journey to Lincoln's Inn Fields, borrowed his £10 and so hastened back to the office to square his accounts.

Yet though times were difficult, Pepys still retained his

pleasures and his social aspirations. The new year saw him sampling the last of the seasonal festivities, calling on the evening of Twelfth Night at his house for wench and lanthorn, and, thus lit and escorted, walking down frosted streets and lanes to his cousin Stradwick, where all the family were gathered and "a brave cake brought us and in the choosing Pall was Queen and Mr Stradwick King". A few days later, as he made his way to the office he was deflected into Harper's by a chance meeting with Will Symons and Jack Price, who introduced him to Muddiman, the newsletter writer and the father, if any man can claim to be, of modern journalism. Here, in many sorts of talk, he stayed till two in the afternoon and found Muddiman a good scholar and an arch rogue, who owned to writing news books for the Parliament and yet confessed—the shocked Pepys noted that night—"that he did it only to get money and did talk very basely of many of them". This however did not stop Samuel from accompanying his new-found acquaintance to Miles' Coffee House in Old Palace Yard where he paid 18*d.* for the privilege of being enrolled a member of the republican philosopher John Harrington's Rota Club. Here he appeared next evening to join in a great confluence of gentlemen taking coffee about a large oval table and listening to "admirable discourse till 9 at night". He came again the next night and on the following Saturday and heard much exceeding good argument against the learned author of *Oceana's* assertion that overbalance of propriety was the foundation of government, but thereafter his attendance fell off and before the end of the month he was noting his opinion that the club would meet no more. The times were out of joint for the abstract discussion of philosophic formulas.[4]

Yet such activities were far more to Pepys' aspiring taste than the vacuities of the ordinary social round. He ever loved a gathering of learned, worthy persons; he was conscious that he was both enjoying and improving himself in such company. And with such thoughts he was content to spend a quiet Sunday at home while he waited for his physic to work, reading in the great Officiale about the blessing of the bells in the Church of Rome—for all his Protestant upbringing he had always a weak spot in his heart for the old Catholic culture. It was otherwise when he was invited by his acquaintance Surgeon Pierce of the *Naseby* to an over-gay party given by his would-be fashionable wife, making his way through the streets thither while Elizabeth hobbled behind him, much troubled with her new pair of pattens. Here he found a rather smart little gathering—much above the level of his ordinary round—two folk pretending to be husband and wife and after dinner a good deal of mad stir, pulling Mrs Bride's and Mr Bridegroom's ribbons with much other fooling, and gentlemen swearing and singing as if they were mad, which he and Elizabeth did not at all like. It was far better to give a return party of one's own in my Lord's lodgings at Whitehall—with tarts and larded pullets, marrow bones and a leg of mutton, a loin of veal, two dozen of larks, a neat's tongue, and a dish of prawns and cheese, all prepared by Elizabeth and Jane—to his father, Uncle Fenner, his two sons, Mr Pierce and all their wives. Here at least there would be no bawdy behaviour in company. Only Will Joyce, as usual, rather spoilt things by talking and drinking too much.

A rather unpleasant background to life that month was provided by Downing's presence in England. Pepys could never be certain when this irritable, restless gentleman might not send for him, even in the midst of a dish of steaks and rabbit, to execute some errand: generally when he arrived he would keep him hanging about for hours till he condescended to notice him. Still it was the salary which Downing paid that made all the other activities of life possible—even the little house in Axe Yard—and so there was no avoiding it. On Monday, January 16th, while Pepys was seated alone at the office engaged in the usual business of doing nothing because there was nothing to do, his employer walked in on him and, mentioning that he was shortly returning to Holland, asked in his usual cold, unencouraging way whether he would care to come with him. He then followed this with the still more embarrassing question whether he did not think that Hawley could perform the entire work of the office alone, to which Pepys was at a great loss to know what answer to give. Three days later Downing sent for him in the early morning to come to his bedside, where, telling him that he had a kindness for him, he announced that he had arranged for him to be one of the clerks of the Council. At this, as he put it, Pepys was much stumbled, for he had no belief in Downing's kindness, and did not know whether to thank him or not; in the end he did so, "but not very heartily; for I feared", he added to himself, "that his doing of it was but only to ease himself of the salary which he gives me". As for the promotion, Pepys thought little of it, for with Monk's army marching south and London on the verge of revolution, a public employment of any kind was not merely uncertain but dangerous.

However, it all came to nothing. At Marsh's Pepys heard that Symons, Luellin and the rest of his old friends, the clerks of the Council, had been turned out and that his own name had been mentioned for one of the vacancies, and a night or two later, on going up to the clerks' room, he was hard put to it to defend himself (which he did in the end with wonted good humour) from the accusation of having tried to wriggle himself into another man's job. Then at the end of the month came Downing's departure for Holland, preceded by a perfect tornado of work for poor Pepys, employed in working out alternative ciphers for this restless employer, who usually sent them back to be done again as soon as they were finished. Early on the morning of Saturday 28th, after sitting up till midnight, Pepys finished his task while his wife, lying in bed, read to him: then carried it in some doubt to Downing, who informed him that he had resolved to leave for Holland that morning. There followed the wild rush of getting his master and his various belongings into the barge at Charing Cross stairs; and in the emotion of the final farewell, when Downing's manner of taking leave proved unexpectedly friendly, Pepys was so moved that he sent a porter post-haste to Axe Yard to fetch his fine fur cap to give him. Happily it was too late to catch him. After all that, it was something of a relief to dine with Luellin on a breast of mutton in the little tavern, "Heaven", at the end of Westminster Hall, and discourse on the many changes which they had both seen and of the great happiness of those who had estates of their own.

Yet had Pepys and his friends known it, the changes that they had seen were as nothing to those they were now about to witness. For all the while the world of Westminster turned restlessly on itself, Monk with his army was steadily marching south, nor did any man know what he would do. Deep in his heart Pepys had his secret hopes: on the morning of January 30th, before he rose, he fell a-singing of Montrose's song, *Great, good and just*, and put himself thereby in mind that this was the fatal day, now ten years past,* that his Majesty died. Then he walked across to Montagu's lodging to set out a barrel of soap to be delivered to Mistress Anne and Jem. Three days later, as he carried £60 home from the

* A mistake, of course; it was eleven.

City for his Lord, he was startled by the sound of guns, and from the window of Mrs Johnson, the sempstress in the Strand, he watched the unpaid infantry face the cavalry and beat them back, bawling out in the street below for a free parliament and their pay. Next day, after piping a little while on his flageolet in St James's Park—it being a most pleasant morning—he stood with Mrs Turner, The and Joyce Norton in the lane at Whitehall and saw Monk's men march in at the end of their great journey. The first stage of England's most English revolution was accomplished.

On February 6th, a Monday, watching from the steps of Westminster Hall, Pepys saw Monk go by, bowing to the Judges (whose law he came unbeknown to all to restore) as he went to wait on the Rump. Outside the little boys in the street cried "Kiss my Parliament" instead of "Kiss my rump", so low in the estimation of the people had their representatives sunk. By the middle of the week—rendered otherwise notable to the family in Axe Yard by Balty's gift of a pretty black bitch, which Samuel liked well enough until he stumbled on traces of its lack of house manners—Monk, obeying the commands of his jealous masters, had marched into the City to pull down its gates and posts. Here he received such unmistakable signs of the spirit of the people as resolved him to wait no longer. On Saturday, February 11th, Monk again went into the City. But this time he left a letter behind him, stating that he was resolved to stand for the immediate restoration of the excluded members of the Long Parliament. This Pepys, hurrying up to the lobby, saw the crestfallen Speaker reading aloud, and the republican Haslerigg coming out very angry while Billing the quaker plucked at his arm with an ominous "Thou man, will thy beast carry thee no longer? thou must fall". Down in the Hall the faces of all men were changed with sudden joy. Then, lest he should miss anything, Pepys hurried into the City, to be richly rewarded as he reached the Guildhall by the great shout of "God bless your Excellence" that went up as Monk came out of the chamber from his audience with the Lord Mayor and Aldermen. All that afternoon, while Pepys canvassed the news with his friend Matthew Lock the composer in an alehouse hard by, the cheering citizens surrounded Monk's troops with gifts of money and liquor. And that night Pepys, in the quiet of Axe Yard, described it all to his Diary:

and Bow bells and all the bells in all the churches as we went home were a-ringing. Hence we went homewards, it being about ten o'clock. But the common joy that was everywhere to be seen! The number of bonfires, there being fourteen between St Dunstan's and Temple Bar, and at Strand Bridge I could at one view tell thirty-one fires. In King-street seven or eight; and all along burning, and roasting, and drinking for rumps. There being rumps tied upon sticks and carried up and down. The butchers at the May Pole in the Strand rang a peal with their knives when they were going to sacrifice their rump. On Ludgate Hill there was one turning of the spit that had a rump tied upon it, and another basting of it. Indeed it was past imagination, both the greatness and the suddenness of it.

All this, and much that followed it—how the boys had broken Praise-God Barebones' windows, how Vane had been ordered to his native Lincolnshire, and how full the taverns were of merry pamphlets against the Rump, Pepys duly reported to his absent patron at Hinchingbrooke. On Sunday, February 19th, dining with his friend Moore, he heard that the secluded members would now come in for certain and that Crewe and Montagu would be great men again. Two days later he reached Westminster Hall just in time to see the miracle happen, the cropped Mr Prynne—after many revolutions a King's man at last—being very conspicuous among the excluded ones as they marched in, his legs a little tangled up with his long basket-hilt sword. That noon Mr Crewe, observing Pepys amid the gaping crowd in the Hall, made him come home with him to dinner and advised him to send at once for Montagu, saying that it was certain he would now be employed again. And at night in Miles' Coffee House beside Westminster stairs, the diarist sitting with Matthew Lock and Henry Purcell and singing a variety of brave Italian and Spanish songs, saw from the window above the river "the city from one end to the other, with a glory about it, so high was the light of the bonfires...and the bells rang everywhere". Only when he got home did he find his Puritan neighbour Hunt a little forlorn and troubled by these omens of change.

With Pepys it was surprising how often a public duty was made to coincide with a private occasion. On the 23rd (Barebones' windows had again been broken on the previous night) he learnt from Crewe that Montagu was chosen a member of the Council of State. He at once wrote to the latter to inform him and next morning, with Mr Pierce to accompany him, set out for Cambridge, whither his young brother John, holder of a foundation scholarship, had just preceded him. For Samuel was the best of brothers: only a month before he had corrected John's speech for Apposition at St Paul's and consulted with his old headmaster, Cromleholme, how to secure him an exhibition. (At much the same time he had sternly rebuked his sister Pall for stealing his wife's scissors and his maid's book.) Since then he had equipped his brother with some of his own books for his University career and bade him God-speed. Now a day later, riding across the wet foul ways through Ware and Puckeridge, he posted after him. At Fowlmere, the travellers slept, whence at cockcrow, leaving Pierce to go on to Montagu at Hinchingbrooke, Pepys continued his journey to Cambridge, reaching the "Falcon" in that town by eight in the morning. An hour later this indefatigable young man was ushering his brother into the presence of his future tutor, Mr Widdrington of Christ's, and supervising the ceremonies attendant on his admission into the College. Thereafter, for the rest of the week-end, life became a little blurred; after an afternoon spent in drinking the King's health at the "Three Tuns", Sam passed on to a very handsome supper in Mr Hill's chambers at Magdalene, where he was still sufficiently sober to notice that there was nothing at all left of the Fellows' old preciseness in their discourse, especially, he added, on Saturday nights. Sunday, though a little damped by the return of Pierce with the disquieting news that Montagu had already left Hinchingbrooke, was otherwise a repetition of Saturday—dinner with Mr Widdrington at Christ's, a great bout of loyal healths at the "Rose" tavern—the whole royal family were this time remembered—and a wind-up at the "Falcon", where, after seeing young John safely to bed, Samuel concluded the day by playing the fool with the lass of the house at the chamber door.

Thus refreshed he hurried back to London. Yet though in his haste he was up by four o'clock on Monday morning, he could not refrain from loitering an hour or two at Saffron Walden to drink from the mazer bowl, inspect the wonders of Audley End and toast the King in the cellars. All these delights, except a parting kiss at the tavern door to the daughter of the house—"she being very pretty"—cost money; and, for one whose total income was little over £50 a year and who had already given that morning a parting gift to his brother of ten shillings, a douceur of two shillings to the housekeeper at Audley End and sixpence (modern readers must multiply these sums by at least five) to the Saffron Walden poor-box seems almost over-generous. But Sam Pepys, the Westminster clerk, liked to do things handsomely when he went abroad.

On Tuesday morning, February 28th, after a night at Epping and an early morning ride through the forest, he reached London. He found Montagu dining at his brother-in-law Sir Henry Wright's, he having been in London ever since Pepys left it on the previous Friday. However he received his young cousin graciously, told him he was glad to see him and sent him out to buy him a hat. Next morning, drinking with Mr Moore at "Will's", Pepys learnt that his luck was in, for Montagu had been chosen General-at-Sea by the new Council.

As happily there was little to do at the office and Downing was far away in Holland, Pepys was free to dance attendance on his powerful cousin. He waited by his bedside at dawn, where many came to honour him—Secretary Thurloe, and Monk's trumpeters to give him a levite—and heard the stirring rumours of all that was passing; the open talk of government by a single person and hopes, more than whispered now, that the King would come again. And on Shrove Tuesday he had his reward, for at Whitehall, where he had gone ahead with Shepley to prepare a fire in Montagu's lodgings, the latter called him alone into the garden and, after telling him how he had tried to persuade his Uncle Robert of Brampton to make some provision for him, bade him look out for some good place and promised his interest. Then he added that he needed someone about him whom he could trust, for secretly he thought that the King would come in, and asked Pepys whether he would come to sea as his secretary.

Bewildered and overjoyed, Pepys made his way to the

office. And here, as though by divine intervention he received an indication of what great things might lie within his grasp, for Hawley brought him a poor seaman who was offering £10 for a purser's post on one of Montagu's ships. Then for a moment Pepys returned to that old merry England of poor artisans, with its peculiar privileges and its humble social round, which, though he knew it not, he was now to leave for ever. For while taking his midday drink at "Will's", in came Mr Day, a carpenter of Westminster, "to tell me", as Pepys that evening recorded, "that it was Shrove Tuesday and that I must go with him to their yearly club upon this day, which I confess I had quite forgot. So I went to the 'Bell', where was Mr Eglin, Veezy, Vincent a butcher, one more and Mr Tanner, with whom I played upon a viol and he the violin after dinner, and we were very merry, with a special good dinner, a leg of veal and bacon, two capons and sausages and fritters with abundance of wine". Then he proceeded to Mr Scott's to join little Jem in the last Shrovetide revels before the morrow ushered in the glooms of Lent and found them all at hide-and-seek about the house, which in the democratic manner of England was "full of tag, rag and bobtail, dancing, singing and drinking". After which in bed with his wife he lay long awake, unable to sleep at the thought of his lord's great expressions of kindness and his own wonderful fortune.

Next morning, however, brought confusion, for on his way through the streets to Mr Crewe's, he encountered a fellow clerk who told him that George Montagu, his patron's cousin, was to be made Custos Rotulorum for Westminster and advised him to put in for the post of Clerk of the Peace. This pleased Pepys, as every new proposition did, and he decided to try for it: there were certainly grave risks about going to sea, nor did he much care to trust

Elizabeth alone in London. But when he spoke to his lord about it, the latter told him that he believed his cousin had promised the clerkship to another and then very frankly gave him the best advice he could, whether to stay or go with him, and offered all ways within his power to do him good, and all with the greatest freedom and love that could be.

Still undecided, Pepys made his way to the office. That evening he went to Fleet Street to see his father, who had returned from Brampton where he had just left his brother Robert very ill. The old man told him that the latter had promised to make him his heir: "I pray God he may be as good as his word", Sam jotted in his Diary. The good news made it easier for him to make up his mind: if he was to inherit his uncle's little property at Brampton, he could afford to take risks. Next day, at the "Dog" tavern, a naval acquaintance whom he encountered offered his experienced advice: to go to sea, to have five or six servants entered on the muster rolls in his name, pay them what wages he pleased and keep their pay. It was admirable counsel. On Friday, March 9th, Pepys informed Montagu that he was willing to accompany him.

Before he could go there was much to be done. At his kind lord's advice, he wrote at once to Downing, asking that his place might be discharged in his absence by Hawley and his friend Moore to each of whom he offered £20 of his £50 salary. As for the safe disposal of his wife, he was so perturbed that, instead of going home early that evening, he stayed drinking at Harper's till ten o'clock, with the result that between his anxiety and his overheated head he could scarcely sleep at all and was forced next morning to register a vow "to drink no strong drink this week, for I find that it makes me sweat in bed and puts me quite out of order". The same morning, however, brought solution, for on visiting his father, whom he found at work in his cutting-house, the old man suggested that he should send his wife to board with the Bowyers at Huntsmore. This highly satisfactory arrangement he then proposed to Elizabeth, just twenty-four hours after his acceptance of Montagu's offer. The poor girl—she was only nineteen—was much troubled at this unexpected turn of events and only agreed to go to the Bowyers after much dispute. But by the evening she had resigned herself to her fate and was busy making caps for her seafaring husband while the wench sat at her side knitting a pair of stockings for him. And on Monday Samuel, despite a bad cold brought on by a sudden change of weather, borrowed a horse at the "White Hart" in King Street and rode down to Buckinghamshire to see the Bowyers. He found them willing to receive his wife and highly solicitous for his cold, making him swallow a spoonful of honey and nutmeg before they put him to bed.

The next few days were full of unwonted bustle and of the business and dignity of his new position. It was a great thing to visit the Navy Office in Seething Lane as the Admiral's secretary and be treated by Thomas Hayter, Esquire, one of the godly officials there, to a fine breakfast at the "Sun" in Fish Street. It was even grander to become an employer of labour oneself: to hire a boy—of the homely name of Eliezer—from Jenkins of Westminster and engage one John Burr to be one's clerk. It was a little disappointing to learn from Montagu that one's predecessor, Creed, was still to be a rival as Deputy Treasurer of the Fleet, but it could not be helped, and anyway it was highly satisfactory to visit Creed in his chambers and take over his books and the Admiral's seal. And for all the work, the endless papers to be sorted and dealt with and the infinity of applications, it was a glorious thing to be flattered and courted by people who a few days before would never even have noticed one. Nor was the new office without its material rewards; five days after his appointment the Admiral's secretary received half a piece from a parson for recommending him to be preacher in one of the State's ships.

There was no record of "nothing to do" in the Diary now. In the scanty intervals of business, Pepys attended to his own affairs: paid his debts and the rent of his house, packed his belongings in a sea-chest lent him by Mr Shepley and bade farewell to his friends and relations. Nor did he forget Elizabeth. In those last days he was particularly kind to her, and when, after he had retailed to her the list of viands which he had just dined upon at Marsh's, she expressed a longing for some cabbage, he at once sent for some. Then to cheer her up he promised to give her all he had in the world, saving only his books* which he left his brother John, in case he should die at sea.

On the evening of Friday, March 16th, Pepys walking in Westminster Hall heard how that day the Parliament had dissolved itself and had gone out very cheerfully, preparatory to the first free general election in England for twenty years; also how a painter had walked into the Exchange carrying a ladder, up which he had climbed and wiped out the inscription under Charles I's statue, "Exit tyrannus, Regum ultimus". Then, while all men talked freely of a king, he went home and, very sadly and solemnly, spent his last night with his wife. Next morning he bade adieu to her company in bed, rose and gave her what money and papers he had and sealed his will for her. So he took her by hackney to the "Chequers" in Holborn, where, after they had drunk together, she took coach "and so farewell".

* All but his French books which he left to Elizabeth.

Chapter V

The Fortunate Voyage

"No life at the shore being comparable with that at sea, where we have good meat and drink provided for us, and good company, and good divertisments, without the least care, sorrow or trouble; which will be continued if we forget not our duty—viz. loyalty and thankfulness."

Rev. Henry Teonge, *Diary*.

It was melancholy to come home, after dining at Mr Crewe's, to an empty house where everything was locked up, but after a busy evening at the Admiralty Samuel was quite ready to be cheerful again. In the absence of his wife it had been arranged that he should sleep with the Crisps, his neighbours in Axe Yard, until it was time to leave for the Fleet. Here he found a warm welcome, old Mrs Crisp all attention and playing over her childhood's lessons on the harpsichord for his delight, a good supper, an attractive daughter and a bed shared with Laud Crisp, the son of the house, in the best chamber, finely furnished. He repaid these kindnesses by soliciting a place at sea for little Master Laud.

Pepys' stay with the Crisps was longer than he expected. A violent storm of wind and rain which began soon after Elizabeth's departure and which half drowned Westminster and poor little Axe Yard, so that boats were rowed up and down King Street, delayed the Admiral for several days. Samuel after his manner made the best of it. When in his official capacity he handed Captain Williamson his commission to be commander of the *Harp*, he received in return a gold piece and twenty shillings in silver. It was most satisfactory. "Strange", he wrote of a company of naval officers and tradesmen who feasted him at the "Pope's Head" in Chancery Lane, "how these people do now promise me anything; one a rapier, the other a vessel of wine or a gun, and one offered me his silver hat-band to do him a courtesy. I pray God keep me from being proud or too much lifted up hereby."

Not that he had much time to grow conceited. "Infinity of business", he recorded, "and indeed for these two or three days I have not been without a great many cares." For a great fleet putting to sea must always bring to those in charge a vast train of business and applications, but when that fleet is setting out to revolutionise a nation's form of government, the press is likely to be overwhelming. So Pepys, to whom his master passed every paper that reached him, found it, for now all men talked openly of bringing in the King and looked to Montagu, with his brother Monk, to do so. Only Robert Blackburne, the Puritan Secretary to the Admiralty, seemed as glum as the clouds that drove all day above Whitehall, for "good men and good things", he told Pepys, "were now discouraged".[1]

But the storm was blowing itself out and it would soon be time to sail. On March 21st Pepys took a short melancholy leave of his father and mother: indeed his mother had so piteous a cold upon her that he doubted if ever he would see her again. When he got home that night, Mrs Crisp was waiting with the best supper she could serve him and a hankercher with strawberry buttons upon it; and poor Kate Sterpin was ready to cry. For when it came to losing him, everyone loved Sam Pepys. Then on Friday, March 23rd, in his riding clothes, his new grey serge stockings, his sword, belt and hose, and surrounded by friends taking leave and bearing presents—one, not content with the gift of a sugar loaf, actually brought his wife, a very pretty woman, for the departing hero to see—he followed his lord to the Tower, where the barges were waiting. About midday they came to Long Reach, where the *Swiftsure* lay at anchor, and as they went aboard, the guns of all the ships sounded to greet them.

Scarcely were they embarked when the Vice-Admiral, John Lawson, came aboard. As there had been some doubt as to his loyalty to the government in the event of any attempt being made to restore the King, it was reassuring to see the respect with which he treated my Lord. Then Pepys went down to his cabin—a noble one, he noted, though a little short to stretch oneself in*—and unpacked his writing things and, with Burr to help him, got down to work. That night he slept well and "the weather being good was not sick at all", yet, he added, "I know not what I shall be". So the future ruler of the English Navy went to sea.

All the next three days, as they lay in Long Reach, the Admiral's secretary sat in his cabin writing letters. He had not even time to drink with two old acquaintances when they visited the ship. Indeed the strain, combined perhaps with the unwonted lilt of the river, made him a little testy at first: it was irritating to see Creed come aboard and dine very boldly with my Lord, though gratifying that he could not find a bed; and when the boy Eliezer spilt a can of beer over all his papers, Samuel gave him a sound box on the ear. Yet the position was pleasant enough, if one only had time to enjoy it: it was a notable honour to receive a letter from Mr Blackburne of the Admiralty superscribed in his own

* As at the outside he was not (if we follow Mr Whitear's deduction about the giantess encountered by the diarist on Jan. 4th and Feb. 8th, 1669) more than 5 ft. 6 in., it must have been a very little cabin indeed.

hand to Samuel Pepys, Esq.—"of which God knows I was not a little proud"—to dine in the great cabin with the ship's officers, taking precedence of all but Captain Cuttance, and to be visited by the latter dignitary in one's very own cabin, where he benevolently sat drinking a bottle of wine till eleven at night, "a kindness he do not usually do to the greatest officer in the ship".

On Tuesday, March 27th, they fell down the river into the Hope, receiving such "abundance of guns" as they passed the Vice-Admiral that Pepys' cabin windows were shattered by the honourable impact. But still the ceaseless work of writing letters and making orders continued—intensified, as poor Pepys soon discovered, by a regrettable tendency on the part of his clerk Burr to take unwarranted leave ashore, whenever the latter element presented itself. At the moment he had found Gravesend.

On April 2nd, the Admiral transferred to his old flagship, the *Naseby*, and Pepys with him shifting his things into a new cabin, little but very convenient with one window to the sea and another to the deck. The work went with him—vast packets of letters to receive in the early morning, commissions to prepare for replacing dissatisfied officers with loyal ones, interviews with merchantmen requiring convoys (we were still officially at war with Spain), passes to make out for mysterious strangers who secretly visited my Lord and seemed, under various pretences, to be all bound for Flanders. Occasionally the monotony was relieved by a present—two private missives each containing a piece of gold from persons to whom he had done a favour, £5 from a newly promoted captain, thirty shillings for writing a commission for another.

Then on the 5th there came a change, sail was hoisted and the low river banks began to slip by. The Fleet was going to sea. All that afternoon Pepys spent on deck, watching the passing coasts of Kent and Essex glimmering in the spring haze. And next night, as they sailed on towards the Spits (Burr as usual had been left behind), Mr Secretary, his day's work done, stayed late walking on the quarter deck with Captain Cuttance, learning sea terms.

But next morning he awoke to see green water, and his naval education took a new turn. For about nine o'clock the wind got up and the *Naseby* anchored among the sands for a while, and, wrote Pepys, "I began to be dizzy and squeamish". At this moment the Admiral, full of sympathy for his overworked secretary, sent for him to his cabin and offered him a plate of oysters—the best he had ever tasted in his life, he explained. No further work was done that day, and, following a fruitless afternoon spent in walking the deck to keep himself from being sick, Samuel at about five o'clock retired to his bunk. Then a hot caudle was brought him, and he slept.

It was calmer on Sunday and at noon the Fleet set sail again. And now Pepys, somewhat recovered, began to see the green horizon opening before him: saw also many vessels and masts and learnt something of the topography of the sea. All afternoon a brave wind blew and leaning out of the Lieutenant's window, he had a good look through the perspective glass at the decks of two East Indiamen, among the occupants of which he was delighted to notice several handsome women. He was finding his sea legs. But the invigorating effect of ocean was not maintained, for later in the afternoon he was again forced to retire, though he managed before the day ended to engage in a spirited argument with the ship's preacher against extemporary prayers.

But on the morrow, sailing all day within sight of the Forelands, he was able to brook a fresh gale far better than he expected, had his first distant view of the French coast and stood on deck when the *Naseby* came to anchor in the midst of the English battle fleet in the Downs: "great was the shout of guns from the castles and ships and our answers, that I never heard yet so great rattling of guns. Nor could we see one another on board for the smoke that was among us nor one ship from another".

Up to this time, Pepys' association with Montagu had been almost entirely of an official kind. But next night, as he was sitting alone in his cabin in a melancholy fit playing his violin—he had not heard from Elizabeth since he left London and his heart was heavy with apprehension—my Lord with Sir Richard Stayner, the Rear-Admiral, came into the coach to sup, and, hearing his secretary playing, called him out to join them. A new bond—and that almost the most enduring passion in the lives of both of them—had come to link these two sensitive and artistic cousins to each other. Next morning Montagu made Pepys breakfast with him in his cabin. And in the afternoon he poured out his heart to his little secretary—made happy himself by the receipt of two letters from his wife—and discussed very earnestly with him the extent to which he could depend on the loyalty of his captains when the time should come to proclaim the King. Thenceforward Pepys was altogether in his master's confidence, secretly aiding him to purge the Fleet of Anabaptist captains and wording the new commissions of the Vice- and Rear-Admirals to give him the maximum of power over them. He loved to listen to the Admiral speaking to him in such a mood, telling him how happy he thought himself to be now at sea, as well for his own sake as that he thought he might do his country some service. He for his part was also happy, even if his kind master sometimes chaffed him, showing him the French coast through his perspective glass and telling him that it was Kent. For he was now trusted and honoured, and all aboard the ship knew it. So, when on Good Friday he had the furniture of his cabin altered, it gave him great joy to see what a command he had over everyone to come and go as he ordered.

Moreover he was thoroughly contented in other ways. The sea suited him, and he was not in the least perturbed by the great gale which swept the coast in mid-April and, unlike the gentleman from shore who dined with my Lord, was never forced again to rise from table. So long as he knew that his wife was well, he was free from all anxiety; "what with the goodness of the bed", he wrote in the midst of the storm, "and the rocking of the ship, I slept till almost ten o'clock...which occasioned my thinking upon a happy life that I live now". Even Burr's further disappearance on shore at Deal did not worry him.

Reading between the lines of his Diary one can see what good company Pepys was that spring. He, Shepley and Will Howe formed a little trinity of Hinchingbrooke friends on board the ship, to which Lambert, the Lieutenant, and Ibbott* the preacher were always admitted. Lambert was a particular favourite of his: he was even privileged to see his manner of keeping a journal. With such boon companions Pepys loved to broach a vessel of ale and be merry: one evening when they were all together young Will Howe pulled out the spigot of the barrel, filled his mounteer with ale and started to drink from it, while Samuel tried to dash it in his face. After which there was a great deal of good liquor flying about, and Sam's velvet studying cap and his clothes got a little spoilt.

* Pepys was sometimes rather worried that he might have gone too far with this worthy parson in their social evenings together: "sensible that I have been a little too free to make mirth with the minister of our ship, he being a very sober and notable upright man". *D.* April 12th, 1660.

But often Pepys' company was of a higher and more decorous kind. Captain Cuttance would sit of an evening in his cabin and, sharing a barrel of oysters with him, catch something of his fine, infectious gaiety. And the fame of his company went further afield: the Vice-Admiral's coxswain came to invite him to dine with his master, and there in the *London's* state room the humble Exchequer Clerk sat down to feast and be merry. Other captains followed suit, Pepys recording his great content to see how he was treated "and with what respect made a fellow to the best commanders in the Fleet".

The round of work was broken by other pleasures. On St George's Day the rough seamen held their sports and Pepys found it pleasant watching them. A few days later he himself succumbed to the fashionable game of ninepins, with which the great ones of the ship were wont to recreate themselves after dinner, and won half a crown. It was a most expensive victory. Thereafter day after day, Pepys played ninepins on the deck, losing now five shillings, now nine, with almost unfailing regularity to Captain Cuttance, to Creed and even to Montagu, who sometimes took a hand at the game: and this when his total worldly wealth did not exceed £40.

Even less able was he to resist the charm of music—singing a good-night psalm with Will Howe before he slept or tuning his violin with Shepley and Lambert in his cabin. But there could be no harm here. One night as he and Howe were playing, Montagu made them come down to him and calling for instruments joined them in a set of Lock's, two trebles and a base, and, that done, "fell a'singing himself a song upon the Rump to the tune of Greansleaves". Thereafter the three had many musical evenings together.

All the while that the Fleet lay at Deal, there passed

through it a continuous stream of mysterious gentlemen outward bound—great cavaliers who had supported the King through evil times and others who had not but were now making up for lost time. It was part of Pepys' duties to supply them with discreet passes and sometimes with ships; as Montagu's confidential secretary, he stood, a kind of usher, in the loyalty corridor to Flanders. But after May 1st there was no longer any need for secrecy. On that day—"the happiest May day that hath been many a year to England"—the King's letter from Breda was read to a bareheaded House of Commons, who at once invited him to return and govern his native land. The tidings of these events reached the Fleet next day; and on May 3rd the Admiral's secretary sat proudly at his first Council of War and read aloud Charles II's letter to the assembled captains. At the end of the meeting, while they were discussing it, Pepys pretended to draft a loyal resolution, which he had taken down at Montagu's dictation beforehand, and presented it to them: this, though several of them were still republican at heart, they passed. Thereafter he had the most glorious afternoon of his life, visiting each ship in turn and, with infinite pomp and trumpeting and cheering, reading the royal declaration to the assembled crews. Before he retired to bed the Admiral capped his joy by showing him the confidential letters written to him by the King and the Duke of York "in such familiar words as if Jack Cole and I had writ them".

With life opening before him in such wonderful fashion Pepys was at work before three next morning, being careful to add his name to all copies of the Council's resolution so that if any of them found their way into print it should be there. In the afternoon Montagu called him into his cabin to read over the letter which he was secretly sending to the King to see if he could find any slips in it: he was learning to rely more and more on his secretary's discretion and judgment. The latter then hurried off to his cabin and wrote down as much as he could remember of this historic document in his Diary, after which he repaired to the deck for a game of ninepins. That night he wrote a letter on his own account to his old crony, Tom Doling of the Exchequer, enclosing a copy of the vote:

Sir,

He that can fancy a fleet (like ours) in her pride, with pendants loose, guns roaring, caps flying, and the loud "Vive le Roys", echoed from one ship's company to another, he, and he only, can apprehend the joy this inclosed vote was received with, or the blessing he thought himself possessed of that bore it, and is

Your humble servant.

It was all very formal and splendid.

On Monday, May 7th, Montagu gave Pepys orders to write for silk flags and scarlet waistcloths, a rich barge, a noise of trumpets and a set of fiddlers. Three days later he sent for him privately and told him that he was commanded to sail to fetch the King. On the 11th the Fleet left the Downs for Dover and next day, without waiting for the Parliamentary Commissioners who were expected from London, weighed anchor for Holland. Before he left Pepys received a letter from his wife and had the unspeakable satisfaction of seeing his name in print in a London pamphlet describing the Fleet's doings at Deal. Burr once more was nearly left behind.

So with the sea he was to serve so well blowing through his being, Pepys watched the vanishing cliffs of Dover and Calais: "and very pleasant it was to me that the further we went the more we lost sight of both lands". Sunday was spent in making ready for the new era, with the Fleet's painters and tailors hard at work removing the Commonwealth harps from the ships and cutting up yellow cloth into crowns and "C.R.s", and in the afternoon good Mr Ibbott prayed for "all that were related to us in a spiritual and fleshly way". Towards evening they came within sight of the Dutch shore.

When Pepys awoke on Monday morning and looked out of the scuttle he could see the sand dunes and beyond the spires of the Hague. Then the sight familiar to so many generations of sea-going Englishmen arriving in a foreign port appeared: and "some nasty Dutchmen come on board to proffer their boats to carry things from us on shore, etc., to get money by us". In the grey mist of dawn the islander in Pepys reacted; but later when the sun rose, the curious child of nature that was more than half of him got the better of his insularity and he was all agog to go ashore. Later in the day he found himself, with leave of absence duly given, in a coach, "wherein there was two very pretty ladies very fashionable and with black patches", jolting over the sandy road to the Hague. The ladies sang merrily all the way, two blades that were with them made very free in kissing them, and Pepys took out his flageolet and piped. It was a pity that in doing so he dropped his rapier stick out of the door: he sent his boy back to fetch it but some horses had been over it and had broken the scabbard. He found the Hague a most fine and smart place in all respects, the houses as neat as possible with maypoles outside every door: it was also very full of English. A friendly stranger showed him round, and at about ten o'clock he obtained admission to see the little Prince of Orange. After that it was pleasant to sup with nine of his fellow sightseers on a sallet and three bones of mutton, and retire to bed with the Judge Advocate of the Fleet, the boy Eliezer lying on a bench beside them. It was all, he added again, "very neat and handsome".

Next day, in the sunlight, the sight-seeing continued. It was entrancing—the burghers with their muskets bright as silver, the trim rows of trees, the pretty baskets which he bought for Elizabeth and Mrs Pierce: "indeed", he wrote, "I cannot speak enough of the gallantry of the town...the women many of them very pretty and in good habits fashionable and black spots". It was a great pity to have to leave it all (though he had just time to buy three books for love of their fine binding before doing so) to go back to Schevelling and the ships. But the Admiral made up for everything, showing Pepys his new clothes, "rich as gold and silver can make them", talking to him all alone for two solid hours on his views on religion, "wherein he is, I perceive, wholly sceptical, as well as I, saying that indeed the Protestants as to the Church of Rome are wholly fanatiqus"; and showing such respect and kindness as he had never known in his life. After supper, the talk continued till the sea grew so rough that Sam was unable to stand and had to go to bed.

After a day of hard work at sea, when even his weekly shave from the barber was interrupted by the arrival of a Dutch Admiral who, speaking no French or English, must needs be entertained in Latin, Pepys managed to get on shore again. This time he was particularly fortunate. He saw the King, who seemed to be a very sober man and who most graciously kissed little Edward Montagu, who had come sight-seeing too, the Lord Chancellor Hyde lying on his bed with a fit of the gout but exceedingly merry, and the Queen of Bohemia. After this feast of royalty—the first of that rare species on whom he had set eyes since childhood—Samuel took coach to the House-in-the-Wood to see the Dowager Princess of Orange's pictures and sing songs in the Echo there. It was all inexpressibly pleasant, the more, as he said, "because in a heaven of pleasure and in a strange country"; never in his life had he been so taken up with a sense of delight.

Moreover the treat was prolonged. An attempt to re-embark at dawn next morning was frustrated by a gale, and, after waiting some hours in the rain for a boat, he returned to the Hague. There was a slight hiatus, however, due to the disappearance of young Montagu, whom Pepys left in the charge of Mr Pierce: hearing that the latter had borne him off sight-seeing to Delft, he took boat to that place. But though he saw the church where Van Tromp lay entombed, and a most sweet town with bridges and a river in every street, he could find no trace of his employer's son and his custodian. Nor was the weight on his mind relieved by the behaviour of a pretty sober Dutch lass upon whom he tried to fasten some discourse in the boat on the return journey and who prudently refused all his advances. Another visit to the House-in-the-Wood cheered him up, but there was still no sign of Master Edward. His anxiety was not removed till next morning when he encountered the young gentleman and the truant Mr Pierce in a shop buying pictures. After which he gave the latter a piece of his own mind.

The storm was still blowing, but as he had been now absent from the Fleet for nearly three days, Pepys resolved to set out for Schevelling early next morning. Before he left the Hague he met his old chamber-fellow of Cambridge, Kit Anderson, in whose rather hectic company he spent several hours in a tavern where they were privileged to enjoy the society of a very promising young lady. Fortunately it was Saturday night and her professional duties with the refreshments prevented her from devoting herself too entirely to her English admirers, and at midnight, though the aspiring Anderson announced his intention of returning to see more of her, Pepys retired to bed. But there was no doubt that the long celibacy and the Dutch sights and wine were proving too much for his far from frigid temperament. After the jolting ride to Schevelling in the early morning, the wind was still blowing hard and so he repaired for a few hours' sleep to an inn where "in another bed there was a pretty Dutch woman in bed alone", but he added regretfully, "though I had a month's mind to her, I had not the boldness to go to her. So there I slept an hour or two. At last she rose, and then I rose and walked up and down the chamber, and saw her dress herself after the Dutch dress and talked to her as much as I could and took occasion, from her ring which she wore on her first finger, to kiss her hand, but had not the face to offer anything more". Then he bade adieu to the shore.

For two more days the storm blew. On the 22nd the wind dropped and the ship's company made ready to receive the Dukes of York and Gloucester on board—both very fine gentlemen they seemed to be. That morning on the quarter-deck the Duke of York as Lord High Admiral, his secretary William Coventry, Admiral Montagu and Samuel Pepys spent a busy hour allotting to every ship its service for the return voyage to England. On one side of the medal one sees a busy little man, conscious of his new-found importance and dancing assiduous attendance on these great ones; on the other the future governance of the Royal Navy brought together for the first time on the *Naseby's* rolling deck.

Wednesday, May 23rd, was the great day. Pepys from the ship watched the vast multitude on the sands that pressed around the King as he made his way to the water's edge—the last surge of returning exile—and was almost deafened by the thunder of guns as the Admiral's barge bore him towards the flagship. He knelt to kiss the hands of the King and the other royalties who accompanied him and saw them all dine in the coach, "which was a blessed sight to see". Afterwards the King to mark the inauguration of a new régime rechristened the *Naseby* after his own name *Charles*, and, while the Dukes went to their stations in the *London* and *Swiftsure*, those who were not to sail put off for the shore, so that in one small boat Pepys could see the receding forms of the daughter of James I, the daughter of Charles I and a little boy who in the far future was to be King William III. Then the Fleet weighed anchor, and "with a fresh gale and most happy weather we set sail for England. All the afternoon the King walked here and there, up and down (quite contrary to what I thought him to have been) very active and stirring. Upon the quarter-deck he fell into discourse of his escape from Worcester, where it made me ready to weep to hear the stories that he told of his difficulties that he had passed through". All these things his humble listener recorded in his Diary.

There were so many people on board the ship that one could scarcely move. But they were all people of great quality, lords and persons of honour, so that Pepys did not in the least mind having to share the carpenter's cabin with Dr Clerke, that genteel and knowledgeable physician, or to crowd with seven other people in to dinner in that tiny space; after all it was not every day that one could mess with such notables as the King's chaplains and physicians, his old tutor Dr Earle and his confidential financial agent, Stephen Fox, or walk the deck listening to the royal jester, Thomas Killigrew, telling merry stories—delightful, even if he were a little blasphemous. And it was a glorious thing to carry a document into the King's own presence and watch him sign it. Amid such joys and wonders they came in sight of English land on the evening of May 24th.

Before the King landed next morning there was a further

thrill in store for Samuel. For going to speak on business to the Duke of York, that kind prince called him Mr Pepys by name and promised him his future favour. About noon the royal brothers landed in their native kingdom. The Admiral's secretary followed them in a smaller boat with one of the royal footmen and a dog that the King loved, which so far missed the significance of the occasion as to forget its manners, which "made us laugh, and me think that a King and all that belong to him are but just as others are". With this philosophical reflection, Pepys completed his part in the most dramatic episode in English history.

So he saw the King pass from the crowded beach and away through the town towards Canterbury—"the shouting and joy expressed by all was past imagination". Then he returned to the ship, to find his chief almost transported with joy at the thought of his share in these events. After that there was something of a reaction. For the great company was now all gone and next day Pepys found himself "very uncouth all this day for want thereof". Indeed the full measure of that fall was perhaps best indicated by the fact that he himself, in the Admiral's absence, dined commander at the coach table and all the officers of the ship with him. Yet even that, when one reflected on it, was a wonderful and almost miraculous position for one who two months before had been proud to eat his dinner with a couple of senior clerks.

Also, though the glamour of the last few days was over, there was a compensation. For a golden shower of royal benevolence now fell on the ships that had brought the King over, and a not insignificant part of it lighted on the Admiral's secretary. On the 23rd, Pepys heard that the King had given £500 for the *Naseby's* crew and officers and another £50 for Montagu's servants. Of the former he secured sixty ducats (about £30) and of the latter seventy guilders. When he made up his accounts on June 3rd he found himself worth nearly £100, for which his heart was glad and he blessed God. The voyage in nine weeks had more than doubled his capital.

Nor was this all. For in those last ten days on board the *Naseby*, after the princes had departed and before he and his master also left, there lay in the air a lively sense of further favours to come. To Montagu, Charles II had sent from Canterbury the King-of-Arms bearing the great order of the Garter, and it was plain that the royal favour was at the command of the man whose ships had brought him home. It was not unreasonable that Pepys, who was now so caressed and trusted by his master, should look for something too. And, as they cleared up the last business of the voyage, played a friendly game of ninepins or rode together in a merry party beneath Dover cliffs, wagering their height against that of St Paul's, Montagu in his reticent way was quick to encourage these hopes. On June 2nd, when Pepys was thanking him for his share of the Duke of York's bounty, he told him that he hoped to do him a more lasting kindness, and added: "We must have a little patience and we will rise together. In the mean time I will do yet all the good jobs I can". Four days later, hearing from London that a clerkship of the Signet had fallen to him, Montagu promised his secretary, and that in the most loving terms, the execution of it in case he could not get him better employment. Then on Thursday, June 7th, came a royal summons to London, and my Lord and his servants made ready to go. Next day they set out, Pepys a little troubled with the King's guitar. The travellers dined at Canterbury, where one of Mr Pepys' many selves took great delight in inspecting the Cathedral and the remains of Becket's tomb, and slept at Gravesend, where another of them kissed a good handsome wench, "the first that I had seen a great while". On Saturday the 9th they came by boat to London, landing at the Temple.[2]

So ended the fortunate voyage. It had brought to Pepys money, opportunity and contact with great folk, acquaintanceship with whom had hitherto been beyond his wildest dreams. It had also brought him while it lasted intense pleasure; important work, good victuals and drink, health-giving breezes, merry company and a complete absence of personal responsibility. Above all his passionate curiosity, his love of new sights and new faces, had been gratified as never before.

Yet in all that voyage in which he found so much, one thing he missed. Once, visiting my Lord's store-room of wine and drink, Pepys had admired the ship's massy timbers, but for the most part the vessel that bore him attracted his notice very little; it was her good fare, important passengers and congenial employment that charmed him. Of the seamen themselves, that rough humorous race apart, of whom Clarendon wrote so feelingly and who had their being all around him, he never spoke nor indeed scarcely seemed aware. The tarry, swearing, droll fellows, who called all things by a peculiar name of their own, rolled so in their gait that a waiting wench or a pressman could tell them half a mile away, sang lustily as they sounded the depths, and, cursing their commanders, bore their ships unflinchingly between the cliffs of Teneriffe into the flame of a thousand guns, were still beyond his ken. For it was not on the wide and dancing waters that a great servant of England's navy was to learn his trade, but in the riverside streets beside the Tower, where the grey Thames flowed outwards with ships upon her breast to meet the sea.[3]

Chapter VI

Clerk of the Acts

"To my wife again...and presented her with my patent at which she was overjoyed; so to the Navy Office and showed her my house, and both were mightily pleased at all things there." *Diary*, July 13th, 1660.

It was good to see Elizabeth, safely come up from the Bowyers to John Pepys' house in Salisbury Court, to take her arm in Lincoln's Inn Walks, and to comfort his former loneliness at night with her presence. Samuel had been troubled for some weeks by news of her poor health, and she had written plaintively how fain she was to be with him and at her house again; "but we must be content", he had told his Diary. Now she was well and restored to his arms. It was a fortnight, however, before the little house at Axe Yard was ready to receive them; till then Mrs Pepys, with her maid and her black dog, lodged at her father-in-law's.

But man, so soon as one hope is fulfilled or one anxiety assuaged, finds something new to vex his heart. So it was that June with Pepys. His wife he had: it was a post he sought now. In this he was not alone, for all England in the summer of 1660 came flocking to Whitehall to see what the miraculous turn of events and the generosity of a king could give. Amid the crowd of suitors in Whitehall gallery and park, little Samuel Pepys took his place; "there", as one laconic entry has it, "walked, gallantly great".

Those who climb seek as a rule some firm handhold by

which to raise themselves. Montagu that June must sometimes have found the attendance of his secretary a little overwhelming, for he was followed by him everywhere. It was wearying for Pepys too: "Court attendance infinite tedious", he confessed, but then it was worth it. For his master was in high favour, was made Master of the Great Wardrobe, a Commissioner of the Treasury and given an Earldom, and at any moment something might come the way of his faithful attendant. In the meantime Pepys did not neglect small gains; when Murford, his old acquaintance of Westminster Hall, took him to a tavern to drink and told of a business by which he might make £5, he was all attention, especially when a day or two later the suitor actually showed him the money. Nor did he refuse to aid Lady Pickering—once so great a personage in his little world but now, through her husband's republicanism, fallen on evil days—when she begged his assistance with his Lord and gave him for his encouragement five pounds of silver wrapped in paper.

On June 18th, Montagu told his secretary that he was on the look-out for the place of Clerk of the Acts of the Navy for him. Pepys was not quite clear what it was, and did not think much about it for some days: after all it was improbable that anything so grand would really come his way. Instead he busied himself with such matters as obtaining contact with a gentleman who was offering £500 for a baronetcy, and the collection of small gratuities due to him for services rendered to sea-captains in their pursuit of commissions. But on the 23rd, Montagu told him that he had definitely obtained the promise of the post for him, "at which", Pepys notes, "I was glad": my Lord also must have been glad. Then the full nature of the promised appointment began to dawn on Samuel, and by next day his mind was entirely taken up with the thought of it.[1]

Straightway he set to work to make certain that the prize so suddenly dangled before him should become his: no stone would he leave unturned to ensure that. He spoke to William Coventry, the Duke's secretary, with whose remote acquaintanceship his naval work for Montagu had endowed him, lobbied everyone he met and followed his Lord about more attentively than ever. Nor were such precautions unneeded. For almost at once obstacles to the fulfilment of his wishes presented themselves. Mr Turner of the Navy Office told him openly that he was after the same place—"he was very civil to me and I to him"—and worse, Lady Monk wrote to Montagu saying that she had promised the office to someone else. But the Admiral proved a match for this all-powerful lady (who was using her husband's unique position to demand a "rake-off" from every aspirant to employment in the state) and wrote back that he believed that General Monk would take it ill if he, for his part, should try to name the officers of his army and that he therefore hoped to have the naming of at least one officer in the Navy. After which there was no further opposition from Lady Monk.

The Clerkship of the Acts was well worth a battle to obtain. In a sense it was the oldest of all the administrative offices of the Navy Office—the department which under the supervision of the Admiralty (then still the secretarial entourage of the Lord High Admiral) built the ships, fed and clothed the men and maintained the dockyards of the old Navy. In the far mists of the past, somewhere in the days when White Rose was fighting Red, there had been first appointed a great officer called Clerk of the King's Ships. In the time of Henry VIII the manifold duties of this functionary had been merged into those of a Navy Board. But one of the four Principal Officers of the latter, though admittedly inferior to his brethren—the Treasurer, the Comptroller and the Surveyor—still bore the honoured name of Clerk of the Acts of the King's Ships. When the outline of all things old vanished in the great deluge of 1642, he and the other Principal Officers disappeared from the pay roll of the state, and their places were taken by a body of Commissioners, who continued to execute the administrative work of the Navy from their office in Mark Lane and sent out, not unprepared, the ships which humbled Van Tromp and sailed into the waters of Santa Cruz. With the Restoration, in the great business of trying to please everyone which was the main concern of the new government of England, it was decided to amalgamate the practice of both the ancient royal and the more recent republican Navy Offices. Independent Commissioners with a roving warrant were still to sit on the Board, but to them were to be added the old Principal Officers—the Treasurer, the Comptroller, the Surveyor and the Clerk of the Acts. Though the latter was both in theory and practice the least of these, and his official salary in the days before the civil wars had been somewhat slender, the perquisitorial possibilities of the post were sufficiently promising to cause a hard-headed man of business to offer Pepys, almost on the very day that his candidature was first discussed, £500 to desist from his application. For one whose total wealth two months before had not exceeded a twelfth part of that sum, Pepys' prayer that night that God would direct him what to do was not unreasonable.[2]

The Duke of York himself spoke to his secretary to dispatch the business, and everyone whom he met gave Pepys joy of his new place as though he were already in it. On June 28th, Sir George Downing received a full release from all contractual obligations to his former clerk: "he is so stingy a fellow", the latter recorded, "I care not to see him". Next day, with the Duke's warrant for the Clerkship of the

Acts in his pocket, Pepys received a shock, for he was told that his predecessor in that office, one Thomas Barlow, was still alive and was coming up to town to claim his place. Though his master bade him get possession of his patent and promised to do all that he could to keep this invader out, his heart sank into his boots.

In the next few days events moved almost breathlessly. On the last day of the month came a letter from Mr Turner offering £150 to be joined with Pepys in his patent and advising him how to make the most of the place and keep out Barlow. Early next morning, a Sunday, there arrived at Axe Yard a fine camlet coat with gold buttons and a silk suit; "I pray God", wrote its proud owner, "to make me be able to pay for it". Success in his candidature was now more vital than ever. Monday brought infinity of business so that Pepys' heart and head were both full. And at seven that night in Montagu's lodgings, there met for the first time the Principal Officers of the Navy and "among the rest", recorded the proud diarist, "myself was reckoned one". There they received their instructions to meet next day and to draw up such an Order of Council as, when passed, would put them into action.

Of those who gathered round the table in Sir Edward Montagu's room all but one had experience of things appertaining to the sea or war. Chief of them was the newly appointed Treasurer of the Navy, Sir George Carteret, who had rendered the most important services to the King in his native Jersey in the early days of his exile and who had held the office of Comptroller of the Navy twenty-one years before in the time of Charles I. Another veteran of those far days was Admiral Sir William Batten, who had been Surveyor of the Navy from 1638 to 1642 and who now, after a somewhat chequered sea career, first as a parliamentarian and then as a royalist, returned at a ripe age to his old post. The Comptroller was as yet unnamed, but the three additional Commissioners, who with a roving warrant were to assist the Principal Officers, had all been nominated by the Privy Council at its sitting that morning. Of these by far the most important was Sir William Penn. He had been born and bred a merchant seaman of Bristol, had first commanded a royal ship in 1642 at the age of twenty-one and had held the great office of General-at-Sea under the Commonwealth. During the last few months of the republic he had gone the same way as Monk and Montagu and had been knighted on board the *Naseby* for his share in bringing back the King. He was still only thirty-nine and was probably the most able officer in the English Navy. It was he who, through his friendship with the Lord High Admiral's secretary William Coventry, had prevailed upon the Council to adopt the administrative practice of both royal and republican days and had drafted the memorandum which laid down the nature and duties of the new Navy Board. The other two Commissioners were Lord Berkeley of Stratton, a distinguished Cavalier soldier, and Peter Pett, who for thirteen years had served as the Commonwealth Commissioner at Chatham dockyard and was the most eminent living representative of the famous family of shipwrights which for over a hundred years had held, through all political changes, the virtual monopoly of building the state's chief ships. He, on Penn's advice, was not obliged to a continual personal attendance at the Board like the other Principal Officers, but continued in his former employment in charge of the great yard at Chatham. The one exception to this galaxy of naval and military experience was the Clerk of the Acts elect, a young man of twenty-seven who a few months before had scarcely known one end of a ship from the other. It was small wonder, therefore, that Pepys had some fears that he would be unable to attain to the great post which his cousin, the Admiral, had so unexpectedly placed within his reach.[3]

Next day his fears were shown to be fully justified. After attempting during dinner to spike Turner's guns by offering him £50 out of his own purse and the benefit of a clerk's place besides, he was greeted with the news that Barlow was on the point of enquiring for Mr Coventry. In terror he hurried to his Lord, who, like the noble-hearted patron he was, assured him that he need not fear, for he would get him the place against all the world. He received further comfort from Will Howe who told him that Barlow was a sickly man who would be incapable of executing his old office in person. After that Pepys was able to write letters for his chief in comparative peace of mind till two in the morning.

Yet before dawn he was up again, soliciting Sir George Carteret, the Treasurer, for his help and then hurrying with Commissioner Pett to the Navy Office in Seething Lane to view the official residences of the Principal Officers: even the worst of them, he decided, was very good. But the fatal fear of losing that which he so much coveted gnawed again at his heart; what if the great ones who were to be his colleagues should shuffle him out of his right to one? And all that evening he spent restlessly pacing in the courtyard of Whitehall, until his Lord came out and told him that the Council had passed the formal orders empowering the new Navy Board to act.[4]

Next day, feeling a little more assured, Pepys agreed to employ Thomas Hayter of the old Navy Office as his clerk. He also obtained much sage and experienced advice from the superseded Secretary to the Admiralty, Robert Blackburne, with whom he walked for an hour or two between the summer showers in St James's Park. And at dinner he learnt from Mr Cooling, the Lord Chamberlain's secretary, of a project which that gentleman had formed "for all us secretaries to join together and get money by bringing all business into our hands". The spirit of a great Civil Service was already abroad in the land.

Yet again that night the promised cup was almost dashed from Pepys' lips. Dr Petty, one of the Professors of Gresham College, whom he had previously known slightly, came to him to inform him that his friend Barlow was now in London, which, with other things this learned gentleman mentioned, put him into an utter despair. Even next day when, in company with Montagu, Carteret and Coventry, he went to take possession of the Navy Office and its papers, his expectations of really securing the job remained almost negligible. But with the week-end hope returned. On Saturday, July 7th, one came to him offering to buy a clerk's place, and Samuel was bold enough to ask £100 for it. A few hours later he learnt that the Council had advanced the old pre-war salaries of the Principal Officers all round, setting his—the lowest of the four—at £350 a year, a sum equivalent to perhaps £1500 in our present-day money. And though on Sunday his campaign was necessarily interrupted, he was a little cheered by the news that a friendly don at Cambridge had procured him a degree as Master of Arts by proxy.

Pepys' great business of the next week was to secure his patent to his office before Barlow could have time to establish his earlier claim. All Monday morning he spent at Sir Geoffrey Palmer's, the Solicitor General's, advising how best to get his bill—the necessary preliminary to the engrossing of a formal patent—drawn quickly; in the evening, the first meeting of the Board at the Navy Office over, he returned to the Temple on the same business. On Tuesday he recruited Montagu into this service, coaxing him to go to the Secretary of State and desire a speedy procurement of the necessary royal signature. The application was successful and the next afternoon Pepys bore away the bill, duly signed, in triumph to the Privy Seal Office, there to have it perfected. Thence on Thursday he took it to the House of Lords and sought out an old cavalier friend, Mr Kipps, whom he had known in the days of his extreme poverty but who was now Seal Bearer to the Lord Chancellor, "a strange providence", Pepys reflected, "that he should now be in condition to do me a kindness, which I never thought him capable of doing for me". Kipps directed him to one Mr Beale in Chancery Lane who would, so he said, engross his patent for him. But in the best traditions of Chancery, Mr Beale pleaded that he had no time. So poor Pepys was forced to run up and down Chancery Lane and the Six Clerks Office, where those who enrolled warrants, pardons and patents lived, looking for someone with leisure enough to do his business. But no one was able to undertake it, for that summer half the public offices in England were changing hands and all their new possessors taking out their patents. By this time Pepys was in despair, for he had discovered that Barlow had already been that day at the Chancellor's Office, threatening to enter a caveat and put a stop to the whole business. Almost in a state of frenzy he hurried back to Kipps' lodgings, only to find him out. At last, at eleven o'clock at night, he procured a musical acquaintance, Mr Spong, who was versed in such practice, to come round to Montagu's lodgings and promise to write out the bill that night. The good-natured man was still at it in his nightgown when Pepys went round to call for it in the morning. All that Friday, though he ate but a little bread and cheese all day, the intensive attack on the entrenched forces of officialdom continued: Mr Kipps at Worcester House secured the Chancellor's "*Recepi*" and Pepys positively ran with it to Beale's for a docket. The latter was very angry at such unusual haste and far from pleased to see that the bill had been written by a hand other than his, but at last, with much importunity and the timely production of two gold pieces—"after which it was strange how civil and tractable he was"—he was prevailed upon to do his part of the business. Further comings and goings brought Pepys back in the afternoon to Worcester House, where by Kipps' help and by dint of pressing through the crowd in Admiral Montagu's name, he found himself in the Chancellor's presence and, beyond all expectation, got his seal passed. He was Clerk of the Acts at last. And far away the King's ships strained at their moorings or swung with the tides.[5]

Then he went away and fetched Elizabeth to share it all. She sat in the hackney coach while he went into Mr Beale's, paid his fee of £9 and then bore out his patent, illuminated and enscrolled, to show her. After that they drove together through the narrow city streets to Seething Lane, and there Samuel showed his wife the house which was now to be theirs. It had formerly belonged to Commissioner Willoughby of the Commonwealth Navy Office and stood overlooking the garden and courtyards of the Office with half a dozen or so other official residences. It was all finer than anything they had ever dreamt of before, with eight or nine rooms and built of brick—as commodious, neat and up to date as any man could desire. And only that morning Pepys had got his brethren of the Navy Board to agree to his having a door made on to the leads, whereon he and Elizabeth might walk together on summer evenings.[6]

So that night Pepys went to bed with greater quiet of mind than he had felt for many a day. As for the ghost of his predecessor, he soon managed to lay that bugbear. For having placed himself in an almost impregnable position, he used it to safeguard himself against any recurrence of danger. A few days later Mr Barlow called on him, an old consumptive man and fair-conditioned, and after some little talk Pepys agreed to allow him £100 a year out of his £350 salary, as and when it was paid. He could afford now to be generous, and it was his nature to make friends. The arrangement suited them both, for Barlow could never really have hoped to have obtained much from his old office: he himself had only held it for a very short time in the far days before the Civil Wars and since then had never had anything from it save a few months' imprisonment by the Long Parliament for suspected malignancy. On the 23rd the two signed a formal agreement, Barlow, who lived in the country, appointing Dr Petty as his attorney to receive the money for him when it fell due. Afterwards they dined together at Pepys' house and were very pleasant with one another.[7]

No time was wasted by the Pepyses in moving into their new quarters. On the day after her husband had received his patent, while he himself made a visit to Tower Hill to order in coals, Elizabeth packed up the household goods and on the next day her clothes. A heavy downpour delayed the trek for a further day, but on the 17th the great move was made, carts carrying the baggage through London, while the Pepyses, accompanied by Mrs Hunt to help them settle in, made the journey in a hackney coach. That night, infinitely pleased with it all, they slept in their new home. And on the very next day the carpenter completed the door on to the leads. No one could say that the new Clerk of the Acts allowed the grass to grow under his feet.

The rise in fortune brought with it new responsibilities. No longer was it possible for simple, harmless Jane Wayneman to do the domestic work for the three of them, and an addition was made to the household in the shape of a boy, Will, who had come to the Pepyses a few weeks before to help them during Jane's temporary illness and who was now retained permanently. This young person may best be described as a caution. At first his employer, who loved anything droll and original, found his vagaries amusing; when he returned late one night and discovered the boy, who was supposed to be guarding the house, fast asleep, he only laughed and had great sport in waking him. But after a short time the novelty began to wear off, and certain of Will's more objectionable characteristics manifested themselves. Towards the end of August, he was caught stealing money in the house, and, when Pepys cross-examined him, he lied outrageously. He was subsequently succeeded by Jane's brother, Will Wayneman, a pretty, well-looked boy and one, his master thought, that would please him well.[8]

Another Will came into the Pepyses' house that July. This was young William Hewer, the seventeen-year-old nephew of Robert Blackburne, the former Secretary to the Admiralty. It was the beginning of a long and honourable association which only death was to close nearly half a century later. Hewer's duties were something between those of a clerk and a personal attendant, and he was employed impartially at the office and about the house. At first he by no means always gave satisfaction: he was inclined to stay out late, occasionally got into bad company and was often very careless; on one occasion his master was partly consoled for the loss of a tankard by the knowledge that Will, whose failure to bolt the door had given the thieves their chance, had lost his own clock at the same time. But the young fellow possessed also a very tender and loyal heart, a thing which no man living was more quick to appreciate than his master.[9]

The appointment to the Clerkship of the Acts was attended for Pepys by other benefits. Nothing could exceed Montagu's kindness to him. The latter made him dine with him all alone and walked with him publicly in the garden at Whitehall, showing him all the respect that could be. On the day after Pepys moved into his new house there arrived for him from Hinchingbrooke half a buck: "it smelling a little strong", the grateful recipient recorded, "my Lord did give it me though it was as good as any could be. I did carry it to my mother, where I had not been a great while,... because my father did lie upon me continually to do him a kindness at the Wardrobe, which I could not do because of my own business being so fresh with my Lord".

Yet this benevolent nobleman—he took his place as Earl of Sandwich in the Lords that July—continued to heap favours on his young kinsman. He himself had been given by a grateful sovereign as one of his minor offices a Clerkship of the Privy Seal. Since he could scarcely condescend to carry out its duties in person, he passed it on, like the buck, to his late secretary to execute as his proxy. Pepys did not, as a matter of fact, expect to make much out of this appointment and accepted it chiefly as a kind of insurance in case he should lose his other office and also to do a kindness to his friend Moore whom he joined with him in the employment. But he was agreeably surprised.[10]

On July 31st Pepys went to the Privy Seal where he found Crofts and Matthews, the two outgoing clerks, making up their books in order to leave the office to their successors for the month of August—the Clerks of the Privy Seal taking their turns of service in rotation. Next day in his Lord's name, Pepys entered upon his month of office, obtaining temporary leave from the Navy Board to enable him to do so. He could scarcely have been more fortunate. For after all the grants of places, lands and pensions which had been made from Whitehall that midsummer, the office of the Privy Seal—usually a quiet, uneventful place—was crowded from morning till night with suitors taking out seals for their patents and commissions. And every seal taken out meant a fee for the clerk who signed it. By the 10th of the month Pepys was reckoning that his new employment was bringing him in about £3 a day—a blessed piece of fortune he accounted it, even though the constant attendance, combined with his work at the Navy Office, kept him so busy that he had no time to write to any of his friends or relations—not even to his Uncle Robert from whom he had expectations. The good work continued right up to the month's end, when he handed over the books to the incoming clerks. When a day or two later he cast up the profits, he found that his Lord's share came to £400 and his own to £132, of which he gave £25 to Mr Moore for his pains. For the second time that year Pepys had doubled his capital in a single month.

All this access of good fortune naturally turned his head a little. On Saturday, August 4th, rejoicing in God's blessing in bringing such a host of fee-paying applicants to the office and a little impatient at the reappearance of his wife's old pains, he bespoke some linen from Betty Lane of Westminster Hall and afterwards took her to the "Trumpet" nearby for a little innocent toying. A week later—this time it was on a Sunday—he went somewhat further and, after treating this buxom and free-hearted young woman to a bottle of wine, he inveigled her into his empty house at Axe Yard and there, as he put it, was exceedingly free in dallying with her and she not unfree to take it. It was an interesting example of the advantage of having two houses, especially on a Sunday afternoon.

But this was scarcely the kind of luxury which a discreet and rising young state official, with his fortune still to make, could afford. Early in August, Pepys cast up the amount he had laid out on his Axe Yard home, finding it to come to about £20, for many people were now offering to take it off his hands—among them no less a person than John Claypole, the late Lord Protector's son-in-law, so strange were the revolutions of fortune. On the last day of the month he agreed to sell the lease to one Dalton, one of the King's wine-sellers, for £41. But before he finally sealed and signed the deed of sale in the presence of landlord Vanly and was so free for ever of his "poor little house", it was to witness one last scene in the vivid and crowded life of Samuel Pepys.

Since their kindness to him before he sailed he had not forgotten his Axe Yard neighbours, the Crisps. Old Mrs Crisp had been to Seething Lane to advise the Pepyses about the furnishing—they were not quite sure of themselves yet—and Samuel had done his best to help young Laud Crisp and had got him a post as page to Lord Sandwich. Early in September the latter was ordered to sea to fetch over from Holland the Princess Royal, who was about to pay a visit to her brother. Before the Fleet sailed Mrs Crisp gave a farewell supper for Laud: Pepys was there, and so also was Laud's aunt, the fair Diana.* As is the way at such parties, a good

* The compiler of the Index to Wheatley's edition of the Diary makes two separate persons of Mrs Crisp's daughter and Mistress Diana, omitting also one reference to the latter (perhaps because she is called Dinah), that of Sept. 16th, 1660. A careful examination of the relevant entries (March 18th, 22nd; Aug. 20th; Sept. 2nd, 4th, 16th, 22nd, 23rd, 1660) has convinced me that Miss Crisp and the frail Diana are one and the

deal of wine was drunk, and after a time Diana began to be wonderfully loving and kind towards him—so much so that he began to suspect that she was not so good as she should be. Much as his puritan soul might deplore such conduct in a nicely nurtured girl, Pepys was not the one to waste an opportunity. Two days later, while visiting his old house, he saw the young lady passing down Axe Lane and beckoned her in. They went upstairs and there he found, in Latin, that "nulla puella negat". Taking the long view it was an unfortunate discovery. And for one moment it almost looked as though its more immediate consequences were to prove unhappy. For a fortnight later, meeting him in the street, Mistress Diana told him that she wanted to speak with him so significantly that he was afraid that it must be about something of which he did not wish to hear. However his fears proved groundless.

Of all this, of course, Elizabeth knew not one word. She knew sometimes that her husband was angry with her, as when he found her clothes thrown carelessly about her room; she knew also that sometimes he was unexpectedly kind. Thus on September 5th—it was the day after the episode with Diana—she was a little impatient about something, whereupon Samuel without a murmur went along with her and bought her a pearl necklace for £4. 10*s*.—"which I am willing to comply with her in", he explained to his Diary, "for her encouragement and because I have lately got money". For the rest she obediently tried to master the lessons he gave her in singing—in his more optimistic moods

same person; the places in which they are both to be met—always in or about Axe Yard—the quick sequel to Miss Crisp's over-loving behaviour on Sept. 2nd in Diana's lapse on the 4th, above all the fact that Miss Crisp drank at Harper's, the very place to which Pepys repaired to seek Diana, all lead to the same regrettable conclusion.

he found her apt in her scales beyond imagination—and lavished all her starved affection on the puppies with which her black bitch presented her.

His official work for the Navy as yet scarcely troubled Pepys. For a little while he was still the official channel through which Sandwich corresponded with his ships at sea. From the latter source came as well as letters occasional presents—"a brave Turky carpet", a jar of olives, a pair of turtle doves for his wife from the penitent Burr brought by his former boy Eli, who was ready to cry when he learnt that there was no chance of being taken into his employment again; indeed Pepys was forced to comfort him with half a crown. As for the Clerkship of the Acts, it was really surprising, considering its salary and importance, how little trouble it entailed. There were Board meetings, generally twice a week, and a moderate degree of correspondence to transact in conveying the instructions of that body to its subordinate officers, such as Clerks of the Cheque, Dockyard Officials, Ships' Pursers. There was also a good deal of calculating the past debts of the Navy for presentation to Parliament—accounting work of a kind for which Pepys' previous experience well fitted him. Penn, in his June memorandum to the King, had defined the duties of the Clerk of the Acts—"Clerk of the Records", he called him—as being that of preparing business for the Board to sign and recording its proceedings. For the time being Pepys was content to leave it at that. He was more interested in the honour and profit of his place than in the work it brought him. When Mr Mann offered him £1000 for his post, it made his mouth water, and he only refused it in deference to the objections of Lord Sandwich, who told him it was not the salary that made a man rich but the opportunities of getting money while he was in place. When at St Olave's Church on the other side of Seething Lane, the churchwardens placed him and Sir William Penn in the highest pew of all, and when a special gallery began to rise at the south wall of the said church for the special and sole use of himself and his fellow officers, he could only offer up a heartfelt prayer of praise to the Almighty that all things should continue so well for him: "I pray God", he added, "fit me for a change of my fortune".[11]

Chapter VII

The Happy Placeman

"At night to Sir W. Batten's and there very merry with a good barrel of oysters, and this is the present life I lead." *Diary*, April 5th, 1661.

On the evening of Saturday, September 8th, after a quiet day spent at home, Pepys was sent for by his colleague Sir William Penn to drink a glass of wine with him at his lodgings next door. A father, with a daughter and two sons, one of whom in course of time became one of the most famous figures on two continents—he was a comely, fair-haired, round-faced man with a youthful expression and a disarming manner. Pepys, after an hour or two of talk, set him down as both sociable and able, and very cunning. He soon saw more of him; sat by his side at the office and in church and walked with him along the river bank when naval occasions took them to visit the dockyards at Deptford or Woolwich—"a merry fellow", he found him, "and pretty good natured and sings very bawdy songs".[1]

Somewhat of a contrast was his neighbour and colleague, Sir William Batten, the Surveyor. A much older man, he had formerly taught Penn his business. Squat and tub-shaped,* he was not a pleasant character, though he could be

* For a description of Batten's appearance we are indebted to Charles II, who on April 21st, 1666, "among other pretty things swore merrily that he believed the ketch that Sir W. Batten bought the last year at Colchester was of his own getting, it was so thick to its length". *Diary*, April 21st, 1666.

merry enough when he chose and was a great man at taverns; "a Presbyterian rogue", Prince Rupert had called him a dozen years before. His favourite resort was the "Dolphin" in Seething Lane, where the officials of the Navy Board and the rich city merchants with whom they contracted were wont to meet and where he could be found any evening quaffing great quantities of sack and telling merry stories.[2]

Both these gentlemen were very much wealthier than Pepys, Penn had an estate in Ireland and Batten a substantial country house at Walthamstow—both had been knighted and both were admirals. He could therefore account himself very happy in finding himself, as he did, so much in their society. His fortune in this respect was partly due to the fact that alone of his colleagues they were his neighbours at the Office: Carteret and Berkeley were courtiers and personal friends of the King, living in the great world of Whitehall, Pett resided at Chatham, and Colonel Slingsby, the newly appointed Comptroller, had a fine house of his own in Lime Street and had therefore no need of official lodgings. Yet there was no real reason why the two knights—the "Sir Williams both", as Pepys called them—should have given him so much of their company, for they could easily, had they chosen, have kept themselves aloof and left the young man and his wife to find their own level with the subordinate society of the Office—the Turners and Davises to whose social sphere they seemed naturally to belong. But there was something irresistibly delightful about Pepys' company; he was so good-natured, so alive and so universally interested in everything and everybody about him. It was this intense relish for pleasure of all sorts that made him so entrancing a companion: unconsciously he communicated his enjoyment of his surroundings to others. Therefore he was much sought after, and when the two Sir Williams and their fine friends sat down to wine they liked to have him with them. "I see", he wrote on September 11th, "we are like to have a very good correspondence and neighbourhood, but chargeable."[3]

Into such company Pepys entered willingly enough—sometimes too willingly. For all his puritan upbringing he had never been averse to good fellowship; in the old days of poverty he and his brother clerks had caroused as far as their slender purses would let them and now there was no financial consideration to stop his drinking deep. But he soon found that it did not agree with him; thus an evening over the walnuts and wine ended ignominiously next morning in Lord Sandwich's house of office where he vomited up his breakfast of pickled herrings. So sometimes on a Sunday he woke with his head aching and his body not well "by last night's drinking which is my great folly"; nor were the ill consequences always confined to himself, for on such occasions he would find fault with Elizabeth, grumble at his food or go to bed in a pet because Jane was out late. Even the latter was apt to suffer from his excesses; after a Christmastide party at Sir William Batten's, where everybody ate and drank too much, Pepys woke in the middle of the night and was ill, so that, as he wrote, "I was forced to call the maid, who pleased my wife and I in her running up and down so innocently in her smock, and vomited in the basin, and so to sleep".[4]

But if good fellowship had its disadvantages, it also had its charms. It was a great thing to return home through the moonlit streets from a dinner-party at which were a lord and many fine gentlemen, piloting home a drunken admiral, and he in so merry and kind a mood that he could scarcely go; to walk with the same noble personage in the day-time through Moorfields in brave talk together watching the young clerks from the office at their sport; to play games in merry company at the "Dolphin", taking forfeits of the ladies by kissing them—"among others a pretty lady, who I found afterwards to be wife to Sir William Batten's son". Into these delights even Mrs Pepys was sometimes admitted; she accompanied her husband to supper at Lady Batten's, and four months after her first arrival at Seething Lane was called on by that personage, a circumstance which pleased Samuel exceedingly. Occasionally there were expeditions to Batten's country house at Walthamstow, where he lived like a prince and treated his guests to such delightful sights as his closet of rarities or a hog fattening. Afterwards one would ride home with Sir William Penn, stopping to drink at Bow or watching him knock down two insolent country fellows who deliberately got in his way—a little undignified Pepys thought it. And once in Penn's two-horse chariot he took part in a race against Batten's coach-and-four, a thrilling adventure even though it ended in the muddying of his new velvet coat.[5]

All this, of course, cost money. When Batten gave a party to celebrate the wedding of two of his servants, Pepys had to be there to share the merriment and make the customary offering—"and I did give 10 shillings and no more, though I believe most of the rest did give more and did believe that I did so too". And when Valentine's Day came round he must needs rise early and knock at Batten's door till the negro boy Mingo opened it and then step upstairs to make Miss Martha his Valentine: out of complacency only, he added, for the lady was past her prime. And when he returned home he found that old Batten himself had done the same for Elizabeth (who cannot have seemed unattractive to a middle-aged admiral), and for the rest of the day they were all very merry together. Yet though it was pleasant enough when Sir William sent Mrs Pepys half a dozen pairs of gloves and a pair of silk stockings and garters for her Valentine, it was decidedly galling to have to lay out forty shillings at the Exchange on the unprepossessing Martha. Still, in such fine company—so long as he esteemed it such—Pepys was ready to do anything, even to dance, which he had never done before, dropping his fiddle and joining in the revelry, while black Mingo in the rhythmic steps of the Congo capered before them.[6]

The dignity of his new position and the miracle of it all were constantly in Samuel's consciousness that winter. He was careful to pick his company, to avoid being seen too much with the puritan Commissioner Pett, who he thought was "going down the wind", and to keep the servants of himself and his colleagues as far behind his own pew in the Navy Office's new gallery in church as he could. It was wonderful for such a one as he to be sworn a Justice of the Peace for Middlesex, Essex, Kent and Southampton (the counties in which the naval dockyards were situated), "though", he admitted, "I am wholly ignorant in the duties of a Justice of the Peace", or to be asked by an admiring don to set one's name to a certificate bearing the signature of a great many honourable persons. It was better still to sit as one of the Principal Officers in conference with the King's Council of Trade in the Mercers' Hall, where a dozen years before he had stood a petitioner for his Paul's School Exhibition, to see Mr Jessop, whom formerly he could scarcely have looked upon, stand in his presence, to be driven in state to dine at the Tower where a Duchess was among the company and many high cavaliers. "Never till now", he wrote after a visit to Deptford dockyard, "did I see the great authority of my place, all the captains of the fleet comming cap in hand to us."[7]

The duties which he was called upon to perform in return

were not onerous. It was sufficient if he observed the bare letter of his instructions and registered (no "mean clerk" now but a clerk in his glory) the actions and decisions of his colleagues, of whose honourable Board, he was quick to remember, he was not a servant but a member. For the present these actions were chiefly confined to reducing the size and expense of the Fleet as quickly as possible, for the long era of naval war with Holland and Spain was over and England was entering upon one of her periodic phases of disarmament. The only difficulty was to find enough money to meet the arrears of the Commonwealth Navy, for neither Parliament nor the nation, after a generation of high taxation, was in a particularly giving mood.[8]

As a result Pepys' early employment at the Navy Board was chiefly concerned with the paying-off of ships and the sale of surplus vessels and stores. He sat with the other Principal Officers while they decided what vessels should be demobilised first and attended the Committee of Parliament which had been set up to supervise the business, suffering to the full the annoyance which all administrators feel at the unreasonable delays and interferences and the unnecessary interrogations of such bodies: "Colonel Birch was very impertinent and troublesome", he wrote of one of its members. A little later he was employed in occasional expeditions in the Office barge to Deptford to help his colleagues at the pay, afterwards observing the merry antics of the seamen as they made their way Londonwards to spend their money. It was not a particularly inspiring occupation, and, as cash ran short, it tended to become a highly unpopular one. At the end of November someone proposed that the growing debt of the kingdom should be checked by paying off all the seamen simultaneously by tickets (payable at a future date) and allowing them 8 per cent. interest until their tickets were cashed. Such a proposal neither commended itself to the Officers of the Navy Board nor to the unfortunate sailors. In the end, so unpopular did the whole business become, the Principal Officers washed their hands of it, allowing the Parliamentary Commissioners to proceed on their own, and confined themselves to an occasional protest at the high-handed manner in which the latter endeavoured to borrow their clerks. As for the seamen, they were so incensed that the politicians had to carry out their work at the Guildhall where the civic authorities could protect them.[9]

For the rest there was a moderate amount of routine: making provision for victualling ships, setting out the winter guard or the several squadrons which bore visiting members of the royal family to and from England and the usual correspondence with the subordinate Clerks of the Cheque, Store-keepers, Master Attendants and Shipwrights at the Dockyards. Occasionally something more eventful would ruffle the placid waters of naval decay; thus on the morning of December 9th, after a night of terrific wind, news was brought to the Navy Office of the loss of the *Assurance* while she lay moored at Woolwich ready to sail for Guinea. The two Sir Williams hurried at once to the scene of the disaster, but Pepys was detained by more clerkly duties in London. However, next evening he found that his wife and Lady Batten had made a bargain to go to Woolwich to see the sunk vessel, and so on the following morning he rose early and went with them down the river in the Office barge, Lady Batten being very fearful all the way because of the wind. Here he saw the *Assurance*—"poor ship that I have been twice merry in in Captain Holland's time"—lying under the water with only her upper deck and masts visible. Later in the afternoon, while his colleagues were considering how to raise her, he performed his first duty as a magistrate, examining a seaman and finding—and perhaps this was a little disappointing—no reason to commit.

Early in the new year of 1661 there occurred an incident of a more stirring kind. On January 8th, Pepys in his comings and goings heard talk of a band of fanatics entrenched at Barnet, but did not believe it. Next morning he was waked at six by people running up and down in Mr Davis' house next door, crying that they were in the City. "And so", he relates, "I rose and went forth, where in the street I found everybody in arms at the doors. So I returned (though with no good courage at all, but that I might not seem to be afraid) and got my sword and pistol, which, however, I had no powder to charge; and went to the door, where I found Sir R. Ford and with him I walked up and down as far as the Exchange." Everywhere the shops were shut and the streets full of Trained Bands, such was the terror that the veriest ghost of the old Roundhead army could inspire.

The rising—it was Venner's—thoroughly alarmed the government. One of its fears was that the malcontents, of whom it was reckoned there were many thousands near London, would seize the naval dockyards and arsenals. The Principal Officers were therefore ordered to set guards in all the Yards, and even the Clerk of the Acts was recruited for this warlike service, accompanying the Comptroller, Colonel Slingsby, to Deptford, on which journey they shared the society of a certain Major Waters, a friend of the Colonel and in Pepys' view "a deaf and most amorous melancholy gentleman, who is under a despayr in love, which makes him bad company, though a most good-natured man". From this rather depressing start the expedition quickly recovered, for once at Deptford the manner of their treatment by the dockyard officials was impressive in the extreme; Pepys was taken home and lodged that night by Mr Davis, the storekeeper, most princelike, and with so much respect and honour that he was at a loss how to behave himself. Next day being Sunday he rested from the labour of choosing captains of the Guard and spent his time, suitably and in some state, attending divine service—the morning at Deptford where he had the ill fortune to hear a cold sermon by a young man who had never preached before, and in the afternoon at Greenwich where the going was better in a good sermon, a fine church and a company of handsome women. Then at night his martial achievements began anew, for no sooner was he in bed than the alarm sounded, and there in the dark yard below he and the Comptroller distributed handspikes to the seamen, who were as fierce as could be. However, no enemy appeared, and after a while England's defenders retired to bed. Pepys spent the following two days more peaceably, and perhaps more usefully, in prying about the yards at Deptford and Woolwich looking at rope, tar and other mysterious substances of which he knew next to nothing; what particularly struck him was the neatness of the houses possessed by the dockyard officials. The reason of this was later to become plain.

None of this work was very serious; Pepys was still no more than a fortunate clerk who had found a good place: for all he cared, he might equally well have been in the Excise or any other department of state, so long as the salary, perquisites and attaching rank were equally advantageous. Yet he made certain modest attempts to make himself master of his job, such as he as yet conceived it to be. In the September after his appointment he wrote to Mr Barlow to enquire the nature of his former duties and received in return a courteous but not very helpful letter. His own predecessor, Barlow explained, had been old and infirm, had also held another post in the royal stables and lived out of town, and for these reasons had come very seldom to the office. As for his own brief tenure of the post, he had a vague recollection that letters from the Lord Admiral and warrants for conferring places were brought (in the intervals between meetings) to the Clerk of the Acts who forthwith gave notice to his fellow Officers ("if they were in town") and presented them to the Board at their next meeting. Afterwards the Clerk was expected to draft suitable replies, pursuant to the Board's decision. Agreements for provisions or for hiring ships were drawn by him, and Petty Purveyance, Barlow added, also belonged to the Clerk of the Acts. Thereafter the letter tailed away.[10]

Yet Pepys was not quite content to be a clerk. He made his old friend of the *Naseby*, Lieutenant Lambert, explain the names and functions of the various parts of the ship from a model of Lord Sandwich's in his keeping and got his clerk Hayter to teach him a few sea-terms. In the latter's company he looked over some old instructions concerning naval administration drawn up by Lord Northumberland in the days before the Civil War and, so primed, had his first dispute with his colleagues as to the prerogatives of his office, having a particularly heated argument with Mr Turner regarding his right to purvey petty provisions; characteristically it ended, after Pepys had carried his point that he should sign all bills for such, in his allowing Turner to continue to purvey them, since he would not have the poor man lose his place. And he was very angry when any affront was put upon the cause he served, particularly at "a most tedious, unreasonable and impertinent" sermon by an Irish doctor on the text—"Scatter them, O Lord, that delight in war", which was scarcely calculated to please the occupants of the Navy Office pew.[11]

But when Pepys tried to apply all that wonderful energy which was his to his work, made a vow to rise by candle-light each morning and busied himself on a project for stopping the growing charge of the Fleet, he received no encouragement from his colleagues. When he bore the project to Sir William Batten's house, he found that gentleman and his colleague Penn drinking and playing at cards, and there was nothing left for him to do but to stand by watching or to join in. After all, who was he to force unwelcome views or work on his seniors? his business was to hold the office so miraculously given him and remain on friendly terms with his colleagues. Not that this was always easy, for he soon perceived that they did not at all care for each other—none the less he resolved to keep in with them all as much as he could.[12]

With one of them, at least, he found no difficulty in being friends. This was the Comptroller, Robert Slingsby, a man of a singularly noble character. He came of an old naval family: his father, Sir Gylford Slingsby, had been Comptroller in the time of James I, and he himself had been bred to the sea. When the Civil War broke out he gave all he had unreservedly to the King whose bread he had eaten. For this loyalty he had suffered wounds, imprisonment and loss of fortune. Now at the age of fifty-one, after twenty years of proscription, he had been appointed to the post which his father had held before him.[13]

Slingsby took a fancy to Pepys. He invited him to his house in Lime Street and over a friendly glass of wine at the "Mitre", falling into a discourse of poetry, repeated some of his verses to him, which Pepys thought were very good. And alone of his colleagues, Slingsby took some pains to interest him in his new profession. He told him what had been the practice of the Clerk of the Acts in former days, mentioning that one of them had been knighted—"of which to myself I was not a little proud"—and read over to him his proposals to the Duke of York for regulating the Navy. For these reasons and because he was of a finer social texture than any of his fellow-workers (for Carteret and Berkeley seldom visited the Office), Pepys paid him a respect which he never gave to Batten or Penn. The latter might be his intimates, but they never commanded his heart.[14]

But save from this one fine gentleman, Pepys received no encouragement to be officious in his business. He therefore devoted his surplus energies to other things. Chief of these was his house. When the wise men of former days had prudently considered the advantages which would accrue to the Navy if each of its Principal Officers was afforded a commodious habitation near the place of his work, they could scarcely have contemplated Mr Pepys' enthusiasm for improving that habitation. For though, in his case, their provision was in the long run repaid a hundredfold, at first it afforded him such absorbing occupation that it became, not a background for his official labours, but a successful rival to them.[15]

So soon as he was settled into the house, almost before Elizabeth had tried her new range and replaced an iron that fell out of the back of it, Samuel was considering ways to beautify and improve it. By the beginning of September, 1660, he had the Office joiners at work reflooring his dining-room. Before the end of the month their labours had been reinforced by those of a company of plasterers, whose devastations were so wholesale that poor Mrs Pepys was forced to remove her bed downstairs: the house, as her husband put it, was in a most sad pickle. None the less, when they had done, the kitchen was so handsome that its owner, employing the phraseology of Mr Valiant-for-Truth, did not repent him of the trouble that he had been at to have it done. Then came the painters, who continued the reign of chaos, till they also had finished their dirty work and the house once again began to be clean.[16]

Though to Elizabeth all these operations must have been highly disturbing, Pepys thoroughly enjoyed them. He would sometimes take whole days away from the Office, while he stood watching his workmen or hurrying from room to room to supervise now this, now that. Sometimes, of course, he had his anxieties: the slowness of the artisans and their objection to co-operating with outside craftsmen who were not of their guild—for the characteristics of the English labouring class have remained a constant factor. But in other respects the idiosyncrasies of his humble countrymen were a great source of enjoyment to him; and when they had done a good day's work he would sit among them and give them drink, delighting in their whimsical, humorous conversation, "it being my luck to meet with a sort of drolling workmen on all occasions".[17]

While the decorations were proceeding within, Pepys maintained a vigorous war against his neighbours who were threatening from without the amenities of his beloved home. Down below were the cellars, a corridor of these running under the houses and providing, not only storage for coal and wine, but the sanitary conveniences of life. Going down into these one October morning to supervise the making of a window, he stepped, as he indignantly related to his Diary that night, "into a great heap of...by which I find that Mrs Turner's house of office is full and comes into my cellar, which do trouble me, but I shall have it helped". Battle was at once joined with his careless neighbour, and after some days of lively recrimination the adjoining vault was emptied. A month later, a new threat arose from the other side of the house, Pepys observing as he came downstairs a great deal of foul water coming into the parlour from under the partition between his domain and Mr Davis'. Without a moment's hesitation he stepped across to his neighbour's to register his protest. The same ceaseless war for the unknown god of sanitation was even waged against Elizabeth's dog, Samuel insisting that the creature (whose habits were no better than those of the mortals around him) should reside henceforward in the cellar. The dispute that followed was only assuaged by Pepys being visited in the night by a dream that his wife had died, after which he could scarcely sleep for anxiety. As a matter of fact his quarrels with Elizabeth generally ended so: and when he started the day by scolding her for putting away half a crown of his in a paper box and then forgetting where she had laid it, he added—"But we were friends again as we are always".[18]

A more serious threat to the household amenities came at the end of October, when Pepys, coming home in the evening from the Lord Mayor's Show, found that Mrs Davis had locked up the door which led on to the leads so that he could no longer use it: apparently his perambulations on the roof had disturbed that lady's privacy. So troubled was he by this news that he lay awake all night brooding on it; next day he hurried to his friend, the Comptroller, to appeal for his help. But for all his entreaties, the Navy Officers at their meeting wisely declined to meddle in anything that might anger Mrs Davis, and the month ended mournfully for poor Pepys, "very heavy for the loss of my leads". Happily before the summer came round again his difficult neighbour had departed and he was able once more to enjoy his favourite walk.[19]

If Pepys wished to make his house neat and proper, he

wanted also to fill it with fine things. When, therefore, his predecessor, Commissioner Willoughby, removed his furniture, he set to work to replace it by goods of his own. He bought green serge hangings and hung them on the walls when the painters had finished, a great bed for his wife's chamber, and gilded leather to upholster his dining-room chairs. And when his father came to visit him, he was overjoyed to see how proud the old man was at his neat house and fine possessions.[20]

These layings out, of course, cost money—far more than the £41 which Pepys had realised from the sale of his Axe Yard house and which he had intended to appropriate for this purpose. Before September was out he was having to break open one of his two bags of £100, his total worldly wealth, and by the end of the next month his cash capital had fallen to £150. But, he added, "I have, I bless God, a great deal of good household stuff". None the less he grew much alarmed at the rate of his expenditure and sought eagerly for ways to increase his income.

Fortune was on his side. On October 19th he sat up late at his accounts and found that Lord Sandwich was £80 in his debt, "which is a good sight and I bless God for it". Other blessings followed. November was a month of windfalls. In two successive days he received £23. 14*s.* 9*d.* from Major Hart for the pay which he drew—for no particular military services, it appears—as a trooper in Montagu's regiment (now disbanded), £11. 5*s.* from Creed as the balance of his sea accounts, and £87. 10*s.* for his first quarter's salary. Of this he at once paid over £25 to Dr Petty for Barlow, but partly recouped himself by retaining a further £7. 10*s.* received for his clerk, Will Hewer. "With this", Pepys very naturally observed, "my heart was much rejoiced and do bless Almighty God that he is pleased to send me so sudden and unexpected a payment of my salary so soon after my great disbursements."

Thus providentially assisted, he was able to continue his layings out on his house. During December he had his parlour painted and gilded—a great improvement it was, and once more he did not repent of the trouble that he had been at, though he had somewhat of a race to get the work finished and the painters out of the house before Christmas. Then to keep down the mice he brought home a cat which Sarah had kept for him at Lord Sandwich's lodgings, and, to increase the dignity of his establishment, graciously invited his sister, Pall, a troublesome, ill-natured girl who was none too welcome at home, to enter it as a domestic companion, being careful to insist on her arrival that she should not sit down at table with Elizabeth and himself lest she should expect it hereafter. The house was now ready for the entertainment of visitors. On January 24th there dined with him the Battens, Sir William Penn, Captain Cuttance and Stephen Fox. It was a very grand affair and cost above £5, and was only a little spoilt by the fact that the chimney smoked.

Altogether Pepys had attained a grandeur of social status which would have seemed quite inconceivable a year before. Even those who best remembered him as he was (save the Joyce brothers who were always jealous) acclaimed his advancement. Lord and Lady Sandwich were particularly gracious, the former not only taking every opportunity of showing his former servant how much he honoured him, but even extending his condescension to Elizabeth whom he now noticed for the first time as Pepys' wife and invited to dinner. As for his kind lady's conduct, nothing could have been more friendly—carefully enquiring of Samuel how he behaved towards Elizabeth's parents and treating her with every conceivable respect.[21]

For a rising man in Pepys' position, the coming Coronation could scarcely fail to be an absorbing event, and as the early weeks of 1661 went by the thought of it began to loom large in his life. One drawback about its approaching glories was the expense; and though in February his capital reached the sum of £350, he was sorely put to it to know where to turn for ready cash. To add to his problem, Lord Sandwich, on a far grander scale, of course, was in the same plight and asked Samuel to act as his confidential agent in raising £1000. This the latter did by persuading a wealthy Puritan cousin, Thomas Pepys of Hatcham near Deptford, to advance £1000. But the cautious lender insisted on Samuel and his Uncle Robert standing security for the debt—an uncomfortable background to life for many a year to come—and, though the Earl of Sandwich was now assured of the wherewithal to buy his coronation clothes, his former secretary was still without his.[22]

Heaven was again on Pepys' side. On March 28th the gentle dew fell, the Treasurer of the Navy paying him £70 cash on a Bill of Exchange obtained from Creed in final settlement of his sea accounts. Moreover he had the good fortune, rare in a Restoration official, to receive his quarter's salary regularly, and this more than covered his normal outgoings, even after paying the £100 a year due to Barlow. The latter, after refusing an offer from Pepys of a capital sum for his annuity, on the ground that it would not be worth while to buy it from one so old and infirm, paid a handsome tribute to the punctual way in which he honoured his obligations, being, he wrote, "very sensible both of your fair and cheerful dealing". Such honest and businesslike conduct struck an aged seventeenth-century public servant as being most unusual. Yet it paid. By the end of May, Pepys reckoned himself worth £500.[23]

Before that date the Coronation had taken place. In a delirium of excitement, Pepys witnessed and recorded it. On the day before, when the King according to custom was to ride from the Tower to Whitehall, he accompanied the Battens and Penns (sending Elizabeth with the Turners to a slightly humbler station in Fleet Street) to Mr Young's, the flagmaker's in Cornhill, where they were accorded a good room all to themselves, a sufficiency of wine and cakes and a fine view of the show. Outside the streets were gravelled and the houses hung with carpets, while every balcony was full of ladies, of one of whom, just across the way, Pepys took a great deal of notice, which caused much sport to his colleagues. His susceptibility was already recognised. As for the procession itself, it was so glorious and dazzling that he had to avert his eyes. Yet he saw the King and the Duke smiling up at the window as they passed: a very noble thing it was of them.

Next day was an even better one for this great sight-seer. He had gone overnight to Lord Sandwich's lodgings at Whitehall to share a bed with Shepley, and was up by four. By closely following Sir John Denham, the Surveyor General, he managed to sneak into the Abbey itself. Here, with much ado—one can picture the eager little man coaxing and bluffing his way forward—he climbed up into a great stand along the north end and there, with the greatest pleasure in the world, sat for seven hours watching the busy sight before him—the raised throne, the fiddlers in red vests, the Bishops in cloth of gold, the massed nobility in their robes—all of which certainly was a most magnificent spectacle. Finally there came the King himself, and close behind him Lord Sandwich bearing the Sceptre. But when sermon and service were done and the great ones passed to the High Altar for the final ceremonies of the coronation, it was a grief to Pepys that from where he sat he could not see them. Nor did he hear much of the music, owing to the ceaseless clamour of those about him, nor even come by one of the silver medals which were flung among the congregation. Then nature after that seven hours' vigil compelling him, he went out before the King and made his way through the vast crowd waiting outside to Westminster Hall. The lawyers and gossips who usually thronged it were gone and in their place were many brave ladies, ranged in scaffolds, in one of which he sighted his wife sitting with a pretty friend of the Bowyers. Here he saw the King and his nobles sit down to eat and, when they had done and armoured Dymock, the King's Champion, had ridden in on his horse and flung down his gauntlet, he managed with Will Howe's help to beg four rabbits and a pullet from one of the tables. After that he climbed up the scaffold and got a kiss from the pretty lady beside his wife. And when it was all over, with the sound of shouting, the trumpets and the violins still ringing in his ears, he went out into the Palace Yard and so to old Bowyer's lodgings where he looked down upon the streets, now all dark, and awaited the fireworks, noting how the City had a light like a glory round it with bonfires.

Then, for the rest of the evening, life became rather confused. There was a pot of ale to be drunk in the company of old friends at Harper's and then a merry gathering in Axe Yard at the Hunts', who had offered Mrs Pepys and her companion a bed and, when the ladies had retired, a walk in the crowded streets, which were full of bonfires and gallant young sparks and their sweethearts, all drinking the King's health on their knees and making the passers-by do likewise. Not that his Majesty's Clerk of the Acts had any objection to doing this, indeed he seemed to like it, and in the end he found himself (he could not quite tell how) in the royal cellars still continuing this loyal occupation. At last, after one of his companions had fallen dead drunk on the floor, Pepys climbed up the stairs of Lord Sandwich's lodgings, but no sooner had he got into Shepley's bed than his head began to hum and his inside to vomit, and the only other thing he could recall before he fell asleep was a feeling that, if ever he was foxed, it was now. Then he slept till the morning when he found his clothes cold and wet and his head in a sad taking; the sage Mr Creed had to prescribe a cup of chocolate for his morning draught to settle his stomach. Yet it was worth it, and, when that night he had finished talking it all over with Elizabeth, he sat down to describe it in his Diary. "Now", he wrote, "after all this I can say that besides the pleasure of the sight of these glorious things, I may now shut my eyes against any other objects, nor for the future trouble myself to see things of state and show, as being sure never to see the like again in this world." Yet even as he wrote, he could not help wishing himself at Whitehall watching the fireworks, the far report of which he could hear borne down the river.

Truth to tell, Pepys could never shut his eyes to the glories of any worldly object. If, as Coleridge said of him, he was a pollard man it was because his gaze was fixed so raptly on the earth, of whose infinite delight and variety nothing could sate him. So he went with equal relish to see a traitor hanged (observing that the poor fellow looked as cheerful as any man could in that condition), to Gresham College to watch the learned virtuosos forgather or to the childlike pomps of the Lord Mayor's Show. A boatman telling bawdy stories as he rowed him home on a pleasant moonlit night, a loquacious one-eyed Frenchman who shared the same hackney coach, a poor Lenten dinner of coleworts and bacon or a quiet Sunday spent at Seething Lane taking physic and reading

French romances, were all alike of interest and worthy of record. When he went to the Theatre, which he began to do frequently that year, and a lady spat backward upon him by mistake, he did not mind at all since he could see that she was very pretty. The gods had been exceeding kind to Sam Pepys.[24]

But when anything really out of the ordinary occurred, Pepys, to whom the most common things were wonderful, became transcended. That spring of 1661 he twice went on pilgrimage, and, as one follows him, the flame of Chaucer's good companions seems to burn in old England again. On both occasions it was his official business that called him forth. Yet it was in no business spirit that he took barge with Sir William and Lady Batten, Mr Turner and Mr Fowler of the Office on the morning of Monday, April 8th, 1661, to visit his Majesty's dockyard at Chatham. Even that night, as they sat round the fire at the Hill House and Batten told ghoulish stories of how his predecessor, old Edisbury, was known to walk o'nights in the chamber Pepys was to inhabit, he was not put out of spirits, though for mirth's sake he pretended to be somewhat frightened: for all his dignity, Sam could never resist a joke at his own expense. Still, when he woke up at three in the morning and saw his pillow, which he had flung from him overnight, standing bolt upright in the light of the moon, he had a momentary shock.

But when it was high day, and he saw the respect and honour in which he was held by all the people of the Yard— "and I find", he added happily, "that I begin to know now how to receive so much reverence which at the beginning I could not tell how to do"—all the ghosts in the chambers of the past could not have scared him. It was a glorious thing to inspect the storehouses, to watch old goods being sold there by an inch of candle and, most of all, to meet at dinner

Captain Allen's two daughters, one of whom was so tall and handsome that he could not refrain from falling in love with her—such a result did a day's absence from Elizabeth have on his susceptible heart. In this delicious company he went over the *Sovereign*, singing all the way, and when he got on board, among other pleasures, putting the ladies of the party into the lanthorn and then going in after them and demanding a kiss apiece as the fee due to a Principal Officer, at which of course there was great mirth. There was even more next night, when he attended a party at which the fair Rebecca Allen was present. For though the music was the worst he had ever heard, he minded it not a bit, for the favours of his charmer, who marked him out for her especial company, kept him in a perfect heaven of delight all the evening. He even tried to dance—though, as he admitted, he made but an ugly shift at it; Rebecca, of course, danced beautifully. When at nine the Battens went home, Pepys remained and continued dancing another hour or two: then he must needs see the Allen family home, which he did, singing at his sweetheart's request all the way and staying till two in the morning, during which time he found many opportunities to kiss her. So inspired, he was in wonderful spirits, and survived even the next day's parting, when he consoled himself by singing, "Go and be hanged, that's twice good bye", and making Lady Batten's maid who rode beside him pretend to be his clerk. When they met two little girls keeping cows by the wayside, Pepys dismounted and made one of them ask his blessing, telling her that he was her godfather, on which she asked him innocently if he was Ned Wooding and he replied that he was. So she knelt down and very simply called, "Pray, godfather, pray to God to bless me", which made him even merrier and caused him to give her twopence. He was much taken with children all the way, buying a pitcher of ale from some little boys who were carrying it to their schoolmaster and asking all the women he met on the road whether they would sell him their little ones, to which they answered No but added that they would give them to him to keep if he liked. Such was the good-humoured social democracy of that which England once was, and such the man who has left us its greatest picture. Nor did he spare to paint its other side, telling us how, as they neared London, he and Mistress Anne, the maid, rode under a corpse that was hanging on the gibbet on Shooter's Hill, "and a filthy sight it was to see how his flesh is shrunk to his bones".

A similar expedition to Portsmouth dockyard at the beginning of May was only less eventful because Mrs Pepys came too. Yet even in his brief account of his journey across the Surrey and Hampshire hills, the traveller communicates to us his joy in that fresh green countryside and its people: how his hat at Newington Ford fell into the water, the jokes with the drawers at the wayside inn about the red-faced minister of the town, the sight of himself and Creed fooling in a Guildford garden after dinner trying who could best jump over an old fountain well for a quart of sack.

So in a life full of incident, variety and enjoyment, Pepys' first year at the Navy Office drew to a close. But before it ended, certain omens of coming change appeared. Ever so little, his growing friendship with Slingsby was making him weary of his intimacy with Batten and Penn. In May he had his first clash with Penn, who while choosing Masters for the Fleet refused to accept one of his recommendations. A week later he witnessed the sequel, when Carteret angrily rebuked the Sir Williams before the whole Board for their presumption in choosing Masters without reference to their colleagues and particularly inveighing against the omission of the very man whom Pepys had recommended. The lesson was not lost on him: henceforward he knew that there were higher powers whose word, rightly invoked, could overrule the omnipotency of the two knights. Deliberately he refrained for some days from visiting the Battens that his absence might raise their opinion of him.[25]

A greater change than these tended to turn his steps into a new path. That June he learnt that Lord Sandwich was to sail at once on a long voyage to the south to put down the Barbary corsairs in the Mediterranean, visit Tangier—the North African station with which the King's marriage-treaty with Portugal was about to endow England—and bring home the new Queen from Lisbon. In a frenzy of haste, Pepys made the necessary arrangements for his patron's departure; begged a reversion of a place in the Wardrobe for his father, and also got the latter an order for £300 of fine cloth which Sandwich was to take with him as a present for the Moors. Then, a little mournfully, he put on his grey cloth suit and faced white coat, made of one of his wife's old petticoats, and accompanied his Lord down the river as far as Erith, where, after singing a little, he took his leave of his friends, Will Howe and Shepley, kissed his master's hands and went aboard the wherry that was to bear him home. "My Lord", he recorded, "did give five guns, all they had charged, which was the greatest respect my Lord could do me, and of which I was not a little proud. So with a sad and merry heart I left them sailing presently from Erith hoping to be in the Downs tomorrow early." As the wherry bore him homewards, Pepys pulled off his stockings and dangled his legs in the water, and stopping awhile to take cherries and wine at Woolwich, fell asleep until the boat slipped alongside Tower stairs. A week-end of rush and anxiety, shipping the cloth off by a Margate hoy to catch Sandwich in the Downs before the Fleet sailed, and thereafter he was left to stand on his own feet.[26]

Chapter VIII

A Man of Property

"To the office all the afternoon, which is a great pleasure to me again to talk with persons of quality and to be in command, and I give out among them that the estate left me is £200 a year in land, besides moneys, because I would put an esteeme upon myself." *Diary*, July 24th, 1661.

A man by the sudden advance of fortune does not divest himself of family ties. Pepys, though he no longer supped regularly every Sunday with his parents as in the old days of poverty, was honourably conscious of his. He had given his sister Pall a place in his household, he had intervened when his father wished to turn Tom out of doors for staying out at night, and had supplied young John at Cambridge with tips, books and learned advice. He had also done his best to compose a violent quarrel between his father and mother, arising out of the old lady's ludicrous jealousy of her husband's supposed relationship with her maid of all work, according to Samuel the most ill-favoured slut he had ever seen. He had no hesitation in telling his mother what he thought of such folly, rating her so soundly that the silly old woman cried, for which he was afterwards sorry. But there was no help for it; she had grown so pettish with age that he did not know how his father could bear it any longer.[1]

There was one member of his family from whom Pepys had expectations. For long he had laboured to please his Uncle Robert of Brampton, had corresponded with him regularly and had at his advice invested his savings with him, being always careful to make out that these were bigger than they were. In return the old yeoman had from time to time made oracular, though somewhat obscure, references to his intention of passing over in his will his second brother, Thomas Pepys of London and the latter's son Tom the turner, and of leaving his estate to his younger brother's heir —in other words to Samuel. The time of the fulfilment of these half-promises now seemed at hand, for old Robert had long been ailing. Indeed lately he had become very tiresome, harassing Samuel with such requests as a demand for his old fiddle for his cousin, Perkin, whose mill near Wisbech had been burnt down and whose only available means of livelihood was to play dances for the country girls on their holidays. However, it was best to comply, though Uncle Robert, his nephew reflected, could easily have afforded to buy a fiddle himself for his beggarly relation. The one haunting fear was that the old gentleman would change his mind— which long residence in the English countryside had made both eccentric and obstinate—or, what was even more probable, that the revolting old woman his wife, who was also ailing, would die before him and enable him (for with these fenmen one could never be certain) to marry again.[2]

But Uncle Robert's end was now at hand. Two weeks after Lord Sandwich's departure, John Pepys received a letter from his sister-in-law that his brother had been suddenly taken dizzy in the head and that his presence by his bedside was urgently required. And on the morning of Saturday, July 6th, Samuel himself was woken by a messenger from Brampton with news that his uncle was dead. He rose at once and, after informing those most concerned, bought a pair of riding boots and repaired to the Post House, whence he set out shortly before midday. By nine o'clock that evening he had covered the sixty miles of road to Brampton, where he found his father, his bereaved Aunt Anne and his uncle's coffin. The latter was beginning to smell a little, so he had it moved out from the hall chimney into the yard; as for his aunt whom he visited in bed, she was in such a nasty ugly pickle that it made him sick to see her. Then he retired for the night with his father, but, with his just sense of what was proper, just managed to stifle his intense desire to ask about the will until the morning.

Next day, a Sunday, they buried the old yeoman. The neighbours came from far and near, and there were ribbons and gloves for them all. They bore the coffin from the untidy little house to Brampton Church, where the parson, not having anything in particular to say of the deceased, spoke for a long time of his honesty. Then they went home to supper.

Uncle Robert had been as good as his word. For though Samuel himself could get little out of the will till after his father's death, the whole of the real estate, for what it was worth, was to come to him in the end. After disposing of half an acre of land at Buckden and £20 a year to his brother Thomas, the heir-at-law, the old man had devised the rest of his land to John Pepys with remainder to his eldest son. But there were over two hundred pounds of legacies to pay first and a charge of £25 per annum in annuities on the little property. The house at Brampton, together with Goody Gorham's alehouse (whenever the old woman should die), were also left for life to John Pepys and thereafter to Samuel.[3]

For the next fortnight Pepys and his father wrestled at Brampton with his uncle's papers, which were in a terrible state of confusion, and, as best they could, bore with his aunt's base, ugly humours. The old woman was a sore trial to them, and her family promised to be even more so. For her husband, on the ground that thirty years before by pretending that her former husband's estate was bigger than it was, she had tricked him into allowing her to dispose of £200 to her sons Jasper and Thomas Trice, had left her nothing in his will but an injunction to his executors to be as civil to her as they could. The first, therefore, of the many anxieties that his uncle's death brought Samuel was the news that Tom Trice was putting in a caveat against him on behalf of his mother. But there was far worse to come. For when old John and he went through the dead man's papers, they found that his estate was nothing like so good as the world believed. Nor could they find anywhere the surrenders of his copyhold land, which without them would pass to the heir-at-law.[4]

Though a visit to the Talbot Pepyses at Impington failed to clear up the situation, the arrival at Huntingdon of the Lord of the Manor, the lawyer, Sir Robert Bernard, made matters only too plain. The latter, after inspecting the will, pronounced that the money due upon the lost surrenders—a matter of £164—and any debts due to the deceased must at law go to the legal heir, Uncle Thomas of London. This, of course, nearly broke Pepys' heart. Nor did a conference with the Trice family at Goody Gorham's do anything to cheer him up, as for all his calm and quiet reasoning he was unable to make any impression on these solid brothers. The most he could get from them was to agree to remove their intolerable mother from the house for a consideration of £10; other matters in dispute between them were left to the law.

Altogether it was a wretched fortnight—the anxiety, his aunt's base, hypocritical tricks, the badness of the drink and the gnats that bit him at night, all helped to depress him. The only piece of comfort was that he was able to engage a steady, dependable farmer of the name of Stankes to act as his father's bailiff. This done, on Monday, July 22nd, he bade farewell and rode back to London, where he found his own private affairs as well as he could expect—which was not anything to boast of, for his sister Pall was grown so proud and idle that she had disorganised the house while Will Hewer had allowed thieves to steal the best tankard. Still it was a consolation, when he returned to the Office next day, to talk with persons of quality again and to be in command. To enhance his value with them he gave out that he had been left an estate of £200 a year.

Other people, besides Pepys' colleagues, formed an exaggerated idea of that estate. There was his Uncle Wight in a snuff because nobody had told him anything about it, or perhaps because he had been left nothing, and his mother, who in the most injudicious way was boasting to everyone, telling them that God knows what was fallen to her, and, what was worse, suiting her expenditure to her tattle. It made Pepys mad to hear her, but he could not very well tell her not to, at least not in public. Above all there was Uncle Thomas and that obstinate, vulgar fellow, his son Thomas the turner, whom Samuel sought out as soon as he reached London but who did not appear at all willing to acquiesce in the peaceful disposition of a property which should by rights have been theirs. And when he showed Moore his great box of papers, which had come up by the carrier from Brampton, his friend predicted that there would be no end to the trouble which the will would give him. As it was, the outgoings on the funeral and legal expenses were already so heavy that he was forced to borrow £40 from Sir William Batten to meet them. It was sad to see one's expectations shrinking.[5]

Meanwhile his father, poor man, was all alone at Brampton, and this worried Samuel a great deal. On August 2nd he got on horseback once again and rode to Cambridge, whiling away the journey by talking with a quaker fellmonger who would tell him how wicked a fellow he had been all his lifetime till God had visited him. Here at the Assizes he took counsel of Roger Pepys: it was best, he felt, to keep these things in the family. His cousin bore him home to Impington for the week-end, where on Sunday morning they plucked fruit in the orchard, while Roger confirmed Moore's melancholy predictions, and listened to a good plain sermon in the parish church, where it was gratifying to notice the reverence with which old Talbot Pepys (still living and like a man out of the world) was treated, the country people all rising as he entered and the parson beginning the prayers by turning to his pew with a "Right Worshipful and Dearly Beloved". On the Monday, Samuel rode on to Brampton where he found his father well and, what was almost better, his aunt gone. The house was now quiet and a great content to them both. And in the two days he was there, by dint of expeditions to Yelling and Graveley, he was able to clear up a few of the outstanding complications that beset the estate. After that he had to hurry back to London, as it was his month of service at the Privy Seal.

Back in his familiar haunts, sitting in the Office of the morning or avoiding it of an afternoon in Captain Ferrers' company at the playhouse, Brampton still haunted him. On August 13th, Pepys and his father, with Uncle Wight as arbiter, met Uncle Thomas and his two sons at Rawlinson's. Here they read over the will, telling Uncle Thomas how kindly their thoughts were towards him if only he would carry himself peaceably and withdraw the caveat which he also, like Tom Trice, had now entered against them. This the wily old gentleman promised to do and the conference ended with drinks all round, for which Samuel paid. But a fortnight later he heard that his uncle and his sons had left suddenly for the country without giving notice to anyone.

It was, in fact, plain that Uncle Thomas—always, observed his nephew, a close and cunning fellow—had somehow got wind of the news that the surrenders to the Graveley copyholds were missing and had gone down to investigate. When the two met again in London early in September at a little blind alehouse in Shoe Lane—a place where Pepys was then quite ashamed to be seen but where to-day the *Daily Express*' new building boldly proclaims itself to the world—nothing was said about the matter on either side, but it was certain that when Graveley Court came on, the jurymen of that village would be privileged to see more than one branch of the Pepys family. On the evening of September 16th, the summons to Graveley came. Next morning Mrs Pepys in a few words persuaded her husband to let her hire a horse and come with him. After one nasty fall on Elizabeth's part in the miry lanes about Puckeridge they came safely to Impington, where John Pepys was waiting to meet them. On the 20th, after a night at Brampton, Samuel repaired to the courthouse at Graveley, where as he expected he found Uncle Thomas and his eldest son. Since he was able to produce no surrenders, the jurymen—a simple company of country rogues—found Thomas Pepys the heir-at-law: in other words the Graveley copyholds of about £25 a year were now lost. The only consolation Samuel could derive was the thought that, if by any chance the missing surrenders should turn up, his uncle and cousin would lose the £70 which they had paid in fines, fees and expenses to make good their claim. And now that he knew the worst, he could at least sleep again at night, and take pleasure in contriving improvements to the house and gardens at Brampton for his father to carry out. So comforted, he and Elizabeth made the return journey to London, noting with some pleasure the minor incidents of travel: the mouthful of pork which they ate at Baldock, and the epicurism of sleep which after the long muddy ride they enjoyed at Welwyn—"there being now and then a noise of people stirring that waked me, and then it was a very rainy night, and then I was a little weary, that what between waking and then sleeping again, one after another, I never had so much content in all my life". No lawsuit could stop the flow of this poet of everyday human sensation.

When all the diminutions and charges of the estate had been added together, it did not appear that there would be much left for his parents to live on: £100 a year at the outside and probably not half that sum for a good many years to come. And when Samuel went through the business accounts, he found still less to be pleased with, for his father's assets just about equalled his liabilities, and what kind of condition his mother would have been in had she been left a widow, he did not care to contemplate. At the end of August he saw the old man off to Brampton, where it was resolved that he should now live, and a day or two later packed his mother and Pall into the country waggon after him. It was an unpleasant business, for his mother, silly simple soul, made a great fuss about going, and Pall, though he gave her twenty shillings and a great deal of good advice, cried exceedingly. The latter he had recently discharged from his household after a troubled scene in which he and his father had both angrily told her that they would have nothing to do with her, till in the end her proud spirit had been so brought down that she had submitted to do whatever they commanded. It was something at least to be rid of her.[6]

But Pepys' family worries that autumn did not end here. For now that his father was gone there was Tom to be settled, and he had grave doubts as to that idle young man's capacity to carry on the shop. To steady him, and secure a little capital for the business, he did what he could to find him a wife. But it was not at all easy; as one prospective father-in-law put it, he had nothing against the match save that the estate with which God had blessed him was too great to give in a marriage where there was nothing on the other side but a trade and a house.[7]

Meanwhile disease was playing havoc with Pepys' other relations. It was a sickly autumn and death was everywhere: one day that August he recorded how all the clerks were at the burial of one of their colleagues—"a very ingenious and a likely young man to live as any in the office". Among the victims were his Aunt Kite, the butcher's widow,* and Aunt Fenner. Both left a small legacy of trouble to Samuel, the former sending for him on her death-bed and beseeching him to look after her daughter Peg—"a troublesome carrion", he soon found her. For this self-opinionated young woman, flatly refusing her executor's advice, announced her intention of marrying a beggarly weaver and what was more, though he washed his hands of her, did so. As for Aunt Fenner, not only did her demise necessitate the Clerk of the Acts' attendance at a very degrading kind of funeral—a little lightened by the beauty of "my father's family being all in mourning, doing him the greatest honour, the world believing that he" (Uncle Fenner) "did give us it"—but it involved him in the humiliation of Uncle Fenner's subsequent behaviour. For within five months of his deprivation, the disgusting old gentleman—who might frequently be encountered at an alehouse, "drinking and very jolly and youthsome"—had taken to himself another wife, and she a

* Her real name was Mrs Julian Clarke, as she had married a second time, but Pepys continued to call her by her first husband's name. *Whitear*, p. 143.

pitiful, old, ill-bred woman and a midwife by trade and altogether a source of shame to Samuel.[8]

But the most serious loss of the autumn was that of Slingsby, the Comptroller. Early in October, Pepys himself was taken ill, coming home on his wedding night intending to be merry and being suddenly seized with a violent pain which kept him in bed for four days. Scarcely was he about again when he was called upon to visit the sick bed of his colleague. On the 24th he heard that Slingsby could no longer speak and two days later that he was dead, "which put me", he wrote, "into so great a trouble of mind that all the night I could not sleep, he being a man that loved me and had many qualities that made me to love him above all the Officers and Commissioners in the Navy".

There were some who fell sick, yet did not die—chief among them Lady Sandwich. In August, Pepys was at her bedside where she lay ill, it was feared with small-pox, while awaiting the coming of a child, and, though he did not tell her of it, his own heart was haunted by an even worse fear. No letters had come from my Lord for several weeks, but there were rumours that he was sick of a fever at Alicante: and God alone knew what kind of condition, with all his debts, he would leave his family in if he should die under that hot and alien sun—to say nothing of that uncomfortable £1000 for which Samuel stood his surety to his cousin at Hatcham. During the lady's illness, Pepys showed great tenderness, visiting her every day and attending (though he had plenty of his own to worry him) to all her affairs. But never a word did he breathe to her of what all the town was speaking of, that her Lord was dead, carefully hiding it from her until sure news had come that he was convalescent. Happily Lady Sandwich recovered also and was delivered of a fine daughter. "But to see in what a manner", Pepys related, "my Lady told it me, protesting that she sweat in the very telling of it, was the greatest pleasure to me in the world to see the simplicity and harmlessness of a lady".[9]

There was another of Pepys' relatives who did not die. That was his brother-in-law Balty, but this seemed no gain. He had an unpleasant way of cropping up as a domestic topic of conversation just when he was least welcome, which was frequently, for he was usually in trouble and always in need of money. In the midst of all the worries of that August, Samuel returned home one evening to find Elizabeth weeping and begging him to do something for her brother. Reluctantly—for she would not stop crying—he promised, but he could not help reflecting to himself that if once he did so, he would never be able to wipe his hands of him again. Nor at that moment had he any surplus funds for financing his wife's ne'er-do-well relations.

For Brampton affairs were still pressing, and that autumn he was forced to borrow a further £100, in addition to the £40 which Batten had already advanced him, to meet legal costs. Among other anxieties, the Trices were now returning to the offensive. They had withdrawn their original caveat and had shown for a time a disposition to be friendly; and on August 23rd—after a glass of wine in an alehouse, which always went a long way with this family—Pepys had actually given Tom Trice, who was a notary, the original will to prove. Yet the question of their Uncle Robert's bond to their mother (according to the dead man's testimony so unjustly procured) still remained distressingly open. That the principal of £200 was legally due there was little doubt, and this Pepys and his father agreed to pay; but the Trices claimed thirteen years' accrued interest on it, amounting to another £200. Payment of this, after taking advice, Pepys resolved to resist on the ground that there had never been any intention on the part of either his uncle or his aunt that the bond should become payable until the time of the latter's death. The Trices flatly denying this, and the lady in question dying and so depriving all parties of a first-hand witness, a lawsuit became inevitable.[10]

On November 7th Tom Trice brought an action at Common Law against the Pepyses to recover the full penal sum of £400, secured by the original bond, and delivered the writ in person to Samuel. All that month the harassed young official spent interviewing lawyers, and these, after the manner of their calling, said some one thing and some another. On Sergeant Turner's advice, he and his father filed a Bill of Complaint in Chancery claiming that Trice's suit was unconscionable in equity and demanding an injunction to prevent him from proceeding in it. Having made the lawyers happy, there was nothing now to do but to await the leisurely course of events: the injunction was duly granted and, attempts at a settlement proving abortive, the case continued as a haunting and expensive background to life for the next two years.[11]

Compared with this extravagance, Pepys' other ways of spending money were comparatively innocuous. But—perhaps because they gave him so much pleasure—he was very anxious about them that winter. His chief weakness was the theatre; he was constantly visiting the playhouses, and even his vows to desist or never to go save with his wife did not stop him. The fine robes and curtains, the tall candles, the skill of the actors, the women in men's clothes with their sightly legs, above all the play itself (Betterton in *The Bondman* he saw over and over again), all were irresistibly delightful, especially to one engaged in litigation with such dull fellows as Uncle Thomas and the Trices. But the failing which worried him most was his tendency to exceed in wine, for it both wasted his time and money and made him ill. The old association with Penn and Batten still led him too often into such temptation. The work of this jovial couple generally ended by midday, and thereafter there was little better for them to do than to dine at the "Dolphin" and make shift to fuddle anyone who joined them. In this task they sometimes had some success with the Clerk of the Acts: once so much so that he was unable to read the usual evening prayers to the household when he returned home.[12]

None the less, Pepys was growing very weary of such company. He dared not shake it off too abruptly, for now that Slingsby was gone the two knights were the only members of the Navy Board with whom he was on intimate terms; the new Comptroller, the aged Cavalier Admiral Sir John Mennes, though he seemed a pleasant old gentleman and a good scholar, was reputed to be an enemy to Lord Sandwich, and was in Pepys' opinion a very poor successor to his dead friend. So he was forced to dissemble. "But, good God", he whispered to his Diary, "what an age this is, and what a world is this, that a man cannot live without playing the knave and dissimulation."[13]

But Elizabeth was swayed by no such prudential motives. She did not like Lady Batten and her daughter's high-handed ways and refused to truckle to them, and Samuel, to do him justice, encouraged her. Across the garden wall, in the gossip of the rival kitchens, in the great weekly battle for precedence in the Office pew, an undying war now began; sometimes, for all its ardours, there were glorious gains, as on the day when Pepys brought back to his wife the news that her proud rival had before her marriage been another man's whore. Of course one tried not to believe such stories, and yet one just could not help it; it was so exactly what one had expected.[14]

So encouraged, Pepys plucked up heart to quarrel himself with Batten. The first serious rift occurred on December 6th when the two knights chose to take umbrage at their young colleague's chaffing them about their intimacy with a serving-wench at a tavern; it was time, they resolved, to put him in his place. A fortnight later they rebuked him because he was absent from a Board meeting, saying that they could not be a committee without their Register—a remark which infuriated Pepys who liked to suppose himself their equal. He also resolved that it was time to act; if he did not do so now, hold himself aloof from them and refuse to crouch at their command, he would never be able to keep himself even with them.[15]

While he prepared to join battle with his colleagues at the Office, he also turned to fight his own failings. A long succession of vows, not always kept, but always manfully fought for, mark the progress of that war. On the last day of the old year he took a solemn oath to abstain from plays and wine. Next day—after starting the year by accidentally striking his wife a great blow over her face and nose as he turned over in bed, "which waked her with pain, at which I was sorry and so to sleep again"—the sight of a handbill, announcing that the *Spanish Curate* was to be acted in the afternoon, proved too much for him and he accompanied young William Penn and his sister to the theatre. (Returning, the father of American quakerism left his sword behind in the coach.) Nothing daunted, Pepys returned to the attack and before the end of January—there had been no more plays—he was recording his thanks to God that since his leaving off drinking of wine he found himself much better, minded his business more and spent less money. On the 31st he was vowing to keep indoors and be conscientious in his attendance at the Office.

A new experience there had recently given him a fresh interest in his work. At the end of the previous November, the Duke of York had sent for the Navy Officers to take their advice, not this time on the matter for which they were most usually summoned—lack of money—but on one much affecting the honour of England, the failure of Captain Holmes to enforce the time-honoured salute to the English flag in the narrow seas. The whole Board was present and the Duke desired each member to state what he knew of ancient practice. When it came to Pepys' turn he could not bear to admit that he knew nothing about it all, so was forced, as he put it, 'to study a lie", and told the Duke's secretary, Coventry, that he had often heard Selden say that he could prove that Henry VII gave his captains commissions to make Danish ships strike to them in the Baltic.[16]

This unlikely thesis Pepys now resolved to prove in writing and present to the Duke, judging it a good way to make himself known. Accordingly on the way home he bought a copy of Selden's *Mare Clausum* and settled down to study it. He found the subject surprisingly interesting and before long became absorbed in it. Soon he began to carry his researches further, canvassed the pros and cons of the case with lawyers and merchants on 'Change, and even asked one of his old Exchequer friends to look up Domesday Book to see if there was anything in it about the dominion of the seas. The whole affair ended in nothing and would be wholly unimportant but for one circumstance. For it awoke in Pepys that deep-seated feeling for history which had always been his and, directing it to the sea, first aroused his lifelong ambition to become its chronicler. Moreover, it profoundly affected his work, for henceforward the Navy, and all that appertained to it, had a new meaning for him.[17]

Chapter IX

Buckling To

"My mind was never in my life in so good a condition of quiet as it hath been since I have followed my business." *Diary*, July 5th, 1662.

At the beginning of February, 1662, there arrived at the Navy Office a small and precious volume containing the formal Instructions of the Duke of York as Lord High Admiral to the Principal Officers and Commissioners of the Navy. It was accompanied by a letter* from the Duke stating that up to the present the prevailing lack of money had "so hardened and emboldened many persons in their negligences and abuses that there was little hope of their amendment", but urging that henceforward, whenever money was available, it should be used to discharge negligent and inefficient officers from the Yards and ships; some of the Yards, it added, were more fit for the purposes of a hospital than those of the King's service. The Instructions themselves—a confirmation with certain additions of those issued by the Earl of Northumberland a generation before—laid down the duties of the Board, forbade its members to engage, or allow their inferiors to engage, in the sale of merchandise to the service, and urged the utmost care in the purchase of naval stores by enquiring frequently as to the market price of masts, deal, hemp, pitch, tar and the like and obtaining weekly returns from the Customs Office of all consignments of such goods arriving

* Dated Jan. 28th, 1662.

in the river. The reason for the last was, as the letter pointed out, to prevent the Principal Officers from concluding contracts with any one merchant before satisfying themselves that there were no other able to furnish the King with the same goods cheaper and better.[1]

The Instructions arrived at the very moment when Pepys' imagination had been first stirred by the past history of the Navy and when he was resolving to apply himself more zealously to his duties in order to diminish his expenses and outdistance his colleagues. These motives were now given an official impress. On the day after the Board met to read over the Instructions, the Clerk of the Acts got himself trimmed and made his way with a new purpose to the Office, where, he recorded, "I do begin to be exact in my duty there and exacting my privileges and shall continue to do so". The next few months were to show him as good as his word.

No longer was Pepys' attendance at the Office confined to unavoidable occasions and Board meetings: henceforward he was there all day. He rose early and stayed late (which nobody else did) and, as is the way of mankind, visited his own virtues on his startled subordinates: when his boy Will failed to call him betimes in the morning, he sent for a rod and beat him soundly. His head was now always full of his work, and he found it a great pleasure and a growing content. Nor did he hurry from the Office any longer when callers arrived at the house: he was better off where he was. "My mind in good ease", he wrote, "when I mind business, which methinks should be a good argument to me never to do otherwise."[2]

To mark the new era, he had his study at the Office altered and his own clerks set in a room apart. Here, with the scene set for the future administration of the Navy, he tidied his files and tore up old papers till they covered the floor of his closet as high as his knees. And to show that he, at any rate, was resolved to obey the Duke's instructions to the letter, he sat up late with Hayter making abstracts of all the contracts made at the Office since he first entered it. He was Clerk of the Acts at last.[3]

So resolved, he did his business with new understanding. He made expeditions to Deptford and Woolwich to set out waiting squadrons or pay off discharged crews, hired ships for the Navy on 'Change and pondered long over the mystery of the Victualler's accounts. And as he wrote and copied and thought, various dark suspicions began to vex his mind. Were not the Treasurer's Officers swindling the King's service—rumours reached him that they were taking ten per cent. commissions on all monies they paid out—and was not Wood, the timber merchant who supplied the Navy with masts, for all his alliance with Batten, a knave? These matters were as yet too high for him to enquire closely into, yet daily they became of greater import in his mind. And within the scope of his still limited authority, there appeared a new zeal; when he found that Griffin, the caretaker, had left the door of the Office open at night, he had serious thoughts of carrying away the screw or the carpet to teach him a lesson before sending for him and chiding him.[4]

The same impulse to work and righteousness appeared in Pepys' private as well as his public doings. Wicked and fashionable leanings on the part of Elizabeth to wear the new perukes, which were then all the rage, were sternly checked: he would only endure it, if they were made of her own hair. As for Will Wayneman, the lad had every reason to be conscious of his master's drive towards self-improvement: for one spring morning he found himself being followed down the cellar stairs, whither he had been sent to draw beer, by the man of righteousness bearing a cane with which he fell upon him and chastised him for his faults, till his sister Jane, alarmed by his cries, came down and pleaded for him. "So", wrote Pepys in his Diary that night, "I forebore and afterwards in my wife's chamber did there talk to Jane how much I did love the boy for her sake and how much it do concern me to correct the boy for his faults, or else he would be undone."[5]

Perhaps the unaccustomed rigidity of the rule which Pepys put on himself soured his temper a little. He had almost bidden farewell to plays, and his amusements were now chiefly confined to the Sabbath—a quiet morning spent over Fuller's *Worthies* or in walking from one church to another, "hearing a bit here and a bit there". Certainly his abjuration of wine appeared to upset his health, and he made anxious notes of the evils incurred by such abstinence: he was even forced to relax his vow a little. One recreation he still allowed himself —music. Ever since the beginning of the year he had been practising singing to himself, morning and evening; it sent him out to his work refreshed and to his bed in peace. That January a higher ambition came to him; he would learn to compose. With this intent he had hired the services of one John Berchinshaw, an Irish music-master. As always with him he had taken to this new pursuit with tremendous enthusiasm, so much so that he even fell to composing airs on a Sunday—"God forgive me!" In February he stumbled on his first song, with his tutor's aid setting to some far-fetched amorous lines the melody of *Gaze not on Swans*. He finished it a fortnight later, paying Berchinshaw on the same day £5 for his five weeks' tuition: a great sum of money, he reckoned it, and one that troubled him to part with. On the same afternoon his master, who had every hope of continuing his profitable employment, showed him in his enthusiasm his mathematical card of the system of music, of which he was inordinately proud. But Pepys was more critical and, though impressed by it, did not believe it to be as useful as its inventor claimed. A few days later he told him so, upon which the outraged artist flung himself out of the room in a pet, his employer being careful not to stop him since he had already resolved to discontinue what was now a needless expense. For he had learnt Berchinshaw's rules by heart and had secured the setting of two of his incomparable songs; the rest of that morning he spent committing them to writing.[6]

The end of the music lessons coincided with another reformation in Pepys' life. All that winter, he had been postponing the unpleasant task of making up his accounts: he was conscious that he had spent far too much and guessed that when he made up his balance he would have an unpleasant shock. With the help of vows he brought himself to the sticking-point, and on March 1st, after paying off the £40 which he had borrowed in the previous autumn from Batten, sat down by himself to the long-postponed task. When he rose he found that he was £100 poorer than at his last reckoning, his capital having dwindled to £500, and that he had spent £250 in six months. Yet, for all his past extravagance, his mind was eased, and next morning in bed he talked long with his wife of the frugal life they would live henceforward, telling her all the wonderful things he would be able to do if ever he could save £2000—to be a knight and keep his own coach, which pleased her mightily. Then he drew up rules for his future expenses, binding himself in the presence of God to keep them faithfully and attaching penalties for failure to do so; "and I do not doubt", he added, "but hereafter to give a good account of my time and to grow rich". So the righteous man awaited the summer of 1662.

Yet, had spring brought no relaxation, Pepys would not

have been Pepys. There was an odd play or two around Easter, and an occasional walk across the fields to the cheese-cake house at Islington, or a dinner at the "Dolphin" on a mighty chine of beef and other good cheer. And towards the end of April he made for the second year running an expedition to the Dockyard at Portsmouth. With infinite difficulty he had prevented Elizabeth from accompanying him, though he was unable to persuade her to retire to the tedious security of Brampton during his absence from town. His old acquaintance of the voyage to Schevelling, Dr Clerke, was of the company, and in the merry humour of that springtime pilgrimage, while cutting asparagus for supper in the garden of their Guildford inn, they called each other cousins by virtue of the name of the one and the office of the other. And when they came to their lodgings at Portsmouth, Samuel reckoned that his new kinsman must be of the oldest and senior house of Clerkes, since all the fleas went to him and none to himself. A day's excursion to Southampton, a good many healths (so many that his eyes were troubled) and the magnificent respect with which he and his colleagues were treated by the natives—he was made a Burgess of Portsmouth and attended a naval service at which there was a special prayer for the Right Honourable the Principal Officers—all gave relish to his stay. The town was full of fine folk expecting the arrival of the Queen and Lord Sandwich from Lisbon, and one evening towards the end of his visit the quick-eyed Samuel espied his old flame, Mrs Pierce, and another lady passing by. To them he sped, carried them to a place of refreshment, feasted them with wine and sweetmeats, waited on them at their lodgings and was exceedingly merry. He even contrived some business to detain him in Portsmouth so that he might enjoy another evening in their society; he and Dr Clerke were particularly intrigued with Mrs Pierce's companion, "she being somewhat old and handsome and painted and fine, and hath a very handsome maid with her, which we take to be the marks of a bawd".

On his return to London, Pepys had a further lesson in the diverse construction of the world. No sooner had he greeted Elizabeth at home, than he washed himself (for it was a very hot day) and sallied out with a letter from Dr Clerke, who had remained behind at Portsmouth, to his lady at Whitehall. He found her a very fine and fashionable woman, so much so that he was quite abashed; "what with her person and the number of fine ladies that were with her, I was much out of countenance and could hardly carry myself like a man among them, but however I staid till my courage was up again and talked to them and viewed her house". The tailor's son was still not always at home in the great world, but he faced it boldly.

After these excitements it was a little hard to settle down again, particularly to the Spartan life which he had marked out for himself. A sudden burst of plays and summer evening jaunts marked the first course of the struggle, and for one moment it looked as though Pepys had surrendered to his own genius for enjoyment: "it is best", he wrote, "to enjoy some degree of pleasure now that we have health, money and opportunity, rather than leave pleasures to old age or poverty when we cannot have them so properly". The new Queen had arrived and all the Court was merry-making, and with her came Lord Sandwich after a year's absence, putting Pepys, who had so carefully tended his interests and befriended his lady and children while he had been away, into a great tremor of joy. But before May was out, Samuel's determination had returned and he was taking out new vows against wine and plays. To signalise the change, on the last evening of the month, after his maid Sarah had combed his head and washed his feet in a bath of herbs, he cut off his moustache.* [7]

So shorn—henceforward, he decided, he would trim himself neatly and cleanly with a piece of pumice-stone—he began the month of June by singing French psalms all a Sabbath morning. Then, once more, he buckled to his business. The initial plunge taken, it was all extraordinarily easy. He rose at five and, after writing his journal for the previous day, made his way to the Office to get everything ready against the next meeting and steal long industrious summer dawns on his sleepy colleagues. When some old acquaintance like Creed visited him with tempting rhetoric about the latest playbill, he had only to think of the happiness his new virtue and application gave him to dismiss him without regret. And every Sunday he read over his vows.[8]

To the King's Navy, this revolution in the habits of its junior Principal Officer brought a wonderful change. For suddenly in its sluggish administrative channels a swift, fresh stream began to flow. The Store-keepers and Clerks of the Cheque and Survey at Woolwich and Deptford, who hitherto had been content to perform only a third of their duties, now found that they were liable to be visited almost weekly by young Mr Pepys, and, when he was not peering about their works in person, received from him a long succession of enquiring, admonitory and categorical letters. In that keen, untiring mind, their time-honoured perquisites took the colour of corruption and dereliction of duty—the deals which they undervalued and then sold, the multitude of servants and decrepit old men whom they kept on the

* "Beard" is the generic term by which Pepys refers to the victim of this operation, but acquaintanceship with the fashions and nomenclature of the period leads one to believe that it adorned his upper lip only.

musters and whose pay they retained, the old cables which they stole and subsequently retailed to the King as new.[9]

Not to his subordinates alone did Pepys confine his criticism. For those rich and powerful beings, the government contractors, were stung that summer as though by a hornet. The flagmakers' genial cheat of charging threepence a yard more than was allowed in their forgotten contracts was ruthlessly exposed, Mr Pepys informing the shocked Navy Board that he could obtain the same materials elsewhere for half the price. Those who supplied the King with tar and oil at their own figure were electrified to see a quick, commanding little figure going up and down their own Thames Street enquiring of all their rivals the current market prices of their commodities. And the great Sir Richard Ford, who provided the Navy with old worn-out yarn, skilfully covered over with new hemp, found himself confronted with the cheat before his very friends, the Principal Officers. For Pepys had secretly gone down to Woolwich to experiment and had come back burning with anger; never again, he resolved, would he have the King's workmen discouraged from representing such palpable corruptions on the part of powerful merchants. And without fear or disguise, he had stood up boldly at the Board next day and laid bare the whole shocking story, so that his colleagues for very shame were forced to stop Sir Richard's bill. It made that great merchant his enemy; he did not care, he had done his duty.[10]

Pepys' zeal was strengthened by his growing dislike of his colleagues, Batten and Penn. If they were idle and corrupt, he would be industrious and honest; they had lorded it over him because they were his seniors, he would show them that in the real business of the Navy he was their superior. He fought them in open office for the prerogatives of his post, and, when Batten tried in his heavy way to snub him, he called him an unreasonable man to his face. He took a special delight in exposing the many cheats in which the stocky, old Presbyterian had a secret part, and he was the more encouraged to do so by virtue of the great battle for precedence which he and his wife so gallantly waged against Lady Batten every Sunday. As for Penn, he had broken with him violently one June morning when the latter with his smooth voice had tried to jockey him out of his prerogative of preparing contracts; a base rascal, Pepys set him down for, and resolved to remember it against him as long as he lived. Henceforward he loathed Penn and all his "base treacherous tricks", though in the face of Sir William's habitual courtesy and his friends at Court, he found it best to dissemble his dislike.* [11]

In his attack on the two Sir Williams, Pepys knew that he could rely in the last resort on powerful support. Ever since his first resolve to apply himself to his business, he had been making advances to the Navy Treasurer, the great Sir George Carteret. Carteret did not like Batten, who came of a social class and schooling very different from his own, and Pepys gained ground with him by expressing his discreet horror at his neighbour's idleness and corruption and taking every opportunity of contrasting his own zeal and integrity. A still mightier ally now came the way of the Clerk of the Acts. On May 8th he heard that the Duke's secretary, William Coventry, was to be added to the Navy Board as an additional Commissioner. At first Pepys had some misgivings:

* "Sir W. Penn came to my office to take his leave of me" (before setting out on a visit to his Irish estate) "and desiring a turn in the garden did commit the care of his building to me, and offered all his services to me in all matters of mine. I did, God forgive me! promise him all my service and love, though the rogue knows he deserves none from me, nor do I intend to show him any, but as he dissembles with me, so must I with him." *Diary*, July 9th, 1662. For a letter written by Pepys to Penn in Ireland in the same spirit, see Tanner, *Further Correspondence*, p. 1.

Coventry was a friend of Penn's whose great naval talents he admired; moreover he was hated by Carteret. The latter was most indignant, regarding the whole affair as an intrigue of Penn's and confided his feelings to his young colleague. But Pepys, despite a natural leaning towards Carteret, decided that his proper policy was to keep in with both of these powerful rivals.[12]

He therefore set out to win Coventry's trust as he had won Carteret's. He soon felt the benefit of doing so. For Coventry was a man after his own heart, full of enthusiasm for whatever he set his hand to and, like him, resolved to do good and to enquire into all the miscarriages of the Office. And with the great name of the Lord High Admiral behind him, he was far better placed than the Clerk of the Acts for so doing. Under his reforming standard Pepys now enrolled himself. And as the jackal and the tiger hunt together, so did Pepys and Coventry. First would the lesser terror go forth to spy out the nakedness of the land: then he would return to fetch his mighty ally to pursue and slay. Thus on a summer's day, when the morning's Board meeting was done, Pepys would clamber into Coventry's coach and drive with him to the Exchange, here to surprise a truant captain whose ship was already due at sea: then, the poor man sent flying in his fine clothes Thameswards, the two reformers would sit down together to a bite of dinner at the "Ship" tavern behind the 'Change. Thus refreshed, they would take boat at Billingsgate and descend on Woolwich, board a warship there—where "found all things out of order and after frighting the officers there, we left them to make more haste"—and then landing discover old Batten going about his Survey, "so poorly and unlike a survey of the Navy that I am ashamed of it, and so is Mr Coventry". After that there would be a glorious hour or two in the Dockyard, measuring timber, surprising clerks in cheats and finding fault everywhere, until it was time to return home again. And as twilight fell on the river and the lights of London gleamed above their bow, the two reformers would talk familiarly together of the business of their Office, and Pepys would reflect with pride on having gained the favour of so great a man.[13]

Yet Pepys the reformer was no mere careerist. There was nothing superficial in his attack upon the abuses of the Navy. Conscious of his own shortcomings, he made it his business that summer to learn his duty. If there were cheats in the King's Yards, it was for him to discover ways to detect them. He would rise early to visit the Ropeyard at Woolwich, there to study the several sorts of hemp and the various methods of dressing them and to make experiments as to their respective strengths, until he felt himself competent to judge between them and to tell at a glance when bad material was being served into the Yards. He taught himself, too, to measure timber, seeking out his old acquaintance, Greatorex, the instrument-maker, to recommend him an able instructor, and buying a rule with which to make his own calculations and nonplus the indignant carpenters of the Yards. When a contract affecting the royal Forest of Dean was to be drafted, Pepys—up at four in the morning—no longer contented himself with the clerical part of his business: he must needs take down Speed's map and make himself master of the geography of the forest. And, finding that in all these new activities a knowledge of mathematics was a first requisite, he went back to first principles and, a rising man of close on thirty, put himself to school. For, having hired one Cooper, a discharged mate of one of the King's ships whom he had known formerly in the *Naseby*, to teach him arithmetic of an evening, he settled down to learn the multiplication tables and rose by candlelight each morning to repeat them by rote until he had mastered them. When his month's tuition was done, he made further use of Cooper, taking him on the river to point out the various parts of the vessels there and getting him to explain the model of a ship which he had found in an old chest in his office and quietly annexed. Nor was he ungrateful to his tutor, for when his lessons were finished he procured the good man promotion as master of the *Reserve*, then commissioning under Captain Holmes. It gave him especial pleasure to do so, for it showed the effects of his constant attendance at the Office, his influence now being so felt in every action that nothing could pass without him.[14]

In his quest for naval knowledge that summer, Pepys made two new friends. The fame of his zeal was beginning to attract the notice of all those who, like himself, felt the humiliation of the age-long corruption of the Navy, and one August morning there appeared at his office a young man of much his own age named Anthony Deane, at that time Assistant Shipwright at Woolwich. Deane promised to discover to Pepys the whole abuse that the King suffered in the measurement of timber, and also to make him the model of a ship. A week later he joined his superior over an early breakfast of eggs at the "King's Head" at Bow and then rode with him into Epping Forest, where he showed him the method of hewing trees and the mystery of half square by which the service was cheated. Such was Pepys' enthusiasm at all this that, while dinner was being served at Ilford, he occupied himself by measuring the tables and furniture according to the rules which his new friend had taught him. Then, after riding down to Barking to view the quay where the timber was shipped to Woolwich, he returned home, still repeating to himself the rules he had learnt that day. As for Deane, he justly reckoned him a most valuable acquisition; a little conceited and apt to decry his colleagues, but honest and able and a useful man to play against the great shipbuilding family of the Petts, who had established such a monopoly in the making of the King's fleets. Henceforward he would give him all the encouragement he could.[15]

His other new friend was of a different stamp. Sir William Warren, the timber merchant, was one of the greatest traders of his day. It was his misfortune to see his rival, William Wood, obtain contract after contract from the Navy Office for his deals and masts, a fact which Batten's lavish housekeeping in London and Walthamstow helped to explain. Warren now beheld in the sudden activity of the Clerk of the Acts, who, he was astute enough to see, had no love for Batten, a chance of ending Wood's monopoly. He therefore began to show Pepys the most delicate and flattering attentions, attuning them carefully to the young man's new enthusiasm. One June evening, after transacting some minor business with him, he offered to show him over his deal ships and carried him down the river, where with great pains (and the most winning disinterestedness) he explained the difference between his various wares—Dram, Swinsound, Christiania—adding many pleasant anecdotes of the manner in which the Swedes cut and sawed them. Thence he took him to his yard and showed him all his deals, spars and balks, till Pepys felt positively proud at acquiring so much new knowledge, and finally to his house where he plied him with mum—wine the young official, true to his vows, refused—and impressed him with his fine possessions. A further lesson followed a few weeks later, when from the nature of the timber the conversation naturally passed to the corruptions of Sir William Batten and the kind of people he employed.[16]

On another evening in July, another caller brought an abuse of a new sort to Pepys' notice—a little shyly at first, but when he saw his readiness to be informed, more boldly. Nearly a century before, Drake and Hawkins had founded the Chatham Chest for disabled seamen, each serving sailor paying sixpence a month from his wages towards its support. Since then grave abuses had crept into its management and at the present time it appeared that Batten, one of the Governors of the Chest, was not only charging large sums of money as private expenses and even as gratuities to himself and creating all sorts of unwarranted offices out of the fund for his friends and dependents, but also retaining monies deducted from seamen's wages in his own hands. Both from the wish to right an injustice and the even greater desire to annoy Batten, Pepys joyfully accepted this new charge and through Coventry's aid succeeded in getting the Duke to set up a Commission for inspecting the management of the Chest. Such officiousness did not make him popular with his colleagues, but among the poor folk who flocked to the Office for wages, employment and redress of grievances, Pepys became known as a kind and good-hearted man.[17]

Confident in his own integrity and the support of his great patrons, Pepys fell furiously that summer upon all abuses, big and little. He wrote to Coventry to tell him how his colleagues absented themselves from their duties so that he was left alone in London, and bored a hole in the wainscotting of his closet to watch the doings of those small fry, his clerks, in their office next door. And that he might discover the better the shortcomings of his colleagues and subordinates, he fell to reading old John Hollond's *Discourses of the Navy*, and found them most entrancing, "hitting the very diseases of the Navy which we are troubled with now a days". For was he not now himself his Majesty's watchdog, to give the alarm against all who troubled his ships and yards?[18]

And he waxed great. His superiors thought well of him

and praised him to one another and to the Duke, who to his extraordinary joy thanked Lord Sandwich "for one person brought into the Navy naming myself"; and on 'Change and in the Yards men spoke of Pepys and Coventry as the pair who between them did all the work of the Office. And all who had business to transact brought it to the Clerk of Acts, knowing that if he took charge of it, it would be carried through. So did his diligence daily gain him ground in his employment. He was no longer the least among his brethren.[19]

And honours came to him. As early as February 15th, 1662, he was sworn a Younger Brother of Trinity House. Before the year ended, a much greater dignity was conferred on him. He had long been wearying of his employment at the Privy Seal: after that first glorious rush of office-holders after patents in his first month of service in 1660, the post had proved a barren one with little to do but sign pardons—"a deadly number of these"—to which no fees were attached. By 1662 almost the only benefit left in the place was the right it carried to a seat in the Chapel at Whitehall—a modest privilege which Pepys occasionally claimed. But for the rest it interfered sadly with his growing work for the Navy. Accordingly on August 17th he relinquished his connection with the Privy Seal. Two days later, he was told that Lord Sandwich had nominated him among many noblemen and other eminent persons as a member of the Commission set up to manage the affairs of England's new possession, Tangier—they included the Duke of York, Prince Rupert, the Duke of Albemarle and Lord Sandwich himself.* Well

* The members were the Duke of York, Prince Rupert, the Duke of Albemarle, Lord Southampton, Lord Peterborough, Lord Sandwich, Sir George Carteret, Sir William Compton, William Coventry, Sir R. Ford, Sir William Rider, Hugh Cholmley, Thomas Povy, Samuel Pepys, Captain Roger Cuttance and John Creed. Routh, *Tangier* 31.

might he tell his Diary that on all hands, by God's blessing, he found himself a rising man. And with him, on his goings and comings, went the panoply of rank, for now he was accompanied by his boy, Will Wayneman, wearing his livery of grey trimmed with black and gold lace and a sword at his side, outshining by far the boys of Batten and Penn.[20]

With all this growing honour, Pepys' wealth did not increase that year quite as rapidly as it might have done. In early June he noted how dearly he wanted to possess a thousand pounds, but could as yet only claim £530 towards it. The month brought a great increase and by the end of it he was master of £650, the greatest sum he had yet known. But for the rest of the year, for all his hopes to make himself a profit out of his accounts with Lord Sandwich—"God forgive me",—his capital remained much the same. For, though his industry tended to bring money his way, his soaring ambition, for all his vows to economise, found powerful ways to spend it.

On the little house that looked across the courtyard of the Navy Office, Pepys' love was still lavished. He had begun the year by hanging pictures and arranging pewter sconces on the stairs and in the entry: a month later he spent an entire morning watching the colliers move his store of coal from its old habitation to his new cellar, and, though Mrs Pepys called repeatedly down to him that dinner was ready, she received no response, and it was three in the afternoon before he could be induced to come up from his grimy, but delicious, occupation. At midsummer he resolved on a far more venturous alteration—no less than the addition of a new storey to his house. So on a July Saturday he laid up his goods preparatory to the workmen coming in on Monday to remove the roof. By July 15th every tile had been lifted, and then was seen the sad fate that befalls the man who ventures to uncover his house upon St Swithin's day. For the rain came down and continued to fall for five days until there was not one dry foot above or below in the whole house, and, cold and wet from dabbling in the water, Pepys was forced to move his soaked belongings to an empty chamber of Sir William Penn's.[21]

Elizabeth he thought it best to move further afield. Though she was anything but anxious to go, he succeeded in persuading her to visit the country until the house in Seething Lane was fit again for habitation. Accordingly on July 28th, he saw her off, with her maid Sarah and the boy Wayneman, from the "George" at Holborn Conduit in the coach to Brampton, finding himself that night as usual troubled and melancholy for her going, so that even Mr Cooper's mathematics lesson failed to console and he was driven before he could sleep to comfort himself with his lute. Three nights later the lonely husband's dilemma was increased, for hearing that Sir William Penn's pretty maid, with whom he had secret hopes—"God forgive me"—of having a bout, had gone unexpectedly into the country, his errant fancy turned upon his old servant Jane, whom Elizabeth had left to look after him; but then doubts intervened, "and I dare not for fear she should prove honest and refuse and then tell my wife". Besides, much as he wanted her, it would be a shame to himself, he decided, to beg a favour of his wench. So, instead, he contented himself with discreetly admiring a most pretty young lady, whom he met in the company of his uncle and aunt Wight and who was quite securely unapproachable; he had also a far from creditable chance encounter with his friend Sarah at Lord Sandwich's lodgings, who was too old a hand at the game—he was careful of course to stop short of the final bastion—and therefore did not matter.[22]

Those who make themselves enemies by their zeal should

not set their hearts too closely on anything of which men can rob them. Pepys had done everything within his power that summer to undermine the prestige of Batten and Penn. His anxiety to improve his house gave them their chance of revenge. Early in September, Penn—one suspects with the greatest joy—buttonholed his young colleague to warn him of Sir John Mennes the Comptroller's anger at the way in which his new storey was shutting out his view and blocking his passage to his house of office on the roof. Next day the old Cavalier himself spoke to Pepys of it, and, taking Coventry with him as a witness, insisted on showing him just how much damage his building operations had caused. Poor Pepys was in a fever of apprehension, so much so that he could not sleep: "the more fool am I", he added sadly, "and must labour against it for shame, especially I that used to preach up Epictetus' rule of Τὰ ἐφ' ἡμῖν καὶ τὰ οὐκ ἐφ' ἡμῖν".

But worse was to come. For Mennes, secretly, as one suspects, spurred on by his fellow admirals, now demanded Pepys' best chamber as a compensation for the damage done him, basing his claim on the fact that it had belonged to the previous occupier of his own house in Commonwealth times. But, though he was so troubled and hurt in heart that he could scarcely eat, Pepys determined to make a fight to save that which he held so dear. Discovering from his plasterer and bricklayer that the room had always belonged to his lodgings, though it had been a while lent to a neighbour by a bachelor republican official, he got his clerk Hayter to write to his two old friends for the history of the disputed chamber. So armed—for both the men of the past obligingly replied, adding their gladness to know that Hayter still held his employment*—Pepys resolved the more to stand to his right.

* Their replies to Hayter will be found in *Rawlinson MSS. A.* 174, ff. 327, 329.

And faced by such an opponent, Mennes tacitly gave way. For though the old gentleman loved to bluster and swear (as he did with a vengeance one morning when from the Board Room window he espied Pepys' workmen putting up rails upon the leads) he was lazy and at heart good-natured and had no wish for a war of attrition. And so the affair gradually lapsed, quietly fading into the limbo of forgotten incidents.[23]

Everything returned to normal. Mrs Pepys came home again, carpenters and joiners laid the floors and wainscots of the renovated house, and the painting and plastering came to an end. Only the glaziers' work remained to be completed and the furniture to be put in place. This also the busy days brought to pass. On November 22nd, the whole edifice of reconstruction was crowned by a new-fashioned knocker which the workmen before their departure fastened upon the front door. And Pepys looked upon it all and saw that it was good.[24]

Chapter X

Pots and Pans

"The fierce Devil of Jealousy, which haunts the houses of married folks, rendering them no less unhappy, dismal and clamorous than the Temple of Moloch, where such children and servants as you most delight in shall pass through the fire of daily contention." Francis Osborne, *Advice to a Son.*

On Sunday, November 2nd, 1662, Pepys lay long in bed, talking with great pleasure with his wife, in whom, he wrote, "I never had greater content, blessed be God! than now, she continuing with the same care and thrift and innocence, so long as I keep her from occasions of being otherwise, as ever she was in her life, and keeps the house as well". But in stating his contentment, he stated also the problem of its maintenance. It was not easy to keep his wife from "occasions of being otherwise".

For Elizabeth by nature was neither careful nor thrifty; one could not even be certain that she was innocent. If left to herself she put things in the wrong place and forgot where they were, threw her clothes by untidily and even left her scarf, waistcoat and night-dressings in a coach returning from some Christmas festivities at Lord Sandwich's— "though" (as Samuel confessed) "she did give them to me to look after, yet it was her fault not to see that I did take them out of the coach". As for her economy, it was erratic in the extreme: at one moment the domestic staff would be threatening mutiny because she had gone out leaving no victuals for them; at another her husband would be forced to put aside his official labours to reduce the size of the housekeeping bills. Nor were her relations with her servants happy. She had taken to the country with her that summer Will Wayneman and Sarah, an admirable maid, tall and well favoured and an excellent worker—Samuel thought her as good a servant as ever came into a house—who had been with them since the previous autumn. While at Brampton, Elizabeth quarrelled violently with both of them; declared that the boy had been guilty of offences not fit to be named and that Sarah was too ill-natured to live with. All this was infinitely distressing to Pepys, who liked to live on good terms with his maids and to sit of an evening in the kitchen in merry discourse with them. Elizabeth made this almost impossible.[1]

Yet there was a deeper cause for Mrs Pepys' domestic unrest than her weariness of Sarah or her dislike of the boy's vices. For like every woman she secretly wished to excel, to be like the fine ladies on the fringes of whose world her husband in his official capacity moved, to keep a gentlewoman as companion, go to plays and have adorers. But the very industry that was carrying her husband forward on his career seemed to shut all these things the further from her. For poor Elizabeth lost both ways: her husband's absorption in his work deprived her of his company and his abjuration of pleasure of other people's. She grew fretful and lonely, until even Pepys began to perceive that something was amiss.[2]

He tried at first to quell her discontent by anger, but then the fire that was in her flamed up and scorched his fingers. One November afternoon, he was disturbed in the Office by a letter from her: angrily he put it in his pocket, guessing it to be some querulous protest against his injustice and meaning to burn it before her face. When he came home that night he would not speak to her but went to bed, sullen and silent.

But in the morning, as he related, "she begun to talk...and to be friends, believing all this while that I had read her letter, which I perceived by her discourse was full of good counsel, and relating the reason of her desiring a woman, and how little charge she did intend it to be to me. So I began and argued it so full and plain to her, and she to resign it wholly to me, to put her away, and take one of the Bowyers if I did dislike her". But, after a little while Pepys, who always knew how to be wise in the last resort, yielded and agreed to his wife's desire to take a gentlewoman as her companion into his household. Nor was he without motives of his own in so doing.

Elizabeth's brother, Balty, had already found the young lady. Her name was Gosnell, one of two sisters, both attractive, vivacious and accomplished at singing and dancing. Doubtful as Samuel was about the whole business, he could not help a secret longing to have so desirable a creature beneath his roof: their little Marmotte, he and Elizabeth in their talk called her. Early in December she came, to depart again almost immediately. For she had been in the house only three days—a delight to Samuel, who kept coming back from the Office at all hours to share her company, and a most graceful sight to behold attending Elizabeth to church—before it transpired that Balty had beguiled the young woman into coming with lying tales of daily visits to Court and plays. Not finding these delights obtainable at the Pepyses', the young lady promptly made an excuse and went home. When next Pepys saw her, she was on the stage. In the meantime he cheered himself up by the thought that the expense of keeping such a one would have been altogether beyond his means and that her departure was really a concealed providence to prevent him from running behindhand in the world. As for his wife, poor wretch, he must find some other way of relieving the tedium and loneliness of her life. Perhaps work would do it.[3]

So the changes in the household followed for the moment a more ordinary turn. Sarah went, weeping piteously and all but causing her kind employer to do so too, and firing a parting shot as he kissed her a last good-night, by revealing that Elizabeth had been giving money and clothes to her beggarly brother. A new cook called Susan arrived, also recommended by the inevitable Balty, for which Pepys liked her never the better—but a good, well-looked lass—and Jane was promoted to the dignity of chamber-maid, at which he was secretly pleased, though he was careful not to say so. And Will Wayneman* for his naughty tricks was to be sent home.[4]

Cold, with the housetops covered with snow—a sight Samuel had not seen for three years—the winter of 1662–3 was a troubled one. It began with hopes and was attended with successive discouragements. At the end of October there had appeared an informer who had given notice to Lord Sandwich of £7000 buried beneath the Tower by one of its republican governors. Sandwich at once sent for Pepys and asked him to act as his agent in the search for this secret treasure. Armed with the royal warrant and accompanied by Mr Wade, the discoverer, and a small party with pickaxes, the Clerk of the Acts made his way Towerwards, and there—being forced like a modern tourist to leave his sword at the gate—spent several days digging in the cellars beneath Cold Harbour. But no treasure was ever found, and neither the King nor Lord Sandwich, nor Wade nor Pepys was ever a penny the richer for the undertaking. "We went away", wrote the last, "like fools."[5]

Then there was Uncle Thomas. This troublesome fellow

* He, or his shadow, reappears for a moment in Anthony Wood's pages as butler to Ralph Sheldon of Weston. Wood, *Life and Times*, II. 294.

and his son the turner were still trying to upset Robert Pepys' will and obtain possession of the Brampton estate which should otherwise have come to them as heirs-at-law. Ever since the beginning of 1662 they had been holding meetings with Samuel, usually with one or other of his Impington relations as arbitrators, with a view to a settlement, but these family conferences had invariably ended with words on both sides. When Samuel, as befitted one of his Majesty's Principal Officers of the Navy, wrote rebuking Thomas the turner for failing to keep an appointment, his cousin wrote back "in the very same slighting terms as I did to him, without the least respect at all, which", added that truly just man, the Clerk of the Acts, "argues a high and noble spirit in him". Yet it was annoying. And when in October he was forced to journey down into the mists of Huntingdonshire to meet Uncle Thomas' action to invalidate the will at Brampton Court, it was still more so. The case was heard on October 14th, and the Jury, carefully primed by the two Thomas Pepyses, were prepared to find that the will had not observed the custom of the Manor and that the estate, therefore, passed to the heirs-at-law. But Samuel had also done his part to smooth the course of justice and in a long private interview on the previous day with Sir Robert Bernard, had obtained his promise to persuade the Jury to put off his uncle's admittance to the estate. This Bernard succeeded in doing, and Samuel was able to return to London feeling that for the moment at any rate his diligence had averted disaster.[6]

Once more the negotiations for a composition were resumed. On November 24th, the parties met in the Temple, Samuel bringing Roger and Dr John Pepys of Impington as his arbitrators. The choice was not a happy one, for Uncle Thomas' champions, not being related as Samuel's were to both parties, were far higher in their demands and incidentally much better acquainted with the terms of the will, and they ended by requesting that he should give a personal bond of £2000 to stand to their award. This he flatly refused to do. After that the conference broke up, and Pepys was somewhat relieved next day when his cousins begged, on account of their dual kinship, to be excused from further arbitration.

But the dispute still remained unsettled, and there seemed a strong likelihood that it would end in poor Samuel being left to support his father and family; a great pull-back to him in his fortune, he reckoned mournfully, it would be. The thought of it troubled him even in his dreams. Meanwhile there were Tom's affairs requiring settlement. In the autumn Samuel had made a further strenuous attempt to marry him off suitably, but the silly creature had elected, of all unreasonable things, to fall in love with his prospective mistress and so entirely to prejudice the match. For Tom in his infatuation had ended by offering on behalf of Samuel, who was to foot the bill, a jointure nearly twice as large as that which he had authorised and, proposed, moreover, to accept a portion far lower than such a jointure would merit. At which Pepys was stark mad and broke off the negotiations. But though he pointed out to his foolish brother that he would not have been as much as £100 the better off for such a one-sided match, the poor fool still moped and whined for his mistress: not even a delicate, fat pig which he gave him for dinner could comfort him.[7]

At the beginning of 1663 the shadow of law lay heavy on Pepys. Once more his Uncle Thomas returned to the attack, suing all the Brampton tenants for rent which they had paid to his father. On February 1st he received an ominous piece of news—that through Lord Sandwich's interest Sir R. Bernard had been turned out of his Recordership of

Huntingdon; this, he feared, Bernard in revenge might well visit on him at Brampton. He therefore hastened to come to a composition. A few days later he again met his uncle and cousin at Roger Pepys' chambers and, laying the whole state of the property very frankly before them, made them an offer. After a day's delay, still higher demands on their part and much talk, it was accepted. It was, from Samuel's point of view, anything but an advantageous settlement, for it deprived him of all real profit from the estate for many years to come, but it offered peace and liberty from litigation, and for this alone was worth having. Good Roger Pepys was so sensible of it that he could not forbear weeping.

It was well to have the family litigation settled, for not only was the Trice suit in Chancery still dragging on, but a more furious legal peril now threatened. For a year past, Pepys had been harassed by the insolences of a scoundrel named Field, whom he and his fellow officers had committed to prison for some ill words against the Navy Office. Since then Field had subpœnaed them, complained of them to the King for disregarding an information he had made to them of embezzlement in the Dockyards and brought an action against each of them for £30 damages for false imprisonment, based on the unfortunate fact that their ex-officio authority as Justices, though it held good in Middlesex, did not run in the City of London. In October, 1662, a verdict was found for Field, and Pepys was informed by counsel that judgment must be given accordingly. However, he trusted that the King would protect him.[8]

Then was seen one of those demonstrations of the majesty of English law and liberty, so bewildering to foreigners accustomed to more absolute forms of government. Pepys and his fellow officers had behaved in all good faith and in pursuance of their duty. On the morning of

February 21st there walked into the Office a fellow, as though upon ordinary business, who pulled out a writ from the Court of Exchequer and calmly informed the Clerk of the Acts that he was his prisoner: "methought it did strike me to the heart", wrote poor Pepys, "to think that we could not sit in the middle of the King's business". However, he put a bold face on it and telling the fellow how he was employed, bade him have a care; at which the latter withdrew to wait for him outside.

There ensued that afternoon the strange spectacle of one of his Majesty's Principal Officers besieged in his house at the Navy Office by bailiffs, while one of his colleagues, the old Comptroller, went peeking up and down Whitehall seeking some authority to rescue him. One thing this legal outrage did, which almost nothing else in the world could have done: it reunited for a moment the Principal Officers. For Sir William and Lady Batten anxiously watched from their window while their old enemy, Pepys, aided by their black servant Mingo, climbed over their backyard wall and sought shelter in their house. Thence he was rescued an hour or two later by the arrival of the Board's solicitor, who reported that the Court's fees had been satisfied and that he was free to go abroad.

A final passage of words followed before the invaders departed—"the most rake-shamed rogues that ever I saw in my life"—the Battens flinging jibes at them from the window, which they answered in as high terms, calling Pepys rogue and rebel and swearing to come again with the sheriff and untile the house. After that, to prove to the neighbours that the business was no worse than it was, the Clerk of the Acts showed himself outside, but it was some days before he could bring himself to walk straight to his own front door or see a man standing in the street without quaking and sweating.

It made him bless God that he was not in that sad condition that many a poor man was for debt, liable to be seized at any moment and thrown into prison. And to comfort himself he relaxed his vow and took a turn at the playhouse to see the *Slighted Maid* and regale himself with the spectacle of a girl dancing in boy's apparel, "she having very fine legs, only bends in the hams, as I perceive all women do". As for the case itself it dragged on for many a weary month, causing poor Pepys a fit of apprehension every time he saw Stint, Field's one-eyed solicitor. One effect of it was to make him write a long paper to Coventry on the "Ill Consequences of the Want of Authority in the Principal Officers and Commissioners of the Navy to act as Justices of the Peace within the City of London".*[9]

In other matters there was small unity between the members of the Navy Board. Pepys' activity of the previous year had temporarily caused his lazier colleagues to bestir themselves: that January, Coventry pointed out to him how marked an improvement there was in Batten's conduct. But this did not altogether please Pepys. He preferred to be thought the only man of business in the Office. And he was therefore quicker than ever to detect the faults of his fellows: certainly his judgments of them in his Diary that year do not err on the side of kindness. Mennes, who visited him so tenderly during a February bout of fever and itching pimples, was set down as a mad coxcomb and an old dotard led by the nose and Batten as the knave who did the leading. Nor did he spare to tell Coventry exactly what he thought of them, easing his mind to him in the Matted Gallery at Whitehall of his discontent "to see things of so great trust

* Now preserved among Pepys' naval letters at Greenwich and printed in Tanner's *Further Correspondence*. Though undated, it plainly belongs to this period.

carried so neglectfully and what pitiful service the Comptroller and Surveyor make of their duties".[10]

They fought each other about many things. Mennes, half-fuddled, took Pepys aside and told him how Penn was urging the Duke to make him joint Comptroller on the ground that the office could never be performed adequately by one man; this, of course, made the old Admiral mad. To vex Penn, Pepys did all he could to prevent this (though time was to show the necessity of the change) and stirred Mennes up to such a pitch that there was no proceeding in the matter. Yet no one knew better than he how incompetent the Comptroller was: "to see", he laughed, "how the old man do strut and swear that he understands all his duty as easily as crack a nut and easier...for his teeth are gone".[11]

Pepys himself had one battle royal that spring. Captain Holmes of the *Reserve* returned in March from the Straits full of complaints of his master, Cooper, whose appointment the Clerk of the Acts had secured in the previous summer as a reward for teaching him arithmetic. Holmes reported that Cooper was a mutineer, a man so ignorant in his duty that he had endangered the ship, and a drunkard. Pepys did not believe it, but, feeling himself concerned in the matter, wrote Cooper a majestic letter, enquiring of the truth of the charges, "so", he explained, "I may neither be misled in the defending you against his reports to whom (as your commander) we ought to give credence till the contrary appear nor in condemning you if you have not deserved it". The upshot was a first-class row at a Board meeting between Pepys and Holmes. The latter, instead of accepting the former's offers of mediation, charged Cooper in the most passionate manner with almost every fault known to naval discipline. Upon which almost as passionately Pepys protested against the injustice of condemning a man unheard and allowed himself the use of some equally high language till Holmes muttered that it was well for him he did not speak so outside. After that the fat was in the fire.[12]

Though Pepys told his Diary his fears, he was no coward. Expecting a challenge, he encountered Holmes two days later at Lord Sandwich's door and, seeing his confusion, walked straight up to him and told him not to go away since he would not spoil his visit. This frank behaviour so disarmed the swashbuckler, who was not accustomed to opposition, that he as good as apologised for his words, and, after the Clerk of the Acts had spoken out his mind, the two fell to quite amiable discourse. Only Cooper was left with any cause of complaint, for Pepys now washed his hands of him as a fuddling, troublesome fellow and one whom he was contented should be turned out of his place.[13]

Yet to a man who he felt deserved well of him he could be a true friend and patron. When in May poor honest Tom Hayter, his chief clerk, was caught at a dissenting meeting-house in defiance of the Act of Uniformity and taken to the Counter, it was to Pepys to whom he turned for help. Nor did he appeal in vain. When Pepys asked him to promise not to commit the same offence again so that he could vouch for him to his superiors, Hayter replied that "he durst not do it whatever God in His providence should do with him, and that for my part he did bless God and thank me for all the love and kindness I have shewed him hitherto. I could not without tears in my eyes", Pepys added, "discourse with him further". But he went straight to Coventry and, by pleading for his clerk, secured a promise of the Duke of York's protection.

Even more strikingly was Pepys' tenderness, when once his heart was touched, shown in his dealings with his father.

The old man visited London again that April to discuss his affairs with his son. Since the composition with Uncle Thomas these were unpromising enough, and on going through his accounts Samuel found that he was spending double his income. He undertook, so far as he could, to make up the deficiency and then, since the total revenue of the estate could not for the present exceed £75 a year, of which £25 was charged on annuities to Uncle Thomas and Aunt Perkin, he explained the whole situation very carefully to his father and Tom, urging the former to "good husbandry and to be living within the compass of £50 a year, and all in such kind words, as made not only both them but myself to weep, and I hope it will have a good effect". It is easy to blame a young man with an income of several hundreds for so sententiously expecting his father to live on a fraction of that sum; but to be just it should be remembered that no man supports poor relations with enthusiasm, and that Pepys, whatever his secret thoughts were, never failed to do so tenderly and manfully.[14]

And just then he wanted money and wanted it badly. For nearly a year his capital balance had remained almost stationary in the neighbourhood of £650: indeed, at the end of February, 1663, it had declined by nearly fifty pounds from its peak of the previous summer. And until a few weeks before he had been confronted with the likelihood of having to support his entire family, mother, sister and two brothers, to say nothing of his wife and her beggarly relations. A man may be pardoned for being frugal and calculating in such circumstances.[15]

With the spring of 1663 Pepys' financial affairs began to look up. A steady increase of about £30 a month carried his capital account forward to the record figure of £726 by the end of May. This improvement was due, not to economy, but to an increase in his revenue. His industry of the previous summer was beginning to reap its reward. For all men who had dealings with the Navy were now aware that the favour of the Clerk of the Acts was a thing worth wooing.[16]

And they wooed. A year before it had been with a stately cake that a Chatham merchant had sought his friendship; now they said it with silver and gold. On a February evening Sir William Warren himself came to the door of the house in Seething Lane, and, leaving a box, went on his way. Opened, it was found to contain a pair of gloves for Elizabeth and for Samuel a fair state dish of silver and a cup with his arms most gracefully cut upon them. The Commissionership for Tangier also proved valuable: there were lucrative contracts to be made for victualling that place, and, according to the custom of the time, those of his Majesty's officers who did the work had to be suitably rewarded by the merchants who made a profit from it. So Pepys: "Which I did not demand, but did silently consent to it, and money I perceive something will be got thereby". He was right. As he came out of Whitehall a week later, a trader whom he had befriended slipped a letter into his hand. "But I did not open it till I came home...and there I broke it open, not looking into it till all the money was out, that I might say I saw no money in the paper if ever I should be questioned about it. There was a piece in gold and £4 in silver." No wonder after such presents that a well-meaning side of pork seemed a little clumsy; it would be a pound of candles or a shoulder of mutton next, he told Elizabeth.[17]

She, poor girl, raised her hopes at these accessions of fortune and returned to the attack to win herself another companion. Such was her desire for one that she even proposed the despised Pall (now engaged at Brampton in such

ELIZABETH, WIFE OF SAMUEL PEPYS

innocent country recreations as making paper baskets). Once more the offending letter was produced—for it appeared that on occasion Elizabeth as well as Samuel made copies of her epistles; it made her husband mad to read it, so piquant it was, and wrote in English and most of it true. Furiously he bade her destroy it, and, when she refused, tore it from her hand and, leaping out of bed, thrust it and the bundle of papers from which she had taken it into the pocket of his breeches, hastily drawing them on lest she should recapture it. Then, before her face, and one by one, he tore up all her papers, even his old letters, and the will in which he had left his all to her, she crying all the while and begging him not to, and he sick at heart to do so and yet passionate with rage to think of the dishonour it would have been to him had anyone found it. After that, rather naturally, there followed on both sides a severe fit of the sulks. Yet before the day ended Mrs Pepys had secured a new moire gown.[18]

And in the end she got her way. After prolonged negotiations and questionings it was agreed that Mr Ashwell's daughter, Mary, then finishing her education at a young lady's school at Chelsea, should come to Seething Lane as Elizabeth's maid. On March 12th, 1663, she arrived—a new cook, Hannah (for Jane Wayneman had left to better herself) entering the household at much the same time. The first impressions were admirable—a pretty girl (but not too pretty), humble and active and "ingenuous at all sorts of fine works which pleases me very well and I hope will be very good entertainment for my wife without much cost". Above all she was musical and played the harpsichord in quite a commendable way, and Samuel, delighted to have a pupil, rushed out to buy her a virginal-book.[19]

Yet, as another great student of human nature in the feminine found, young ladies, who in their first acquaintance are all silent modesty can desire, in their familiar play too often prove to be as loud as hogs in a gate. So it was with Ashwell—"a merry jade", Samuel, who was quick to bring out the playfulness of any young woman, noted before she had been a week in the house. Not that he minded: so long as she remained a novelty he was delighted with her. But before long certain distressing results of her presence manifested themselves. For one thing he found himself slipping, all too contentedly, into a round of pleasure which took him from his business and cost money: the resurrection of his old fiddle and the purchase of a bass viol, cards, which Ashwell taught the family to play of an evening, and as summer drew on a good many jaunts—walks to the Half Way House at Rotherhithe to gather cowslips beside the river, or to Woolwich to hear the nightingales sing, rides amid the fashionable throng in Hyde Park on a horse which proved rather too mettlesome for Samuel's modest skill, and even a visit to the new Theatre Royal in Drury Lane. This last seemed to entrench on his vows, still renewed and read over every Sabbath, though he skilfully managed to avoid his forfeit by reminding himself that the Theatre Royal had not been in existence when he had sworn to avoid the playhouses. But he knew that he had done wrong.[20]

And worse: for Elizabeth also began to be seduced by this itch for pleasure which Ashwell had brought into the household. She too played cards, asked for jaunts and plays and craved for variety and amusement. Moreover, encouraged by Ashwell's presence, she began to assert herself; and when her husband reproached her for failing to keep the house clean, she called him "pricklouse". To quiet her and keep his power over her undisturbed, he was forced to lay out money to buy her clothes.[21]

With the same excellent intention, and also because

Ashwell, fresh from school, had a very fine carriage and put his wife to shame by contrast, he encouraged Elizabeth to take dancing lessons. He could scarcely have made a more disastrous mistake. On April 25th, Pembleton, the dancing-master, first appeared—"a pretty neat black man". He had soon completely turned Elizabeth's little head. Though, in the eyes at any rate of her husband, she was anything but adept at dancing, she became so conceited that she even refused to listen to his criticism. Moreover she made him take lessons too, till the entire household was engaged (at some expense) in practising the steps of corantos and treading country dances. Nor did Pembleton's skill fail, for he soon had Samuel also thinking that he was like to make a dancer. "I think I shall come on to do something in a little time", he wrote proudly.

But when his wife made the dancing-master come twice a day and would think of nothing else, Pepys began to grow angry. A day or two later he came home to find the two of them alone above, not dancing now but talking. At once he was in a fire of jealousy, scarcely able to work or sleep, blaming his own folly yet ashamed to tell Elizabeth what ailed him, and so desperate that he made a hundred excuses to discover evidences for his suspicions, even to prying to see whether she "did wear drawers". Yet in his very agony there was something noble in the mind that could see so clearly its own meanness and frailty: "for which I deserve to be beaten if not really served as I am fearful of being, especially since God knows that I do not find honesty enough in my own mind but that upon a small temptation I could be false to her, and therefore ought not to expect more justice from her. But God pardon both my sin and my folly herein".[22]

It was his old disease again. Once or twice in the past year or two it had returned—notably in the autumn of 1661 when his wife had encountered at the theatre a son of Lord John Somerset whom she had known in France before her marriage and who had put Samuel into a fever of apprehension by giving her a bracelet of rings and trying to make a secret appointment with her. A little later Captain Holmes' appearance had caused a recurrence of his alarm, and he had even had some fears of mild Mr Hunt of Axe Yard, whom he had once found in a room alone with his wife. But nothing had ever been as bad as this. On May 19th, the Pepyses, accompanied by Ashwell and the inevitable Pembleton, made an evening's expedition by water to the Half Way House for a game of ninepins, and here Samuel's "damned jealousy" again took fire at seeing Elizabeth and her friend (who were on the same side) take hands, though he admitted that it was probably only in sport. Yet it was typical of his curious, alert mind that even at such a moment as this he sat up for several hours over his Diary recording, not only his jealousy, but, at vast length and wealth of detail, his impressions of the Mint where he had been sight-seeing that morning.[23]

Next day when he went home from the Office at noon, there was Pembleton dancing. Later in the afternoon, after dining at Trinity House, he saw the fellow sneaking away from his house, having dined there, nor did Elizabeth by saying nothing of this circumstance allay his suspicions. And in the evening there was Pembleton again for another lesson.

Pepys expostulated, but his doing so only led to such high words on Elizabeth's part that he made a vow not to reproach her again until her month of dancing was over—after which, he resolved, there should be no more of it. But when she used the word "devil", he felt bound to tell her that she must not use such language; then, to his horror, she merely mocked him—in Ashwell's presence too, so that he was powerless to protest at an insult for less than which he would formerly have struck her. "So that", he wrote, "I fear without great discretion I shall go near to lose too my command over her, and nothing do it more than giving her this occasion of dancing and other pleasures, whereby her mind is taken up from her business and finds other sweets besides pleasing of me."

There was no release from the torture even on Sunday. For when Pepys went to church, hoping to enjoy the sight of a pretty lady who was staying with Peg Penn, he could see nothing during the sermon but Pembleton in the gallery leering upon his wife: moreover she curtsied back at him and then pretended she had not seen him. Two days later, returning unexpectedly from the Office, he discovered the two of them in circumstances which forced him to conclude that there was something more than ordinary between them, which so upset him that for some time he wandered like one distracted in a torment of jealousy between his office and his home, flying now and then to write a few words in his beloved Diary for comfort—telling how his trouble was so great that "I know not at this very moment that I now write this almost what either I write or am doing, nor how to carry myself to my wife in it, being unwilling to speak of it to her for making of any breach...nor let it pass for fear of her continuing to offend me and the matter grow worse....This is my devilish jealousy, which I pray God may be false, but it makes a very hell in my mind, which the God of heaven remove or I shall be very unhappy". And unhappier still he was, for when in the afternoon he again sneaked back from the Office, they were again alone in the house. Secretly he crept upstairs to see whether any of the beds were out of order; they were unruffled. Not that that contented him. And that night he spoke not one word to his wife.

But Elizabeth knew what ailed him. When next morning she took hold of him as he slipped out of bed and asked him what was the matter, he taxed her with her indiscretion, "but she quickly told me my own, knowing well enough that it was my old disease of jealousy which I disowned, but to no purpose". Later in the day he found her in a musty humour, enquiring of him in front of Ashwell when he would be coming home, as she wished to postpone Pembleton's dancing lesson till then, not venturing to have him in the house save when he was there. It all made life exceedingly difficult: however Samuel put as good a face as he could on it, sent a lofty message round to the house when Pembleton arrived that he was detained at the Office, and, when he finally joined the dancers, did his best to appear merry and unconcerned lest the fellow should publish his shame about the town. And then, as it was the last evening of his month, Elizabeth paid her master off, and he was cleared.

Yet Pepys' troubles were by no means over. For Elizabeth understood nicely how to turn the tables on him: declared her jealousy of Ashwell, of whose company he knew well he was too fond, and, whenever he tried to reassert himself, relied on that young woman's presence to snap her fingers in his face. Altogether it was a sadly changed Elizabeth whom he had now to wife, and bitterly did he curse his folly that he had ever let her learn to dance or given her such a companion as Ashwell to rouse her dormant spirit. The only hope was to send her away to the country for a while and trust to time to cure her. And this at least he was able to persuade her to.[24]

Nor till she went was he free of his jealousy. The dispatch of the boy on an unknown errand, his wife's absence from the house on a visit to his father's, the return of Pembleton to give a farewell lesson before she left town, all put him into the old fever. Once more he lay abed to make sure that Elizabeth put on her drawers before she went out, "which poor soul she did, and yet I could not get off my suspicions". And not till he had packed both her and Ashwell into the country coach for Brampton on June 15th was his mind eased. There were no other travellers, he was relieved to see, but some women and a parson.

Then, though his heart was troubled for her absence, he was at peace. He did not worry that afternoon when Lord Sandwich turned to old Mennes and said, "Sir John, what do you think of your neighbour's wife?"—looking straight at Samuel—"do you not think that he hath a great beauty to his wife?" Rather he was glad, and very proud. For at Brampton, this coveted beauty was surely quite safe.

With Elizabeth safely stored, Pepys saw a new régime of work and success opening before him. Midsummer Day had come with a sense of time passing and nothing done: now he would amend. So he renewed his vows and took an additional one of peculiar ferocity against strong drink of all kinds until November: "God send", he prayed, "that it may not prejudice my health". Then he settled down to rise early and apply himself to his business: to refresh his mind, he read over all the office correspondence since his first appointment, entering the more important letters into his own private manuscript book. He was already laying the foundations of his great collections of sea papers and—though this had scarcely yet taken shape in his mind—of a future history of the Navy. He also renewed his attack upon the abuses and corruptions of the service. With his new scale for measuring timber—delicately adorned by Mr Cocker with a brass almanack and other ingenious devices—he became a perfect terror in the Yards. The King's sleeping ships felt his presence too; when on a visit to Chatham, he swooped down on warship after warship to find not an officer aboard nor a single man awake. And once again he opened fire on his colleagues, and, since Penn lay bedridden most of that year with gout and so escaped his broadsides, the brunt fell on the Surveyor. "I will not", Pepys wrote indignantly—though the offending contractor sent him a barrel of sturgeon to appease him—"have the King abused so abominably in the price of what we buy by Sir W. Batten's corruption and underhand dealing." Pett of Chatham was also added that summer to Pepys' gallery of ill-favoured portraits—a man of words and little else, he found him. All of which, of course, did not tend in certain quarters to make Pepys popular. But at Court and among the merchants on 'Change, his name now passed for one that did the King's business wholly and well.[25]

Yet all was not well with Pepys. Whether it was the wet summer—it scarcely ceased to rain for four months—or the unsettling effect of Ashwell and Pembleton, he could not truly settle to his work again. Even the early rising soon went by the board. Something in him craved for pleasure and that, alas, pleasure of no seemly kind. For since his wife had departed, he had fallen into the habit of making a bad use of his fancy with whatever woman he had a mind to, and nightly, the day's work done, he drew them to him in his lonely bed. One day he went to the Court to see the Maids of Honour coming out from a riding expedition, "talking and fiddling with their hats and feathers, and changing and trying one another's by one another's heads, and laughing. But it was the finest sight to me", he told his Diary, "considering their great beauties and dress that ever I did see in all my life. But above all Mrs Stewart" (who was the King's new favourite) "in this dress, with her hat cocked and a red plume, with her sweet eye, little Roman nose and excellent taille, is now the greatest beauty I ever saw, I think". That night, before he slept, he fancied himself to sport with Frances Stewart.[26]

But there was another favourite of the King's, seen also that day, who had long found favour in Samuel's eyes. Ever since he had first set eyes on her at the theatre, Barbara Palmer, Countess of Castlemaine, had thrilled him: never enough, he told himself, could he admire her beauty. Even the sight of her smocks and petticoats hanging up to dry in the Privy Garden at Whitehall had power to fill him with a strange rapture. When she was out of favour with Charles, though Pepys disapproved strongly of their association, he was sorry, and, when she was restored to her old position of power and shame, he was glad in spite of himself.* It was almost a romance.[27]

Not that Samuel Pepys was a man to be satisfied with anything so insubstantial as a passion for a woman to whom he had never spoken. There were in London certain acquaintances of his earlier days, who doubtless if put to it would prove as frail, if not altogether as fair, as the inaccessible Castlemaine. With one of these, Betty Lane, he fell into talk on a late June day as he walked among the stalls in Westminster Hall; and when the girl told him that she never went abroad with any man as she used to do, he invited her to join him over a lobster at the Rhenish wine-house in Cannon Row, where he so towsled and fondled her that a passer-by, observing their dalliance, flung a stone at the window and cried aloud—"Sir, why do you kiss the gentle-

* "But strange it is how for her beauty I am willing to construe all this to the best and to pity her wherein it is to her hurt, though I know well enough she is a whore." *Diary*, July 16th, 1662.

woman so?", upon which he quickly slipped out of the back way—unobserved, he hoped.[28]

Thereafter he was ready to seize whatever pleasure of this kind he could find—provided always that it was attended with safety. A girl met in a casual encounter in a tavern, pretty and very modest, was fit for three or four quick kisses—"God forgive me, I had a mind to something more". Becky Allen, now come up to town a married woman, pale and tall, was eagerly desired, though no opportunity offered; little Betty Howlett, whom he had long jestingly called his wife, was followed across Palace Yard in hopes of a little dalliance; Penn's pretty maid coming into the Office to fetch a sheet of paper was caressed and kissed. Almost any woman was food for his fancy in this hot humour; on more than one occasion he went abroad hoping to light upon some lady of pleasure—"but blest be God there was none"—and once, when Miss Lane sought for was not to be found, he retired to bed, soaring between wake and sleep into the realms of high treason and sporting in fancy with the Queen.[29]

All this, of course, was kept to the back streets of his life: never entered that high plateau of existence on which he contended with Penn and Batten or waited on the heels of Coventry and Carteret. Yet when his naval occasions brought him into the neighbourhood of an attractive woman, he could not keep his heart from coveting her. So—"God forgive me"—he must needs muster the Yard at Deptford on purpose to find out one Bagwell, a carpenter, and strike an acquaintance with him, for his wife, who had called at the Office on some small errand, was a pretty woman and he wanted her to come again. A little later he got himself asked to their little house—they all agog, of course, to honour so great a man; they seemed to live prettily, he noticed with approval, and before long were asking him to get the husband a better ship. And Mrs Bagwell, he was glad to observe, was a virtuous modest woman. Which was a great deal more than could be said for Miss Lane, whom he met about the same time, took to the "Crown" in Palace Yard and there had his full liberty of towsling and tumbling (but again risked nothing) while she unabashedly employed her hands about his person to his great content. Of all of which he was afterwards, as he walked home in a mighty sweat, heartily ashamed: never again, he resolved, would he so demean himself.[30]

Never again! A fortnight later he took her on the water, treated her to a variety of meats and drinks at the "King's Head" at Lambeth marsh, and was all but carried too far on that swift, subterranean stream of life which ran so invitingly beneath his wearied feet; "I was very near it, but as wanton and buxom as she is she dares not adventure upon that business, in which", he added strangely, "I very much commend and like her". For deep at heart, Pepys was a Puritan, and man can still be one thing and love another. Yet it was not chastity—"fair silver-shafted queen for ever chaste"—which he saw with admiration in that tawdry, living wench, but common prudence. Which, after all, is a kind of virtue.[31]

Mrs Pepys came home. She returned at two days' notice—far sooner than Samuel had expected her, having quarrelled violently with both her father-in-law and Ashwell, whom she had gone so far as to box on the ear, getting a handsome cuff in return. For that young woman scarcely anything was now too bad, and her mistress could talk of nothing else but her iniquities. It was Elizabeth's old foible, so distressing to her husband, of fastening lies upon her maids. Accordingly Ashwell departed on August 25th. Nor was Samuel altogether sorry to see her go. For now he would be able to discipline his wife again and bring her back to her business.[32]

A series of domestic disasters accompanied Ashwell's departure. Hannah the cookmaid also went, in a huff, Mrs Pepys carefully searching her luggage before her somewhat dramatic departure to see that nothing was stolen. A maidless interregnum was interspersed—relieved is not the word—by a brief return of Susan, who unhappily proved since her departure in the previous spring to have acquired the habits of a drunken slut; and then by old Goody Taylor, the daily. With such auxiliaries to life, it was a sad distracted house to which Pepys returned of an evening. But even worse followed. For brother Tom, appealed to, procured from the parish of St Bride's in which he resided a small charity girl of the name of Jinny, "of honest parents and recommended by the churchwardens". The impress of local authority proved a deception. For no sooner had Jinny been cleansed of her lice by Elizabeth and nobly arrayed in the neat clothes provided by her master, than she promptly ran away. Next morning Samuel made his indignant way to his brother, and bade him recover his clothes and get the girl whipped. The majestic machinery of English local government was again set in motion, and at a cost to the community of sixpence the Clerk of the Acts received his clothes and the charity girl her chastisement.[33]

Meanwhile Samuel's attempt, maintained amid domestic revolutions—"we have no luck in maids nowadays", he recorded after the sudden departure of yet another cook—to break in his wife continued. It was uphill work; at first Elizabeth was disinclined to her business, neglected her housekeeping and with base suspicion regarded her husband's continued structural alterations to the house as mere devices to keep her indoors and away from the pleasures she craved.

Even Pembleton reappeared to vex him: there, on the first Sunday after his old pupil's return, he was in church again: and "Lord! into what a sweat did it put me". A fortnight later a horrid thing happened. In the afternoon Pepys from his commanding station in the Navy Office gallery saw Pembleton come into church, look up and then, not seeing Elizabeth (who had stayed at home), go out again. He could not follow him, for his dignity demanded that he should sit out the sermon, which he did in a fever of impatience picturing the worst. But when, service over, he hurried home, all seemed well, there being no sign of any visitor and Elizabeth waiting to receive him with those endearments which Christian men, their devotions over, expect from their wives.*[34]

Gradually, having nowhere else to go, Mrs Pepys drifted back into the ways in which her husband would have her walk. Perhaps it was an autumn expedition to Brampton, which Samuel was forced to take on his father's business, that brought about the reconciliation. For on the eve of his departure, having said to her at supper, half in jest and half in fondness, "What! shall you and I never travel together again", she took him up and came with him. And on the way down, at their inn at Buntingford, she was suddenly taken ill, "and became so pale and I alone with her in a great chamber there, that I thought she would have died, and so in great horror, and having a great trial of my true love and passion for her, called the maids and the mistress of the house". Happily it proved to be nothing worse than the

* "Impatient all the sermon. Home and find all well and no sign of anybody being there. And so with great content playing and dallying with my wife." *D.* Aug. 30th, 1663. By some curious oversight the entry for this day (as also for those of Nov. 26th, 1661; March 25th and May 13th, 1662) was omitted from the Wheatley edition of the Diary.

effects of drinking cold beer on a hot day and "after a little vomit, she came to be pretty well again". After which, she settled down to her business and became mighty mindful of her house, even putting up the hangings of her new closet with her own hand.[35]

The same autumn which saw the recomposure of Samuel's domestic life saw also the end of his long suit in Chancery against the Trices. For finding, on taking advice at the Six Clerks Office, that his case, through his long neglect of it, was in a very bad way, he resolved to yield as much as he decently could and to settle the affair. On October 27th, at the "Pope's Head" tavern, he offered £80 in settlement of the £200 interest on his uncle's bond claimed by the Trices; the latter demanded £150, and after much discourse on both sides a compromise was reached at £100. It was a great sum to part with, but it was good to have peace and be free from the lawyers.[36]

There was another matter to be settled before the year closed. For some time Lord Sandwich's behaviour had been causing increasing comment. In the previous spring, to convalesce from a serious illness, he had taken lodgings in the riverside village of Chelsea. His landlady, Mrs Becke, had a daughter, Betty. And when he recovered, whether it was the country air or Betty Becke, Lord Sandwich stayed on, absenting himself more and more from Court until even the King took notice of it. Rumours, of course, soon reached Pepys. After a talk with Will Howe he had no doubts: "I perceive", he wrote, "my Lord is dabbling with this wench, for which I am sorry, though I do not wonder at it, being a man amorous enough, and now begins to allow himself the liberty that he sees everybody else at Court takes". It was certainly a liberty that Pepys allowed himself, for he also had a Betty. But he seemed to forget the fact, for he came to the conclusion that it was his solemn duty to reproach his Lord for his frailty. Or perhaps it was not so much the frailty as the neglect of his business which was the real offence: after all Lord Sandwich was many thousands of pounds in debt, of which Samuel himself was owed £700, and his only chance of setting his affairs in order was by assiduous attention to his duties. Moreover there was the public scandal; Mr Moore told Pepys that his Lord exhibited his dotage on the slut at Chelsea even in the presence of his daughter, Lady Jemimah. And of deliberately exhibiting his own frailties, Samuel himself was never guilty; when Lady Jem saw him leading his own slut Betty Lane down to the boat at Westminster Stairs, he was heartily ashamed of the encounter and did not so much as speak to her.[37]

Still for all this moral superiority towards his patron, he could not quite bring himself to approach him. It would perhaps be better to leave it: "I am very sorry to see that my Lord hath thus much forgot his honour, but am resolved not to meddle with it...let him go on till God Almighty and his own conscience and thoughts of his own lady and family do it":—this should be his last word. But soon the tales from Chelsea grew worse: walking out on a September evening, thinking to meet Mistress Lane, Samuel encountered Ned Pickering who for three or four hours poured into his eager ear "the whole business of my Lord's folly with this Mrs Becke at Chelsea, of all which I am ashamed to see my Lord so grossly play the beast and fool, to the flinging off of all honour, friends, servants and everything and person that is good, and only will have his private lust undisturbed with this common whore, his sitting up night after night alone, suffering nobody to come to them...his carrying her abroad and playing on his lute under her window and forty other poor sordid things". It was disgusting.[38]

By November, Pepys could bear it no longer, and once again he resolved to speak to his patron and tell him of his shame. It was easier now, for his moral sense had had a bracing medicine in the meantime, God Almighty having justly smitten him with a great pain in the head, breast and ear one stolen evening while he sat lewdly sporting with Mistress Lane beside a draughty tavern window. In the light of this visitation his own infirmities had become patent to him; "it grieved my heart", he told his Diary when he found his wife working hard at her house, "to see that I should abuse so good a wretch, and that it is just with God to make her bad with me for my wronging of her, but I do resolve never to do the like again". It was therefore still easier to see the frailties of others. On November 12th, after an inspiriting dinner with Mr Moore, he took coach to Chelsea, fully intending to broach the matter. Yet somehow, when he came to the point, his heart misgave him and he said nothing. Instead he went home and wrote Sandwich a letter of reproof. And three days later, after somewhat ill-advisedly discussing it with Will Howe and reading it over to Moore, he took his courage in his hands and sent it off.[39]

It was a brave letter and an honest one. In one of his charged and telling phrases, he spoke of "the duty which every bit of bread I eat tells me I owe to your Lordship", and went on to relate the ill-natured talk which Sandwich's long absence from Whitehall had caused. Then, boldly, he spoke of the cause of that abstention:

Another sort, and those the most, insist upon the bad report of the house wherein your Lordship, now observed in perfect health again, continues to sojourn, and by name have charged one of the daughters for a common courtizan, alleging both places and persons where and with whom she hath been too well known, and how much her wantonnesse occasions, though unjustly, scandal to your Lordship, and that as well to gratifying of some enemies as to the wounding of more friends I am not able to tell.

Once only did the writer deviate from the path of rectitude: when he assured his patron that no one but himself was privy to what he had written.

In anxiety and pain, Pepys awaited the upshot. Four days passed before he could summon the resolution to approach his Lord. There then occurred a rather painful scene. At first that reserved and austere noble spoke calmly and with apparent kindness, thanking Pepys for his care of his honour: then he demanded the names of those from whom he had heard these rumours. Confused and muttering excuses, Samuel told him Pierce the surgeon, Ned Pickering, Mr Hunt of Axe Yard, and his maidservant Ashwell from Chelsea School. And when he again spoke of his tenderness for his master's reputation, assuring him that nobody in the world knew of his letter but himself, Lord Sandwich sharply interposed that he must give him leave to except one. Poor Pepys was caught out in his lie and wept. "I confess", he wrote mournfully that night, "I think I may have done myself an injury for his good, which, were it to do again, and that I believed he would take it no better I think I should sit quietly without taking any notice of it."

Yet, though it cost Pepys many a wakeful night and it was long before his Lord quite forgave him, the letter had its effect. A week after he sent it, he heard that Lord Sandwich was leaving Chelsea for good. Another month and he ventured to approach that nobleman for the loan of his coach to ride in the funeral cortège of his cousin, Edward Pepys of Broomsthorpe, brother of his old benefactress, Mrs Turner. It was granted. Two days later when the procession assembled in Salisbury Court, the coach was waiting for the Clerk of the

Acts with six fine horses to draw it. As he drove through the City, Samuel felt that in some measure he was forgiven.[40]

So the year ended. Things after all were looking up. At the Office, Pepys' reputation was on the rise again, and, after a period of some neglect, he was throwing himself once more into his business and taking delight in it. And during the last two months he had been able to save money, and his capital had increased to £800, though of this all but £100 was on loan to Lord Sandwich—a fact which, added both to natural loyalty and the other £1000 lent to the Earl for which he stood surety, helps to explain his anxiety for all his concerns. At home, too, the horizon was fairer than it had been for at least a year. To fill her mind, he had taken to giving Elizabeth evening lessons in arithmetic and the use of the globes. She had also such occupations as the making of marmalett of quince, and once even persuaded herself (but not Samuel) that she was with child. So he wrote of their pleasure in one another's company, "and in our general enjoyment one of another, better we think than most other couples do".[41]

Chapter XI

The Arming of Mars

"To the Coffee-house with Captain Cocke, who discoursed well of the good effects in some kind of a Dutch war and conquest (which I did not consider before, but the contrary) that is, that the trade of the world is too little for us two, therefore one must down." *Diary*, Feb. 2nd, 1664.

If men have good angels, Pepys' must have worn tarry breeches. Whenever the urge of his many loves became too insistent or Elizabeth too tumultuous, the sea called him. It was so in the winter of 1663–4. Early in October, Mr Cutler, one of the great merchants of the Exchange, told him in a coffee-house that there was a likelihood of war with the Dutch. "I hope we shall be in good condition before it comes to break out", was his unspoken reply.[1]

The first three years of Pepys' service at the Navy Office had been years of retrenchment. During the Commonwealth epoch the cost of the Navy had risen to the unprecedented sum of £20,000 a week, and at the Restoration the Navy debt had amounted to another three-quarters of a million. Foremost of the demands made by the English people of its new government was the reduction of armaments and taxation. The core of that government's difficulties lay in the fact that it could meet neither of these demands efficiently without credit. For as long as the servants of the state were unpaid, however corrupt, inefficient or superfluous they might be, they could not be dismissed, and, as long as the unpaid balance of their wages kept accumulating, the ultimate burden of national taxation remained the same.[2]

In 1660 and 1661 Parliament made provision for the standing charges of the government, of which the Navy was the greatest. But it made none for the debts of the past, with the result that the King's Officers were forced to meet the deficit either by leaving bills and wages unpaid or by borrowing at exorbitant rates at a time when there was no machinery of public credit and when to anticipate its revenue by so much as a single year cost the Crown 10 or 12 per cent. on the amount advanced. We who live in an epoch when governments finance current expenditure out of the expected earnings of unborn generations can scarcely comprehend an age when lenders dared not count on the repayment of a state debt for more than a few years ahead.

To make matters worse, the taxes voted by Parliament for the support of the Crown brought in only about two-thirds of the estimated amount. Each of the opening years of the Restoration, therefore, saw a deficit of something like 33 per cent. of the supposed revenue, a chasm which was bridged partly by borrowing from greedy bankers and partly by leaving poor seamen and merchants unpaid and compensating them with bills to be met (at interest) by the future. For the rest, the government, as it became conscious of these deficiencies, sought as best it could to reduce expenditure, regardless of national needs. Those who live from hand to mouth, with the bailiffs at the door, can scarcely be expected to have much regard for the future.

In the first years, therefore, of the reign of King Charles II, the government looked to the Principal Officers of the Navy to reduce expenditure. Their main business was the laying-up of ships and the paying-off of men. That the logical end of this policy was not reached was due partly to the fact that money for these purposes was so slow in coming and partly to the personal interest shown in the Fleet by the Duke of York and his secretary, Coventry. Otherwise, by the time of the outbreak of the Dutch War, there would have been no Navy at all. As it was, in the spring of 1663 the Principal Officers were instructed to reduce its annual charge from the £374,743, which Pepys and Hayter had recently estimated it to be, to £200,000. The politicians in Parliament were particularly insistent on this.[3]

Thanks largely to the work of Coventry and Pepys, and to the integrity of Southampton, the Lord Treasurer, and Carteret, the Navy Treasurer, the debts of the service were by the end of 1663 substantially reduced. One result of this was to enhance the credit of the Navy Office in the City. Another was an improvement in the terms of contracts with the merchants who supplied the Fleet and Yards. And in the preparation of these a leading part was played by Samuel Pepys.[4]

Among the ancient duties of the Clerk of the Acts was the rating and recording of all contracts; the actual making of them was, of course, performed by the Board at its sittings. Yet the more that the former applied himself to his business and the less his fellow officers did to theirs, the greater his influence in this all-important matter of giving out contracts became. For when any question arose at the Board, Pepys, fresh from the initial negotiations with the contracting merchant and with his head stored with the figures of current prices, gleaned in his daily expeditions to Thames Street or the 'Change, or of past contracts culled from his carefully-kept memorandum books, was more than a match for dissenting colleagues. By 1664 it had become a matter of comment and grievance to him that the Board refused, for once, to proceed in a contract which he had recommended to them. Probably no previous Clerk of the Acts had ever held so commanding a position.[5]

It was in the summer of 1663 that Pepys first realised the magnitude of the power which his industry had made his. On July 16th, he induced the Board to make a great contract with his new friend, Sir William Warren, for forty thousand Scandinavian deals at £3. 17*s.* a hundred. Two months later he completed a still greater contract with the same merchant for £3000 worth of masts—the best bargain of the kind, he proudly recorded, made for the Navy in the past quarter of a century. "But, good God!", he added, "to see what a man might do, were I a knave, the whole business from beginning to the end being done by me out of the office and signed to by them upon the once reading of it to them without the least care or consultation either of quality, price, number or need of them, only in general that it was good to have a store." The nature of committees has altered little with the ages.[6]

Yet his colleagues did not always remain so quiescent. Though they were unwilling to take the pains that Pepys took to get something done, they were ready enough to criticise when that something was done—especially when their own private interests were injured by his action. So Batten, finding his favourite Wood damaged by Warren's good fortune, took the opportunity of Pepys' absence on a flying visit to Brampton and Wisbech, to inveigh against his contract for masts, declaring that the stores were already over-clogged with these. In this he was supported by both Pett and Mennes, who denied the Clerk of the Acts' carefully argued claim that Warren's timber was better than his rival's. But Pepys was able to secure the powerful support of both Coventry and Carteret, whom he convinced in long, reasoned letters. Not only, he showed, were Warren's masts from 5 to 7 per cent. cheaper than Wood's, with a further saving of £220 in freight since they were already lying in the river, but their purchase broke the monopoly of a merchant who had long been holding the King up to ransom "at prices unfit to be mentioned". Moreover, he added with a shrewd undercut at his foe, Batten, the King could be certain that in buying Warren's masts, they would have the unusual advantage of being most carefully inspected by the Surveyor, since that gentleman was so anxious to prove them bad.[7]

So—beginning the new year with a mighty laugh at his pompous Uncle Wight's being out in his grace after meat—Pepys entered upon 1664 resolved to master every contract made by the Office. He fought Batten over and over again, defying him and all his experience, on such diverse matters as the plastering and glazing of the Navy buildings, the size of canvas, the abuses of the merchants who supplied the Navy with flags and pendants. He attacked him in the flank over the old scandal of the Chatham Chest for sick seamen—the Surveyor's weakest spot—and ranged indefatigably over such novel ground as the purchase of poop lanterns and the control over the disbursements of Deputy Treasurers. And when Batten and his son-in-law, Castle, the timber merchant, counter-attacked with carefully circulated rumours that Pepys, former employee of the republican government, was favouring his fellow-traitors, the angry Clerk of the Acts went to infinite pains—sitting up till four in the morning, cold and alone by a guttering candle till his head ached—to make himself such a master of the whole complicated question of masts—the respective merits of Gottenburg (whence Warren's goods came) and New England, the ratio of their diameters to their length, the proper method of preserving them, whether wet or dry—as should confound them and all their knavish tricks for ever. Such industry was invincible. On July 21st he smashed Batten by persuading the Board to sign a contract for a thousand Gottenburg masts, the biggest of its kind ever made. It was not surprising that a fortnight later the gratified Sir William Warren offered to go half shares with him in all contracts made in the future.[8]

Indeed Pepys' application was handsomely rewarded. He began the year 1664 with £800; by March 31st this sum had risen to £900, by the end of July to £1000. Such increase was not derived only from his salary. On January 1st he had found awaiting him the best New Year's gift he had ever known, a bill of exchange for £50 from a deal merchant, a consignment of whose goods he had bought for the King at the entreaty of his old friend Luellin. But he was careful to add, in telling the tale to his Diary, that the bargain had been very much to the advantage of the service and that neither this nor any other gift could induce him to do the King a wrong. And with true seventeenth-century honesty, he made Luellin a present of two gold pieces wherewith to buy himself a pair of gloves.

And soon other rich and honourable things came his way. A pair of gloves, for instance, from Warren, wrapt up in paper: feeling something hard in the fingers, Pepys refrained from opening them till his wife had left the room, "and by and by, she being gone it proves a pair of white gloves for her and forty pieces in good gold, which did so cheer my heart that I could eat no victuals almost for dinner for joy to think how God do bless us every day more and more". It almost seemed as though one was in the presence of a miracle.[9]

Again, one February day when Pepys had successfully, and to his great content, prevailed against Sir William Batten at the Office for the King's profit, there came to him a silver state cup and cover from Mr Falconer, the Clerk of the Ropeyard at Woolwich. This was followed ten days later by a case of very pretty knives from Mrs Russell, a woman contractor. A barrel of mighty oysters, a timely gift of £20 from Captain Taylor to comfort his heart when it was low, a pair of pretty silver candlesticks—these were the visible marks of God's goodness to the virtuous man who followed his business.[10]

Most profitable of all was Tangier. The shipowner who wished his vessel to be chartered for carrying troops or provisions to that remote garrison town did well to approach the youngest and most active member of the King's Commission: he would find him both courteous and helpful. And for these, his additional pains, Pepys expected his reward from those who reaped the benefit of his industry. In the seventeenth century there seemed nothing wrong in this. Nor, for all the commissions he received, was Pepys ready for one moment to overlook any neglect or omission on the part of any contractor, however open-handed. And it must be added that for every ten pounds he made, he could by unscrupulous dealing have taken a hundred.[11]

In 1664 Tangier brought two notable accessions of fortune. One was a noble pair of flagons from the Victualler, Mr Gauden: over £100 he found them to be worth when they were weighed. The other was even better—the promise of a share in a new contract for victualling the garrison, offered by the Plymouth merchants Alsopp, Lanyon and Yeabsly. If Pepys could get them the contract at three shillings and a penny halfpenny per man per week, he should have £150 a year; if at three shillings and twopence, £300. He succeeded, and at the higher price. Then Alsopp fell sick and died—"a sad consideration to see how uncertain a thing our lives are, and how little to be presumed of in our greatest undertakings"—and the partnership was dissolved. It seemed as though the contract would come to nothing: it was at least a comfort to have the rival Victualler's flagons in one's keeping. But all ended well, the partnership was revived, and Pepys was left with the promise of £300 a year, "without", he added, "the least wrong to the King". And he had the flagons as well, which the generous-minded Gauden gave him leave to keep. Small wonder that he looked on Tangier as one of the best flowers in his garden.[12]

Not that all this wealth was without its cares. Never before had he known what it was to have a large sum of money in his keeping. Once at night in Elizabeth's absence he heard noises in the house and, sweating till he had all but melted to water, furiously rang the bell. But neither of his maids answered, and he began to think that they had been gagged. At last Jane arose, and it transpired that it was only the poor dog looking for somewhere to lie. "These thoughts and fears I had", he recorded, "and do hence apprehend the fears of all rich men that are covetous and have much money by them." To avoid a repetition of such alarms, he contemplated banking the money with the goldsmith, Backwell, who was offering 6 per cent.; but here also Pepys was doubtful. For Backwell might die or become bankrupt. "It is a strange thing to observe and fit for me to remember", he noted with philosophical acumen, "that I am at no time so unwilling to part with money as when I am concerned in the getting of it most."[13]

With all this came an increase in worldly state. In the spring of 1664 Pepys was put into the new Corporation for regulating the Royal Fishery, a very honourable, though not a particularly lucrative, appointment. Perhaps the most satisfactory thing about it was the proof it gave that he was regaining favour with Lord Sandwich, to whom he owed the inclusion of his name in the Commission. His attempts to recover his old position had not hitherto been too successful. When at the beginning of the year he had humbly waited on his Lord, intending to invite him to dinner, he had been treated with marked coldness; so much so that he had decided to forbear laying out his money on such a treat. It would be better, he resolved, "by grave and humble, though high, deportment to make him think I do not want him". This Samuel had endeavoured, but it had gone against the grain. It was a relief, therefore, to see this mark of his friendship, and still more to receive a blessed visit one April day from Lady Sandwich, even if he did, in his eagerness to greet her, find this dear lady—to both their embarrassments—making a fugitive use of the chamber-pot in his dining-room. It was also good to be taken notice of by the Duke of York, whom up to the present Pepys had ever been afraid to meet, but who now distinguished him with a long discourse on the price of naval materials. It made him very happy to see how his estimation in the world grew every day more and more. Happily it also made him a philosopher: "I pray God give me a heart to fear a fall and to prepare for it!"[14]

Certainly he needed philosophy, for he had his crosses. There was Uncle Wight, for instance. This not very prepossessing old gentleman had recently taken to hinting that he hoped that Mrs Pepys was with child and that, if she should be, he would make it his heir. Samuel was naturally gratified, for though his uncle's tastes were distressingly bourgeois and his society revolting, his fortune was substantial. Thereafter Uncle Wight was perpetually appearing at the house in Seething Lane, and caressing and kissing Elizabeth with most pressing enquiries as to her condition. "I do not trouble myself for him at all, but hope the best and very good effects of it", noted Samuel.

But it presently appeared that his uncle's wish to see Elizabeth a mother was accompanied by a desire to forward the process in person. For one spring afternoon the pious old merchant, after ascertaining that her husband was safely employed in his official duties, called on her, and commending her body proposed that they should set to work to have a child between them, adding that he would settle £500 on her and that for all he knew the thing was lawful. The lady thought otherwise and summoned her husband. He, after much consideration, decided that it would be better to say nothing about the affair.[15]

Then there was Tom. A little while before, Samuel had been warned by a gipsy that one named Thomas would shortly injure him; a week later came a request from his brother for a loan of £20. It was the second of its kind that he had craved within a few weeks. Poor Tom! The shades, though Samuel knew it not, were closing round him. The little business in Salisbury Court was failing and the tares which he had sown were ripe for reaping. In January he fell sick, it was feared with a consumption; but he was about again in February, with all his books, papers and bills lying loose on the parlour table. The recovery was but temporary. It was the despised Joyces and kind Mrs Turner who brought to Samuel a month later the news of how desperately ill Tom really was. Moreover they whispered into his ear that it was the pox, shamefully got and secretly concealed, that had brought him to this pass.[16]

In an agony of shame Pepys hastened to his brother's bedside. There Tom lay, scarcely able to recognise him and babbling idly, and his face plainly showed that he was dying. Next day he did not know him. He lingered one more day, and Samuel, who had wept when he could not say who he was, had the satisfaction of conversing with him once more for a little while. Moreover, the foul aspersion cast on the dying man by a careless doctor and Mrs Turner's hasty talk was proved baseless, and so glad was Samuel of this that he sent for a barrel of oysters on which he and the watchers dined and were very merry. That evening the end came. "About 8 o'clock," Samuel wrote—"my brother began to fetch his spittle with more pain, and to speak as much but not so distinctly, till at last the phlegm getting the mastery of him, and he beginning as we thought to rattle, I had no mind to see him die, as we thought he presently would, and so withdrew and led Mrs Turner home, but before I came back, which was in half a quarter of an hour, my brother was dead. I went up and found the nurse holding his eyes shut, and he poor wretch lying with his chops fallen, a most sad sight, and that which put me into a present very great transport of grief and cries, and indeed it was a most sad sight to see the poor wretch lie now still and dead, and pale like a stone. I staid till he was almost cold, while Mrs Croxton, Holden, and the rest did strip and lay him out, they observing his corpse, as they told me afterwards, to be as clear as any they ever saw, and so this was the end of my poor brother, continuing talking idle and his lips working even to his last but his phlegm hindered his breathing, and at last his breath broke out bringing a flood of phlegm and stuff out with it, and so he died."

After that they buried him: the grave-digger with ghastly civility offering—if Samuel would give him sixpence for his pains—to jostle together the other corpses, still not quite rotten, to make room for him. A hundred and twenty who were bidden came to the funeral and about thirty who were not: they all had six biscuits apiece and as much burnt claret as they could drink. "Anon to church, walking out into the street to the conduit, and so across the street and had a very good company along with the corpse."

Yet was not quite the last of Tom, for a legacy of trouble remained. A few weeks after his death, Samuel received a mysterious visit at the Office from his father's old servant, John Noble; smelling the business he took him home and there learnt how Tom had got his maid Margaret, "an ugly jade", with twin bastards, and how, to save him from being blackmailed and to pay for farming out the surviving child, Noble had advanced him ten pounds. This had never been repaid, at least so Noble maintained. With the anxiety arising from this roguish business poor Samuel was saddled for many months. Then there were Tom's debts, which much exceeded his assets and which it was left to Samuel to pay, who had already lent his brother £87. These involved him in much acrimonious correspondence with two of his relations, his cousin Scott who acted as his father's attorney in administering the dead man's estate, and his cousin Dr Thomas Pepys of Impington, who had charitably but rashly advanced Tom money and now demanded its immediate repayment from Samuel. The latter was nearly driven mad by this foolish creditor's importunities—"doating coxcomb", "puppy", "foul-tongued fool" are among the epithets with which he labelled him in his Diary. On his side the doctor went so far as to accuse his cousins of falsifying the inventory of the dead man's goods in order to defraud him,* and spoke of Samuel embezzling his half shirts, worth 24 shillings, which had accidentally been omitted from the inventory, and

* "As for the pewter, you carry that away or give it where you please, to defraud the creditors, and wrong your own credit, which once was good but it stincks now by your base actions. Be you assured, if you give not a new and true inventory, without concealing or cloaking anything, no, not the new cloak which made of the reliques of the High Sheriff of your county's livery, expect a summons at the Civil Law as well as at the Common." Dr Thomas Pepys to John Pepys, May 21st, 1664; *Rawlinson MSS. A.* 182, f. 340.

threatened a lawsuit. Altogether Pepys was not sorry when at the beginning of the next year Dr Thomas also died—"a shame to his family and profession, he was such a coxcomb".[17]

Pepys himself was ill that year. He had suffered a good deal of spasmodic pain in the previous autumn, which made him fear the return of his old complaint, but his surgeon, Hollier, had assured him that he had no cause for anxiety. But one day, in the May of 1664, he was seized at the Office with an excruciating pain in the lower part of his back and belly, as bad as any he could remember. Driven to bed, he took a clyster and lay for two or three hours, crying and roaring in his anguish until, getting up by chance upon his knees, his pain began to diminish. But during the next fortnight it continued to recur, and when the fits were upon him he could neither break wind nor make water. Sad and out of content with all the world, he sent again for Hollier, who to his sorrow told him that, though he had previously thought it impossible, he believed he had the stone again. In vain, now, seemed his hopes of wealth and fame.[18]

In his despair, he placed himself in the hands of a new physician, Dr Burnett, who pronounced that the complaint was not a recurrence of the stone, but an ulcer in the kidneys or bladder. When John Pepys heard the news he wrote to his son in an agony of apprehension: "Dear child, for God's sake let me beg of you that you will have Mr Holyard's advice and some able doctor of his acquaintance with as much speed as you can, and to beg a blessing from the Lord that your life may be preserved, for what a sad condition should your poor old father and mother be in if the Lord should take you before us". Samuel had reasons of his own for sharing his parent's anxious hopes. Seeking Hollier again, he received comfort. For by this time the doctor had again changed his mind; it was only the cold in his legs breeding wind that caused the pain; the thickness of his water was due to overheat in his back, and in short the whole trouble was the result of his walking about of a morning in nothing but his dressing-gown. So do the doctors in their wisdom fool us. A week later Pepys set aside a Sunday to the drinking of three bottles of Epsom water; thereafter he felt fine.[19]

It was well that he did so. For, as 1664 went by, it became clear that war could no longer be averted. Everywhere the Dutch and English were at loggerheads. Captain Cocke, the great hemp-merchant, put the situation in a nutshell when he declared that the trade of the world was too small for both nations and that one or other must go down. On April 18th Pepys heard that the Jews were insuring against an outbreak of hostilities; three days later the House of Commons resolved, on a report from the Committee of Trade, that "the wrongs, dishonours and injuries done to his Majesty by the subjects of the United Provinces by invading of his rights in India, Africa and elsewhere," were the cause of the decay of the nation's trade. The first orders from the Admiralty to the Navy Office to buy stores and set the ships in readiness followed at once.[20]

The Clerk of the Acts did not share his countrymen's optimism. He knew too much. "We all seem to desire it", he wrote of the universal longing for war, "as thinking ourselves to have advantages at present over them; for my part I dread it." For he was aware that the Navy was anything but ready.[21]

But what he could do to make it so he did. He sat long at his office till his head was ready to burst and his eyes recoiled from the hieroglyphics that swayed before them in the flickering candlelight: even his Sundays were recruited into the service. Though there was little joy in such grinding labour, something iron in the man gave him courage to go through with it. At moments he despaired: money was lacking, the King's business was everywhere ill done and the corruptions of the Navy were endless. As for his colleagues, though Penn became a new man and, thanks to his service in the first Dutch war, was much demanded at the Court and Admiralty—a fact not much to Pepys' liking—Batten and Mennes became more impossible than ever. Indeed the preparations for war showed up Mennes in a far worse light than before, the old man proving quite incompetent to cope with the work that now poured in on him. Sometimes it made Pepys pity him for his dotage and folly: at others it maddened him that the King's business should be ruined by such an old fool.[22]

His own part Pepys performed with admirable zeal and discretion. As soon as the talk of war got into the air, the contractors began to enhance the price of their commodities, knowing that the King would now be forced to deal. They met their match in the Clerk of the Acts who, by coaxing, threatening and playing off one against the other, made it his business while prices were still reasonable to push through purchases of as large a supply of naval commodities as possible. It was a yeoman service. Even his open-handed friend Warren felt its effects, Pepys beating down the prices of his masts till he was angry; "at best it may be but a losing contract," wrote that merchant, "you drive your bargains so extreme low". For when the safety of his country was at stake, Pepys was a true Englishman.[23]

On one occasion, however, his zeal outran his discretion. On July 14th a terrible piece of news reached him: that he had fallen under the displeasure of no less a person than the Lord Chancellor, Clarendon, the greatest subject in the kingdom. In the course of his duties he had given Deane instructions to mark the best trees in Clarendon Park for selling: these, it now appeared, were part of the royal property vested in the Chancellor. Full of horror, the Clerk of the Acts straightway sought out the great man, accosting him as he came out of his dinner and telling him that he was the unhappy Pepys who had fallen into his high displeasure. That night by appointment he waited on Lord Clarendon after the latter's business was done. "Come, Mr Pepys," said he, "you and I will take a turn in the garden." There the gouty old vizier of England and the young Clerk of the Acts walked in close converse for an hour, and when their talk was finished, the trees in Clarendon Park had received a new lease of life. A few days later Pepys gave Deane his revised instructions. "Lord!" he told his Diary, "to see how we poor wretches dare not do the King good service for fear of the greatness of these men."[24]

In other matters public spirit was fortified by vows. These in their turn were supported by the forfeits which Pepys set himself for their non-fulfilment. Plays were allowed but once a month: the idle practice of buying books was prohibited for long periods altogether. Just occasionally he would make an outflanking movement on his own conscience; once he lent Creed, who was dining with him, the money to take his wife and himself to a play—"a fallacy... never to be more practised, I swear". At other times when he failed, the Poor Box gained; the sinful purchase of two volumes of maps cost him nine shillings for the price and another five for his forfeit.[25]

In one particular he was not so successful. For brief periods his vows with difficulty saved him from Mistress Lane and her ilk, but temptation had only to show her full face and he fell. In January the fair Betty by yielding too far gave him a nasty shock, and he half expected to hear ill news of the effects of the encounter. Happily all proved well, but his nerve was shaken. Before he would venture again, she must marry. Remembering that his old colleague Hawley admired her, he did everything he could to advance his suit. Betty, however, flatly refused to have him: she could not bring herself, she said, to love anyone as dull. "The match", observed the disgusted mediator, "...will not take, and so I am resolved wholly to avoid occasion of further ill with her." But at midsummer, while Elizabeth was away on her annual holiday at Brampton, he heard that Miss Lane had chosen a mate of her own, a sorry simple fellow called Martin. "I must have a bout with her very shortly to see how she finds marriage", he noted that night. Nor did he delay, for next afternoon, after a busy morning of making naval contracts, he slipped away to her lodgings to give her joy of her wedding, and found her as willing as he could wish. Two days later, feeling in an idle and wanton humour and not having the courage to accost one of the pretty wenches who smiled at him from the doors of Fleet Alley, he repeated the experience. It was all very mean and sordid.[26]

Touched, perhaps, by a spark of some purer fire was Pepys' passion that summer for little Jane Welsh, his barber Jarvis' maid. In the previous winter he had come to a resolve to go abroad in better clothes—a velvet cloak, a new black cloth suit trimmed with scarlet ribbon very neat, silk tops for the legs and many other fine things; these, he felt, would much enhance his dignity. To the same end, he had invested in one of the new-fashioned periwigs—a daring venture which had cost him many an anxious thought as to its reception by his neighbours and colleagues,* but happily

* "Up and to my office, shewing myself to Sir W. Batten and Sir J. Minnes, and no great matter made of my periwig, as I was afraid there would." *D.* Nov. 4th, 1663.

"I found that my coming" (to church) "in a periwig did not prove attended by nothing worse than the Duke of York's declaration that Mr Pepys was so altered by his new periwig that he did not know him. This same took him from time to time to his barber's at Westminster for such improvements and reparations as occasion demanded, as for instance its cleansing of nits, a number of which little creatures appear to have made it their habitation. These visits brought him far too frequently into the society of Jarvis' wench, Jane. Though of humble station, she was very attractive: at least so Samuel found her. On one of his visits—it was the anniversary of Cromwell's crowning mercy—having the luck to find her alone, he persuaded her to meet him in Westminster Abbey during sermon time on the following Sunday. But, when on the chosen Sabbath Samuel paced wearily up and down the Abbey till six in the evening, no Jane came. However he returned to the charge next day and, after ascertaining when her master and mistress would be out and filling in the time by looking at the tombs in the Abbey with great pleasure, he spent two hours alone in the house with her, "kissing her but nothing more". The following Sunday saw a repetition of the same hopes and the same disappointment. And though on the morrow when he called again and found her cold, he told himself that it was no great matter, there was no doubt that his heart was touched. "A strange slavery that I stand in to beauty", he wrote, "that I value nothing near it."[27]

So he had to console himself with carpenter Bagwell's wife. Earlier in the year, when that lady had visited the Office on an errand for her husband, she had had the privilege of being stroked under the chin by the Clerk of the Acts.

so strange to the world as I was afraid it would, for I thought that all the church would presently have cast their eyes all upon me, but I found no such thing." *D.* Nov. 8th, 1663.

Now in the autumn she suffered the further honour of being kissed. "She rebuked me for doing it", that versatile official recorded, "saying that, did I do so much to many bodies else, it would be a stain to me." None the less, she did not seem to take it at all badly. He persevered. Next time she came, he caressed her, soothing her with many kind words and promises of getting her husband a place. Before long he got her to an alehouse in Moorfields, where further caresses followed, but no compliance did he receive from her in what was bad, "but very modestly she denied me, which I was glad to see and shall value her the better for it, and I hope never tempt her to any evil more". So strangely are the threads of good and evil interwoven in human hearts. Yet still the indomitable Clerk of the Acts kept his course. Five days later he was making a further assignation.[28]

As for Mrs Pepys, she was a loser all round. Not merely did her husband deceive her, but he still showed himself jealous of her association with anyone else—even with Will Hewer and Admiral Penn's schoolboy son, the future Quaker chief. The affair of Pembleton had sadly shaken him. He could not rid his mind of a haunting fear, so concisely expressed by the mentor of his youth, Father Osborne, that during his absence at Office or Yard, some gaudy wasp or liquorish fly would have a lick at his honey pot. Combined with overwork, the suspicion tended to make him ill-tempered, marred the learned serenity of the connubial geography lessons and led to unnecessary quarrels over such trivialities as the weekly washing day, the lace poor Elizabeth aspired to tack on her gown or the twenty-five shilling pendant which she bought herself. On one occasion, he even pulled her by the nose: the poor wretch, he recorded, took it mighty ill.[29]

Happily his wife's absence at Brampton worked a cure,

and when she returned in August—he riding out to Stevenage to meet her—it was to a much more peaceful home. Better fortune, too, attended the family domestic arrangements. The little girl Susan proved "a most admirable slut", and though Bess left on her own in September, she was more than compensated for by Jane Birch, the new cook, "a good natured, quiet, well meaning, honest servant" after Samuel's own heart. And there were two notable additions to the household in the autumn; a new companion for Elizabeth, named Mercer—a young woman of very different stamp to Gosnell or Ashwell, found for the Pepyses by Will Hewer who lodged at her parents' house: a musician, moreover, of no mean promise, who played well on the harpsichord and had a good ear and voice. The other was Tom Edwards, a lad whom Pepys' friend Captain Cooke, the court musician, had procured for him from the choir of the Chapel Royal. At present he was still a schoolboy, "that talks innocently and impertinently", but his master proposed to make a clerk of him if he did well. In the meantime he was to serve in the house: it was a great joy to be able to maintain one who had such a thorough knowledge of music. "Never since I was housekeeper", wrote Pepys, "I ever lived so quietly, without any noise or one angry word almost."[30]

All the while, with war becoming ever more imminent, Pepys was toiling from dawn till nightfall, and often long after, at the Office. The joys which he recorded so contentedly or stole with such keen relish were crowded, after all, into a few fugitive hours and fade into insignificance beside that imposing background of labour. That August he was rising regularly at five, making long expeditions down the river and working feverishly to set out the squadron which was ordered to sail for Guinea. All men's discourse was now of war in the highest measure, and hopes rose and fell daily with each successive piece of news. Sandwich was already at sea—much to Pepys' alarm who feared he might die with all his debts upon his head—and the Duke of York announced his intention of going too. And with the heir presumptive of England hoisting his standard in the Narrow Seas, the eyes of the whole nation were focused on the Navy.[31]

And at his desk in the Office at Seething Lane, writing ceaselessly, sat the little man who every day became more and more the pivot of all this activity. Of the life of the sea itself—the sailing of the fleets, the training of the guns, the ordering in battle of the dogged courage of the seamen—he knew nothing. But with the departure of Coventry and Penn with the Duke of York for the Fleet, he became in practice, though not in name, the pivot of that administrative machine without which not a single ship could set out from port. As Coventry put it to him before his departure, the weight of dispatch now lay on him; Berkeley was a figure-head, Batten too corrupt, and as for old Mennes, he was like a lapwing—"all he did was to keep a flutter to keep others from the nest that they would find".[32]

On November 14th Pepys remained at the Office, infinitely busy, till midnight. During the day news was brought that a ship of masts of Sir William Warren had been stopped and seized by the Dutch. On the morrow, the Clerk of the Acts, that he might not be too fine for the business he had resolved on that day, left off his fine new clothes lined with plush (that had cost him £17) and put on his old black suit. Then, his morning's work done, he made his way to a little blind alehouse in Moorfields where he met Bagwell's wife: "and there I did caress her and drink, and many hard looks and sooth the poor wretch did give me, and I think verily was troubled at what I did, but at last after many protestings by degrees I did arrive at what I would, with great pleasure". Four days later Admiral Teddiman sailed into Portsmouth with twenty captured Dutch merchantmen. "The war", wrote Pepys, "is begun: God give a good end to it."

Chapter XII

First Blood

'So ends this month with great expectation of the Hollanders coming forth, who are, it seems, very high and rather more ready than we. God give a good issue to it!" *Diary*, Feb. 28th, 1665.

"Soon as ever the clock struck one", wrote Pepys on January 1st, 1665, "I kissed my wife in the kitchen by the fireside, wishing her a merry new year." He had just finished the old one by casting up his accounts and finding himself by the blessing of God worth £1349, £500 of which had come to him in the last twelvemonth: "the Lord make me forever thankful to his holy name for it". He had torn up his old papers, summarised every aspect of his worldly affairs and added in longhand in a blank page of his Diary the names, births and deaths of his father's and grandfather's children. He had also been particularly careful to destroy anything that seemed not worth the keeping or not fit to be seen should it please God to take him away suddenly! Now, with a clear past and a hopeful heart, he waited, pen poised, to record the future.

The last few weeks of the old year had been troublesome enough. So busy that he could hardly sleep, sick for want of food, with head and eyes aching, he had borne the burden of the Office on his shoulders so long as the Fleet remained at sea. Then, at the beginning of December, the rivai navies returned to their harbours, the islanders, whose strategic position athwart the trade routes of their rivals had given them many rich prizes, claiming their enemy's retirement to port as a victory but Pepys noting more soberly that it was merely the result of the weather. This opinion, of course, he discreetly kept to his Diary, though in a letter to the triumphant Penn at Portsmouth he ventured on a mild jest, begging next time he went to sea "that a little mischief be done, for our good friend, Captain Cocke's sake, paymaster to the sick and wounded".[1]

His arduous service, coupled with the frosty weather which had brought up pimples and pricks all over his body and put him into an agony of wind, had again soured his temper. He had flown at old Mennes for his folly, telling him roundly and boldly what he thought of him, bidden his wife dismiss good-natured Bess because she had forgotten to set out his clothes in the morning and, when that long-suffering spouse ventured to return a cross answer to one of his complaints that she did not command her servants, had struck her over the left eye such a blow as made "the poor wretch cry out. Yet", he added, "her spirit was such as to endeavour to bite and scratch me. But I coying with her made her leave crying, and sent for butter and parsley, and friends presently one with another, and I up, vexed at heart to think what I had done, for she was forced to lay a poultice or something to her eye all day, and is black, and the people of the house observed it". There was certainly this to be said for Samuel as a husband; that his attitude to his wife was full of variety and surprise and that, when he offended, he at least had the grace to be sorry for it. But when a fortnight later he told himself that he had as pretty, loving and quiet a family as any man in England, he was probably overstating things.[2]

For this good and worthy household chief took little of his pleasure at home. This he preferred to share with other partners—with Jane Welsh, the barber's girl, with whom he continued to make fugitive rendezvous (almost invariably broken by the elusive little cockney) and for whom that Christmas he told himself he had "*grande envie, avec amour et passion*"; with Betty Martin who was always ready to sneak home from Westminster Hall with him and, in her husband's absence, let him do what he would with her; with Mrs Bagwell, who was more difficult to capture but who yielded as inevitably in the end. Jane Welsh gave herself up to another sweetheart, a sorry fellow and poor, and so—after one brief hour of fondling in a riverside tavern—eluded Samuel for ever; Bagwell, in one of her periodic, despairing attempts to recover her lost virtue, strained his forefinger, so that for a day it was in mighty pain, but gave in as she always did on his promising to write a letter to Lord Sandwich to advance her husband to a better ship. As for the buxom Betty, Pepys grew tired of the ease with which she fell; wrote contemptuously of her pitiful poor lodgings in Bow Street and had the effrontery to confess himself "sick of her impudence". For a moment he was almost bored by his own powers. And as all this roving love was interfering with his work, he made a vow to "*laisser aller les femmes*". "Thereby", he wrote, "I may follow my business, which and my honour lies a'bleeding."[3]

There was certainly plenty to be done. The war had multiplied the work at the Office almost beyond computation. The variety which fell to Pepys' share is mirrored in the official correspondence which from this time onwards he so carefully kept or copied. Some of these letters are better described in his own words as "volumes". The supply of stores of every sort—blocks, and oars, colours, sails, rope, anchors, cables, ironwork, tobacco stalks for gun wadding (an ingenious makeshift of his own); of men—able men for boatswains', gunners' and carpenters' mates to be gathered in the river, pressed men to be kept by soldiers till the ships were ready to receive them, fishermen to be smuggled away from the vigilant eye of the City's Water Bailiff; of all the things which a great fleet demands and war devours, Pepys' epistolary pages are full. When they failed, he was quick to plan new means of supplying them. A complaint (in an awful hand from the new Commissioner at Portsmouth) that the shrouds were so ill-fitted that the ships' masts were often broken as a result, set him exploring the possibilities of erecting stoves* in his Majesty's Yards. He visited the ropemaker Stapely's rope-ground at Limehouse, got a bricklayer to accompany him with a measure to the principal stoves in the City and pumped two Dutch masters, whom he discovered drinking in a tavern, on the practice of ropemaking and stoving, subsequently writing to Coventry the most elaborate treatise on a highly technical process of which a few weeks before he had known nothing whatever. He even turned his attention to shipbuilding. Having formed high hopes of the capacity of his ingenious friend, Mr Deane (now by his recommendation Master Shipwright at Harwich), he exerted himself to bring him forward as a shipwright in opposition to the all-pervading tribe of Petts. In March, 1665, Deane submitted a design for a new ship. Anxious lest it should be rejected by the expert from Shipwrights' Hall, by whom such designs were examined before final approval, Pepys privately submitted his protégé's draught together with that of a rival competitor to an experienced shipbuilder, asking him to give his views on them. Though much approving the other, the expert, on seeing Deane's design, declared that the man who made it had never built a ship in his life, and Pepys in great distress wrote to Deane pointing this out and enclosing both his own and his

* Kilns for putting ropes in to make them pliable.

rival's draughts so that he might amend his own accordingly. Ultimately this somewhat unconscionable proceeding helped to give a great naval architect to England: two years later, when Deane's vessel was finished, the King and the Duke of York agreed in saying that it was the best ship ever built.[4]

Not that Pepys allowed any partiality to his favourites to blind him to their defects. He knew that Deane, for all his talent, was conceited, self-opinionated and quarrelsome; men are so made that their great virtues are weighed down by as great failings until with age they attain to mastery over themselves. So when the new Commissioner, Captain John Taylor, appointed to the Navy Board to supervise the Yard at Harwich, was setting out, Pepys, anticipating trouble, wrote to Deane to be particularly careful to maintain good relations with him. In the same way he kept up a constant correspondence with all those subordinates whom for their industry he had advanced in the service, encouraging them with praise when they deserved it and admonishing them whenever they failed. Nor did he exclude old servants of the Commonwealth from his patronage: indeed these, having early learnt the lessons of industry, obedience and punctuality required in an official in the hard school of the republic, were more often than not his favourites. When Coventry, holding that all hands would be needed for the work of war, got the King and Duke of York to appoint two of them, Colonel Thomas Middleton and Captain Taylor, as additional Navy Commissioners in charge of the Yards at Portsmouth and Harwich, Pepys zealously defended the appointments against Mennes and Batten at the Board. For different reasons, he welcomed the addition of another Commissioner, the mathematical courtier, Lord Brouncker, believing a little over-hopefully that he would help to check the corruption of his colleagues.[5]

Pepys' greatest difficulty lay, as ever, with the merchants who supplied the service. Like others before and since, these saw in the coming war a golden opportunity to turn their country's necessity to glorious gain. Sometimes they compelled the government to buy all their stores or none, whether it wanted them or not: at other times the ships and yards were starved because they neglected to lay in sufficient provisions. And always they tried to enhance the price. "Mere's cheap man", wrote Pepys of one aspiring contractor, "is so unconscionably dear that we cannot agree to his price for timber or plank": therefore, he added, the Navy Office must look elsewhere. But sometimes there was nowhere else to look. By April, 1665, the Board was forced to pay one merchant £55 a ton for hemp in order to keep the dockyard hands at Chatham in work.[6]

Yet whenever he could, the Clerk of the Acts fought the profiteers and beat their prices down. He was even ready on occasion to act against his own purse to save the King's, and warned his friend, Warren, that if he joined with his rival, Castle, who was making over 25 per cent. on every load of timber served, in rigging the price of masts against the government, he would abandon him. Not that he actually did so, for in December, 1664, a contract was concluded between Warren and Castle and the Navy Office for supplying 1500 loads of timber, but Pepys at least went to enormous trouble to ensure that the contractors did not cheat the King of a penny more than was necessary, as his voluminous papers on this contract—to-day preserved in the Bodleian Library—go to show.[7]

After all, in an aristocratic age, a young official, without high family backing and wealth, could not afford to carry his zeal too far. He had to live, hold his place and accumulate that saving capital (on whose possession depended security, independence, future power) which he so coveted. Therefore it was best not to quarrel too far with such friends as could help him to achieve these hopes. On February 6th, 1665, he made a firm league with Warren to serve him (and himself) in all just ways within his power; "and I think he will be a most useful and thankful man to me", he added. A week or so later he defended him against Mennes, who had alluded to the great timber-contractor as a "cheating knave". Warren showed how grateful he was by rewarding his young friend with much admirable and confidential advice—as not to do anything suddenly but always to consult his pillow before he resolved on any important step. And there were also other and more substantial rewards which the kindly merchant saw fit to make.[8]

It was really surprising how easy it was to make money, now that the needs of the Navy had become so universal. A little private trading on his own account in supplying flags to the service brought Pepys a profit of £50 on his outlay: and with great honesty too, he reflected, for he had saved the King double that sum. One might use one's influence to secure priority of payment to a navy contractor for some long due debt: "the thing most just", he wrote of one such application; "perhaps I may undertake it, and get something by it, which will be a good job". Or a merchant might require to send a valuable freight beyond seas: a word in the right quarter would secure the vessel that bore it from the press-gang or provide it with a convoy, and the trade of the kingdom be thereby enhanced and one's own interest served at the same time: Warren promised Pepys £100 for the protection of a single ship. And what noble gifts there would be awaiting one on one's return home in the evening: two large silver candlesticks and snuffers from Mr Harris, the sail-maker, a couple of state cups worth £6 each from

Burrows, the slopseller, or the neat silver watch from a hopeful solicitor, whom Mrs Pepys so injudiciously received at the door and presented with a receipt. This last present was for a short while a wonderful source of enjoyment to the Clerk of the Acts: "but Lord!" he wrote, "to see how much of my old folly and childishness hangs upon me still that I cannot forbear carrying my watch in my hand in the coach all this afternoon, and seeing what o'clock it is one hundred times". Of course he was careful not to take anything which his conscience told him was a bribe: when Deering, the plank merchant, offered him twenty gold pieces to dispatch a contract, Pepys refused it, and only accepted it a month or so later with the greatest regret.[9]

Yet, in all his garden, Tangier still remained the finest flower. There was always something to be made from this remote yet convenient place, and at the meetings of the governing Commission, Pepys, as the youngest and most active member and the one with the greatest knowledge of the ways of contractors and merchants generally, contrived to get the lion's share of whatever was going. In the winter of 1664–5 he had been disappointed in certain hopes which he had entertained of being made a Commissioner of Prizes —"a visible increase of encouragement", he had described the coveted office in a letter to Coventry. A far richer source of profit was now to fall to his share.[10]

For some time the incapacity of Thomas Povy, the Treasurer of the Tangier Committee, had been growing increasingly apparent. Pepys, who had at first been much impressed by Povy's commodious way of living—his splendid furniture and cabinet work, his grotto and vault, his bath at the top of the house, his manner of eating and drinking—had tried to help him straighten his affairs, but was forced, fine accountant as he was, to confess himself beaten: "such accounts", he observed, "I never did see; or hope again to see in my days". When he was attacked in Committee, Povy defended himself so badly that he merely left everyone wondering whether he was a knave or a fool or both. Finally in March, 1665, after one particularly troubled meeting, in which many high and shameful words were spoken, he begged Pepys to step aside and then and there offered him his post on condition that the profits of it should be shared between them.

After some thought, for he was conscious that the war was likely to make his work at the Navy Office worth all his time to him, Pepys accepted the charge. The Dukes of York and Albemarle, Lord Sandwich and the rest of the Committee agreed without a dissentient voice to their colleague's promotion: the first declared that he would trust his industry and discretion as soon as any man's in England, and Lord Fitzharding (the King's new favourite) was seen to whisper something about him—it seemed to be flattering—to Secretary Bennet across the table. Coventry assured him that it would do him much good by making him known to the greatest persons in England, whereas at the present he was buried at the Navy Board among four or five others. So, two weeks after the official declaration of war on the United Provinces, the Clerk of the Acts of the Navy found himself also Treasurer of Tangier. It took many hard and precious hours, stolen from his office at Seething Lane, poring over complicated figures before he felt himself master of his new business, but, once mastered, it was worth it. Throughout 1665 Pepys' capital mounted rapidly. So also did his household goods. On July 7th he made a special note in his Diary of what a condition it had pleased God to bring him to that he could number in his cellar two tierces of Claret, two quarter casks of Canary, a vessel of Sack, a vessel of Tent, another of

Malaga, and another of White Wine—more he believed than any of his name now alive had ever possessed at once.[11]

Moreover, he deserved it. Did not everyone unite to sing his praises, from Mrs Bland the merchant's wife whom he helped with a passage in one of the King's ships to her husband in Tangier,* to William Coventry "whose profession of love and esteem for me to myself was so large and free that I never could expect or wish for more"? Nay, even the Duke of York took the trouble to tell him to his face how much he valued him, while Lord Sandwich, who had apparently quite forgotten that perilous letter, used him at dinner with the greatest solemnity in the world, "carving for me and nobody else and calling often to my Lady to cut for me, and all the respect possible". The very virtuosos of the Royal Society honoured him (or themselves) by electing him to their number, so that he was enabled in his scanty leisure moments to enjoy the educative and delightful spectacles of a hen drunk with the Florentine poison or an abortive child preserved fresh in spirits of salt† in the company of the most learned and worthy persons in England. Sometimes he could scarcely believe it all, sitting in Committee with his hat on while his old superior, Mr Sherwin, stood bareheaded before him: "I thank God I think myself never a whit the better man for all that", he added. In a way it was all a kind of miracle—the miraculous providence of God: it certainly seemed so that February when Mr Barlow, that good,

* "Really Sir", wrote that enchanted lady of a naval captain who at Pepys' command had given her passage, "he did treat me with that respect that if I had been the greatest lady in England he could not show me more, and clearly it was upon your account." Mrs Bland to Pepys, March 21st, 1664; *Rawlinson MSS. A.* 174, f. 95.

† Pepys must have been wrong here; it cannot have been spirits of salt that preserved the abortive child.

honest pensioner, died, "for which, God knows my heart, I could be as sorry as is possible for one to be for a stranger by whose death he gets £100 per annum....I have cause to bless God and do it from the bottom of my heart".[12]

All the while the preparations for the first summer of the war went forward. The four great wants of England's Navy were money, men, materials and meat, and Pepys' letters during the spring of 1665 ring the changes on these needs. Money he had done his best to supply a few months earlier when, in company with Sir George Carteret and Sir Philip Warwick of the Treasury, he had helped to cook the Navy estimates for Parliament, "studying all we could to make the last year swell as high as we could". In November, 1664, the House had voted £2,500,000 for the war, to be spread over a period of two and a half years: a great sum it seemed at the time, but as early as December 3rd Pepys predicted its inadequacy. Nor was it speedily available: long and valuable weeks were spent in discussing the means of raising it and many wearier months in doing so. By February the Clerk of the Acts was reporting to Coventry that the Service was running apace into the old ill-effects of bad payments. Merchants, whose bills were outstanding, refused to renew their contracts save on exorbitant terms to cover the risk of non-payment; others declared their inability to supply at all until recouped for their previous expenditure. "What we shall shortly do without better payments", Pepys wrote to Coventry, "I am at a loss to guess, or add to your other melancholy meditations so heavy a one as this, but it's come already that people under their hands have said 'Pay me for what you have had and I'll trust you further.'" When he pleaded before the Privy Council for the needful supplies, he was only met by signs of amazement and discontent. "Why, what means all this, Mr Pepys," cried the old Lord

Treasurer, holding up his hands; "this is true, you say, but what would you have me do? I have given all I can for my life. Why will not people lend their money? Why will they not trust the King as well as Oliver? Why do our prizes come to nothing that yielded so much heretofore?" And this was all the answer he could get.[13]

All this Pepys attributed to the idleness and incapacity of those in high places: "one of the saddest things that, at such a time as this, with the greatest action on foot that ever was in England, nothing should be minded". Yet, though with his cautious and logical intelligence he saw the inevitable consequences of such financial constipation better than any other man, he lacked the high imagination, given to very few, to pierce to the heart of the cause and find in it, not the extravagance of the Court or the laziness of the great, but that fatal duality of sovereignty which paralysed England's action from the Restoration to the Revolution. Later he was to change his views; for the present he set down his troubles to the carelessness of his superiors, of which there was certainly all too much. But the truth of the matter was that, so long as the King who controlled the executive had no power to make Parliament give him money and no machinery of credit to bridge the gulf between current expenditure and future income, a prolonged national war could only end in bankruptcy.

For the moment, want of men was even more serious than want of money. All through the early months of 1665, the Navy Office and the King's Captains were seeking for seamen. On January 15th Pepys, with Coventry and three admirals, was one of a little delegation of five who pleaded before the King and Council that the Turkey Company's ships might be prevented from leaving for the Mediterranean, since of 30,000 sailors needed to man the Navy, 26,000 had to be found from the merchant marine. In the eastern counties, where the war was popular, there was no difficulty in recruiting, but elsewhere the press-gang brought in far from satisfactory material—poor landsmen "fitter to keep sheep than to sail in such great ships" who when caught as quickly deserted, so that Coventry in despair wrote that nothing but hanging would man the Fleet. And among the lobstermen, trawlers, trinkers and hebbers of Greenwich and Barking Pepys, making good the deficiencies of his Majesty's Navy, took his fishy way.*[14]

With the victualling of the Fleet he was still more actively engaged. Though the responsibility for provisioning the Navy lay with the civilian Victualler, Dennis Gauden, the Navy Office was expected to supervise his efforts, and with Penn and Coventry much at sea and Mennes and Batten increasingly incompetent, a large burden lay on the Clerk of the Acts—the greater because he had no subordinate machinery with which to oversee the Victualler's agents at the ports. Indeed he was often quite alone at the Office, bearing the whole weight of this as of other matters: "sat all morning and I did most of the business there, God wot", runs one of his typical entries. "Let your letters be directed to the Board or myself", he told Coventry, "for twenty to one to me they will come at last. But 'twas spitefully done", he added, "to give you this counsel just now when, by my being alone, the Board and Mr Pepys are all one."[15]

Twice that spring was the Fleet got out to sea, and to this

* Witness Pepys' long and detailed survey, dated March 5th, 1665, and now preserved in his letter-book in the National Maritime Museum at Greenwich, of the Thames fishing trade and the claim of its brethren to be free of the press. Among the arguments which he advanced against this claim was the heavy unemployment among the fisherwomen—"the greatest nursery of lewd women, beggars and bastards about the City". *Greenwich MSS.* p. 161 *et seq.*

great end were all Pepys' efforts directed—"laying about us all we can to meet the spring with a good fleet", as he himself put it. Rising at six or earlier every morning, securing lighters to carry stores and provisions (he even contrived to make a little profit for himself out of his industry), or going down the river at midnight to hasten out the victualling ships, he was the life and soul of the administration; "the right hand of the Navy here", the Duke of Albemarle—left in charge of the Admiralty while the Duke of York was at sea—styled him. No wonder the King called him by name to speak to him of the service whenever he saw him, and the old Lord Chancellor stroked him on the head.[16]

On April 21st the Fleet, with the Duke of York, Coventry and Penn as Captain-General aboard the *Royal Charles*, sailed for the Dutch coast, hoping to entice the Dutch out to battle: "God go along with them", was Pepys' prayer. But, unfortunately, what did not go along with them was enough beer: as Coventry had gloomily prophesied, Mr Gauden had ensured that the Fleet should not stay long abroad. On May 15th, the thirsty sailors returned home.[17]

Once more Pepys busied himself frantically in preparations to get out the Fleet. Meanwhile the Dutch put to sea. On May 24th they fell in with the English Hamburg convoy, which was bringing home the naval stores then so badly needed in England from the Baltic, and captured them. The efforts to get out the English Fleet were redoubled, and on May 30th the Duke of York, with 109 warships, 28 fireships and 21,000 men weighed from the Gun Fleet. Pepys leant back, as it were, with a sigh of relief. He had done his part "carefully and faithfully. One word more I have", he wrote to Coventry, "which is to commit the whole matter, and the many noble lives hazarded therein to the protection of the Almighty".[18]

Then next day—it was June 1st—he put on his new silk camlet coat, the best that ever he had worn in his life and one that had cost him £24. Thus arrayed he made his way to Westminster Hall, where, in his words, he took "the fairest flower and by coach to Tothill Fields till it was dark. I 'light, and in with the fairest flower to eat a cake, and there did do as much as was safe with my flower, and that was enough on my part. Broke up, and away without any notice, and, after delivering the rose where it should be, I to the Temple and 'light and there took another coach and so home to write letters, but very few, God knows, being by my pleasure made to forget everything that is". Save for a drive with Elizabeth and Mercer in the coach and a single play, it was the first he had had for many a week. "Take it then in your own merry mathematics", he had told Coventry, "I have heard no music but on Sunday these six months."[19]

On June 1st the rival navies came in sight of each other off the Suffolk coast. Early on the morning of the third, the English then having the weather gauge, the action began at a distance of 14 miles N.N.E. from Lowestoft. All that day "the two most mighty and best appointed Fleets which any age had ever seen, disputed the command of the greater half of the globe, the commerce of nations and the riches of the Universe". While they did so, the noise of the cannon trembled in the summer haze, passing across the farms and villages of Suffolk and Essex, until it reached London. Then, as Pepys' contemporary Dryden recalled it, "everyone went following the sound as his fancy led him; and leaving the town almost empty, some took towards the Park, some across the river, and others down it, all seeking noise in the depth of the silence". As Dryden and his companions rowed towards Greenwich, little undulations of sound, "like the noise of distant thunder or of swallows in a chimney", reached them. Then they ceased and were heard no more.[20]

Pepys heard them, going about the City on his naval occasions; heard too by letters from Harwich that the fleets were engaged, and thought much and with deep anxiety of his cousin and patron, now commanding the Blue Squadron, and of the Duke of York and Coventry upon whom all his worldly hopes rested. "I tremble at what the consequences of it may be, should the Fleet come home in the condition we hope to put our enemy into", he had told the latter a few weeks before, and he trembled now. Happily his anxiety was tempered by one of those internecine battles in which administrative England delights to engage in time of peril, and, while the great ships poured forth their broadsides on the deep, Pepys at home lustily defended his clerk, Hayter, who at this most opportune moment had been committed to the Gatehouse by the Council for unwittingly infringing some technical regulation. And he had to stand bail for him in £100 before he could get him out.[21]

For five days no certain news came. Letters from the coast towns showed that the battle had drifted eastwards, but that was all. Rumours of victory, to which Pepys gave small credence, ran the round of the Exchange; others that Lord Sandwich had been killed. It was oppressively hot—hotter than he could ever remember; on the 7th, while Elizabeth with Mercer, Mary the cook, Tom Edwards and Will Hewer were refreshing themselves on the river, the thirsty Clerk of the Acts tried to buy himself a glass of whey at the New Exchange and it was only with the greatest difficulty that he could obtain it. Later that day he noticed in Drury Lane two or three houses marked with red crosses upon the doors; the Plague, despite all attempts to keep it out, had come to town, brought over from Holland where it had been raging in the previous year. "It put me into an ill conception of myself and my smell", he wrote as he sat up waiting for Elizabeth's return, "so that I was forced to buy some roll-tobacco to smell and to chew, which took away the apprehension."

Next afternoon, Thursday the 8th, the long-awaited news came. Pepys was at the Lord Treasurer's at a conference with the goldsmiths when he heard of it: that the Dutch had been totally routed, and that the Duke of York, Prince Rupert, Lord Sandwich and Coventry were all safe: news that put him into such joy that he forgot all other thoughts—the heat, the want of money, the plague-stricken houses in Drury Lane which he had so carefully warned Elizabeth to avoid when she went out to dine at Will Joyce's. Then, as soon as the bankers had departed, he hurried across to the Cockpit, where he found the Duke of Albemarle like a man out of himself with content. By and by a letter came in from Coventry to the Duke, who flung it unopened to Pepys to read.

It was almost too good to be true. The Dutch neglecting to use the weather gauge for two days had lost it by the morning of the 3rd to the English, who then attacked, the two battle lines gradually closing with each other. The Dutch flagship, with the High Admiral Opdam on board, had blown up and by nightfall over twenty of their great ships had been taken or destroyed. The rest had escaped to their harbours, the victorious English, though with shattered masts and torn sails and rigging, riding victorious along the Dutch coast. The Dutch had lost, it was believed, eight thousand men, the English less than eight hundred, though among the dead were the Earl of Marlborough and Rear-Admiral Sansum, and the Earl of Falmouth (the King's dearest friend), Lord Muskerry and Mr Boyle, all three killed by a single shot while standing beside the Duke of

York. Vice-Admiral Lawson, too, had been wounded, but it was hoped not mortally. The letter ended with urgent demands for stores of all kinds to be sent down to the coast against the Fleet's return. Unfortunately the Dutch had not been totally destroyed and there was no mention of Lord Sandwich's services. For the rest, a greater victory had never been known.[22]

This letter and others methodical Mr Pepys copied out in his memorandum book, also making a summary of it in his Diary. Then, with his heart full of joy, he spent the evening with Lady Penn and her children, who were "not a little puffed up" at the good success of their father. Together they lit a great bonfire at the Navy Office gate and were exceedingly merry.

Such, at least so far as it touched the life of Samuel Pepys, was the battle of Lowestoft. Later news fully confirmed the extent of the victory. When the Duke of York and his courtiers, all fat and lusty and ruddy by being in the sun, returned to Whitehall, Pepys learnt more: how the great ships with their powerful guns had performed the real business, "they quite deadening the enemy", what brave things Captain Jeremy Smith in the *Mary* had done, and how basely (this from his cousin's own mouth) Lord Sandwich, who had led the van almost the entire day and had broken the enemy's line, had been treated in being omitted from the printed relation of the battle. Poor Lawson's wound turned out to be worse than had been supposed; and, despite visits from the King and Mr Pepys, he died at Greenwich on June 25th of "a fever, a thrush and a hiccough, all three together, which are, it seems very bad symptoms". Coventry, more fortunate, was knighted and sworn a Privy Councillor.

Pepys also was stirred to battle by the events of that month. Some while before, in learning his business, he noted that,

WHITEHALL FROM ST. JAMES'S PARK

in "speaking in matters distasteful to him that we write to, it is best to do it in the plainest way without umbrages or reasoning, but only say matters of fact and leave the party to collect your meaning". In June, 1665, he gave a remarkable example of how thoroughly he had mastered that lesson. For some time Commissioner Pett had been grumbling at the great contract for masts which the Navy Board at Pepys' recommendation had concluded with Sir William Warren. He now wrote formally charging the Board with neglect. He received in reply a most unexpected letter. "Sir," wrote Pepys, "in answer to yours of the 12th...I must own myself much surprised to find so severe a reflection upon the whole Board in the business of masts, as if they, contrary to your frequent advice, had committed some such heinous neglect in the contracting with one man for our supply of masts that it needed a public declaration of your incense thereon."

"What I have to say", he continued, closing into column formation, "is this:

1. That to this hour I never heard you, either publicly or privately, oppose this contract or offer any better or other, saving one with Mr Shorter, which he upon treaty did voluntarily decline....

2. That at the time of the making this contract, Mr Wood and others were summoned, but none would entertain our supply....

3. That no contract appearing in my books for 15 years backward (so well as things were done then) equals this in cheapness and other circumstances of advantage to the King.

4. That it was made deliberately, and by His Royal Highness' particular approbation, as well as full advice of the Board....

Lastly. I have this further to vindicate the Board with, that as you never did propose any other way so I am ready to make good, that at the time and since, no English merchant but Sir W. Warren was, and has been, able to serve us with that quantity and sort of masts as he has done upon that contract, and therefore no contrary advice of yours (if you had given any) could have been of use to us."

"You will please to pardon this unusuall style," he concluded, "it being upon a matter extraordinary and in defence of the whole Board against a very untimely and, I think, unjust a charge....

I remain, Sir, Your very humble servant

Samuel Pepys."

It was the first of those tremendous epistolary broadsides, leaving his enemy raked, dismasted and without the power of reply, which in the course of the next seven years raised the young Clerk of the Acts to the highest administrative position in the Navy. Already the war was bringing out the inner man of action and dogged determination which was the very core of Samuel Pepys.[23]

Chapter XIII

Mr Greatheart

"Thou shalt not be afraid for any terror by night: nor for the arrow that flieth by day; for the pestilence that walketh in darkness: nor for the sickness that destroyeth in the noon-day. A thousand shall fall beside thee, and ten thousand at thy right hand: but it shall not come nigh thee."

Psalm xci.

"I have never lived so merrily (besides that I never got so much) as I have done this plague time." *Diary*, Dec. 31st, 1665.

During the month of June the plague increased rapidly. On the 10th it had entered the house of Pepys' good friend and neighbour, Dr Burnett of Fenchurch Street. A week later, as he drove home from the Lord Treasurer's, the hackney coach in which he was riding came to a sudden stop and the coachman staggered down, crying that he was struck sick and scarce able to see. Next day at church Mr Mills preached a sorry sermon to prove that there was a world to come. Many who heard him were soon to discover this truth for themselves. By the 21st the streets were full of coaches and waggons, packed with goods and people, rumbling over the cobbles for the country. The London Bills of Mortality for the last week showed that 267 had died of the plague.

Pepys, like his neighbours, took precautionary steps. Packing off his mother, who was on a visit to town, to Brampton, he took lodgings for Elizabeth at Woolwich at the house of William Sheldon, the Clerk of the Cheque. Thither, with her maids Mercer and Mary, she departed on

July 5th, leaving Alice and little Susan to look after the house in Seething Lane. Samuel remained: he had his work and was resolved to stay. He bade farewell to Coventry, who with all the rest of the Court was also leaving (save old Albemarle who remained serenely behind at the Cockpit) and, with a due sense of the solemnity of the times, put his estate in order and prepared himself for death.

Yet instead of dying he lived, and lived as even he had never lived before. During the past six months work had almost banished pleasure from his life. But now pleasure returned, flowing in like a summer tide over the waiting sands of life. On a late June evening he revisited Vauxhall, noting his sober contentment in this escape from business, "which with the air and pleasure of the garden was a great refreshment to me and, methinks, that which we ought to joy ourselves in". So in the last days of June he resolved that he would shut his office henceforward while it was still daylight and enjoy what remained of the pleasant evenings of summer. The departure of all the great world from London made this easier.

In the first week of July the mortality from plague increased to 700: in the second to over 1000. Pepys knew these things and was afraid. But they did not stop him from driving Mary, the girl from the "Harp and Ball", by coach to take the air at Hampstead and Highgate; "much pleased" he was "with her company, pretty and innocent, and had what pleasure almost I would with her". Nor did it keep his entranced feet from seeking the house of Mrs Bagwell at Deptford when he visited Woolwich to see his wife—a little strange he found the latter to his wonder and distress, but on his admiring her drawings, all was well again.[1]

He had a new source of delight that summer. Before he left London, Lord Sandwich—now about to sail with the Fleet—sent for Samuel and, propounding a match between his daughter, Lady Jemimah, and Sir George Carteret's eldest son, asked him to approach that gentleman in the matter. Delighted at the prospect of being of use to his patron and of cementing an alliance between him and his powerful colleague, he informed the latter's friend, Dr Clerke, "which he (as I knew he would) took with great content: and we both agreed that my Lord and he, being both men relating to the sea, under a kind aspect of His Majesty, already good friends, and both virtuous and good familys, their allyance might be of good use to us". Thereafter matters had proceeded rapidly. Within three days, Pepys, hastening between Lord Sandwich and Sir George Carteret, had negotiated a settlement eminently satisfactory to both sides. What was more, both the King and the Duke of York were delighted.

At the beginning of July, Lord Sandwich, having signed and sealed the necessary writings, departed for sea, leaving "honest Mr Pepys" in charge of the remaining negotiations. During the next few weeks the latter became in consequence a most important social personage. No longer, when he visited the Treasurer of the Navy, was the conversation confined to the melancholy topic of the Office debts; when official matters were done, he would venture on "a little merry discourse of our marrying business". It was indeed a subject on which the seventeenth century delighted to dwell. And what a wonderful change he now found in the proud and awe-inspiring Carteret!—"so light, so fond, so merry, so boyish", he could scarcely believe he was the same person.[2]

On July 9th Pepys, in his capacity as deputy for the prospective bride's father, waited on Lady Sandwich at the Carterets' country house at Deptford. He was received with the most extraordinary civility by Lady Carteret: the most kind lady in the world she seemed to be. And her generosity to the prospective bride proved it. "But Lord! to see how kind my Lady Carteret is to her!" wrote the entranced Pepys; "sends her most rich jewells, and provides bedding and things of all sorts most richly for her, which makes my Lady and me out of our wits almost to see the kindnesse she treats us all with, as if they would buy the young lady."

An even greater joy followed on July 15th—a summons to stay for the week-end at Dagnams in Essex, the seat of Lady Wright, Lady Sandwich's sister, where the bridal party was to reside until the wedding. Pepys had the privilege of escorting the bridegroom there. For all the magnificence of the occasion, he was a little disappointed in his charge. "But Lord!" he wrote, "what silly discourse we had by the way as to love-matters, he being the most awkerd man ever I met with in my life as to that business." He himself could have taught him so much. After that, when old Lord Crewe after supper proposed that the young people should be left alone "to begin their amours", Pepys advised against it, "lest the lady might be too much surprised". So instead he led the young gentleman up to his chamber, where he asked him how he liked the lady, "which he told me he did mightily, but Lord! in the dullest, insipid manner that ever lover did".

Next morning—it was Sunday—Pepys, deeply conscious of the honourable responsibility which had devolved on him as the bridegroom's trainer, returned to the charge. Walking up and down the gallery with him, he told him what to do: how he should take the lady always by the hand to lead her and what compliments to pay her when, as he warned him would be the case, he would be left alone with her. But, alas, though young Carteret thanked his kind mentor profusely, frankly admitting how much he needed training, neither coming nor going to church had he the confidence to take his lady so much as once by the hand, so that Pepys was forced to give him a gentle rebuke. After dinner the great ordeal came, and the young folk were left for the first time together—"and a little pretty daughter of my Lady Wright's most innocently came out afterwards, and shut the door to, as if she had done it, poor child, by inspiration". But when next day Pepys asked Lady Jem how she liked the gentleman she blushed and hid her face, and the utmost that she could be brought to say was that—she would readily obey her father's and mother's commands. One is left with the impression that Pepys derived a great deal more pleasure from the week-end than the lovers: he certainly made the Carterets shout with laughter with the account he gave them of it all when he returned to Deptford.

Nothing could decrease Pepys' enjoyment of an affair so full of honourable entertainment, fine journeys and noble company—not the swelling Bills of Mortality, nor melancholy plague-stricken London with its coachless streets and its bells ever tolling across the sweltering air, nor the frightened inhospitality of the great in their sanctuary at Hampton Court. He was out to enjoy every moment of it: even the chilly midnight hours when the Carterets' coach, returning from Dagnams to Deptford, missed the ferry at the Isle of Dogs and he and Sir George and his daughter, Lady Scott, refusing to be daunted, pulled up the glass and, resolving to make a frolic of it, slept and picnicked with great content in the coach! On the last day of the month, leaving his office, Pepys hastened with Sir George Carteret to the wedding and, being again stranded in the Isle of Dogs, arrived just too late for the ceremony. But he was in good time to eat the wedding dinner, undress the bridegroom (with many a merry jest) and see the young people to bed. "I kissed the bride in bed", he related, "and so the curtaines drawne with the greatest gravity that could be, and so good night. But", he added, "the modesty and gravity of this business was so decent, that it was to me indeed ten times more delightfull than if it had been twenty times more merry and joviall." Next morning he hurried up to see the young people and found them both red in the face and well enough pleased with their night's lodging. It was a wonderful wedding—"the only occurrence I ever mett with", he assured Lord Sandwich, "begun, proceded on and finished with the same uninterrupted excesse of satisfaction to all partys". As for his own part in the transaction, he had never spent so happy a month in his life—"with abundance of joy and honour and pleasant journies and brave entertainment and without cost of money". It was hard to believe that plague and war were really raging.[3]

Not that Pepys could be always content with such decorous delights. Returning from the wedding, he fell to a little love-making on his own (of a quality very different from that of young Carteret), sending for his maid Susan to comb his head on a Sabbath morning and then, to use his own curious phrasing, "nuper ponendo mes mains in su des choses de son breast, mais," he added with admirable caution, "il faut que je leave it lest it bring me to alcun major inconvenience". A few days later, interspersed between the usual interludes with Mrs Bagwell (who could now count on being visited whenever the Clerk of the Acts went to see his wife at Woolwich, so conveniently adjacent were his Majesty's dockyards to one another), he tried his hand on a young married woman named Robbins, daughter to old Delkes the waterman, who had called at the Office to get her husband exempted from being pressed to sea. At her first visit, he only managed to kiss her, but on a second occasion he was more fortunate. But the height of his August felicity came in a dream (3000 had perished of the pestilence that week) when he dreamt that he had Lady Castlemaine in his arms and was admitted to all the dalliance he could desire with her, and "then", added the happy philosopher, "dreamt that it was only a dream, but that since it was a dream and that I took so much real pleasure in it, what a happy thing it would be if when we are in our graves (as Shakespeere resembles it) we could dream, and dream but such dreams as this, that then we should not need to be so fearful of death as we are this plague time".[4]

Mrs Pepys, though she did not know the reason, gained greatly by these amorous encounters. When her husband visited Woolwich on August 14th, he presented her with a diamond ring (given him by an old acquaintance in return for procuring him a purser's place). A week later she with her two maids ("which are both good wenches") importuned Samuel to buy her a pearl necklace; this also he consented to do, for he had an appointment with Bagwell later in the day. She was even gaining a little freedom, though he was no less jealous than before; there was a great quarrel that autumn over a mysterious letter from an unknown man found in her possession. But he was learning wisdom. When the maids, threatened with dismissal, gave as was their wont mysterious hints about Elizabeth's gaddings abroad with certain Frenchmen, or dark clouds gathered in his mind about her relations with Browne, the drawing-master, Samuel did his best to forget them, being unwilling, as he wisely said, to vex himself in a strange place at a melancholy time.[5]

And all the while, plague and war were riding across his world. Even during the wedding festivities at Dagnams, some young gallants of the place, on passing a close curtained coach in a narrow lane and thrusting in their heads to ogle the pretty modest gentlewoman within, saw a ghastly female figure ("in a sick dress and stunk mightily") being borne to the pest-house. At Combe Farm near Greenwich human bodies lay unburied, while armed watchmen forbade any to come in or go out, "this disease making us more cruel to one another than if we were dogs". By the end of August the London Bills of Mortality for plague alone had risen to over 6000. 'Change was deserted, corpses were carried openly through the streets in the daytime and there were no boats upon the river. In terror, the remaining Principal Officers of the Navy petitioned that their meetings might be held at Deptford or Greenwich. Only Pepys remained quietly at Seething Lane, making his way, a little fearfully, through the stricken streets, but unshaken in the pursuit of his work and pleasure; once he was even impelled by his insatiable curiosity ("God forgive me") to walk into Moorfields to see if he could observe any corpses being taken to the plague pit. He made much of it in his letters to others—the horror, the uncanny silence of the streets, the gruesome stories—but, as the pages of his Diary show, he did not let it interfere with his business. "You, sir, took your turn at the sword," he wrote to Coventry, "I must not therefore grudge to take mine at the pestilence."[6]

For the needs of the Navy continued to demand his unflagging attention. In July, after a month of hurried effort, the Fleet had been got to sea again under Sandwich—with Penn as Vice-Admiral—in the hopes of intercepting De Ruyter's Atlantic squadron and the richly laden Dutch East India ships as they sneaked home to Holland round the coasts of Scotland and Norway. Rumours of an engagement from time to time reached England; then early in August came the news, as humiliating to the expectant islanders as it was heartening to the Dutch, that the great De Ruyter with his weather-beaten ships had given Sandwich's waiting fleet the slip and got safely into the Ems. By the middle of the month worse followed; that an attempt to seize the Dutch East India ships as they lay in the neutral harbour of Bergen had failed through a diplomatic misunderstanding at Copenhagen, Admiral Teddiman's squadron, which Sandwich had dispatched to effect the seizure, being repulsed by the guns of the Danish forts which he had been told would be silent. England's belief that the victory of June had given her command of the seas had proved a delusion. The Dutch, heartened by the return of their hero, De Ruyter, were preparing to challenge her again in the North Sea, and her own Fleet was forced to return to harbour for the ignominious, but unchallengeable, reason that its victuals had given out weeks in advance of the time allowed for by the victualling contract.[7]

Once more, there followed ten days of breathless action for the naval administration until the clamour of the country could be appeased and the Fleet once more be got to sea. De Ruyter was known to have sailed for Bergen to fetch home the East Indiamen, and the honour of the nation, as well as its hungry Treasury, urgently demanded that he should be intercepted. Pepys in particular had especial reason to pray for a speedy sailing, for his patron Sandwich was being universally assailed for the ill-fortune which had attended the Fleet. His prayer was answered. "My Lord", he wrote to Lady Carteret on September 4th, "is gone to sea with a noble fleet, in want of nothing but a certainty of meeting the enemy."[8]

There followed ten anxious days, while all England waited desperately lest the enemy should get back to harbour with its guarded treasures before Lord Sandwich could find them. Pepys, who knew what it had cost to set out the Fleet again, was particularly apprehensive. Then, on September 10th, while he was spending a lazy Sunday with his wife at Woolwich, there came an express with glorious tidings: that Lord Sandwich had met with part of De Ruyter's fleet, divided and driven off its course by a storm, and captured two of the great East India ships and six or seven others—a noble prize. As though on air Pepys walked the intervening miles to Greenwich, where the Navy Office and his own temporary lodging were now established, and there supped at Captain Cocke's house in the society of Lord Brouncker and his mistress, Sir John Mennes, Sir W. Doyly and Mr John Evelyn of Sayes Court, Deptford. Never in all his life had he spent so merry an evening, for the news after the long suspense had put them all into an ecstasy of joy, particularly old Mennes, who loved to be merry, and quiet sober Mr Evelyn, who kept making up comic verses so aptly and fast that they nearly died of laughing, which, related Pepys, recalling that uproarious scene, "did so stop the mouth of Sir J. Mennes in the middle of all his mirth (and in a thing agreeing with his own manner of genius) that I never saw any man so outdone in all my life; and Sir J. Mennes's mirth too to see himself out-done was the crown of all our mirth". It was, he decided, one of the times of all his life when he was fullest of the true sense of joy.[9]

More good news followed on the 14th when a letter arrived from Solebay that the Fleet had returned with a dozen or so more prizes, including four battleships and a thousand men, taken from the storm-scattered Dutch in a further encounter. A more daring Admiral than Sandwich might perhaps have done more; flung his Fleet against De Ruyter and ended the war in an overwhelming victory. But, battling against storms on a perilous enemy coast, with rich prizes in store and his own victuals running short, he had decided that he was not justified in forcing an engagement. He accordingly sailed for his native land with his prizes intact, closing his journal of the voyage with the words *Deo Gratias*. For the moment, so far as that plague-tortured land could be grateful for anything, it was the feeling of England.[10]

To those Englishmen most concerned, however, the prizes brought trouble even greater in extent than the half million pounds of precious spices which they were worth. It was an old custom of the Navy that captured merchandise lying between decks should be divided on reaching port among the common seamen—a rule easy enough to understand in days when a poor man had no postal address and disappeared from official ken as soon as he was paid off. But the officers had to await the official award of the Royal Commission for Prizes. Knowing the financial difficulties of the Restoration government and the notorious good nature of its Prince, and perhaps envious at the unseemly scramble which according to wont was already going on between the decks of the captured Indiamen, the commanders of the victorious Fleet decided to take a short cut to their reward. At a Council of flag-officers held in Lord Sandwich's cabin on the voyage to England, it was decided to resort to an immediate share-out. Penn, the Vice-Admiral, was particularly insistent on the advisability of this course, and the majority of the Council supported him. Sandwich carelessly, and perhaps not unmindful of his own debts, acquiesced. The King's allowance, he had no doubt, would follow when asked for. It was, as he afterwards told Pepys, so much easier to keep money when once got of the King than to get it when it was too late. But such a course as he now adopted was too easy even for the government of a monarch who confessedly liked to be easy and see everyone about him so.[11]

As soon as the ships anchored off the Buoy of the Nore, the Admirals, following the example of the common seamen, began to help themselves. It was a disgraceful scene. Between decks the sailors had finished their plunder, and soon the taverns along the riverside were filled with poor wretches offering bags of cloves and nutmegs at prices which would make any grocer's mouth water. In the holds their superiors now thrust more capacious hands, tossing and tumbling and spoiling all things in their haste to come at the finer goods. Sandwich and Penn both annexed plunder to the value of £4000, the other Admirals of about £2000 each. One or two, including Sir George Ayscue and stout Christopher Myngs, stood out, refusing to touch a pennyworth of wealth so irregularly distributed, but the rest had no such qualms. Then, on September 21st, the two great Indiamen were dispatched with the remainder, and greater, part of their treasure to Erith to be dealt with as the Prize Commissioners and Officers of the Customs saw fit.[12]

It was not long before Samuel Pepys appeared on the scene of all this wealth. Four days after the ships berthed he came to a resolve to go down to the Nore. With Lord Brouncker and the merchant Captain Cocke as his companions he at once embarked on the *Bezan* yacht. After sailing merrily all night, they came at dawn within sight of the Fleet—"a very fine thing to behold, being above 100 ships, great and small, with the flag-ships of each squadron, distinguished by their several flags of their main, fore or mizen masts". When they went aboard the *Prince*, Lord Sandwich was still in his night-gown; however he received them kindly, telling them at some length how ill-provisioned the Fleet was and how there was not a drop of beer left. After that the visitors nosed about the ship for themselves. Before they departed again in the evening Pepys had borrowed £500 from Will Howe, the Admiral's Deputy Treasurer, in order to buy in partnership with Captain Cocke £1000 worth of mace, nutmegs, cinnamon and cloves from Sir Roger Cuttance, the captain. It would prove, he was assured, a most profitable business.

The voyage home was less prosperous. For one thing, no sooner had Pepys got aboard the yacht, overjoyed with the good work he had done that day, than he was overcome with sea-sickness and "began to spue soundly and so continued" till the vessel reached the calm of the Medway. For another, when they came to Greenwich next morning, it was found that Captain Cocke's boy had retired to his bed with a headache—"a bad sign it seems". The alarm proved a false one, but it was a nasty shock. That week the plague deaths in London reached the record figure of over 7000.

For the first few days after his new purchase, Pepys' chief anxiety was lest he should be cheated by his partner. Indeed, when Lord Sandwich landed on September 22nd, he stole a march on Cocke by cautioning the Admiral against him and persuading that easy-going nobleman to sell him direct another £1000 worth or so of goods. Then with Cocke to accompany him he again went down the river to the Fleet to make further bargains to the extent of several thousands with Cuttance and Penn. By the 27th Cocke was offering him £500 for his share of the profit, and Pepys was standing out for £600.

On Sunday, October 1st, Pepys made a further step down to the Fleet and got Lord Sandwich to give him a warrant to remove all the goods which he and Cocke had purchased with full power to dispose of them as they pleased after paying the customs. Moreover, he obtained his Lord's assurance that the King fully approved of his action in breaking bulk, for he had been growing a little uneasy. So relieved was he that returning in the yacht that night he was not in the least put out by the snoring of his companions in the crowded cabin: "but Lord!" he recalled, "the mirth which it caused to me to be waked in the night by their snoring round about me: I did laugh till I was ready to burst".

Yet next day Pepys was made aware that all was not well. Visiting Lord Brouncker and Sir John Mennes on board the captured East Indiaman at Erith where in the holds the greatest wealth lay in confusion—pepper scattered through every chink, cloves and nutmegs up to the knees, silk in bales and boxes of copper—he found them full of envious complaints about the pillaging of the ships, and, though he did his best to pacify them with a little tactful talk about the honest money that might be made by these goods, he was left with an uneasy feeling. Two days later the good news that the plague had decreased was overclouded by a rumour that Captain Cocke's goods had been seized by the King's officers. Even in decimated London there were far too many people talking about the disposition of the prizes for Samuel to feel comfortable.

Then the clamour began. On October 7th, after a hard worrying day at the Office, Pepys spent a busy evening housing two waggon-loads of prize goods which had just arrived at Greenwich from Rochester. While he was so engaged, two officers from the Customs House appeared and demanded the goods. Pepys showed them his *Transire*, but they refused to accept it and, after some hot and angry words, the incident closed with their locking up the goods and giving the parish constable the key. Two days later with great difficulty Pepys got his belongings freed, only to have them at once seized again by another official. Next day worse followed when four more waggon-loads were arrested opposite Greenwich church in front of a large crowd. That same evening Pepys heard disquieting tales of what was going on at the Court at Oxford; how Myngs and Ayscue had complained of the conduct of their fellow commanders and how the King and the Duke of York had disavowed Lord Sandwich's action. He wrote at once to the latter to tell him; "I pray God", he added, "there be no foule meaning towards your Lordshipp in it".

A visit to the ships at Erith in the morning showed how much there was. Here was Mr Seymour, one of the Commissioners for Prizes, "mighty high" and declaring that all the purchased goods must be forfeited: Pepys in the heat of the moment took him up shortly, only to regret it a moment later lest it might show how much he was involved—a circumstance about which he was now keeping as quiet as possible. Soon he learnt more: that royal orders had been given to examine most severely into the destination of all goods taken from the ships, that twenty warrants were out for their seizure with penalties against all who should sell them and that all Captain Cocke's goods were detained.[13]

All this had happened at a moment as inopportune as any that could have been imagined. Even before the grip of the plague had tightened, the position of the naval administration for lack of money had been serious. In June Pepys had had to suppress a strike among the unpaid dockyard hands at Woolwich; at Portsmouth at the same time the ropemakers had discharged themselves for want of money and tramped into the fields to make hay, and this in the midst of a great naval war. But since the spread of the plague the situation had become infinitely worse; the trade of the whole kingdom was paralysed and the taxes had dwindled into nothingness; there was no one to advance any cash and no Parliament to vote any. By September the only business left to discuss at the Navy Board was the want of money. The sick and wounded lay in the streets unfed and untended (the kind-hearted Clerk of the Acts gave the poor wretches good words and a little money as he passed by) and the Office at Greenwich was assailed all day by the "horrible crowd and lamentable moan of the poor seamen that lie starving...for lack of money". When Pepys, perplexed to the heart to see them, went out he was followed by a hundred of them, cursing, swearing and praying: Batten, less fortunate, had his cloak torn from his back while his black servant, Mingo, and Marlow, the Office messenger, were beaten in the open street. "The whole company of the *Breda*", wrote the Clerk of the Acts to Coventry, "are now breaking the windows of our office...swearing they will not budge without money. What meat they'll make of me anon, you shall hear by my next."[14]

The dockyards were in the same plight—dock and rope men both revolted, declaring they would not work an hour longer without money, and not a wheel or a hammer going in all the three Thames yards. The stores were empty, prices were soaring,* and contractors everywhere refusing to supply commodities. The charge of the Navy since the beginning of the summer, Pepys reckoned, had been over a million and there was no sign of any money coming in. The one hope of King and nation were the captured prizes, and when stories of the great wealth that had been plundered from them got abroad, the fury of the people was boundless.[15]

At this moment, news arrived that the Dutch Fleet had put to sea. On October 7th Pepys heard that it was off Solebay, eighty strong. Next day, he received urgent orders from Albemarle to get out the warships lying in the river, but, when he sent for their captains, he found that of twenty vessels only seven had men or victuals enough to sail. Everywhere the tale was the same: the ships were leaky, unvictualled and unrepaired. Old Albemarle blustered and fumed, laid the blame on Sandwich, whom he disliked and who had

* Hemp that had been £41 a ton before the war was now selling at £55, tar that was £10 a last was now £14. 10*s*., and masts had risen 33 per cent. above their former value. Pepys to Sir Philip Warwick, Oct. 8th, 1665; Tanner, *Further Correspondence*, p. 59.

gone to plead his case before the King at Oxford, and swore in his absence to go to sea himself. But it all ended in nothing, as Pepys had foreseen it must; it would only, he wrote to Sandwich, "have discovered too much of our nakedness, for, after all, a Fleet could not have been got out nor kept out".[16]

The popular clamour against Sandwich now became greater than ever. Men said that he had deliberately refrained from crushing the Dutch Fleet in September in order that he might bring home his prizes and plunder them; now, they cried in derision, he had fled to Oxford, leaving the enemy in possession of the seas. Happily bad weather intervened on the side of England, and the Dutch, who had been boasting that their foes were brought so low by the plague that a man might run them down with his finger, retired to their own harbours.[17]

But Sandwich must down. Maddened by the long agony of the plague—that October, though the Bills of Mortality were steadily decreasing, the sick walked the streets with open sores and poor people sat plastered and muffled up at every fourth or fifth door along Kent Street—the nation had resolved on a scapegoat. When Parliament met at Oxford, a bill was brought in to make it a felony to break bulk, and someone spoke of voting a great sum to the Duke of York, £10,000 to Prince Rupert and half a crown to Lord Sandwich. Pepys trembled for his poor patron. His enemies rejoiced at his imminent fall, and these included Coventry and the Duke of York, who as Lord High Admiral had furiously resented his high-handed action over the prizes.[18]

Sandwich was saved by the King, who remembering his many services gave him a pardon, allowed him to retain the profits of his prizes (which had he but waited would have been his legal due) and, to cover the shame of his resignation from the command of the Fleet, appointed him Ambassador

Extraordinary to Spain. But before all this had happened, and while his patron's downfall seemed certain, Pepys had hastily and as best he could covered up his traces. It was the easier for him to do so owing to the high repute in which he stood for his constancy to his duty during the plague; when his superiors were daily expecting to hear of his death they were scarcely likely to blame him for corruption. On November 13th while the going was still good—for Cocke, through his help, had managed to regain possession of the purchased goods—he got his partner to agree to buy him out, lock, stock and barrel, for £500 profit. The transaction gave him "extraordinary inward joy", as well it might, for on an outlay of some £1800 he had gained over 20 per cent. on his money. By the end of the year he seemed, thanks to his superior speed and adroitness, to have cleared himself of the whole business, and could that Twelfth Night with a light heart slip a clove, the mark of the Knave, into Captain Cocke's share of the cake, "which made some mirth because of his lately being known by his buying of clove and mace of the East India prizes". It was a good jest.[19]

Indeed Pepys had reason to smile as 1665 drew to a close. For, despite all the distractions of the year, war, plague, national poverty, he had thriven mightily. In December alone his wealth had increased by over £1000—£500 through the settlement of his prize accounts with Cocke and £500 through an unexpected gift from Mr Gauden, the Victualler, for whom he procured the payment of £4000 due on account of victuals for the Tangier garrison. At the end of each month, as he made up his balance, he returned his delighted yet pious thanks: "the great God of Heaven and Earth be praised". He had stayed at his post in London, faced the pestilence and monopolised all business. And in six months he had increased his worldly wealth from £1450 to over

£4400. If anything could clearly demonstrate the miraculous goodness of God it was this.[20]

There were also other marks of His goodness. With the coming of the cold weather at midwinter, the great world began to flow back to London, wheels rolled on the grass-grown streets, the 'Change was once more crowded, "But Lord! what a staring to see a nobleman's coach come to town", wrote the recording mortal, rejoicing in it all. "And porters everywhere bow to us, and such begging of beggars! And a delightful thing it is to see the town full of people again." The Pepyses returned to London and saw their old friends. There were a few missing, of course, like Aunt Bell, who, poor soul, had perished in the pestilence. But most of Samuel's relations had been well enough off to escape: it was to such as them that Mr Mills, returning to his stricken parish after six months' absence, preached his sermon of excuse for being the first to leave and the last to return—"very poor and short", as the Clerk of the Acts, who had taken especial care to attend to hear what he had to say, reported. And it was to such as Pepys that the King on his return to the capital paid honour. "Mr Pepys", he said, "I do give you thanks for your good service all this year, and I assure you I am very sensible of it."

Nor was it a small service. At the height of the plague, when the Office was surrounded by clamorous seamen and the universal bankruptcy of rule and purse had driven his colleagues to despair, Pepys had made it his business to define and attack one of the principal causes of the Navy's troubles. Three times that year when victory had seemed within England's grasp the Fleet had been forced to return to harbour through shortage of provisions. The want of victuals at sea even more than the want of money on land had been the bane of the summer's campaign.[21]

As early as August Pepys had summoned Mr Lewes, Dennis Gauden's chief clerk, before the Navy Board to give an account of this failure. The latter denied that his master had been guilty of any shortage in delivery and offered to produce the Purser's receipts for every ship to show that the full amount had been served in. And, on the whole, well-informed contemporary opinion supported him. According to the commercial lights of his day, Gauden was an honest man, and though, like everyone else, he was cheated by his agents, there were few complaints against the quality of his provisions. His failure lay in the fact that he was quite unable to supply the required quantity. It was, in fact, beyond the scope of any one man to do so, especially at a time when the State depended for its supplies on the credit of its contractors. Before the war Gauden's had been good enough to victual a peace-time establishment of 3000 men, but it was insufficient to provide for one of twelve times that number; in fact, as he himself put it, he was not "in a capacity unless supplied with money to make the provision necessary"; it was "too much for any man's purse".[22]

All this Pepys reported to his superiors in a long letter addressed to Carteret and written on the day after his interview with Lewes. (It was August 25th and the plague lay heavy on the little streets around Seething Lane, where the Clerk of the Acts all alone was writing.) In tabulated form he showed how far the provisions on board the Fleet had fallen short of Gauden's estimate of a month before.* Pease,

* Gauden's original estimate, dated July 26th, 1665, is among the Rawlinson MSS. in the Bodleian Library (*Rawlinson MSS. A.* 174, f. 231); Pepys' letter to Carteret of August 25th is printed on pp. 51–3 of Dr Tanner's *Further Correspondence of Samuel Pepys*. A study of the two shows how accurate and honest Pepys was in his official statements and how great was his genius for summarising a document.

fish, butter and cheese which Gauden had assured him would feed the men till the end of the first week of October would, by Lord Sandwich's present computation, expire in the middle of September, while beef, pork, biscuits and beer had already given out. Though further provisions were being shipped at once, the same evils would undoubtedly recur unless immediate steps were taken to alter the victualling system. "Were I to advise", he wrote, "some vigorous person (qualified as I think I could name one) should tonight before tomorrow be put upon visiting all the Victualler's stores and contracts relating to each victualling-port in England, by which the King should... thoroughly know his strength once in three weeks or a month, whereas now the honour and wealth of King and kingdom depend without cheque upon the understanding, credit, diligence, integrity and health of one man, whose failure in any of these five circumstances inevitably overthrows all." He meant nothing against Gauden, he added, who had done all he could. But it was not an individual's profit or reputation that was at stake but the safety of the whole kingdom. For Pepys had firmly grasped the truth that, if a soldier marches on his stomach, a sailor swims on his. Without attention to this particular, no Fleet could remain at sea and no crew be true to its duty. Long after, in stately language, he enshrined this material truth (so patent to a fenman) in his Naval Minutes: "Englishmen, and more especially seamen, love their bellies above anything else, and therefore it must always be remembered in the management of the victualling of the Navy that to make any abatement from them in the quantity or agreeableness of the victuals is to discourage and provoke them in the tenderest point, and will sooner render them disgusted with the King's service than any one other hardship that can be put upon them".[23]

Various remedies were now put forward, and it was left to Pepys as the man on the spot to deal with them. The Duke of York's proposal was that several other merchants should be asked to join with Gauden. But this was easier said than done. For, as Gauden had found from experience, the victualling of the Fleet was attended by too many risks and uncertainties for anyone to be anxious to undertake it. Pepys, in obedience to his instructions, tried to induce four of the biggest merchants in the country, Josiah Child, Sir William Rider, Sir John Bankes and Thomas Beckford, to join the Victualler and all refused: the risk was too great. Moreover, before there was any possibility of getting anyone to enter into partnership with Gauden, it would be necessary to make a thorough inventory of all his goods, and this would take time.[24]

Another suggestion was to put the whole victualling business into the hands of a Royal Commission, as had been done during the first Dutch war. But here also were difficulties. Where, Pepys asked, were four or five men of the necessary experience, "joined with integrity, diligence and activity", to be found? And even if they were found, what certainty would there be that they would manage things any better than Gauden was doing by himself? During the last year, he wrote to Albemarle, who was in favour of a Commission, Gauden had declared for almost 39,000 mens' victuals, "and therein a greater work hath been performed by him alone than ever was done in the last Holland's war when managed by a joint-partnership of half a score the ablest and aptest men of that time, and with less complaint as to the quality of his provisions and (which is more) with a greater credit by him given to the Crown than is to be expected from any body of Commissioners, and many degrees greater than was ever given by the former contractors,

Mr Gauden declaring under his hand that of £474,000 due to him from his Majesty for his...victualling...in the last year's action, he is at this day unpaid by £125,000". It was all true enough, though one cannot quite rid the mind of the uneasy recollection that two months after writing this letter Pepys received a present of £500 from Gauden.[25]

Perhaps he protested a little too much. But he had an attractive plan of his own, and one which he now brought forward. "My proposition is", he continued, "that a person should be established at every victualling-port, on behalf and at the charge of his Majesty, as a Surveyor of the Victualler's action in that port,...obliged to give a true account hereof weekly to some one or more officer...to that purpose provided by the King at London, who, upon comparing all these with the state and stations of the Fleet, may be ever furnished to answer any questions touching the sufficiency or defect, disorder or any other circumstances relating to the Victualler or his stores." What did it matter if secretly Pepys meant, as he confided to his Diary, to do himself "a job of work in it"? If he was doing himself a service, he was doing England a far greater.[26]

All this was written so clearly, so reasonably and convincingly and withal with such force and sincerity, that no one was prepared to oppose it. A week later it was read before the King and his Cabinet at Oxford and entirely approved—"with complete applause and satisfaction", as Pepys put it. Then, being asked to name persons suitable for employment as Surveyors at the ports, he wrote again to Albemarle to suggest that the salaries which it was proposed to allow them should be first named, to prevent, he explained, "the upbringing of the salary to the person" or, as Mr Chappell the first transcriber of this invaluable letter suggests, to make quite sure that the "job of work" which he had in mind was going to be worth his while. The Surveyors at Dover, Plymouth and Yarmouth should get £100 a year, he thought, those at Harwich and Portsmouth £150, and at London £200, "and". he added carefully, "he that shall receive the weekly accounts from all these and keep a constant and general check over the whole victualling action—£300". The ground thus carefully prepared, he wrote to Coventry to offer himself as Surveyor-General. "The truth is", he modestly explained, "I know one, that if you shall think fitt to have it propounded to I dare go farr in assuring you that the work shall be done to your minde, for I am sure he will take paines at it, and (which is more) will by his other occasions be ever at hand, both for the ready receiving as well as giving directions and answers in all matters relating to his business. His emploiement in another capacity I confess is very full, but halfe the trouble which this will adde will be saved by the ease it will bring him in the many letters, orders, messages, and mental labours he is now exercised with, for want of an easy and thorough understanding of the victualling action, and the first letter of this man's name is S. Pepys. And now, Sir," he added, "as I cannot say but I have an eye to the reward, and would be glad honestly to get more than I do by increasing my pains, while God Almighty gives me health to do it...." The letter had the desired result. On October 27th, 1665, Samuel Pepys was offered the appointment of Surveyor-General of Victualling for His Majesty's Navy at an additional salary of £300 a year.[27]

Scarcely less admirable, though unhappily far less useful in its results, was Pepys' statement of the plight of the Navy for lack of money. Being commanded in October to give an estimate of the year's charges, he had done so with great thoroughness under the various heads of wages, victuals, ship-building, wear and tear, dockyards, wounded and prisoners. He took particular pains to show how the increased cost of the Fleet, which was over a million since the spring, was due to the enhanced price of commodities and that in its turn to the delay and uncertainty in payments. In October came the news that Parliament, suitably impressed by these laboriously garnered figures, had voted a further million and a quarter for the war, to be paid at the rate of £50,000 a month. But it was one thing to vote money, another in the existing state of the nation to raise it, and for the moment the Navy Office remained penniless and without credit. The full realisation of these things came on October 26th, when the two Navy slopsellers frankly declared their inability to provide the seamen with clothes for the coming year unless their debts for the past two and a half years, amounting to over 50 per cent. of the value of clothing supplied, were met. "As for the slops", Pepys wrote to Coventry, "I...do with all my heart grieve for the seamen that want them, but reflecting upon men that have trusted the King with above £16,000,...I know not how to blame their not trusting us. Were there not other considerations", he added, "more ominous than the increase of enemies or the dread of the continuance of God Almighty's displeasure, I should go on in my little matters with good cheer. But evils there are which, if not remedied,... will ruin us had we but half the present enemy."[28]

For Pepys was beginning to see the haunting horror that was to dog his country until the inevitable end came: that without money the Navy could not be kept at sea. Talking that November with Carteret, he frankly stated his belief that it would be impossible for the King to set out a Fleet next year and that all must come to ruin, and Carteret agreed. In the middle of a national calamity and a deep trade depression, England found herself committed to the most elaborate and expensive naval war which the world had yet seen, and with no other financial machinery for meeting its costs than the antiquated system of parliamentary aids and subsidies which she had inherited from the middle ages. It has been reckoned that the Dutch, with their more modern commercial apparatus, expended over twice as much on the sea war of 1664–7 as the English government.

Most of this, of course, was hidden from Pepys and his fellow officials at the time. They only knew that money was wanting and that the Navy must be ruined unless it was found. William Coventry, the most able of them all save Pepys himself, proposed as a remedy an elaborate and doctrinaire scheme for paying bills in course, placing each debt as it accrued in strict order of seniority on a rota which should be open to public inspection—a system which, as Pepys very carefully and tenderly pointed out, might have saved a great deal of trouble if applied four years back but would now be entirely useless when bills were accumulating at the rate of £23,000 a week and the unpaid debt of the Navy ran into several hundred thousands of pounds. What was needed at the moment was some method of persuading merchants to extend their credit, so that the Fleet could be sent to sea next year. Nor was it very easy to see how this could be done, since the scarcity of money was so universal that the whole credit of the kingdom had fallen into the hands of two or three great bankers; the East India Company itself was only able to advance a paltry £26,000 to the government on the security of the Dutch prizes by dint of borrowing £18,000 at exorbitant rates from Messrs Backwell and Viner. "So long as we and the world", Pepys mournfully concluded, "must be subjected to these bankers, I do despair of compassing it."[29]

Partial salvation came through an ingenious makeshift of

Sir George Downing's for raising goods on credit by the simple device of apportioning all the supply voted by the new Act of Parliament to the payment of capital and interest on the value of any money or merchandise that should be supplied to the government on the strength of that Act. The expedient did not commend itself either to the Treasury, which regarded it as an invasion of its prerogative, or to the bankers who felt that they were being short-circuited. Nor was it of course viewed favourably by the existing creditors of the government, who were thus debarred from obtaining any of the new £1,250,000 for the payment of their existing debts. But for a time it worked, because, as soon as these creditors saw that their only chance of getting any ready money at all was by serving in goods on the security of the new Act, the flow of necessary commodities to the Navy began again, and by the spring of 1666 over £800,000 in goods and money had been advanced.

It was Pepys who more than anyone else first persuaded the angry and distrustful creditors of the Navy Office to lend on the security of the Act. At first he himself had opposed it: how, he asked Coventry, could anyone be persuaded to lend to the government at 6 per cent. who had to pay the bankers 8 or 9 per cent. for cash with which to buy the needed goods? But a long talk with his old master, Sir George Downing, helped to convince him that the scheme had possibilities. Downing, by flattering him and appealing to his patriotism, succeeded in persuading him much against his will to try to obtain goods on the security of the Act; "But when", wrote poor Pepys, "he came to impose upon me that without more ado I must get by my credit people to serve in goods and lend money upon it and none could do it better than I, and the King should give me thanks particularly in it, and I could not get him to excuse me but I must come to him though to no purpose on Saturday, and that he is sure I will bring him some bargains or other made upon this Act, it vexed me more than all the pleasure I took before". None the less Downing was right, and when Saturday came Pepys, put upon his mettle, announced that he had got Sir William Warren to promise the government two shiploads of badly needed Norway goods to the value of £3600. Downing then, with matchless effrontery, asked him to lend another £200 on his own account.[30]

Through all these distressing and wearying transactions, Pepys' path was lighted by love. There was little Miss Tooker, the daughter of the house next door to his Greenwich lodgings, whom he delighted to have in with his friends of an evening to sing and dance and whom after a while he took to petting by himself—"dallying with her an hour, doing what I would with my hands about her. And a very pretty creature it is". Of more mature vintage was Mistress Judith Penington—"a very fine witty lady,...and indifferent handsome". She also took a liking to the lively little Clerk of the Acts and admitted him to several exciting freedoms, such as talking and playing by her side as she sat in her smock and petticoats by the fire in her lodgings.[31]

From these furtive delights, his work happily was quick to call him. As Surveyor-General of Victualling Pepys was now responsible for ensuring that a fleet of 35,000 was provisioned in the coming year, the greater part from London, Portsmouth and Harwich, with smaller contingents from such remote places as Plymouth, Milford, Newcastle and Kinsale. He had to overcome the Victualler's natural aversion to supplying more provisions while over a hundred thousand pounds was still owing to him—an achievement only made possible by Downing's aid and by an assignment of £200,000 on the new Act. He had to select and supervise the new

Surveyors who were to work under him in each of the ports. And finally he had to justify his own appointment by devising some plan to check the embezzlements of dishonest pursers and agents and so end the appalling wastage of victuals that went on between the shore and the ship. These tasks were anything but easy.[32]

Of all the mysteries appertaining to the Navy none was greater than that of the Purser's trade. Earlier in his career at the Navy Office, Pepys had tried to master its intricacies, but had found the method of making up Pursers' accounts almost beyond his comprehension. The ship's Purser derived his name from the Bursar of the early Christian communities, and the first Christian Bursar was Judas Iscariot. Not all the tribe inherited the failings of their great founder, but the nature of their calling made his temptations theirs. And such was the absurdity of the existing system in the Navy that, as Pepys' clerks, Hayter and Wilson, demonstrated to him, a Purser who did not cheat the King or the crews he served was bound to lose money.[33]

To this intricate business, Pepys now cheerfully applied himself, confident that after a few days he would master it and be able to propose some far-reaching plan to reform the whole system. He was soon disillusioned. Early in December he had a long discourse with Richard Gibson, a man of great experience in this side of naval administration whom he had appointed Surveyor of Victualling at Yarmouth. At the end of the interview Pepys confessed himself ashamed that he should "go about the concerning myself in a business which I understand so very, very little of and made me distrust all I had been doing today". All December he spent revising his ideas and enlarging his knowledge. He examined Commanders, Pursers, ancient Cheques and Stewards, Account Clerks, all of them very secretive about their own malpractices but ready enough to blab about those of their colleagues. By the end of the month his observations were ready for paper.[34]

Very early on the morning of January 1st, 1666, Pepys rose and began to dictate to Tooker, the Office messenger, the great report on "Pursery" which he proposed to give to Sir William Coventry as a New Year's present. He began to do so at five a.m. and ended, without stopping for food or drink, at three in the afternoon. Clearly, and at great though never unnecessary length, he put before Coventry the reasons why it would be perilous in the middle of a war to inaugurate any entirely new system and discussed the respective merits and defects of the three methods hitherto employed in the Navy. That then used, by which every ship's Purser was bound by bond, compelled to give security for his accountableness and controlled by the captains and muster-masters, he condemned without mercy, "in that it supposes a work to be done upon terms demonstrably to the prejudice of the doer". Under such a system, he showed, the Purser could only make a livelihood by professed cheating, either by embezzling provisions and using "all the artifices he can...to find ways of charging the defects of provisions upon the King", or by making a tacit agreement with the Captain to connive at his own fraudulent practices in return for the Captain's allowing his. "Hence", wrote the wise Surveyor-General, "comes an extra provision of great candles, white biscuit, Cheshire cheese (and it may be Parmesan), butter, strong beer, wine, poultry, fresh meat, and what not, for the Captain's table....Hence it is the Purser is obliged to concur with the Captain in the over-ratings of his servants, in his admission of unable persons to serve His Majesty upon terms of half pay. Hence it is so many supernumeraries are crowded upon the ship; so many runaways continued upon the books." He himself, though "no worshipper of the old say-saws of the Navy", much preferred the ancient system which had been abandoned at the time of the Civil War, by which a Purser, though subject to check in respect of pay, was put under no other obligations in respect of victuals beyond that of maintaining the ship at its full complement of men during the time for which it was victualled; if the supplies gave out first, the cost of making good the deficiencies would then fall on his shoulders and not on the King's; and, since anything that he could save would be to his own profit, he would have every incentive for making them last as long as possible. By this means, Pepys argued, the continuance of the ship abroad would become the Purser's profit, and fleets would no longer prematurely return to harbour with the excuse that their victuals were exhausted. Nor would the Purser be any longer under a "servile necessity" to conspire with the ship's commander to cheat the Crown, "for he will naturally reckon all unuseful men entertained for the Captain's profit burdensome to him in consuming his victuals, as much as indeed they are to the King in taking up wages". In short, as Pepys said, "my work is likeliest to be best done by him whose profit is increased by the well doing of it without increase of charge to me that employs him". The strong tenacity to actual fact and proved experience (based always on the common manifestations of human nature and never on abstract doctrine), so typical of the Englishman, underlies every line of this great memorandum.[35]

It is an illumination of humanity's wonderful diversity that the man who wrote it should, as soon as his task was done, seek the company of Lord Brouncker and his mistress to find there the refreshment he needed—the society of a certain enchanting little actress of the name of Knepp, to laugh with her and hear her sing her little Scotch song of "Barbary Allen". And when, most reluctantly, he had torn himself away to return to the Office, he must needs, when the merry crew came out of Brouncker's lodgings, clamber into the crowded coach in which Mrs Knepp was departing and there get her upon his knee and play with her till he had perforce to set her down at the door of that sulky fellow, her husband the jockey. The good company of that winter had brought his old love of music back with a rush; and inspired by Knepp's roguish, sweet face and the society of musical friends, he had set some lines from the play, *The Siege of Rhodes*, to music to make his song of "Beauty Retire". He taught Knepp to sing it, which the baggage did most rarely—"and a very fine song it seems to be", he decided. She wrote him little notes under the name of "Barbary Allen", and he replied, signing himself "Dapper Dicky".[36]

But for most of the hours of the day this selfsame Dapper Dicky was the little man who sat busily at his desk in Seething Lane getting out his Majesty's Fleet against the summer of 1666. All February and March he was engaged in stating the debts of the Navy so that money might be wrung from the Treasury to pay them and credit enough be found to supply the Service's clamorous needs. At times even he grew despondent, as after one troubled meeting at the Lord Treasurer's where it was shown that the certain debt and charges of the Navy were £2,300,000 with an expectancy of only £1,500,000 to meet them: not the sight of the Queen sitting at cards among her ladies could cheer Pepys after that. Everything went awry through this lack of money—even good Mr Evelyn's ingenious and benevolent plan to establish a Naval Hospital, which would ultimately, its author claimed, save the King £4817 a year at an initial outlay of £1400. And "yet", as Pepys sternly put it, "the work must be done". France, fearing from England's victories of the previous summer that she was like to establish a naval dictatorship, had joined her enemies, and the Danes seemed like to follow suit. It looked as though in the coming year the Fleet would not only have to fight the Dutch but protect English shores from invasion.[37]

Meanwhile Pepys pressed forward his plans for reforming the Purser's trade and waxed indignant at the delays caused by the supineness of those in high place. "Is it that the frauds practicable in the expense of £425,800...are not worthy our preventing?" he asked Coventry. "I cannot dissemble my sense of this neglect of ours, for upon my word it wrings me hard to observe what a dust our penny wisdom will raise now and then, while we can permit the King to suffer our pound follies to the hazarding of the whole service." His was the language which great administrators have used in all ages. And to his own erring subordinates he wrote stern and bracing letters: "I will not dissemble with you because I love you", he told his friend Deane, who had been getting himself into trouble at Harwich. "But upon my word, I have not spared to tell the Board my opinion about this business, as you will shortly see."[38]

At other times, like a dog, he returned to his vomit. One day, hearing that Mrs Martin was back in town, he loitered about Westminster Hall till she appeared, subsequently accompanying her to her lodgings where, he cryptically tells us, "I did what I tenais a mind pour ferais con her". Afterwards she asked him to lend her five pounds, which, as soon as he had secured it with an adequate pawn, he obligingly supplied. But a week later when he repeated his enjoyment, he observed that the woman had grown to be very bad and that it was positively dangerous to have anything to do with her. For such perilous delights it was safer to substitute a jaunt to the cake-house in Hyde Park with the beauties, Pierce and Knepp, or an evening of sweet merry singing with the latter, since "music and women I cannot but give way to, whatever my business is". And though he deplored his frailty, he could not think it very heinous provided always that he did not cause scandal or allow it to interrupt his labours—"knowing", he said, "that this is the proper age of my life to do it, and out of my observation that most men that do thrive in the world do forget to take pleasure during the time that they are getting their estate, but reserve that till they have got one and then it is too late for them to enjoy it".[39]

Yet when he felt his pulse for pleasure beat too high and saw his work threatened, he set his will against his erring heart and conquered it. "But Lord!" he wrote, "what a conflict I had with myself, my heart tempting me a thousand times to go abroad about some pleasure or other, notwithstanding the weather foul. However I reproached myself with my weakness in yielding so much my judgment to my sense, and prevailed with difficulty and did not budge, but stayed within and to my great content did a great deal of business." Even Mercer and his wife were now set to work ruling paper for the office to earn pin-money, "which makes them work mighty hard". And as the summer approached and the rival fleets prepared to put to sea, he spent his time setting all things to rights—getting his long-delayed Pursers' plan put into execution, making his report to Coventry (after a lengthy internal struggle and great pains) on the state of the victualling and writing yet another solemn letter—to the Duke of York this time—on the want of money, stressing "the excessive rates we are forced to give for everything the service wants, the merchant resolving to save himself in the uncertainty of his payment by the greatness of his price". Nor, when he could be spared from his desk, did he fail to take boat and so to his proper place "by water among the ships".[40]

As in the previous year, the early days of June, 1666, saw all England awaiting the event of a battle at sea. Sandwich had departed some months before as Ambassador to Spain—Pepys spending a very honourable, though, owing to a house party of young people pillow-fighting, a somewhat disturbed week-end at Carteret's woodland pleasance at Cranborne to bid him farewell—and his command of the Fleet had been taken by the Duke of Albemarle and Prince Rupert. The change marked a departure in policy; henceforward the "tarpaulins"—the old rough Commonwealth captains who had been bred to the sea—were to be superseded wherever possible by new men—gentlemen trained to military virtues, whose ardent and fighting spirit, it was held, would compensate for their ignorance of navigation. At the moment this revolution in policy was hailed with joy: later, when experience had proved its error, it became part of Pepys' life-work to reverse it.[41]

The first augury of the new joint-command was not happy. A French fleet was expected in the Channel and an invasion was feared, and it was resolved at Whitehall to detach Rupert with twenty ships from the main fleet to watch the "Monsieurs". The mistake, though in part directed by necessity, was swiftly punished. On June 1st the Dutch under De Ruyter, ninety sail strong, anchored in the Straits of Dover. Despite his inferiority of numbers, old Albemarle, who had beaten them a dozen years before and despised them heartily, at once, and to their intense surprise, attacked them.

This event, in Pepys' graphic phrase, put the Navy Board into a toss. Desperate messages had already been sent off to Portsmouth to recall Rupert; and on June 2nd all repaired to Greenwich to hear the guns. Various rumours, true and false, came from the coast to London—how Rupert had been sighted off Dover seeking the enemy, how three great Dutch ships had been seen in flames, and how Sir John Harman in the *Henry* (with Balty St Michel, whom Pepys had recently sent aboard as Muster Master) had been surrounded by a Dutch squadron and had only extricated himself by incredible gallantry.

On Monday, June 4th—that morning the waiting crowds in the Gravel Pits beyond the Park could plainly hear the guns—the first fugitives arrived from the Fleet. Pepys had just got home to dinner when he was informed that two seamen were waiting below: on going down, he found them to be Lieutenant Daniel (whose wife's lips he had already tasted at the Office) and a wounded comrade, fresh from Harwich where they had been landed the previous night—"his face as black as the chimney and covered with dirt, pitch, and tar and powder, and muffled with dirty clouts, and his right eye stopped with okum". In great excitement Pepys took coach with them to Whitehall—all London gaping to see them—and, leaving them in Coventry's lodgings, hurried out into the Park to find the King. There he was able to tell him that Rupert had joined with Albemarle; Charles was so delighted that he took Pepys' hand as he talked and later poured out the contents of his pockets into the palms of the wounded sailors.

Two days later came further news—alas! false. For some hours all the bells of London rang for a great victory—half the Dutch fleet destroyed and the rest in flight—and Pepys, who passed the joyful story about St Botolph's Church, was almost beside himself with relief and delight, though, he added, "that which pleased me as much as the news was to have the fair Mrs Middleton at our church, who indeed is a very beautiful lady". That night he supervised his neighbours as they let off fireworks at the Navy Office gate, taking great pains to persuade the womenfolk to fire serpents and taking the thick with the thin—the pretty, sprightly, dark Miss Tite and the "long red-nosed silly jade", her sister. But next day the sad truth followed: that after a four days' battle "we are beaten, lost many ships and good commanders; have not taken one ship of the enemy's, nor is it certain that we were left masters of the field": not even little Miss Tooker's unresisting company all that afternoon in his chamber could recover Pepys' spirits. Old Albemarle, for all his stolid courage, had half-shattered England's fleet, losing twenty ships and 8000 men, in his attempt to show the superior virtues of military courage.[42]

England was deeply mortified by the news and as much cast down as it had formerly been elated, for the later official reports, Englishwise, failed to emphasise the very severe losses suffered by the Dutch in their victory. Everyone fell to blaming the government and the commanders. Pepys, catching at every wisp of naval gossip, recorded it all in his faithful journal. How the seamen condemned every part of the Duke's manner of fighting, his first rash attack, his clumsy tactics, his running his ships aground; how the hero of the hour, the wounded Harman, had advised against the engagement; how the Dutch exulted, carrying a captured English Admiral up and down their streets in triumph; how men declared (and this was balm in Gilead to Pepys) that, had Sandwich been in command, things would have been otherwise. Perhaps the most illuminating discourse of all came from Penn, who being a "mere tarpaulin", had been banished from the Fleet by the military chiefs. "The whole conduct of the late fight", he said, "was ill", two-thirds of the captains had been dead against the fight (which might easily have been delayed till Rupert's arrival), but dared not say so for fear of being called cowards. And he was particularly insistent on the lessons of the disaster; that the commanders must fight in line, instead of promiscuously, that they must not desert ships in distress and that individual vessels must not return to port to refit in the midst of battle. Pepys, who a few weeks before had been complaining that "the falseness and impertinences of Sir William Penn would make a man mad to think of", was much impressed; dimly he had the justice to realise, for all his jealousy and hatred of him, that his colleague was a great seaman.

Meanwhile the Dutch were left masters of the sea. Then was seen for a while how great England can be in adversity. Faced by a league of hostile powers and threatened by invasion, she threw all her crippled strength into the task of getting out her Fleet again. In that service none was more forward than the Clerk of the Acts. On the very day that the news of the defeat arrived he received his orders from the Duke of York. For the next few weeks he was working early and late, writing and dictating letters, wheedling City merchants for money and credit and dispatching vessels with victuals and stores down the river to where the damaged Fleet lay. By June 26th he was writing that though the Dutch battle fleet was for certain at sea again, England would not be much behindhand. On one thing, at least, he was resolved: that no care or pains on his part should be spared. Yet even at this frantic juncture, he could spare a moment to abuse his colleagues, writing to tell Coventry how old Batten had left the Office to pay the Yard at Harwich, where there was already a Commissioner and a Paymaster: "I presume nevertheless", he added, "he means no farther than Walthamstow" (his country home).[43]

To this harried period we owe one of the greatest passages of the Diary. Among the chief problems of the Navy Office in getting out the Fleet was the want of men: many of the unpaid seamen, recruited from the roughest elements in the population, were deserting; one traveller described how he had overtaken four or five hundred of them tramping up the London road. The press-gang was kept so busy that the streets were empty of all but women, and the very messengers from the Office were seized as they went about their business —"a great tyranny", the kind-hearted Clerk of the Acts thought it, as he saw poor patient labourers and householders torn from their weeping families and thrown into jail. Yet there were others who were willing enough to be gone. Among such Pepys now made a strange encounter—"one of the most romantic that ever I heard of in my life and could not have believed but that I did see it". It was at the funeral of gallant Admiral Myngs, mortally wounded in the battle, and now laid to rest among the humble folk from whom he had sprung. After the service, Coventry and Pepys, who had condescendingly come down to this poor parish, were about to drive off when, as the latter tells us, "about a dozen able, lusty, proper men came to the coach-side with tears in their eyes, and one of them that spoke for the rest began and says to Sir W. Coventry: 'We are here a dozen of us that have long known and loved, and served our dead commander, Sir Christopher Mings, and have now done the last office of laying him in the ground. We would be glad we had any other to offer after him, and in revenge of him. All we have is our lives; if you will please to get His Royal Highness to give us a fireship among us all, here is a dozen of us, out of all which choose you one to be commander, and the rest of us, whoever he is, will serve him; and, if possible, do that that shall show our memory of our dead commander, and our revenge'". Their listeners could hardly refrain from weeping.[44]

On July 19th Pepys heard that the Fleet had sailed, his brother-in-law Balty, miraculously preserved in the first engagement, with them. Thereafter he and his colleagues lay big with expectation of the issue of the fight which must ensue when the two navies met at the river's mouth. The first definite news arrived on the 29th—a Sunday. Pepys was in church when a messenger came up to the gallery with a letter addressed to Batten, who was at his house whither he forwarded it. "But Lord!" he wrote, "with what impatience I staid till sermon was done to know the issue of the fight, with a thousand hopes and fears and thoughts." But when service was over and he came out, the bells were ringing and all the town was full of victory. It was not, it later turned out, much of a one, but sufficient, Pepys thought for the day—"enough to give us the name of conquerors and leave us masters of the sea, but without any such great matters done as should give the Duke of Albemarle any honour at all or give him cause to rise to his former insolence".

Two weeks later, after a late and somewhat childish party at which he and his friends in their play smutted each other with candle grease and soot till they looked more like devils than decent citizens, the Clerk of the Acts was called up early by further encouraging news—a letter from Coventry telling how Robin Holmes had burnt a hundred and fifty Dutch merchantmen lying at anchor between Vlieland and the mainland and had done damage to the extent of nearly a million pounds. Yet it was the English misfortune in this war to see all their triumphs obliterated from memory by titanic calamities, and, just as the Plague the year before had overshadowed the victory of Lowestoft, so now the recollection of Holmes' bonfire was to pale into nothingness in the light of a vaster conflagration.[45]

From the contemplation of these pleasing tidings Pepys was

roused abruptly and rudely. He had recently, with some cause, congratulated himself on the success of his victualling venture; two fleets, he wrote to the Duke of York, had been provisioned, without the least delay or a single complaint from the commanders, and with victuals enough to keep the ships at sea till October, "in better condition than ever fleets were yet". Now at the latter end of August the Fleet suddenly returned to Solebay and there arrived at the Admiralty a furious letter from the Admirals to the King, "a most scurvy letter", declaring that their requests for provisions were merely met by long invoices from Mr Pepys which, they maintained, were a poor substitute for food and drink. However, after being called before the King and Council, the injured Surveyor-General was able to show that he had duly dispatched the missing victuals and that any delay was due to the fact that the fiery Admirals had altogether neglected to keep him provided either with intelligence of their movements or with any documentary account of their needs. Indeed, Pepys, had he wished, could have produced a letter dated a few days back from Prince Rupert's secretary apologising for his delay in writing and paying a high tribute to his own administrative efficiency.* So always does the wise and foreseeing man of the pen triumph over the impetuous swordsman. Coventry, as befitted his vocation, exerted himself strenuously in Pepys' defence, and the Admirals received almost as hot a broadside from the Navy Office as from De Ruyter's guns.[46]

In all other matters, indeed, Pepys that summer of 1666 stood in high repute. His credit at the Office had continued to rise, as had also his worldly wealth. He had begun the

* "You are a person so very punctual yourself that you deserve to be very punctually dealt withal." J. Hayes to Samuel Pepys, August 19th, 1666, *Rawlinson MSS. A.* 174, f. 207.

year with £4400; by the end of July his capital was nearly £6000. He had had several fortunate windfalls—£320 from Warren, another £200 from some new City friends, the Houblon brothers, and £200 from Yeabsly on the account of Tangier. He had even ventured (a little timorously) on investment: had banked £2000 with Viner during a rather nervous eight weeks, thereby earning £35 interest, and a little later reinvested it with his friend Warren in a purchase of some ships on the security of the new Act. Moreover his household goods were steadily increasing: he had had his own and his wife's portraits nobly painted by Hayls, and in August he had expended money and much busied his thoughts on furnishing a new closet for himself. No wonder, as he surveyed his fine possessions and his rising estate, that he found cause for congratulation and gratitude. "So home", he wrote, "to dinner, where I confess, reflecting upon the ease and plenty that I live in, of money, goods, servants, honour, everything, I could not but with hearty thanks to Almighty God ejaculate my thanks to Him while I was at dinner, to myself."[47]

Chapter XIV

The Master Chronicler

"And Paul's is burned, and all Cheapside." *Diary*, Sept. 4th, 1666.

On the first day of September, 1666, a Saturday, Pepys with his wife, Mercer and Sir William Penn, took the afternoon off from the Office and went to the playhouse. There they were horribly frightened to see young Killigrew and some of the wild young sparks from Court, but, by concealing themselves, they escaped detection. Then, after a merry jaunt to the cakes and meadows of Islington, the Clerk of the Acts returned home, his mind dwelling much on the thought of gilding the backs of his books in the carved and glazed presses which Sympson, the joiner, made for them that summer. His new closet, he reflected, had been set mighty clean against the morrow, when he was entertaining guests to view it for the first time, and all his worldly affairs prospered. The wind was blowing strongly from the east, after long drought.

About three o'clock on Sunday morning Pepys was called from his bed by his maids, who had sat up late setting things ready against the day's feast, with news of a fire in the City. With his unfailing curiosity, he slipped on his nightgown and went to the window to look; he judged it to be at the backside of Mark Lane and, after watching for a little while, went back to bed.

He was up again by seven, and when he looked out the

fire seemed to be further off than it was and smaller. So he went to his closet to see that everything was ready for his party. Here the little maid Jane Birch (now returned to the household) came to him to tell him that they were saying that over three hundred houses had been burnt in the night and that the fire was now raging along the steep slope of Fish Street above the Bridge.

He made himself ready and went out, walking up to the Tower, where he got Sir John Robinson's little son to take him up one of the turrets whence he could see what was taking place. Half a mile to the west lay London Bridge with its northern houses all in flames and a great fire blazing between Thames Street and the river, where a huddled infinity of timber-built, pitch-coated little houses and warehouses of oil, tallow and spirits provided fuel enough in that dry, windy weather to light all London. His heart misgave him at the sight and was full of trouble for little Betty Howlett—now married to young Michell, the bookseller's son, and living near the "Old Swan" in the very heart of those flames—and for his old sweetheart Sarah who dwelt upon the Bridge; his loves were being burnt out like wasps.

He went down and spoke to the Lieutenant of the Tower, who confirmed his worst fears: then took boat and went up through the Bridge, seeing as he passed through the steep piers the houses of his friends blazing beside the water. As he watched, unconsciously the great artist that was within him took possession of his being; and for an hour he remained as an eye-witness for posterity storing up all he saw—the scorching, untamable, giant flames, the householders crazy to remove their goods, flinging them into lighters alongside or into the very river itself, the "poor people staying in their houses as long as till the very fire touched them and then running into boats or clambering from one pair of stairs by the waterside to another". Even the pigeons, the watching eyes of the poet beheld, were loath to leave their houses but hovered about the windows and balconies till their wings were singed and they fell down. The flaming shadow of death, roaring like a giant, was driving the love of home and property from their age-long habitations before his very eyes.

But when he saw that no one in that universal desire of each man to save his own was making any attempt to stay the fire, which the wind was driving into the heart of the City, the administrator took command of the artist, and he bade the boatmen row him swiftly to Whitehall. Here he found them all at chapel, but, giving his tidings, he was brought to the King and the Duke of York, to whom he told what he had seen, saying that unless his Majesty gave orders that houses should be pulled down nothing could stop the fire. They seemed much troubled and commanded him to go to the Lord Mayor and bid him destroy all in the path ot the flames. With this errand he drove to St Paul's and then walked through the narrow panic-stricken lanes till he found that unhappy magistrate, with a handkerchief about his neck, crying like a fainting woman: "Lord! what can I do? I am spent; people will not obey me. I have been pulling down houses, but the fire overtakes us faster than we can do it". And then walked on. His useless errand accomplished, Pepys also walked on. Once more as he did so the artist came out, seeing the flying distracted crowds and the churches filling with goods borne thither by people who at this time, had things, he reflected, been otherwise, should have been quietly praying within. Then, it being midday, he went home to entertain his guests. But his dinner party was not a success, for the hearts of all those who sat down were elsewhere and Pepys' intention that they should please themselves with the sight of his fine new closet was not fulfilled. And as soon as they could, they went away.

Once more Pepys went out into the streets—"full of nothing but people and horses and carts loaden with goods, ready to run over one another, and removing goods from one burned house to another". He saw familiar friends passing through that troubled kaleidoscope of driven humanity, the King and the Duke of York in their barge going down the river to take command of their kingdom, the Thames crowded with goods of all sorts—"and there was hardly", he noted for the instruction of posterity, "one lighter or boat in three...but there was a pair of virginalls in it". Then, as it grew dark, the air filled with flakes of fire, and he and Elizabeth, unable to endure the scorching heat any longer, crossed the river to a little alehouse on Bankside and there watched that terrible spectacle. As night deepened, the fire seemed to grow "more and more, and in corners and upon steeples, and between churches and houses, as far as we could see up the hill of the City, in a most horrid, malicious bloody flame, not like the fine flame of an ordinary fire....We staid", he wrote, "till, it being darkish, we saw the fire as only one entire arch of fire from this to the other side of the bridge, and in a bow up the hill for an arch of above a mile long; it made me weep to see it. The churches, houses and all on fire and flaming at once; and a horrid noise the flames made and the cracking of houses at their ruin".

When at last they went home, with a bright moon in the sky and fire all over the earth, they found poor Tom Hayter, who was always in trouble, come with a few of his goods which he had saved from his house in Fish Street Hill to take shelter with his master. Pepys gladly offered him a bed and received his goods, but with the fire creeping north and east as well as driving westwards with the wind, he felt that it was time to move his own; the yard was already full of Sir William Batten's carts come up from Walthamstow. So all night long the household tramped up and down the wooden stairs, carrying money in iron chests into the cellar, and bags of gold and boxes of paper into the garden. Hayter trying to sleep in the troubled house, the carts rumbling into the yard from the country, the smell and crackling of fire and the moon looking down serene on the bewildered doings of men, made up the sum of this night. Before it ended, the fire was raging from Queenhithe in the west to Cannon Street on the north, and eastwards beyond the lower end of Botolph Lane.

At about four o'clock on Monday morning, the Clerk of the Acts, riding in a cart of Batten's, packed high with his goods and arrayed only in his nightgown, set out for Bethnal Green. Here at Sir William Rider's, already crowded with the belongings of his friends, he left his most treasured possessions (among them the volumes of his Diary). Then through the crowd of flying people and carts, he fought his way back to the burning City. All that Monday, a glorious summer's day, he and his poor wife, weary and dazed for lack of sleep, packed up their household goods and, bearing them over Tower Hill, loaded them into a lighter at the quay above Tower Dock. Meanwhile the fire burned ever more fiercely, spreading northwards to devour all Lombard Street, the Poultry and Cornhill, and tumbling the Royal Exchange and forty churches in that universal ruin. Beside the river it ran westwards a further half-mile to Baynard's Castle, but its easterly advance was restricted by the wind. Yet even here it crept along Eastcheap and Thames Street, a couple of hundred yards nearer Seething Lane.

In the midst of all this horror Mrs Pepys, like a woman inspired, contrived to give Mercer notice. That young lady (whose breasts, though she knew it not, her husband had of late taken to fondling as she dressed him of a morning),* had without leave, but very naturally, gone to help her mother move her things. Elizabeth, tracking her down, had upbraided her furiously, at which Mrs Mercer had shouted back that her daughter was no prentice girl to ask leave every time she went abroad. The angry housewives in battle, while the great fire pursued its course less than a quarter of a mile away, was the last scene in Mercer's sojourn. She departed that night, while her erstwhile master and mistress lay down in turn to snatch a few hours' sleep on a little quilt of Will Hewer's in the Office.

Tuesday, the 4th, was the greatest day of the fire. Ranged now far to the north its flaming battalions poured westwards in irresistible strength over the doomed City. Early in the morning it reached St Paul's, and, while the leaden roof poured in streams of burning lava into the nave below, flames leapt rejoicing across the valley of the Fleet on to the wooden houses of Salisbury Court and St Bride's, all but encircling the Duke of York and his soldiers, who were gallantly blowing up houses on Ludgate Hill, in an inescapable ring of fire. Eastwards the foe came up both sides of narrow Thames Street with infinite fury, while Batten and Pepys dug a deep pit in the Navy Office garden, in which to lay one his wine and the other his papers and Parmesan cheese. Threatened with the immediate destruction of his home, Pepys that afternoon received sudden inspiration—to send for the naval dockyard hands from Woolwich and Deptford, to pull down houses and save the Office. He communicated these thoughts to Sir William Penn, who was sitting melancholy by his side in the garden. The latter

* "...they being the finest that ever I saw in my life, that is the truth of it". *D.* June 19th, 1666.

at once went down the river to summon this help, while Pepys (even at this juncture methodically taking a copy) wrote to Coventry for the Duke's permission to pull down houses, there being an ancient rule of the City that whoever destroyed his neighbour's dwelling should be at the expense of rebuilding it.[1]

That night the fire was in Fenchurch Street to the north of the lane and had already reached the "Dolphin" in Tower Street. Pepys and his wife sat down to a last sad supper in their house with Mr Turner, the Petty Purveyor, and his wife as their guests. Somehow they contrived to be a little merry. Only when they looked out, the horrid glamour of the sky, "all in a fire in the night", terrified them almost out of their wits; it looked as though the whole heaven was in flames. Throughout the night, the sound of explosions kept them from sleeping: the authorities, bent on saving the powder store in the Tower, were now blowing up houses all along Tower Street. At two in the morning, after again lying a brief while on Hewer's quilt in the Office, Pepys was called up with news that the fire was at the bottom of Seething Lane. There being now no hope, he took his wife, Will Hewer and Jane, with £2350 in gold, by boat to Woolwich. Then leaving them at Mr Sheldon's in the Yard (after charging his wife and Will never to leave the room in which the gold was lodged without one of them to keep watch on it) he returned to London to survey the ruins of his home.

But when he got back at seven in the morning his house and the Navy Office were still standing. The men from the Yards, whom Penn had brought up in the night, had done their business; and at Barking Church, its porch and dial already burnt, the fire had been for the moment at least stopped, though from the north flames still threatened. Then, the artist overcoming even the man of property, Pepys climbed to the top of the rescued steeple and surveyed the scene—"the saddest sight of desolation that ever I saw, everywhere great fires, oil cellars and brimstone...burning...the fire being spread as far as I could see it".

Then, having good hopes that the worst was over—for everywhere the King and the Duke of York with their soldiers and volunteers had been opposing its course with rope and powder—he dined on cold meat at Sir William Penn's, the first proper meal he had eaten in three days, and walked abroad to see the town. Over the smouldering ruins he made his way, as his fellow diarist, Evelyn, did two days later, clambering over piles of smoking rubbish, the ground so hot beneath his feet that it scorched the soles of his shoes. Fenchurch, Gracechurch and Lombard Streets were all dust, the Exchange a blackened skeleton, and Moorfields full of poor wretches sitting among their goods. He noted Anthony Joyce's house still burning, the buckled glass that had fallen from the windows of the Mercers' Chapel and the poor cat, its hair all burned off its body, which he saw being taken out of a hole in a chimney. So he went home, and, as the air was still full of flying sparks, and rumours were abroad of Dutch and French spies carrying fireballs to spread the flames, he set the dockyard men to guard the Office all night, giving them beer and bread and cheese. Then he fell asleep, all sense of time lost.[2]

But that wonderful curiosity did not allow him to sleep long, and he was up before five. At the gate of the Office as he went out, he met Gauden, the Victualler, hurrying to beg the aid of his men to fight a new fire that had broken out at Bishopsgate. So Pepys went along with his dockyard men and helped to put it out, which they did in a little while; it was strange, he reflected, to see how hard the women worked fetching water and how they would then scold for a drink and be as drunk as devils. Then, his work done, and being all in dirt from head to foot, Dapper Dicky took boat to Westminster to buy a shirt and some gloves and get himself trimmed. And as he went up the river he saw the sad sight of the ruined shores, with no house standing from Tower Bank to the Temple. Of the old City within the wall, scarcely a sixth part remained; thirteen thousand houses had been burnt, leaving a hundred thousand people homeless.

Such was the strange and terrible interlude which broke the course of Pepys' life. He for his part had been wonderfully fortunate—"the Lord of Heaven make me thankful and continue me therein!"—his goods, scattered at Woolwich, Deptford and Bethnal Green, were all safe, and when, a week later, the dockyard labourers had ceased to tramp all night through the Office and his house was made clean, he brought them all home by cart and barge (all save two little sea-pictures which were somehow mislaid) and to his infinite joy lay with his wife in his chamber again. Only, he added, "I do lack Mercer or somebody in the house to sing with". But though he tried to entice her back, the lady would not return.[3]

For though Pepys might resume the even tenor of his ways—though he might go abroad in fine clothes again* or in a single afternoon (less than a week after the fire ceased) enjoy both Martin's wife and Bagwell's—the background of his life was changed for ever. Around the Navy Office still stood the familiar houses, and at Westminster and at Whitehall there were trees and green grass and the wonted dwellings of men. But between the two lay a vast wilderness of horror. Walking or riding from Whitehall one approached it, as one visitor to London recalled, passing the untouched

* "Up betimes and shaved myself after a week's growth, but Lord! how ugly I was yesterday, and how fine today!" *D.* Sept. 17th, 1666.

palaces of the nobility which still lined the south side of the Strand. But once through Temple Bar and a double line of houses ended two hundred yards away in a desolation of blackened rubble and white ashes, stretching as far as the eye could see and broken only by the ruin of old St Paul's and the tottering towers of churches. Here for many months the stench and smoke of subterranean fires assailed the traveller, nor was it safe at night to pass by for fear of the lawless and homeless men who lurked among the shadows; half a year later when his Majesty's Clerk of the Acts had occasion to pass through the ruins, he sat in the coach with his sword drawn.[4]

But being English, Pepys dwelt as little as possible on all this. From shades and horrors he turned to the normal and familiar; recorded cheerfully, even before the fire was fully burnt out, how house property in his part of the town was soaring in value, how the citizens congregated at the still standing Gresham College to gossip and bargain, and what speedy plans were being made for rebuilding the City. Of that mysterious country, whose horrid landscape he had seen for a brief while, he did not speak; only in dreams, lying (when the memory of it was still fresh) in Penn's naked bed with nothing but his drawers on, or long after beside Elizabeth in his own familiar room, did he revisit it with the fear of fire in his heart.[5]

Chapter XV

England Unarms

"But that, that he tells me of worst consequence is, that he himself did hear many Englishmen on board the Dutch ships speaking to one another in English; and that they did cry and say, 'We did heretofore fight for tickets; now we fight for dollars'." *Diary*, June 14th, 1667.

Meanwhile the war continued. Just before the Fire the English and Dutch fleets had been in sight of each other in the Channel. Rupert, cautious for once, failed to attack at a critical moment; the high wind which drove the flames at such speed through the City kept the English ships in harbour, and the Dutch soon after returned to their own coast. So ended the summer campaign of 1666 and the last chance of the English obtaining that annihilating sea victory which alone could compensate them for their sufferings before their own internal ills overwhelmed them.[1]

For those ills were now acute. Even before the Fire Pepys had come to accept the want of money as inevitable, recognising that the only business left for the Office was to file petitions and appease duns, and that the Treasury could do nothing to help the Navy until new supplies could be got from Parliament. And now, though Parliament was about to meet, it was hard to see how even that terrible and puissant assembly could raise taxes from a nation sunk under the twofold ruin of plague and fire.[2]

Terrible and puissant Parliament seemed to be to the despondent officials of the bankrupt Navy. It met on September

21st, and Pepys, more nervous and prescient than any of his colleagues, feared that they all would be turned out of their places. For the Commons, with their Hotspurs enquiring into all things, were in a nasty temper; men said that the King had received two millions more for the war than he could account for, and, though these accusations were not supported by figures, they were universally believed. Accounts were called for, and Pepys was kept hard at work, even on Sundays—honest Hayter having "no mind to, it being the Lord's Day, but, being told the necessity, submitted, poor man!"—drawing up a statement of the charge of the war; £3,200,000 he showed it to have been up to date, of which nearly a million was still owing. But the Commons were by no means disposed to accept the Navy Office's statement without examination; and soon the great Sir George Carteret was making his way humbly to St Stephen's with his book of accounts under his arm, and Pepys following suit. On October 2nd he was sent for by the Committee of Navy Accounts; while waiting outside, he gave Penn's boy his confidential book of papers to hold; picture his horror when later he discovered that the fool of a boy had delivered it to the doorkeeper of the House: it made him "stark mad, considering all the nakedness of the office lay open in papers within those covers". Happily, after an anxious hour or two, a little bribery released the incriminating volume from the custody of the doorkeeper, and next day, in comparative ease of mind, the Clerk of the Acts underwent his first cross-examination by the politicians, "and did make shift to answer them better than I expected". With admirable courage and presence of mind, quietly and effectively, he bore the brunt of their questionings all day, without the least support from his colleagues, and when the Committee rose he was undefeated. Shortly after the

Commons were induced to vote a further £1,800,000 for the war—a great sum, Pepys observed, were it not for the debts which swallowed almost all of it.

For these had reached what were in those days titanic dimensions. Pepys, speaking before the King at Whitehall on an October Sunday, dwelt long on the Navy Office's total incapacity through the lack of money and the helpless condition of the Fleet; he spoke well, he thought, but when he sat down, Rupert sprang up in a white heat and declared that he had brought home his ships in as good a condition as any had ever returned to harbour, on which the gallant little Clerk of the Acts replied that he was sorry to have offended his Highness, but he could only repeat what had been reported to him by the Surveyors. After which there was a long and awkward silence. But the only upshot of it all was that the King allocated a sum of £5000 to the Navy Office—an amount so absurdly inadequate that it was quite useless. But till the money voted by Parliament could be collected, it was all there was.

In despair, while unpaid sailors rioted outside the Treasury or swarmed angrily around the Navy Office to the terror of its inmates, Pepys contemplated resignation. Bluntly he told the Duke of York that he must not expect any further service from him and his colleagues, for without money it was impossible to give it. Even the few hundreds which he asked to satisfy a small part of the debt of the broom and reed men, that there might be enough credit to bream the ships' bottoms, were denied him, the Navy Treasurer turning up his eyes as if he had asked a million. Everywhere the affairs of the nation were drifting to ruin; the Fleet in such a condition as to discipline—swearing, drinking and whoring—that, as grim old Commissioner Middleton put it, it was as if the Devil commanded it: the merchants giving up all trade for lost, and men deploring that the old valour of England was spent and worn out. Pepys, wearied with the distraction and confusion of the times, wished himself with the little he had got safely settled at Brampton, "where I might live peaceably and study, and pray for the good of the King and my country".[3]

Yet he did not retire. Seeing that his importunate requests for money merely irritated those in authority, he gave over, drew in his horns* and, after one last despairing letter to the Duke of York in November, for a time left the doomed Navy to its fate. Instead he surrendered himself to less harrying occupations. It was better by far to spend an evening at home playing upon one's lyra viol with great pleasure and peace of mind than to waste long and fruitless hours in the service of an ungrateful country; to entertain noble and titled guests in one's fine house with reflections that no joys that life could offer could really exceed this—"eating in silver plates and all things mighty rich and handsome"—to make one's colleagues green with envy to see themselves served from that selfsame plate (even if Lord Brouncker did afterwards mutter some ignoble remark about its origins)—"all I have and do so much outdo for neatness and plenty anything done by any of them".[4]

At other times the company he entertained did not so much please Mrs Pepys. When Mesdames Pierce and Knepp dined, she was mighty pettish, so that these two spotless ladies remarked with astonishment on her ill-temper; and when Sam returned from seeing them home he found her

* When Carteret repeated to him the Chancellor's critical enquiry "how it [do] come to pass that his friend Pepys do so much magnify all things to worse", the Clerk of the Acts took warning. "I must have a care", he noted, "not to be over busy in the Office again and burn my fingers." *D.* Oct. 20th, 1666.

strangely out of order, reproaching them "as wenches, and I know not what". It was most mysterious. Yet Pepys could not help admitting that he was always glad to see Knepp—the best company in the world he found the jade—to hear her sing his new song "*It is decreed*", to gaze and listen to her as she performed on the boards of the King's Theatre. Indeed in the opinion of Lord Brouncker, who liked a pretty face as well as Pepys, she was coming on to be a great actress. To have her with him Samuel gave a dinner to some of the chief players: there was Henry Harris, who sang an Irish song with great effect, and Captain Rolt, and Knepp herself deliciously disguised in the dress and vast straw hat in which she had just been acting the country maid in the *Goblins*; there were also four fiddlers (who would not accept less than thirty shillings) and, to appease Mrs Pepys, Pembleton himself to lead the dancing. And the crown of the evening came, after Mercer had sung the most ravishing Italian song over the supper table in the Office, when Pepys went upstairs to bid good-night to Mrs Knepp—who being taken a little sick had been put to bed by his wife—and, after waking her, handled her breasts and kissed her and sang a song with her as he lay beside her on the bed.[5]

It was not always that his delights were so innocent. There was Mrs Bagwell, who was now only too ready for his business (he had got her husband a better ship as he had promised)—"con much voluptas", as he phrased it in the peculiar jargon in which he recorded his loose amours. There was Mrs Martin, grown into "la plus belle moher* of

* In Joseph Wright's *English Dialect Dictionary* [1903], "maur" or "mohr" is defined as a Suffolk term for a woman or girl. Of more general use was the word "mauther", meaning "a girl just growing into motherhood, especially a great, rough, awkward wench". But an equally possible explanation is that Pepys was using the Spanish word "mujer".

the orbis", so much so that Pepys, who apparently could get all the pleasure he wanted without pushing things to perilous extremes, was somewhat taken aback. He was also a little put out when her husband, that vain, silly fellow for whom he had got a place, went swaggering across Westminster Hall with some new-purchased gewgaw so that all the people laughed at him: Pepys feared they might suspect him as the cause of this unmerited wealth. And when Mrs Martin was out of the way having a baby, her little sister Doll Lane proved herself to be made from the same mould. Contrary to all expectation, Pepys found that he could do what he would with her and might, he added, have done anything.

Indeed Pepys was decidedly promiscuous in his loves that autumn. Having withdrawn his superfluous energies from the task of defeating the Dutch, he was now ready for anybody. "Our Sarah", formerly of the household in Seething Lane and who had recently taken a shoemaker to her legitimate bosom, as well as her little sister, the maid of the "Swan"; Mrs Burrows, the pretty widow of a naval officer whose dead husband's ticket he had helped to get paid and whose modesty he slowly undermined—in a coach ambling across the Acton and Paddington fields, or at the Office, and, most sinister of all, in Mrs Martin's lodgings; young Mrs Daniel, whose husband's promotion he so obligingly nursed and whose clothes, after carefully shutting the door, he so disarranged when she visited the Office; even Penn's daughter, Peg Lowther whom he towsled and kissed, were all fuel to feed his "mauvais flammes". In a single December week, he took his pleasure of Doll Lane (immediately after a most improving talk with Mr Evelyn on the vices of the King and Court), of Mrs Martin and Mrs Daniel.[6]

Yet it would be wrong to deduce from these ragged and miscellaneous affairs that Pepys was an all-triumphing Don

Juan, draining the last dregs of amorous pleasure and sparing none. A wonderful way with women, he certainly had; when his neighbour Mrs Turner, deprived of her lodgings by Lord Brouncker, came weeping to him for comfort, he had her laughing in a few minutes.* His vitality, his sensitive and varying emotions and his unquenchable zest for life were irresistible. But the strange intermixture of revelation and omission in Wheatley's edition of the Diary has left a false impression of the nature of Pepys' love affairs. For except for one or two, they were strictly (if such an adverb be here permissible) limited in their scope: his early training had left behind it a mind fortified with inhibitions. To go beyond a certain point—albeit that sometimes his passions and the opportunity of the hour carried him further, leaving him afterwards humiliated in himself and despising his unfortunate victim—was shameful. Worse, it was dangerous. Even in his bewildering, truthful exposure of himself Pepys cannot quite bring himself to put down in everyday black and white the record of his own infirmities; while admitting that he, with his fine clothes and imposing carriage, did for a moment kneel down and grovel in the mud, he does so in a different language as though the lapse had in it something of unreality—a dream, the freak of an unguarded moment, a lapse into the irresponsible years of childhood. So that the confessions are written in a strange jargon of tongues, French, Greek, Spanish, Italian, Latin—with toy words scattered meaningless throughout them—till one reads with wonder in that baby language the naïve confession "she would not suffer that je should poner my mano above ses jupes which je endeavoured".[7]

All this, of course, had little to do with the heart: much

* "So that I perceive no passion in a woman can be lasting long." *D.* Jan. 29th, 1667.

with the body. As a distinguished surgeon and Pepysian scholar, Sir D'Arcy Power, has pointed out, much of Pepys' incontinence was probably due to the injury done in his youth to his genito-urinary system by the removal of so large a stone from his bladder. And he had always been of a warm nature—a very hot little boy, he remembered himself as being, subject to breakings out of heat in his body, and continued prickings and itchings when the weather grew warm. Yet he suffered also from an exceedingly susceptible heart, and, when female beauty touched his imagination—as it was quick to do—he foolishly fell in love. As he had done two years before with Jane Welsh, the barber's maid, so he did this winter with little Betty Michell, who in her youthful days as Mrs Howlett's daughter of Westminster Hall had struck him as having so marked a resemblance to his wife. He had begun one August Sunday when after treating her at the "Old Swan" tavern he had had two or three long salutes of her out of sight of her husband. She, also like his last love, was inclined to blow hot and cold, and to keep him waiting at unkept trysts; after one such wasted afternoon, he had a quaint adventure: "but pretty!" he relates, "how I took another pretty woman for her, taking her a clap on the breech thinking verily it had been her". But Betty was an old friend, and, in his desires as in his work, Pepys knew how to be patient. As he observed of the modesty of another lady that winter: "time can hazer la the same as it hath hereto others". In October, sampling the pleasures of her lips, he found her "mighty modest", in early December, returning in a coach with her from the christening of Mrs Martin's child (who that lady believed, or pretended to believe, was his) he got her, with some ado, to employ her hands in a way scarcely compatible with any woman's modesty. Three weeks later, in another coach with the moon shining, he repeated the pleasure, "she making many little endeavours para stir su main but yielded still. We came home", he added, "and there she did seem a little ill, but I did take several opportunities afterwards para baisser la, and so good night".[8]

Yet he was still in love with her and much afraid lest she should find his advances too bold. It was, however, less the lady's fastidiousness which proved the obstacle than her husband's very natural suspicions. In February there was a disturbing adventure. Pepys had invited Betty in the presence of young Michell to join his wife and himself at the New Exchange in a shopping venture. When Betty arrived, Elizabeth was not there, for the simple reason that Samuel had never asked her to be. He made an excuse, bought her a dressing case at a cabinet-maker's and then settled down to enjoy himself in her company. But late that evening as he took her home by coach, a thought struck him: what if her husband had sent to Seething Lane to enquire for her and, finding her not there, have given not only himself but Mrs Pepys occasion to think strange things. Betty womanwise dismissed the idle thought, and Samuel saw her home. Here he discovered that his fears were well founded, for Mr Michell announced that he had just sent his maid to Seething Lane to enquire when his wife would be back. In haste Pepys took his leave (Betty whispering behind her husband's back that if he would say that they had come by water, she would make up the rest) and hurried home, there in a sweat pacing up and down before the entry wondering what on earth he should say to Elizabeth. But, as God would have it, while he walked to and fro in this agony, a little woman came stumbling up the steps in the dark, and asked the way to his house. Recognising her voice, he told her that her mistress had gone home. Then with his heart full of joy at his good fortune, he betook him indoors to his own wife. After that, the "affaire Michell" somewhat languished.[9]

In his relations with his own family, Pepys was seen to far better advantage. Three years before, at the time of Tom's death, he had discovered among Tom's papers some highly scandalous letters, written by his brother John, full of "foul words" and "crafty designs" against himself. He had sworn at the time never to forget the injury. But now that John, down from the University and about to start his career, was in need of his help he forgave him, sent for him to town, gave him money and a canonical cloak and cassock and looked about for some such clerical preferment as should befit a young graduate of Cambridge. He even gave him lessons in pronunciation, lent him his favourite *Faber Fortunae* to translate, and questioned him, scholarwise, on mathematics and optics. And when one day the young man, who had been spending the winter at Seething Lane, fell down in a dead faint pale as death (he explained afterwards that something had come into his stomach very hot), Samuel was quite astounded at his own brotherly love: "I never", he tells us, "was so frightened but once, when my wife was ill at Ware upon the road, and I did continue trembling a good while and ready to weep to see him". The same anxious solicitude appeared in the early spring of 1667 when his mother, who had long been sinking, fell dangerously ill. Even in sleep the thought of her visited him, dreaming himself kneeling beside her bed, laying his hand over hers and crying, she almost dead, "and so waked, but which is strange, methought she had hair over her face and not the same kind of face as my mother really has, but yet did not consider that, but did weep over her as my mother whose soul God have mercy of". Two days later he received news that on the very day of his dream she had died and that her last words had been—"God bless my poor Sam!" "The reading hereof", he recorded, "did set me aweeping heartily, and so weeping to myself awhile, and my wife also to herself." After which the tearful pair consoled themselves by recalling what a comfort it was that the old lady had not survived her husband or she would have been left altogether on their hands. The subsequent funeral expenses Samuel bore out of his own purse, emptying a £50 bag to do so—and it was a joy to him to see that he could part with such a sum without much inconvenience, at least, without any trouble of mind.[10]

So also towards his father, Pepys kept the simplest and most homely of the commandments, honouring him all the days of his life, though he well knew his faults and weaknesses. "So home", he had written at the time of Tom's death, "and find my father come to lie at our house and so supped and saw him, poor man, to bed, my heart never being fuller of love to him, nor admiration of his prudence and pains heretofore in the world than now to see how Tom hath carried himself in his trade; and how the poor man hath his thoughts going to provide for his younger children and my mother. But I hope they shall never want". That resolve Samuel faithfully honoured. He bought his sire a horse, made up his income by £30 a year—"I do not think I can bestow it better"—and did all within his power to make him happy; and when the old man came to London, he would gladly have had him stay for ever, such innocent company did he find him. Even Pall he did his best for, busying himself to find her a husband and offering to give her a dowry of £500. Had it been possible he would have had her marry his old schoolfellow, honest country parson, Dick Cumberland; he would gladly, he said, have given a £100 more with her to so excellent a fellow, but Dick was poor and, anyhow, averse to marrying. Poor Balty St Michel also came in for his share of his brother-in-law's growing benevolence. Since his good service in Harman's beleaguered flagship, Pepys had felt far more kindly disposed towards the young man. He was delighted when Balty's name was mentioned in the presence of the Duke of York as that of the best Muster Master in the Fleet and deeply sympathetic when he found that he was troubled lest, in his absence at sea, his somewhat flighty little wife should dishonour him. He gave him good counsel and help, though not quite to the extent of offering to house his lady—for what, he reflected, would he do with her if Balty were killed?—and got him made Deputy Treasurer of the Fleet, a truly great promotion. A good man, he now found him, willing to take pains and very sober.[11]

Of his near relations she who received the least share of his tender kindness was his wife. It was not that he did not love her—deep in his heart, as time was to show, he did above all others in the world—but he could not bring himself to exert himself to please her, nor help regarding her as a fool. He tried to teach her to sing, but her ear was so bad and he had not the patience to coax her to do better as he would have done with a stranger. Yet he was frank with himself over the causes of her failure—"I do find that I do put her out of heart and make her fearful to sing before me".

Nor was he kinder to her in other matters. When he came home to dinner and found her in a silly dress of a blue petticoat uppermost and a white satin waistcoat and hood, he was very angry—though he was less peevish when he had eaten—and when contrary to his orders she went abroad in the flaxen hair that was now all the mode, he almost burst with rage, swore in God's name several times—"which I pray God forgive me for"—and even shook his fist in her faec: at which she, poor wretch, was much surprised. Still she contrived, as she usually did when his anger went too far, to make something out of it, and next day traded a promise to discard her white locks for money to buy lace. Another bargain she secured in the spring of 1667—a convention on her husband's part that whenever he spent money on Knepp or any other lady, he should give as much to her. It proved an admirable economy.[12]

All this while the affairs of the nation were in a sad plight. 1666 had closed in universal gloom: even the King's musicians were starving. Nor did 1667 open with any brighter hopes. Everyone was full of distrust: when the Court spoke of the danger of foreign invasion, the City laughed at the alarm and affected to regard it as a mere plot to get money. Corruption was everywhere: great and small alike scrambled to make what they could before the end came. When the Navy Officers tried to prevent the sale of some captured hemp and timber by the Commissioners of Prizes, knowing that they would subsequently be forced to buy these identical goods from the purchaser at prohibitive prices, Lord Ashley,* who was out for his rake-off, flatly refused to obey the King's orders and went on with the sale—"a most horrid evil and a shame", Pepys thought it. Yet he himself was not above forcing through the Board, against even Coventry's protest, a more than doubtful contract for using one of the King's ships to bring back hemp from Genoa, because he had been promised a commission from Captain Cocke if it was signed. Even his fellow Commissioner, the old Puritan Taylor, offered the Clerk of the Acts ten pieces of gold. But when the flagmakers, Young and Whistler, approached him with a box containing £100, he felt that matters had gone too far and, thinking it unsafe to put himself in the power of such men, flatly refused it.[13]

* Afterwards the great Earl of Shaftesbury.

Truth to tell, Pepys continued to thrive though the nation drove every week nearer to the rocks of bankruptcy and the Navy lay helpless for lack of money. During the winter of 1666–7—as barren a one as England had ever known—his capital, despite heavy expenses, steadily increased—"for which the Holy name of God be praised". True, owing to the State's failure to pay its bills there was a distinct falling off of his income in certain directions: contractors who were owed tens of thousands could scarcely be as lavish with presents as in the earlier days of the war. And, owing to an unhappy tendency on the part of that merchant to favour Brouncker as well as himself, Pepys had definitely broken with Warren: he would rather, he declared angrily, lose him altogether than that he should hold any man's friendship higher than his. But kind Gauden, the Victualler, despite the universal shortage of cash, found it worth his while to continue his benevolence to the official who was both Surveyor-General of the Navy and Treasurer of Tangier (giving him £500 a year for the first and £100 for the latter), and Mr Lanyon, the Tangier merchant, secured him another £300 on their old contract.[14]

But if Pepys could grow rich in such times, the King could not. Before 1666 ended the Council, relying on the negotiations for peace which were proceeding with France and Holland, was contemplating the necessity of laying up the Fleet during the next summer; nor indeed did any other course appear financially possible. There was no money in the Treasury, and, as Pepys himself said, without money the King's work could not go on. Before the final decision to lay up the Fleet was taken, he made one last despairing appeal for funds. For it still hurt him to see his handiwork perish, and it was not only of his own £300 that he was thinking when he complained of the lot of poor Mr Lanyon who had given the Navy credit for £8000 and received not one farthing in return; "the King's service is undone", he wrote, "and those that trust him perish: these things grieve me to the heart". In another letter to the Duke of York he summarised the current position; in four months the Navy Board had been able to make only four paltry contracts of not more than £2000 in all and had received but £1315 for the discharge of debts of over £150,000, while the total debt of the Navy was in the neighbourhood of a million; unless £526,000 were allocated at once, to set out a fleet would be impossible. The letter at least, he observed, discharged the Navy Office from blame for the inevitable consequences which must ensue if the money was not forthcoming. (Coventry went even further and resigned.) But Pepys might as well have asked for the Great Wall of China. The only result was to fray the tempers of those from whom he begged; as he himself frankly admitted to Carteret whose secretary had been rude to the Navy Board's messenger: "I confess that to be importuned for money, when money is not to be had, is a provoker". Certainly the old Lord Chancellor found it so, as he listened to the Clerk of the Acts' renewed complaints, though he had the justice to declare that no man in England was of greater method nor made himself better understood: a great compliment, Pepys thought it.

On March 6th, 1667, the government officially acquainted the Navy Office of its intention to lay up the battle fleet. Instead it was resolved to strengthen the harbour fortifications and rely on a few flying squadrons from the northern and western ports to cripple the Dutch by preying on their commerce.[15]

Of the advantages to be derived from plundering Dutch merchantmen, Pepys—though under no delusion as to the probable result of laying up the fleet—was already something of a judge. In the previous autumn he had become joint proprietor with Penn and Batten of a privateer, the three having successfully begged the loan of the vessel, the *Flying Greyhound*, from their good-natured sovereign. The proceeding had naturally caused a certain amount of criticism, and Pepys had had to write to Mr Deane to refute a "treacherous mistake" on the part of a prying official at the Harwich yard and point out that, though his Majesty had been graciously pleased to lend the ship with her furniture and guns during the winter, he and his fellow adventurers were bearing the full expense of her wages and victuals out of their own purses.

To provide additional capital for their "private man of war", the Principal Officers got the merchant, Sir Richard Ford, to bear a third of the cost. There was some doubt at first as to how best to employ her: for a time there were thoughts of sending her on a trading voyage to the Madeiras, "the profit being certain and occasion honest". There was also a certain amount of bickering about the crew, old Batten declaring that he would withdraw unless his son was made Lieutenant. But in the end the *Flying Greyhound* set out, with the complaisant Mr Martin as Purser and a certain pirate of the name of Hogg as Captain, with a roving commission to prey on Dutch merchantmen.

Unhappily the Captain interpreted his commission rather too liberally and, though the privateer brought in several rich prizes, the subsequent "proving" of them before the Prize Courts involved her owners in a great deal of anxiety. Two Swedish prizes proved a particular source of trouble: the Swedish Resident (a gentleman who, it appears, slept in mittens and a fur cap) gave battle on behalf of his injured countrymen, intimating, however, that he was ready to be bribed. On which Sir William Penn made "a long simple declaration of his resolution to give nothing to deceive any poor man of what was his right by law" but ended in saying that he would do whatever the others did. The three eminent adventurers of Seething Lane thereupon authorised Sir Richard Ford to offer the protesting diplomat up to £350 for his silence, Sir Richard also making a speech protesting his virtue and praying God for a curse on his family if he was privy to any knavery. However it appeared that the bribe was not sufficient, for the case went to law and the judge who struck Pepys, just even when his own interests were at stake, as a very rational, learned and uncorrupt man, gave it in part against them.

There was also some trouble when, in her rovings in the Channel and North Sea, the private man-of-war of his Majesty's Principal Officers chanced to light on ships which were claimed as prizes by even loftier adventurers. There was the Vice-Admiral, for instance, who demanded one of the *Flying Greyhound's* victims at Plymouth, and, worse still, Prince Rupert, with two of whose privateers Captain Hogg had chosen, most unwisely, to consort. An even worse shock befell the owners when they discovered that Hogg and his merry men had been engaging on a little piracy on their own account at the expense of their paymasters: it appeared that Hogg was the "veriest rogue, the most observable embezzler that ever was known". But it may be added that he had many competitors.

In the end Pepys decided that it would be better to take what profit he could and get out of this rather too exciting company while there was still time. After hearing Batten boast that he was going to sell his share of the prizes for £1000, Pepys boldly offered him his for £700. This, to his great joy, Batten after a little bargaining closed with at £666. 13*s.* 4*d.* But (to anticipate) there was a further trial in store. For after the *Flying Greyhound's* operations had been brought to a close by the end of the war, the owners formed the hopeful plan of begging her altogether from the easygoing monarch as a reward for their patriotic services. Then a most disturbing thing happened. For on September 17th, 1667, old Batten came raging to Pepys with tidings that their partner, Penn, had secretly got an order from the King for the ship for himself, "which is so false a thing and the part of a knave as nothing almost can be more". Happily all ended well. For, after a very outspoken interview with Penn "wherein I was plain to him and he to me", that thoughtful Admiral suggested as a compromise that he should use his influence with the Duke of York to beg another royal ship for Pepys alone. This was duly accomplished and the quarrel between the Principal Officers was appeased by the transference of his Majesty's ship, the *Maybolt* galliot, fitted out (through Sir William Penn's forethought) as though for a long voyage, to the private ownership of Samuel Pepys. The warrant which attested the gift bore long and loving testimony to his public services.[16]

While these were being rendered, the English government laid up the main Fleet. The great ships were moored in the Medway, a boom set across the river to protect them and the coastal forts strengthened. Meanwhile squadrons to prey on Dutch commerce were fitted out at Plymouth and Hull, and the peace negotiations pressed forward. But so sluggish was the pulse of English government now become that scarcely one of these things was adequately accomplished. The great ships were berthed too low in the river, the chain at Upnor was carelessly fixed and months were allowed to elapse before the work on the forts, ordered as far back as December 1666, was begun. And everywhere, the sailors on the ships left in commission, the dockyard hands, the labourers with their ropes and spades, flatly refused to obey the orders of a government which never paid them. Nor can they be blamed: Pepys, looking out of the Navy Office window, saw a poor seaman, half-starved for food, dying in the Yard.* The unpaid oar-maker at Portsmouth dockyard came to Commissioner Middleton crying and wringing his hands to beg that he might be made a labourer to save him from arrest for debt, the soldiers recruited for service overseas hid themselves rather than sail, and the Navy Office could think of nothing better to do than provide alibis and study excuses against the inevitable disaster which all foresaw.[17]

In May, when financial famine had reached nightmare dimensions, the first hope of relief came. On the 16th the old Lord Treasurer, Southampton, died—a good man, but one for whom his task in a new and changing age had proved too great. The government acted with something approaching vigour and put the Treasury into Commission with the capable Downing as Secretary. The new Commissioners were mostly young and active and at once began to enquire into the existing system with a view to a thorough overhaul of the state's financial machinery. Before the end of the month the Navy Office was receiving demands for an exact account of the expenses of the Office from the Restoration to the present day together with an estimate of what weekly and monthly sums were necessary to release the Fleet from

* An even more terrible record occurs in a letter of April 4th, 1667, written by Commissioner Taylor of Harwich dockyard to Pepys... "men really perish for want of wherewithal to get a nourishment. One yesterday came to me crying to get something to relieve him. I ordered him 10*s*. He went and got hot drink...and so drank it and died within two hours". The heart is still sore at such a relation. Tanner, *Further Correspondence*, p. 172.

debt. "We are", wrote Pepys in his abstract of their instructions, "to be moderate as we can without prejudice to the service."[18]

To him, at any rate, it was a wonderful relief—"the happiest thing that hath appeared...for the good of the nation since the King came in". Under the stimulus of hope the Clerk of the Acts became a new man, embraced again those toils which in despair he had long neglected and fell roundly to business. He also renewed the old spirited war against his colleagues, and from happy discourse with Mrs Turner and others collected damning matter against them: how Penn had risen from a pitiful origin with a dirty slattern for a wife whose stockings had hung about her heels, how he had bribed and plundered his way to his present position, how he was the most false fellow that ever was born of woman, how Pett turned up the white of his eyes while he spoke—sure sign of his treachery; how Lord Brouncker and his whore, Mrs Williams, owed for almost everything, even their butter and cheese. Yet, such was God's goodness, all these scurvy fellows treated Pepys with honour and respect. "I am a happy man", he wrote, "that all of my fellow-officers are desirous of my friendship." And with such stimulating reflections he returned to work—even on Sundays.[19]

But the reformation of the Treasury and the moral recovery of Mr Pepys were alike too late. On June 3rd the latter, after pausing in his morning's labours to give his neighbour, Parson Mills, who was after two livings, an introduction to Sir William Coventry—"which was a service I did, but much against my will, for a lazy fat priest"—sat down to a good plain dinner at the Trinity House, Deptford. Here among others was Mr Evelyn, and after the feast these two worthy men talked awhile of the alarming news that the Dutch were at sea with eighty men-of-war and twenty-five fireships. Five days later, despite anxious hopes in Seething Lane that the wind had scattered them, they were officially reported off Harwich: at much the same time their guns were heard at Bethnal Green. Military steps (for naval there could be none) were now taken to repel them, and all the young Hectors of the Court went posting off to Essex—to little purpose, thought Pepys, but to debauch the country women thereabouts. On that day, Sunday the 9th, the weather being hot, the Clerk of the Acts, after attending divine service in the Abbey and paying a profitable visit to Mrs Martin, took a boat to Barn Elms and spent a solitary and philosophical evening among the riverside trees reading a translation from the Spanish. When, late, he reached home, he found orders awaiting him to send fire-ships down the river.

Next day it was reported that the Dutch were at the Nore, and the Navy Officers bestirring themselves hurried down to Greenwich to dispatch men and ships. For once they had some money, but owing to the fact that no one would believe them, they were able to make small use of it, and in the now familiar atmosphere of idle despair, nothing was done. "It is an admirable thing", commented Pepys, "to consider how much the King suffers and how necessary it is in a State to keep the King's service always in a good posture and credit." The morrow was to provide a still more striking demonstration of the truth of this dictum.

That evening, restless with anxiety, Pepys went down the river to Gravesend. Here he found the Duke of Albemarle with a great many idle lords and gentlemen, pistols and other "fooleries", awaiting the assault of the Dutch Fleet. But at the moment that force was elsewhere—landing eight hundred men at Sheerness, before whom the unpaid garrison of the place fled precipitate. Still unconscious of this disaster, though the offals of sheep borne up the river by the flood showed all too well what the Dutch had been doing, Pepys returned mournfully to London, consoling himself on the way by reading Mr Boyle's new book on Hydrostatics—an excellent work he found it and truly comforting: only a few days before, when Elizabeth had been in a rage, he had read it aloud as she upbraided him until she was quite silenced. But it did not silence the Dutch.

On Tuesday the 11th there were many letters at the Navy Office, including one from Commissioner Pett, "in a very fearful stink for fear of the Dutch and desires help for God and the King and Kingdom's sake". Lord Brouncker and Sir John Mennes accordingly left for the front. Pepys, after getting off some fireships from Deptford, went home to dinner and then, by the luckiest of chances, calling on Mr Fenn at the Navy Treasurer's office, found that some money had just come in and secured £400 of outstanding salary. Then, spying Mercer, he followed her through the dusty streets: it was not a moth* that the Clerk of the Acts chased that day. The rest of it he spent industriously hiring fireships and dealing with Coventry's frantic letters and wondering what was happening on the Medway, where the great ships lay beyond the boom. And that night the drums of the Trained Bands sounded in all the streets: they were knocking up the taverns for Falstaff and his fellow captains to come forth and lead the King's levies.

Next morning the Dutch broke through the chain across the Medway and, under the ineffectual fire of the shore

* "Sir H. Cholmly...tells me...that the night the Dutch burned our ships the King did sup with my Lady Castlemayne at the Duchess of Monmouth's, and they were all mad in hunting a poor moth." *D.* June 21st, 1667.

batteries, bore down on the deserted English warships. These the dockyard men had refused to tow up the river as ordered, having been more profitably occupied in moving their own belongings to safety. The *Royal Charles*, once the *Naseby*, was taken and a number of other men-of-war fired. Late that afternoon the news reached London; "which struck me", wrote Pepys, "to the heart".[20]

Chapter XVI

Aftermath

"Comes a damned summons to attend the Committee of Miscarriages to-day, which makes me mad, that I should by my place become the hackney of this Office, in perpetual trouble and vexation, that need it least."
Diary, Feb. 11th, 1668.

The night of Wednesday, June 12th, that saw the Dutch lying in triumph in the Medway, saw Pepys in a determined mood. When all the house was abed, he took his father, who was on a visit to London, and his wife up to the latter's chamber and there, shutting the door, told them what he had resolved. The Navy Office, he explained, and probably the country, was doomed; the only thing to do was to save what cash he had by him, leaving such of his property as lay in the King's hands, on account of Tangier or the new Act, for lost. Having in two years seen plague and fire, he must now prepare himself for revolution. And meanwhile his wife and father should ride with the money bags to Brampton.

Next day he took his measures. Elizabeth and John Pepys departed with £1300 in gold in their night-bag and many strict orders how to hide it. Will Hewer was sent early to Backwell's and managed to withdraw another £500 of his master's money before the run on the bank began, and an hour or two later Gibson, the clerk, set out after the Brampton travellers with a thousand more gold pieces under colour of an official express to Sir Jeremy Smith, the Admiral in command of the northern squadron at Newcastle. All day long people kept coming in and out of the Office, all with various rumours and all in alarm—the King and Duke of York among them. And all day long, as he listened and looked attentive, the Clerk of the Acts' mind dwelt anxiously on his scattered possessions—on the girdle containing £300 which he had painfully wrapt beneath his clothes round his body, of his noble flagons which he had sent in haste to Kate Joyce's, of that precious night-bag jolting beneath the seat of the coach which bore his wife and father along the North Road. He did not know what to do with his silver, since it was too late to change it for gold; sometimes he thought of flinging it into the privy, but then wondered how he would get it again when he and his colleagues were turned out of the Office. For this now seemed inevitable; indeed, he thought, they would all be lucky if they did not have their throats cut.

Meanwhile the public alarm grew. Travellers from Chatham bore tidings of burning English warships, of unmanned English guns, of English seamen who stood on Dutch decks and shouted to their countrymen on shore that they had fought hitherto for tickets but now they would fight for dollars. And in the streets of Wapping seamen's wives cried aloud that such things were a punishment for not paying their husbands. The City was in a panic, and rich men everywhere were moving their money bags. At any moment, it was said, the Dutch, having scuttled England's fighting ships in the Medway, would violate the Thames and, with their guns playing in the very Pool of London, avenge Holmes' bonfire of the previous year in a blazing pyre of English merchantmen. In terrified haste ships were sunk to block the fairway below Woolwich and Blackwall, but in the general chaos of that moment they were the wrong ships; and vessels laden with badly needed naval stores were sent to the bottom in preference to the empty tonnage that lay alongside. But none of the public miscarriages, real and imaginary, of which men spoke in those terrible days, weighed more heavily on Pepys' mind than did that private one, the news of which reached him on June 19th when his wife returned to London. For she, it seemed, with his foolish father, had buried his gold in the garden at Brampton, not at night but in full daylight, during church time on Sunday morning when any passer-by might have seen. It put Pepys into such trouble that he would neither sup with nor speak to his wife all night.[1]

He had other things to worry him. On the day Elizabeth returned he was called before the Council Board with all his Medway papers to bear witness during the examination of Commissioner Pett who, having been ordered to draw the great ships up the river to safety, had employed himself on the fatal day in using what boats there were to remove his private models from the doomed vessels. Pepys, though conscious of his own innocence, was so doubtful as to what might happen that he gave Tom Hayter his keys and instructions for disposing the rest of his money before he left for Whitehall. The whole Council was present and, in his anxiety to ensure that the victim should be Pett and not himself, he was more harsh than was decent (as he confided to his all-judging journal) to his fellow officer. For which, he added, "God forgive me". When he came out, the crowd outside the Court gazed curiously at him so that he was forced to smile lest it should be supposed that he, not Pett, was the prisoner. And next day it was rumoured about the town that he was in the Tower. For once in his life Pepys was glad if he met nobody*; when he and Coventry encountered each other at

* "I met with none I knew, nor did desire it." *D.* June 25th, 1667.

St James's nearly a fortnight after the calamity they scarcely dared look each other in the face.

Not that many thought that Pepys was really to blame. For though all the world cried out on the Navy Office for a pack of knaves and fools, the general consensus of opinion was that the Clerk of the Acts was a decent, industrious little fellow who knew his job and had done his best. When he told Sir Thomas Harvey, the latest of his colleagues (and one who had purchased his place) that for his part he would not mind being turned out so long as the nation escaped ruin, Sir Thomas answered: "That is a good one, in faith! For you know yourself to be secure in being necessary to the Office".[2]

Meanwhile the war continued to its ignominious end. De Ruyter, bearing off the *Royal Charles* from the Medway as trophy, declined to venture higher up the Thames and contented himself in riding with a hundred sail across the mouth of the river—"as dread a spectacle as ever Englishman saw", wrote Evelyn, "and a dishonour never to be wiped out". While he remained there all trade was at a standstill; coals sold at £5. 10*s*. per chaldron and the poor grew daily more restive. Varying rumours, true and false, reached the Navy Office: how the Dutch had landed at Harwich, how they were now at Yarmouth, how they had been seen off Dover, how they were in great squadrons everywhere—at Portsmouth, at Plymouth, at Dartmouth—till old Batten cried with a great oath: "By God I think the Devil shits Dutchmen". But it all came to an end, for after a last unsuccessful attempt on Harman's part to avenge himself on De Ruyter by a fireship attack, ill-timed and timorously executed, the war closed in August with the Peace of Breda. And though the actual treaty was not unprofitable for England—it brought her New Amsterdam, now rechristened New York—recent events had made it inglorious enough, and the last word was with Pepys who, in his private journal, epitomised the affair for himself and posterity: "thus in all things, in wisdom, courage, force, knowledge of our own streams, and success, the Dutch have the best of us, and do end the war with victory on their side". The Clerk of the Acts had served his apprenticeship in war. Like young Arthur Wellesley a hundred and thirty years later, he had at least learnt what not to do.[3]

For the moment the mellow harvest of experience and knowledge had still to mature, and that August, while the last formalities of the peace treaty were being completed, Pepys, as a Principal Officer of a Navy that no longer kept the seas, had little to do except to play. Fearful as he was of the future, when an angry Parliament must meet to demand vengeance, he made the best of his chances and of the last fleeting weeks of summer. Coaxed by Penn on August 1st to the theatre for the first time since the Medway incident, he saw over thirty plays in three months, once in a single week visiting the playhouse six times. He bought fruit for Knepp and Mrs Pierce when he sat beside them at the King's House, nearly died with laughter over *Sir Martin Marr-all*, which he saw over and over again, and much approved a piece which ended with a dance of ladies in a military manner. Out of doors he pursued the innocent pleasures of the season with equal zest, taking his wife and Jane by boat to the Half-Way House in the cool of the evening to see how beautiful England could be even in defeat (catching thereby a glimpse of a lovely face seen for a moment in the little lane that ran from Redriffe into the fields) or rowing with them to Lambeth and Barn Elms, "very fine and pleasant, only", he added with an unusual twinge of distaste for that women's company, "could not sing ordinary songs with the freedom that otherwise I would".[4]

Of all the expeditions he made in that aftermath of battle, one survives for ever—a part of England's common legacy of pleasure. It was on a July Sunday that he and his wife—she was late dressing herself which vexed him—taking pretty Miss Turner and Will Hewer, to say nothing of a good store of wine, beer and cold fowl, set out at five in the morning in a coach for Epsom. It was a fine day and they had much pleasant discourse on the way, particularly of the pride and ignorance of Sir William Penn's family. At Epsom they drank the waters (with capital results), attended church and dined merrily, sleeping awhile in the midday heat when they had done. "And so", continues Pepys, "the women and W. Hewer and I walked upon the Downes, where a flock of sheep was; and the most pleasant and innocent sight that ever I saw in my life. We found a shepherd and his little boy reading, far from any houses or sight of people, the Bible to him; so I made the boy read to me, which he did, with the forced tone that children do usually read, that was mighty pretty, and then I did give him something, and went to the father, and talked with him and I find he had been a servant in my cousin Pepys' house, and told me what was become of their old servants. He did content himself mightily in my liking his boy's reading, and did bless God for him, the most like one of the old patriarchs that ever I saw in my life, and it brought those thoughts of the old age of the world in my mind for two or three days after. We took notice of his woollen knit stockings of two colours mixed, and of his shoes shod with iron shoes, both at the toe and heels, and with great nails in the soles of his feet, which was mighty pretty: and, taking notice of them, 'Why', says the poor man, 'the downes, you see, are full of stones, and we are fain to shoe ourselves thus; and these', says he, 'will make the stones fly till they sing before me'. I did give the poor man something, for which he was mighty thankful, and I tried to cast stones with his horn crook. He values his dog mightily, that would turn a sheep any way which he would have him, when he goes to fold them: told me there was about eighteen score sheep in his flock, and that he hath four shillings a week the year round for keeping of them: so we parted thence with mighty pleasure in the discourse we had with this poor man, and Mrs Turner, in the common fields here, did gather one of the prettiest nosegays that ever I saw in my life. So to our coach, and through Mr Minnes's wood, and looked upon Mr Evelyn's house; and so over the common, and through Epsom towne to our inn, in the way stopping a poor woman with her milk pail, and in one of my gilt tumblers did drink our bellyfulls of milk, better than any cream, and so to our inn, and there had a dish of cream, but it was sour, and so had no pleasure in it; and so paid our reckoning, and took coach, it being about seven at night, and passed and saw the people walking with their wives and children to take the air, and we set out for home...talking and pleasing our selves with the pleasure of this day's work." So, little guessing how many thousands unborn would ride in fancy that same way beside them, they came to London town, resolved to keep a coach and often take their pastime this way.[5]

In this season even church-going was made to serve for delight (all the sweeter for the turmoil of the past and the fear of what was to come), for these were months of pleasure. So on an August Sabbath, Pepys turned into St Dunstan's and there standing by a pretty, modest maid laboured to take her by the hand and body; this she would not allow but edged away from him. Undeterred he followed until she took pins out of her pocket to defend herself—"which seeing

I did forbear, and was glad I did spy her design". But the diversity of creatures with which God's world is peopled afforded in a pew close by another pretty maid, not, it seems, so modest, who returned the glances of the friendly stranger and permitted him awhile to hold her hand. And so, he tells us, "the sermon ended, and church broke up and my amours ended also".

Scarcely! For love, if such it may be called, continued to play its part in his life. While the thunder of the Medway guns was still in his ears and he feared an attack on the Navy Office, Pepys could not refrain from secretly playing the fool with his maid Nell or toying with Mrs Daniel beneath her petticoats. And that September he engaged in what was almost an orgy of amatory adventure. Even a nasty shock administered by that dangerous Mrs Martin, who so inconsiderately (and in her husband's absence at sea too) informed him that she was with child*, had not lessened his zest for this kind of pleasure. Betty herself, Doll Lane, Mrs Michell, and the maid at the "Swan" (who cried out in alarm at his rough wooing), were all alike his quarry. Rejoicing greatly, and scarcely now pausing to regret, he pursued them.[6]

Poor Mrs Pepys was not pursued, though Samuel sometimes pretended that she was: he was disturbed, for instance, by certain unsettling reports of the morals of a young Guardsman named Coleman, who had accompanied her in the coach from Brampton—"a very rogue for women as any in the world", he heard he was. One day in August Elizabeth came to him and in a most pointed and disagreeable way informed him that she was in a certain periodic

* When three days later he heard that all was well, he was as glad of his escape as he was of the successful issue of the peace negotiations with Holland. *D.* July 6th, 1667.

state of health, and bade him remember it. "I asked her why, and she said she had a reason. I do think by something too she said to-day that she took notice that I had not lain with her this half year, that she thinks that I have some doubt that she might be with child by somebody else, which God knows never entered into my head....But I do not do well", he added with sudden wisdom, "to let these beginnings of discontent take so much root between us." Only a few weeks before, finding her in a dogged humour, he had given her a pull by the nose and some ill words so that she had followed him to the Office in a devilish manner and only with great difficulty had he been able to coax her home again "to prevent shame".[7]

With the coming, in September, of a new companion, Deborah Willet, a fresh domestic era set in. Pepys had at first been averse to his wife having another lady's maid, but had been much consoled when told that the prospective candidate was pleasant to look upon. As soon as she came, he was conquered. For Deb was a charming little girl. Just out of a school at Bow, she was already mistress of a sweet, solemn deportment, the more winning because she was so young and tiny—as grave a little thing as ever he saw in his life, he thought. She made a great change in his habits: he was always at home now, walking in the garden with his lady and her little attendant, as befitted a kind and serious husband, though Elizabeth herself formed her own impressions as to the reason for this unwonted behaviour—so much so that Samuel began to fear that the newcomer would not be suffered to remain. But she stayed, for the little creature won both their hearts, and when her aunt—quite a fine lady, extraordinarily well carriaged with a most imposing store of conversation about the Court and fashions—came to call at the year's end, she found Deb firmly established in the household at Seething Lane. Indeed the good woman took great pleasure to see how her niece's breasts had grown since her coming—"which", as Pepys said, "was a pretty kind of content she gave herself". He himself felt a strange content too as he surveyed his wife's demure attendant—gave her her first kiss, which she took with so pretty a humour as made him love her mightily, got her to comb his hair nightly by the fireside (he liked, he said, to have her fiddling about him), and when his wife, as sometimes happened, was unaccountably angry with her, gave her good advice and dried her tears. And as, in the manner of that day, she helped to undress him, he made certain advances to her which she repelled so gently and modestly that he could scarcely bring himself to attempt more.[8]

These were his pleasures, but when Parliament reassembled in October, the old round of work and trouble began again. The event was preceded by a feverish outburst of economy and accompanied by changes at the Office. Pepys himself, always alive to the spirit of the moment, was quick to draw in his horns; as early as July, he had gracefully anticipated necessity by resigning his Victualling employment and salary; he was just in time, for on the very next day he heard that a letter was being prepared for abolishing all war offices. Economy was the watchword of the hour: ominous orders appeared at the Navy Office to provide details of all increases in official salaries during the past quarter-century, and Coventry propounded a plan for reducing the annual charge of the Navy to £200,000. He also suggested that Pepys should lend some of the profits made out of the private man-of-war, which the King had loaned him, back to the Crown on the security of the "new Act"—an outcome of the economy campaign which the Clerk of the Acts did not at all appreciate. Yet, though he tried to pass off this unwelcome proposition by a "merry answer", Coventry remained persistent, and he was forced to comply*.[9]

On October 10th Parliament met, in a slightly better temper than would otherwise have been the case, owing to the King's timely dismissal of the hated Lord Chancellor. But it was still palpable enough that, as Pepys mournfully put it, bloody work was like to be, and soon every government official was industriously employed in preparing his own defence by blaming his colleagues: indeed so much activity among the employees of the state had not been known for years. To this rule of universal treachery Pepys proved an exception. For one thing, for all his fears, he was confident of his own innocence and knew that his reputation stood far higher than that of any of his colleagues: for another his pride was touched by these outside attacks on the abuses of his Office. With admirable courage and industry, he set himself to prepare a defence, not of himself alone but of the whole Office. For nothing would rid him of the conviction that it was an injustice to charge a department with non-performance of duties, the wherewithal to perform which had never been supplied.[10]

For this reason, Pepys took especial pains to defend the Navy Office against the accusation that certain of its members—Brouncker in particular—had discharged seamen at Chatham by ticket. These negotiable bills, issued in lieu of wages and payable at a future time, had long been a source of grave discontent; poor seamen, without cash to buy the necessities of life, were sometimes compelled—so bad was the government's credit—to sell their tickets to innkeepers and tradesmen for little more than half their value. Purists,

* After consulting the list of subscribers to see how much others had advanced, he lent £300, since no smaller sum, he decided, would consort with his dignity.

among whom the politicians were numbered, were bitterly opposed to this practice; it was, they argued, both an insult to the state's credit and an injustice to the seamen. But, as the practical defenders of the system pointed out, so long as there was not enough cash for the administration's needs, the sailors must either be paid by negotiable paper bills or starve. And, as Pepys in his unanswerable defence insisted, to blame naval officials for taking the only measures open to them at all, was a cruel injustice. He himself had taken a strenuous part in trying to right the abuses of the ticket system: indeed earlier in the year he had incurred some odium by procuring, in the face of considerable opposition, the dismissal of James Carcasse, one of the Clerks of the Ticket Office who had been guilty of corruption. It was among his many trials at this time that this malicious and cunning fellow should appear as his accuser before the Parliamentary Committee of Miscarriages.[11]

Yet if Pepys' innocence was not sufficient to save him from the enquiring politicians, his wonderful industry, method and power of reasoned presentation were able in the end to save not only himself but his colleagues. All day long, till his eyes were ready to fall out of his head, he sat with his clerks preparing notes, citing orders, collecting precedents, vexed to the heart that so honest a business should bring him so much trouble and determined to spare no pains to refute these unjust charges. He was often afraid, almost always uneasy, and altogether lacking that high-hearted joy in battle against odds which is the glory of a Montrose, a Cromwell, a Lincoln; it was not in Pepys' nature to embrace martyrdom as a lover. "Were I but well possessed of what I should have in the world", he wrote, "I think I could willingly retreat and trouble myself no more with it. I do plainly see my weakness", he added with just introspection, "that I am not a man able to go through trouble as other men are, but that I should be a miserable man if I should meet with adversity, which God keep me from." Yet, just as he had faced the pestilence from which others had fled, so now he confronted an angry Parliament—sadly, with fear and yet with unshakable courage and constancy. Danger might damp his zest for life, but it revealed the rock of manhood that, fenman that he was, was the central bastion of his being.

Three times that October and November did he face the accusers of his Office in Parliament, standing bareheaded before Committees of the House and with outward calm and courage defending himself and his companions. And each time, though the night before his head and heart were full of thoughts and he slept but little, he acquitted himself nobly, winning praises even from those furious scapegoat-hunters, the politicians; he was so clear in his arguments, so plainly master of his subject, so engagingly frank. Knowing exactly what he wished to refute or prove and refusing to be drawn into perilous by-paths, he was more than a match for his divided and somewhat confused examiners. "But Lord!" he wrote with contemptuous discernment, "what a tumultuous thing this Committee is, for all the reputation they have of a great Council, . . . there being as impertinent questions and as disorderly proposed as any man could make."

In these encounters, whether in refuting the accusations about tickets or removing the blame for the Medway disaster from the door of the Navy Office, Pepys was manfully aided by his cousin Roger of Impington, who warned him from day to day of the suspicions and intentions of his fellow-members. From his own colleagues Pepys received but little help, though he defended them wholeheartedly—even giving poor, frightened Pett advice to enable him to protect himself from his unjust accusers. But he received his reward, for, when on December 19th the House adjourned till February, Pepys was left, not merely in place, but with his position more assured and his reputation higher than it had ever been before. Even the able but self-opinionated young Sir Robert Brooke, chairman of the accusing Committee, had been conquered by the good temper, clear categorical reasoning and frank answers* of the Clerk of the Acts; he would make him, he said, "the darling of the House". And rough old Colonel Birch, the erstwhile Roundhead, declared to his face that he knew him to be a man of the old way for taking pains.[12]

Among his colleagues there were many changes. Carteret had resigned his thankless task at the Navy Treasury as far back as June, being succeeded by Lord Anglesey, an old Parliamentarian; and Coventry, who had led the hounds against Clarendon, and was aiming for great place, had already laid down his secretaryship to the Duke of York: for one dazzling moment Pepys had toyed with the rumour which was whispered about the town that he should step into his shoes. But he had kept his head with the reflection that he was now in "the best place that ever man was in to please his own mind", and that he could never bear the separation from his wife which personal attendance on the Duke would entail. Yet had he accepted, it is curious to reflect, the whole future history of his country had perhaps been changed, for with his shrewd, steadying guidance the tragedy of James of York and England might never have been enacted.

* One of Pepys' categorical answers to Sir Robert Brooke is worth citation. Brooke's question was whether Pepys believed that the want of money had been so great as to necessitate the discharge of men by ticket. "If by want of money your intentions be it's not being supplied to this Office", was the answer, "I do not only believe but know it." Pepys to Sir R. Brooke, Dec. 10th, 1667. Tanner, *Further Correspondence*, 184–5.

Other changes there were too at the Office. That which Pepys most ardently desired, the departure of the doting Comptroller, Sir John Mennes, did not occur, for the old gentleman, after giving every appearance of dying in July, recovered and moreover succeeded in defeating the various assaults which his colleague behind the scenes prepared to drive him from his post. But in October Batten passed from the mortal scene after a short and sudden illness, Pepys a little repenting his long warfare with him now that he was really gone, "partly out of kindness, he being a good neighbour, and partly because of the money he owes me upon our bargain of the late prize". The latter, the old business of the private man-of-war, gave him much trouble before it was over and many a long, painful interview with his old foe's widow and executrix, but in the end this also, like most of his birds, came home to roost.[13]

For in that penniless and enquiring time, Pepys still contrived to prosper. October, which saw him feverishly digging up his buried gold in the garden at Brampton by the light of a dark lantern—his wife and father had forgotten where they had laid it, and some of the bags had rotted, scattering their precious contents in the damp earth—brought a seasonable windfall of £200 from his Tangier partner, Yeabsly. Better still Warren, from whom he had long been divided, chose that November to return to his old allegiance, bringing him a present (for past services, he explained) of fifty pieces of gold, which he accepted with many protestations of integrity. The gift was more pleasing in that it showed that the City Fathers regarded him as a man to be reckoned with, whatever the hotheads in Parliament might charge against his Office.

Pepys had his financial troubles, of course: even he found it difficult that winter to get possession of his salary. In December he was petitioning for arrears amounting to £500; in February he was adding a whole book of travelling expenses incurred in various kinds of attendance on the King and Duke of York, the Lord Treasurer, the Commissioners of the Exchequer, the Duke of Albemarle, the Lords of the Council, Parliamentary Committees—he was careful to omit nothing —"a continual expense of coach-hire and boat-hire,... arising frequently to 6/8 and sometimes more in a day". As has been well and often said, Pepys was the father of our Civil Service.[14]

In other ways too—for if in certain little matters he was somewhat costly, he did his duty, knew his work, stood by his colleagues and Office in time of trouble and never spared himself when he believed his country had need of his labours; this also has become part of the tradition of the permanent secretariat of England. February, which witnessed the re-assembly of Parliament, was a month of dreadful Committees. Commissioners of Accounts, demanding figures, angry and inquisitive members prying into the innermost intimacies of the Prize scandal of 1665, a Committee of Miscarriages which ranged happily and destructively over the whole field of suspected abuses—payment by ticket, private trading by state officials, bribes, privateers—all demanded Pepys' daily attendance. On him fell the burden of rebutting all charges. And as one watches that heroic fight, unsparing labour day and night, cool, courageous bearing, none the less noble because in his inner soul he was often afraid, one forgets the petty corruptions, the bullying days at home, the sly salacities of the secret hour in coach and tavern, and remembers only the great heart that dared to wage it and the cool head that triumphed over the enemies of his Office. Grumble he sometimes did, writing to the Duke of York of the troublesome life he was forced to lead dancing attendance on one Committee after another; retirement to country peace and quiet—"a good book, and a good fiddle and I have a good wife"—he often contemplated, tired he was always, "for I am weary", he said, "of this life". But he stood fast.[15]

On February 28th the angry Commons decided that the Principal Officers of the Navy should be ordered to answer for the crimes of which they were accused at the Bar of the House on the following Thursday. Pepys at the thought of that terrible ordeal wished himself a great way off—"who am least able to bear these troubles, though I have the least cause to be concerned in it". Then for five days he betook himself to the work of preparing the defence of the Office, for his colleagues were too busy excusing themselves to think of anything else. At ten o'clock on the eve of the dreaded day he went home, weary and dull and sick, feeling that he could do no more, and lay down on his bed. But sleep came but fitfully and after three hours he waked, "never in so much trouble in all my life of mind, thinking of the task I have upon me,...and what the issue of it may be".

So he lay tossing restlessly till five in the morning, when he called to Elizabeth to comfort him, which she at last succeeded in doing, making him resolve to resign his post and endure the trouble of it no more. Then at the Office with his clerks he huddled over a few more notes, took boat with the faithful Hayter and Hewer to Westminster and joined his waiting colleagues. As the summons had not yet come he drank half a pint of mulled sack at the "Dog" and added a dram of brandy bought from Mrs Howlett's stall in Westminster Hall. A little before midday they were called into the lobby. The House was full and alight with expectation.

There, when the Speaker had read the Report of the Committee, with his fellow officers standing taut and anxious about him and the Mace lying on the table before, Samuel Pepys began the defence of the Navy Office. And, as he stood there, a miracle happened; all doubts and fears fell from him and he spoke with a wonderful ease and certainty, "most acceptably and smoothly and continued at it without any hesitation or loss but with full scope and all my reason free about me, as if it had been at my own table, from that time till past three in the afternoon, and so ended without any interruption from the Speaker". Then they withdrew.[16]

As they came out of the chamber, his colleagues whom he had saved and all those within hearing crowded around him, crying up his speech as the finest ever heard. It almost looked as if a vote acquitting the Principal Officers would be taken then and there, but Pepys had spoken so long that there was something of a stampede of members to their dinner, and the few who returned later were so drunk that such professed enemies of the Office as Sir Thomas Littleton were able to prevent the House from dividing. But nothing could rob Pepys of a wonderful triumph. When next morning he called on Sir William Coventry, the first word that that statesman said to him was "Good morrow, Mr Pepys, that must be speaker of the Parliament-house", adding that the Solicitor General had declared that he was the best speaker in England and that men were saying that he had but to put on a gown and plead at the Chancery bar and he could not fail to earn less than £1000 a year. When he went abroad, which he did a good deal that day, everyone hurried up to congratulate him; one member of Parliament swore that he would go twenty miles to hear such a speech again, another that the whole kingdom would ring with his abilities, and a third, his cousin George Montagu, outsoaring them all, embraced him, declaring that he had often before kissed his hands but now he would kiss his lips, for they were those of another Cicero. Even the King came up to him in the Park and congratulated him, and told his friends that he thought he might teach the Solicitor General. Everywhere, at the Court, in the House, on 'Change, men spoke of his great performance. No wonder that the delighted, but prudent little man noted in his journal his resolution "not to make any more speeches while my fame is good—for fear of losing of it".[17]

Chapter XVII

The Heel of Achilles

"A strange slavery that I stand in to beauty, that I value nothing near it." *Diary*, Sept. 6th, 1664.

For nine weeks after the great speech, Parliament continued to sit, and Pepys and his fellow officers were subjected to the inconvenience of those eternally changing humours which in all ages have been the attribute of the politician in assembly. He hung about a good deal in the lobbies, danced attendance on various committees, took careful steps to conceal the traces of such bribes as he had received, and made a clean breast, gaining some further reputation by his careful account of what had happened, of his share in the Prize Scandal of 1665. And when Penn was impeached, he, who had hated him so much in the day of his prosperity, stood by him and consoled him as best he could, sitting with him of an evening when the day's work was done. His success had made him at once more confident of himself and gentler. The former quality was seen one April afternoon as he took water from the Privy Stairs at Whitehall to Westminster when the King, calling down to ask him where he was going, he boldly answered: "To wait on our masters at Westminster", at which there was much laughter. Afterwards he was a little frightened of his temerity, for fear that any member of the House was within hearing. But the cloud of politicians passed in early May when the King adjourned the Houses, hoping that "their recess would put them into a way of accommodation". It was a pleasant thought. Thereafter there was peace.[1]

Indeed a strange calm now fell upon the Navy Office; reflected, too, in Pepys' attitude towards his colleagues. Once more, after long and bitter absence, he visited Lord Brouncker's house and sat there, asking many questions in mathematics which the other did him the pleasure of answering as they drank together. And with Penn his relations became almost affectionate: he shared a coach with him and his family to take the fresh Stepney air and spent long hours at his house when his gout kept him indoors: it was quite like old times. The only thing Pepys would not do was to eat his neighbour's victuals—because of their sluttery, he explained; but he was not in the least averse from petting his daughter, Mrs Lowther, as he obligingly pulled off her wet shoes for her. And, as though to signalise the good humour of that peaceful May, which even the treachery of the weather could not tarnish, he cheerfully lent Lady Sandwich £100, although he admitted that he never expected to see it again*.[2]

In such a mood Pepys turned to his philosophy of pleasure —"the height of what we take pains for and can hope for in this world", he had written, "and therefore to be enjoyed while we are young and capable of these joys". It was in keeping with his habit of making all that life offered serve his turn, that he now found, in the very misfortune which was threatening to end his career, the excuse for devoting more time to the joys of existence. For some time his eyes had been causing him grave anxiety; as far back as the previous autumn he had been driven to consult Turlington, the spectacle maker. With the work of defending the Office, the

* A few months before he had been most reluctant to advance Lord Hinchingbrooke a similar sum.

trouble had been intensified; every week they grew more tired. The entries in his beloved journal grew shorter, and reading for pleasure he had for a time to abandon altogether. Deprived of books, he had found compensation by returning to his old passion for music. It proved joy enough. One day, listening to the wind music in Massinger and Dekker's *Virgin Martyr* all the sensitive love for ordered sound which was part of his diverse being was transcended; "it is so sweet that it ravished me", he wrote, "and indeed, in a word, did wrap up my soul so that it made me really sick, just as I have formerly been when in love with my wife; that neither then, nor all the evening going home and at home I was able to think of anything but remained all night transported, so as I could not believe that ever any music hath that real command over the soul of a man as this did upon me; and makes me resolve to practise wind music and to make my wife do the like". So entranced was he that he fell to inventing a new theory of music—one better and simpler, he thought, than any which had yet prevailed in the world: it seemed almost within his reach as he sat with his musical friends about him listening to that masterly performer, Mr Banister, playing for his delight first on the theorbo and then on his flageolet.[3]

So now in the early summer days of 1668, he made his weary eyes an excuse for recreation. Fourteen times in April and sixteen times in May did he visit the playhouse—pricking down the Echo song in the *Tempest* which gave him such delight, seeing "Nell in her boy's clothes mighty pretty" and stepping up to Harris's, the actor's, dressing room at the Duke's House when the play *Love in a Tub* was done. Inevitably the theatre led to Knepp, and this, since Elizabeth was taking a holiday at Brampton with her maids Deb and Jane Birch, was not attended by inconveniences. He drove with the fascinating creature in a hackney coach through the Park, after the play was done, kissing her a little tentatively, half because he was not certain how she would take it and half because she was so covered with paint that his Puritan soul revolted at it; he sang with her at the Grotto in rural Kensington; took her to the Tower to see the lions and regaled her on lobster and wine at the "Cock". Before long he grew bolder: in a dark coach at night ventured an advance, the lady opposing but little; her skin, he noted, was very soft. Two nights later in an arbour at Vauxhall he explored still further. Yet he who had braved the assembled Commons of England was still afraid to venture all with a wanton actress, and an overbold hand as she slept (or pretended to sleep) on a pallet in the dark at Mrs Pierce's, an immodest offer not pressed too far in a coach returning from Marylebone Garden and a kiss which, finding her from home, he gave her pretty maid was all the injury he ever did to Mrs Knepp. Reading those strange polyglot passages which record the excited hopes, fears and pleasures of these encounters, one is left with the feeling that the lady was a little disappointed. Yet this extraordinary man, after an afternoon partly spent in chasing a pretty woman with a wanton look from Duck Lane to Newgate Market, could note with genuine horror how rudely the young gallants accosted the ladies at Spring Garden; it troubled him, he declared, to see the confidence of the vice of the age.[4]

It is pleasanter to record the genuine kindness with which a man, so frail and enslaved to a corporeal weakness, could behave towards those who were bound to him by ties of blood and social obligation. When the hated Anthony Joyce, overcome by his losses in the Fire and the drudgery of his new life as an innkeeper, died after an attempt to drown himself, Pepys behaved with the utmost tenderness and delicacy towards his unhappy cousin, Kate; comforted, counselled and befriended her and, anticipating a verdict of *felo de se* by which, according to ancient law, the dead man's property would be forfeit to the Crown, hurried to the King and obtained his promise that the deceased's estate should be granted to his widow and children. In much the same way he did his duty by Pall. Two winters past, Ensum, the rustic lover whom he had bought for her, with the promise of a dowry of £500, had died. With admirable perseverance Samuel had ever since tried to find her a substitute—no very easy task, for his sister, he observed, was growing old and ugly. Hewer, to whom he first broached the subject, had refused the flattering invitation with "mighty acknowledgements", but after several essays Samuel landed another Huntingdonshire neighbour for poor Pall, one John Jackson, a kinsman of her deceased lover. And now in May he went down to Brampton for a week-end to visit his father and survey the newly-married couple. It was a pleasing prospect; for his sister, now so happily set up by the dowry he had given her, had grown fat and almost comely (though mighty pert and proud, he thought), and Jackson was all that he could desire—a fond husband and a substantial man, nephew to rich Mr Phillips and about to set up at Ellington as a grazier on his own account.[5]

The expedition whetted Pepys' long-starved appetite for travel: he would take a holiday, ride abroad and see the world. On June 3rd he begged a week's absence from the Duke of York (gladly granted him with a highly flattering royal comment on his diligence in the King's business), and two days later with Will Hewer, Mr Murford and his cousin Betty Turner, who also took a sparrow, to accompany him, he set out for Brampton to pick up his wife and Deb. Then on Monday, June 8th, 1668, with his family about him, Pepys set out to travel across England.

Having left his journal at home, Pepys' record of that pilgrimage is a little scanty. Sometimes we have no other entry but of the petty cash he expended—the 2*s.* bounty for the roadmenders by the wayside, the 19*s.* 6*d.* reckoning for supper at Newport Pagnell, or, maybe, Buckingham*—the narrative of his days, usually so meticulous, here in this holiday mood grows a little hazy—the 6*d.* expended on the poor. But palpably it was all intensely enjoyable. Oxford he voted a very sweet place—the schools and library, the strawberries, Chichele's picture at All Souls', the buttery at Brasenose, the physic garden, the sack, Friar Bacon's study—a "mighty fine place; and well seated, and cheap entertainment". Then he hurried his party on to Abingdon for the night, meeting by Bagley Woods many scholars going home from Custard Fair in the quietude of a June evening. And after supper with his company—one can see the grave solemnity of little Deb dancing before him—he called for the town music, sang and danced.

Then with their landlord to guide them, they went over the lonely downs towards Hungerford, noting the good trout, eels and crayfish which graced that watery town. And so all day, travelling south across the high chalk lands on to the Plain, guided by that divine steeple which rises before the traveller between the rounded breasts of the hills. Towards night they found themselves among the ramparts of ancient fortifications—so prodigious as to frighten Pepys who, ever enquiring, wandered alone among them in the

* There is plainly some mistake in his entry for June 8th, 1668. He started in the morning from Brampton, drank to the tune of a shilling at Bedford and then, according to his own account, went on to Buckingham and slept at Newport Pagnell. As he was travelling to Oxford, this is obviously wrong: no man travels from Buckingham to Oxford by Newport Pagnell.

dusk. But when he came to the "George" Inn at Salisbury, he found good diet and a silk bed to lie in.

Something lyrical informs the laconic entries of the next day, a Thursday, or perhaps it is but the mood of the interpreter whose heart still thrills to the echo of that beloved land of chalk hill and stream, sweetest paradise of old England, Wiltshire. While the coach-horses rested, with the three women mounted behind Will Hewer, Murford and the guide, brave Mr Pepys riding single, the holiday party made its way to Stonehenge. A shepherd woman, kindly rewarded by 4*d.*, went before, leading the horses. The great stones duly impressed; Pepys gazing up at them thought them as prodigious as any tales he had ever heard of them and "worth going this journey to see: God knows what their use was! they are hard to tell, but yet may be told". Then by Lord Pembroke's house at Wilton they returned to Salisbury, to rejoin the coach and pay the reckoning. "Which was so exorbitant, and particular in rate of my horses, and 7*s.* 6*d.* for bread and beer that I was mad, and resolve to trouble the mistress about it, and get something for the poor, and come away in that humour—£2. 5*s.* 6*d.*, servants 1*s.* 6*d.*, poor 1*s.*, guide to the stones 2*s.*, poor woman in the street 1*s.*, ribbons 9*d.*, washwoman 1*s.*, sempstress for W. Hewer 3*s.*, lent W. Hewer 2*s.*" It was expensive, yet it was worth it. And before they left the "tall-spired town", Pepys wrote to London to excuse his not coming home; he was resolved now to see Bath, and, it might be, Bristol.

"Thence about six o'clock, and with a guide went over the smooth plain indeed till night; and then by a happy mistake, and that looked like an adventure, we were carried out of our way to a town where we would lie, since we could not go as far as we would. And there with great difficulty came about ten at night to a little inn, where we were fain to go into a room where a pedlar was in bed and made him rise"—how, as they woke him, the humble man must have blinked at these important, jovial travellers—"and there wife and I lay and in a truckle-bed Betty Turner and Willet." Next day they passed into Somerset, Elizabeth and Deb, who were both west-country born, rejoicing mightily and Pepys commending the landscape, "as indeed it deserves". In the first village of the county through which they passed, he called two or three little boys and listened with great pleasure to their strange speech: childlike himself he made one of them kiss Deb and another say the Lord's Prayer—"hallowed be thy kingdom come". At Norton St Philip, in a more solemn mood, he viewed the tomb of a Knight Templar, recalled the story of the Fair Maids of Foscott, and listened to the church bells, "and they mighty tuneable". So before nightfall they came to Bath—the town of stone, and clean, and the streets narrow.

At Bath Pepys, as befitted one so curious, had a great experience: he had a bath. Nor did he do it by halves: for he stayed in the steaming water for two hours. Wrapped in a sheet and parboiled, he was carried back in a chair to his inn; he felt a little shocked, for all the crowded company there and the many fine ladies in the bath, at so singular and questionable a practice; "methinks it cannot be clean", he wrote, "to go so many bodies together in the same water". Then for an hour he lay at his ease and sweated, while the town music—5*s.**—played before him.

But by eleven o'clock this indefatigable tripper was once more on the road—to Bristol, a place which he had long wished to see. He found it "another London"—the second

* The sergeant of the bath got 10*s.*, and the man that carried the party in chairs to the bath 3*s.* 6*d.* Considering the value of money then, they did not do badly. *D.* June 13th, 1668.

greatest city of the kingdom—with so many houses that one could not see the fields, a fine cross like Cheapside and a handsome fellow who trimmed one for two shillings. Only what was curious was that the carts were without wheels or horses but were drawn on sledges by dogs, lest the rumbling of the wheels, he was told, should disturb the Bristol milk —that golden velvet wine which lay in the vaults below.

A special feature of the visit to Bristol was the hospitality of Deb's uncle, a man so like one of the sober, wealthy, London merchants that Pepys was entranced with him. He entertained the travellers to dinner, showed them the Custom House and quay—where they inspected a new ship a-building—and took them to the street where Deb was born. "But Lord!" wrote her happy employer, "the joy that was among the old poor people of the place to see Mrs Willet's daughter: it seems her mother being a brave woman and mightily beloved". And when one poor woman, hearing that Deb was come, ran up to them with tears in her eyes and speechless with joy, Pepys was so moved that he also wept: "I protest that I was not able to speak to her (which I would have done) to have diverted her tears". The visit ended with a fine entertainment from this noble merchant, of strawberries and venison pasty and abundance of brave wine and, above all, Bristol milk. And so by moonlight they returned to Bath.

To London too. For the best of holidays must have an end, and, after seeing Avebury, Marlborough, Littlecote, Reading and Maidenhead, Pepys on June 17th, just twelve days after he set out, returned to his familiar haunts. He was in fine fettle after his holiday. When Lord Anglesey, the new Navy Treasurer, had the temerity to hint that his holiday had been too prolonged, the Clerk of the Acts recorded that he did not care a turd.

But Mrs Pepys also had been set up by her airing, and

this had its inconveniences. Her prolonged freedom from domestic harness had given her new ideas, and Samuel's last day of pilgrimage had been somewhat spoilt by sad reflections on his wife's impertinent mood, "got by this liberty of being from me, which she is never to be trusted with, for she is a fool". Next day she was in a melancholy, fusty humour; it appeared that she had heard how in her absence at Brampton he had been carrying people—Knepp and Pierce for instance—to plays and treats. That night she rose weeping and sobbing and, leaving Samuel, ostentatiously fled to Deb's bed, and on the morrow it all came out in a passionate torrent of tears and words: how she had a request to make him, how she would go to France and live there out of trouble, how he loved pleasure and denied her any and, as Sam cryptically put it, "a deal of do". Growing wiser now he said nothing, but with very mild words and few suffered her humour to spend till she grew quiet and began to be friends again. And by Sunday the house was once more at peace, and he dined with his wife and Deb alone, "merry and in good humour, which is, when all is done, the greatest felicity of all".

One thing Samuel's holiday did not do—effect any real improvement in the state of his eyes. Three days after his return he was forced to confess that he could no longer work by candlelight and that he must take present advice or be blind. Once more he sought out Dr Turberville, who discoursed learnedly about his eyes—which was certainly a comfort—gave him drops and prescribed pills and bleeding. But the trouble still continued and his heart grew sad and the entries in his journal shorter. One day that July he showed a fellow official his skill in drafting a paper in shorthand and made him marvel at it: "God knows", he added, "I have paid dear for it in my eyes".

Relief came for a time through the agency of certain tubulous spectacles made of paper or soft leather, of which experiment had recently been made by the Royal Society and which Pepys now tied to his eyes. He bought orifices for them at Drumbleby's and set the women of his household at work making them. And by their help he was once again able to sit late at the Office and make the long detailed entries of his doings in the diary which he loved.[6]

It was well for the Navy that it was so. For after a year of shaken and unhoping despondency, the powers-that-were plucked up spirit. Once more the word "Reform" was in the air. The first hint of it had come before Pepys left on his western tour, when he and Coventry had paced up and down the Matted Gallery at Whitehall one rainy afternoon discussing possible improvements, of which the removal of old Mennes from the Comptrollership loomed largest. Now in July the Duke of York took up the cause of reformation. Pepys was quick to trim his sails to this new and hopeful wind. On the 24th of the month he held a long and secret consultation with the Duke in his closet at St James's and showed him the failings of the Navy Office, advising him to call his colleagues to account for their neglect. Before the interview ended, the Duke requested him to draw up a letter for him to sign to the Navy Board stating clearly where each of its members had failed in his duty.

This was the work of August 1668. All that month Pepys was busy drafting the Duke's great letter of enquiry and reform. With his lieutenants Hayter, Hewer and Gibson to aid him, the first administrator in England sat early and late, reading old instructions to Principal Officers, compiling lists of miscarriages, and drafting and copying his long record of idleness and error. On the afternoon of Sunday the 23rd, after he had looked over the letter (by the aid of his tube) to his own extraordinary content, he made his way by appointment to St James's, where the Duke was waiting for him. There he read it aloud, and when he had finished his royal listener poured out his thanks and in "words the most expressive" told him how he would always have a care for him and desired his advice on all future occasions. Though he knew it not, Pepys' fortune was made. As for the letter, the Duke commanded it to be transcribed and sent to the Navy Board.

That something of the kind was in the wind his colleagues already suspected, though they did not yet guess that the blow, when it fell, would come from Pepys. Outside there was much talk of a revolution at the Navy Office: Captain Cocke, ever a great man for rumour, had been whispering up and down the town that the Duke of York would soon be driven from the Admiralty and all things be governed by a Committee of the nominees of the reigning favourite, the Duke of Buckingham, and by the factious spirits in Parliament. It seemed likely enough that Pepys among the rest would lose his place, and he himself seemed to expect it, for at the month's end he wrote to his father not to give away the furniture at Brampton to Pall since he might soon have occasion to live there. He was not much perturbed at the prospect, for in any case he believed that his eyes could not be long preserved.

Meanwhile the bombshell which he had prepared for his colleagues was ready, as Mr Wren's man, Billing, working in the utmost secrecy, copied it from Pepys' draft into his own hand so that none should suspect its origin. On the 28th the Duke himself presented it to the Board. Next day it was formally opened and read. The Clerk of the Acts' colleagues were no longer in the dark; they knew the evidence of his handiwork too well—there was no mistaking that clear and exhaustive style*. Yet there was also no denying the truth of its accusations nor resisting the powerful agency through which it reached them. And each man sat down anxiously to draw up his own defence.

As soon as the Duke received these, he sent for Pepys and asked him to go through them with his secretary Wren. Rather naturally they were full of evasions, with a few sly digs at himself, but all, as he added, to no purpose. Then at the Duke's request he sat down to prepare a further letter of rebuke from the Lord High Admiral in reply to their excuses.[7]

Meanwhile Pepys was engaging in administrative battle against foes far more formidable than his broken colleagues at the Office. Early in September he had started to draw up a new agreement with Gauden for victualling the Fleet. But he encountered unexpected opposition from one of the new Commissioners of the Treasury, Sir Thomas Clifford, a rising Hotspur, who was eagerly seeking out abuses with a view to remoulding the kingdom to his own heart's desire. It was a strange encounter, for two men more unlike each other never lived than the foreseeing little Clerk of the Acts and this passionate Devonshire gentleman. Pepys refused to be browbeaten, told Clifford that the information on which he was relying was a flat untruth and, though troubled at his own boldness, stuck to his guns. A few years before he would never have dared to oppose the will of so powerful a man, the greater because behind him stood the might of the all-ambitious Duke of Buckingham, who was using

* Pepys was not particularly disturbed that they did suspect him. "I met Lord Brouncker," he writes on August 30th, "who I perceive, and the rest, do smell that it comes from me, but dare not find fault with [it]; and I am glad of it, it being my glory and defence that I did occasion and write it."

Clifford as a battering-ram to overthrow his enemy, the Duke of York. But experience, growing financial independence, and the tragedy of his failing eyesight were all conspiring to make a changed man of Pepys. With the Duke of York's help, he carried his point and secured the renewal of the victualling contract for Gauden. "I know", wrote Pepys, "I have done the King and myself good service in it."[8]

He was glad for his own sake that he had, for just at this time his financial affairs were rather troubled by Lord Sandwich's return from Spain. During his embassy that nobleman had run still more heavily into debt, and almost his first action on landing in England was to write to Pepys for an immediate loan of £500. Pepys had too much grace to refuse, but it troubled him deeply to jeopardise any of his hard-earned savings at a time when his own future position was so insecure. Such was his emotion at this sudden call on him that, standing by a candle to seal a letter, he accidentally set light to his periwig: the noise of unwonted crackling led to the discovery of this catastrophe only just in time.[9]

Yet such trials faded into nothingness beside the domestic calamity which befell Pepys that autumn. September had been a month of more than usually furious love-making; it had begun with the performance of an inspired horse, encountered at Bartholomew Fair, which, being bidden by its master to select that member of the company who best loved a pretty wench in a corner, had gone straight to Samuel. That very night as he went home, Pepys confirmed this piece of equine intuition by beckoning a "wench that was naught" into his coach and with a modest shilling purchasing such part of her professional repertoire as was compatible with his own safety. Later in the month he tried his hand with varying success on Mrs Daniel, Mrs Knepp, his maid Jane Birch, Doll Lane and his neighbour Miss Turner. The latter was a new conquest. Walking in his garden on an autumn night she proved ready to toy and be toyed with, opposing his encroaching hand with nothing but a seeming aversion—a merry kind of opposition, he deemed it, as struggling gently she yielded. He might, he believed, have had all.[10]

But there was another conquest for Pepys to make, and that nearer home. One August evening he got Deb as she undressed him to play with him in the way he wished—"with great pleasure". The little creature was serving her first perilous apprenticeship in life. Then in September Elizabeth bore her away from London on a visit to cousin Roger's at Impington, who had long been importuning the Pepyses to stay there for the autumnal joys of Stourbridge Fair. In early October Samuel himself made a trip to the country to welcome home Lord Sandwich, discontinuing his Diary for nearly a fortnight while he did so. It was not till October 10th that the family was reassembled in Seething Lane.[11]

Three nights later, after his wife had finished reading to him, he had Deb in to comb his head and, while she did so, he took the freedom to explore. There was scarcely any opposition. Home to him, with this demure little lady to love, was becoming a very pleasant place: Elizabeth too was strangely quiescent. He was making it pleasanter, too; laying out money on a fine tapestry set of the apostles to hang in his closet, employing painters and plasterers to beautify still further his dwelling, setting up pictures (Cooper had painted his wife that summer) and fine draughts of ships. Moreover he was about to buy a coach. Then, when the scene was set, Nemesis struck. On the evening of October 25th, after a peaceful Sabbath day spent in rejoicing over his new possessions, Pepys called Deb as usual to comb his head. "Which", as he recorded, "occasioned the greatest sorrow to me that ever I knew in this world, for my wife coming up suddenly did find me embracing the girl con my hand sub su coats..... I was at a wonderful loss upon it and the girl also."[12]

Chapter XVIII

Atonement

"It is much the best for my soul and body to live pleasing to God and my poor wife, and will ease me of much care as well as expense."

Diary, Nov. 20th, 1668.

At the first glimpse of that revealing sight Mrs Pepys had been struck mute with amazement. When her voice at last returned, it was husky with anger and she said little. Nor, not knowing for certain how much she had seen, did her husband. About two in the morning the storm began. Weeping she woke the erring male by her side, whispered to him that she was a Roman Catholic and had received the Holy Sacrament, and then raged on from one thing to another, crying and reproaching him that he should prefer a sorry girl before her. All which Pepys bore patiently, promising all fair usage to her and love henceforward, and swearing that he had done her no hurt. Towards morning they were silent for a while and slept.

Then with his heart full of trouble for poor Deb, whom he feared he had undone (his wife swearing that she would turn her out of doors), he was forced to visit St James's to wait on the Duke of York, who was pressing him to finish his reply to the letters of his fellow officers. The Duke's own enemies were daily growing more clamorous and unless naval reform came soon from within, it was plain that it would be imposed from without. Already a Commission was being drawn up for suspending Lord Anglesey and putting the Navy

Treasurership into the hands of Sir Thomas Littleton and Sir Thomas Osborne, creatures of Lord Arlington and the Duke of Buckingham. The heir-presumptive, feeling his position threatened, turned to Pepys to save him.

But from the consequences of his own folly and frailty Pepys could not save himself. When he came home he found a gloomy house, his wife discontented, the girl sad, and no words spoken between them. Once more his bedfellow woke him in the night and in bitter words swore she had seen him hug and kiss her handmaiden. Thinking it best to yield a little, he admitted the former but no more: he had been indiscreet, he explained, but would never be so again. And on his own he offered to give it under his hand that he would never see either Knepp or Mrs Pierce again.

His excessive susceptibility was his undoing. In his tremendous anxiety to appease his wife, he made her realise what she had never realised before—her power. Ruthlessly she grasped it. On the second evening after the fatal discovery she caused a candle to be lit in the chimney and by its light ranted at him all night long, threatening in the highest terms to publish his shame: meekly he bore with her, telling her all he dared and by good words and fair promises bringing her to a semblance of peace. In the morning, before with sleepless eyes he went out to his day's labours, he scribbled a hasty note to Deb (with whom he had now no chance of exchanging speech) to let her know how much he had confessed.

But there was no real peace in the household in Seething Lane. Samuel's own heart was sore, for his wife, for his own shame, for little Deb whom he had desired and had wronged and who he feared would be ruined. He could scarcely analyse his own feelings: it would be better, he knew, for his wife's peace of mind and his own that Deb should go and yet he could not bring himself to let her do so. Over the supper table on these painful autumn evenings, Elizabeth would watch his eyes to see if they strayed to the girl's, which, he confessed, they "could not but do now and then, and to my grief did see the poor wretch look on me and see me look on her and then let drop a tear or two, which do make my heart relent at this minute that I am writing this with great trouble of mind, for she is indeed my sacrifice, poor girl".

In due course she went. Mrs Pepys interviewed her aunt and it was arranged without scandal or quarrel. She did not tell her husband, who dared not ask when she was to go, nor did she let him speak with her, but superintended his dressing and undressing in person, watched him from room to room and kept his mind in an agony of suspense. Once he contrived to fling a note to Deb, advising her not to confess and to deny that he had ever kissed her, which he still continued to do to Elizabeth: "I did adventure upon God's pardoning me this lie, knowing how heavy a thing it would be for me to be the ruin of the poor girl and next knowing that if my wife should know all it were impossible ever for her to be at peace with me again and so our whole lives would be uncomfortable". Yet he found that he still wanted Deb as much as ever, could not help smiling at her when she looked at him and could not bear to think of losing her: "the truth is", he admitted, "I have a great mind for to have the maidenhead of this girl, which I should not doubt to have if je could get time para be con her. But she will be gone and I not know whither".

Yet before she went there was a further shock for Pepys. Shaken by her mistress's ceaseless examinations, Deb gave way and confessed everything. After that a tornado broke out in the house. That night Mrs Pepys upbraided her husband bitterly and told him of all the temptations which she had resisted out of faithfulness to him—particularly mentioning the solicitations of Lord Sandwich (who had wooed her as befitted his rank through the agency of Captain Ferrers, his master of horse), and of Lord Hinchingbrooke, "even to the trouble of his lady"—all which he acknowledged and was troubled at and wept. But no penitence availed: in the night Elizabeth rose screaming, crying that she would never sleep again and kept on raving till Samuel, crying by now as heartily as she, promised her that he himself would bid Deb be gone and show his dislike for her.[1]

After that there was no postponing Deb's departure. Next night Elizabeth again started up "with expressions of affright and madness, as one frantic", and on the following morning Samuel, with tears in his eyes, called up Deb and discharged her in the presence of the presiding she-judge, advising her to be gone as soon as she would and never to see him again. On Saturday, November 14th, just within three weeks of the fatal discovery, she went. Pepys did not have a chance of saying good-bye or of slipping the little money which he had secretly wrapped up in paper into her hand, for on the morning of her departure his wife ordered him to go out without passing through the kitchen and, when he ventured to expostulate, instantly flew into such a rage, calling him rotten-hearted dog and rogue, that he at once crumpled up. Only all that day at the Office his heart was sad and he could not forget the girl nor cease to wonder where she had gone. Still it was a comfort to come home at evening to a house once more at peace and to sleep in content beside an unprotesting wife. "I must here remember", he noted, "that I have lain with my moher as a husband more times since this falling out than in, I believe, twelve months before, and with more pleasure to her than I think in all the time of our marriage before."

But still his mind ran on Deb. And as soon as the week-end was over, and with a full realisation of the risk he was taking, he set about to find her. From some chance words of his wife, he had gathered that she was lodging with one Dr Allbon in Whetstone Park, a notorious region between Lincoln's Inn Fields and Holborn, and one which it troubled him mightily that she should be in. Hither on Monday morning, abandoning the Office, he repaired, but could hear nothing of Allbon till, recalling that Elizabeth had said something of his having once lived in Eagle Court, he sent Drumbleby's boy there and discovered that he was a poor broken fellow that dared not show his head or reveal his whereabouts lest his creditors should find him.

Work at the Office detained Pepys all Tuesday, but on Wednesday he resumed the search. With difficulty and great cunning, he tracked down a porter who had carried a chest of drawers to the poor doctor's new lodgings, and by dint of telling him that his business was not with his employer but with a little gentlewoman, one Mrs Willet, that lodged there, he got the fellow to bear her a message imploring her to see him. Meanwhile he himself anxiously paced up and down the courtyard of Somerset House awaiting the answer. It came: that he might see her if he would, but no more. At this Pepys could not command himself, but as soon as it was dark took coach and drove to her lodgings. She came out to him and there, in the coach, he comforted himself. In perhaps the strangest of all his strange confessions, he tells of that secret encounter. Once more his hand strayed "sub su coats". "I did nevertheless", he adds, "give her the best council I could, to have a care of her honour and to fear God, and to suffer no man para avoir to do con her as je have done, which she promised." Then he gave her twenty shillings and an address through which to communicate, and went home to Elizabeth rejoicing*.

Again his sins discovered him. Next day, after a busy morning at the Office, he returned home as cheerful as a schoolboy and raced upstairs to see how the upholsterers were getting on with their work of hanging his best room. Here he found his wife weeping. When he asked her the reason, she turned on him, calling him all the false, rotten-hearted rogues in the world and let him understand that she knew he had been with Deb. For a time he denied it, but at last discharged his heart of the whole wicked business and confessed. Throughout that afternoon he remained with his wife above stairs in their bedchamber, enduring her threats and vows and curses. Sometimes she swore that she would slit the nose of this girl: sometimes demanding three or four hundred pounds that she might be gone from him that very night, or else she would make the world know of it. "So", he wrote, "with most perfect confusion of face and heart, and sorrow and shame, in the greatest agony in the world I did pass this afternoon." At last he called up Will Hewer, and made him privy to it all; the poor fellow cried like a child at this falling out between his master and mistress and obtained what Samuel could not, that Elizabeth should forgive him on condition that he would promise in writing never to see Deb again. "So before it was late, there was beyond my hopes as well as desert, a tolerable peace." That night he took his pleasure of his wife and gave her content. And on his knees (for long an unwonted exercise) he began

* "and there told my wife a fair tale, God knows, how I spent the whole day, with which the poor wretch was satisfied." *Diary*, Nov. 18th, 1668.

to pray God for grace "more and more every day to fear him and to be true to my poor wife".

There were two further humiliations for Pepys before he had done. Next morning when he went abroad, he was accompanied by Will Hewer who, by agreement, was now to go with him everywhere: Elizabeth would not trust him out on any other terms. And when at dinner he came home, thinking to have a further degree of peace, he found his wife in a new rage, calling him all the bitter names she could devise, and even striking him and pulling his hair. True to his resolution he bore with it and by silence and weeping at last prevailed with her to be a little quiet. But after dinner she fell into a worse fit than ever, swearing again to slit the girl's nose, until at last Will Hewer came up to appease her, and poor Samuel flung himself in a sad, desperate condition upon the bed in the blue room and lay there while they spoke together in the other room. At last it came to this, that if the repentant sinner would call Deb "whore" under his hand and write to her that he hated her and would never see her more, his wife would believe in his penitence and relent. Even this he agreed to do, protesting only at the word whore. But Elizabeth was obdurate. It was left to Hewer to save the situation by winking at his master until he had made him understand that he might safely write whatever his wife demanded, since he would not deliver the letter. So Pepys wrote it and received his wife's forgiveness and promised her never to go to bed henceforward without calling upon God upon his knees—"and hope I shall never forget to do the like all my life; for I do find that it is much the best for my soul and body to live pleasing to God and my poor wife, and will ease me of much care as well as much expense". And next morning Will, like a good and faithful servant, delivered his master's message to Deb that he would see her no more, but brought back his letter unopened.[2]

The world outside, of course, never guessed a word of what was happening within the finely furnished chambers of the Clerk of the Acts' house. It saw him sitting with authority in the Office, going with assured gait up and down the town, entering the private apartments of the Duke of York and talking earnestly with the latter's secretary. On the day before Deb departed, he had given Mr Wren his draft of the Duke's reply to his colleagues' excuses; perhaps the connubial trials through which he had been passing had made him sharper than usual, for Wren found it necessary to mollify certain hard terms in it and make it "somewhat sweeter" before his royal master could present it to the Board. There was much talk of drastic reforms pending at the Navy Office; Penn, it was announced, was about to retire and to go into partnership with Gauden in the victualling business; others said that Pepys would soon follow suit. He, for his part, seemed quite ready to go. His eyes were growing worse and his jealous wife daily more urgent for his retirement to the country.[3]

On one thing Pepys was determined: that if he stayed, the Office should become more a place of ease, and less of slavery, than it had been. No longer would he bear the burden of doing the work of inept superiors. With this resolution he set himself, as Christmas drew near, to dislodge the aged Comptroller. The latter had recently made his task more difficult by rising without the least warning at a Board meeting and complaining of the lack of respect shown to himself at the Office—a speech calculated to delight Sir Thomas Littleton, who was on the look-out for Navy Office delinquencies. A fortnight later the old gentleman repeated his folly, so that Pepys wrote in despair that, for his life, he could not keep Sir John Mennes from showing the weakness of the Navy Board to its own dishonour: "it do vex me to the heart". As for the Comptroller's work, it was simply never done: Warren's accounts, which it was his duty to inspect, had remained unpassed for months. Pepys therefore persuaded Brouncker to join him in impressing on the Duke of York the impossibility of defending the Navy Office unless Mennes were removed and an experienced sailor brought in to fill Penn's place when he also departed.[4]

There was still one experienced member of the Board besides the Clerk of the Acts, the formidable Colonel Middleton, who had recently come up from Portsmouth to succeed the dead Batten as Surveyor. With him Pepys had a furious quarrel. For some time Middleton had been complaining that Will Hewer had been saddling the Navy for reasons of his own with contracts for unnecessary kerseys and cottons, and he now came into the open with "a most scandalous letter to the Board, reflecting", wrote the indignant Pepys, "on my Office". The latter at once gave battle on behalf of his clerk (at that time accompanying him everywhere, "like a jailor, but yet with great love"). For ten days he wrote letters, collected notes and did everything within his power "to make Middleton appear a coxcomb". Then on December 18th he unmasked his batteries and shattered him before the whole Board. Middleton took it very well. As soon as he saw the strength of Pepys' defence he became calm as a lamb and craved his pardon. After which there was peace—more, perhaps, than there had been in the Office for many a day. "So", Pepys records, "Middleton desiring to be friends, I forgave him, and all mighty quiet, and fell to talk of other stories, and there staid, all of us, till nine or ten at night (more than ever we did in our lives before, together)."[5]

At home, however, peace was still delayed. That very

night returning to bed from the friendly gathering round the Office table, Samuel found Elizabeth in a new fury; someone had told her that Deb was going abroad in mighty fine clothes and that a friend had been giving her money. He had much to do to pacify her. Though she had allayed his Protestant fears as to her religion by attending Communion, her anger was still burning beneath the surface, ready to flare up at the least alarm to her jealousy. When he went abroad with her in a coach or to the theatre, he dared not so much as look at the pretty faces about him lest she should take fire; his very dreams were supervised, as she lay by his side, listening to his every movement and murmur*. Patiently he accepted it all as his just due; he would take his punishment without complaining and never, he resolved, "be catched loving anybody but my wife again". And since it takes two to make a quarrel, the year ended in something approaching domestic calm.[6]

Moreover, there was the coach. For that noble and splendid thing, so long desired, had come at last. Even the remembrance of Deb could scarcely deprive Elizabeth of her satisfaction in so glorious a possession. For long Samuel had contemplated its purchase. Some months back he and she had been mightily taken with a little chariot they had seen in the street and had resolved to have one like it. A few days before the disaster of Deb he had taken the plunge and, after inspecting several desirable vehicles, had agreed to buy one for £53. But it turned out that, knowing nothing about coaches at all, he had been handsomely swindled, his choice being both heavy and old-fashioned. Fortunately he was

* "She being ever since our late difference mighty watchful of sleep and dreams, and will not be persuaded but I do dream of Deb and do tell me that I speak in my dreams and that this night I did cry 'Huzzy' and it must be she." *D.* Dec. 5th, 1668.

saved by the elegant and experienced Mr Povy, who just in time pointed out its defects and prevailed upon him to change his mind and purchase an elegant little chariot of the very latest model. It held four, was very light, and was covered with leather. It was duly stabled in Sir Richard Ford's yard. And on November 30th Mrs Pepys, driven by the coachman in a livery of green lined with red, went abroad "to take the maidenhead of her coach".

There were, of course, some who murmured—the Creeds, for instance, on whom Elizabeth was careful to call, and Sir William Warren who, on seeing it, expressed a pious wish that his old friend might not contract envy by its possession. But Pepys replied that it was plainly to his profit to keep a coach and that it would be hard, after eight or nine years of such employment as his, if he were not able to do so. And in this spirit he resolved that he would not be contented with hired horses, but buy a pair of his own.

Once more Pepys had a new experience. At the horse market at Smithfield, he discovered that there was a species of craft and cunning in the purchase and sale of horses of which he had never dreamed. Happily he was again helped by his friends. On December 12th for £50 he became master of a splendid pair of black horses—"the beautifullest almost", he thought, "I ever saw". And though there were disadvantages in this as in all things—the 40 shillings he was forced to pay for a new panel of glass (shattered no one knew how), or the fore-wheel bolt that broke in Holborn and left him and Elizabeth sitting stationary in the coach while the horses went on—it was many weeks before the new possession ceased to be a source of conscious delight to him and his wife.[7]

Altogether Pepys was very grand that New Year. No longer did he filch his pleasures in secret drabbing in low taverns: instead he took his ease in his fine house and entertained his peers. Seven times in the January of 1669 did he feast his friends, carefully suiting his entertainment to their quality. On the 23rd he gave a singularly pleasing dinner-party with Lord Sandwich and his son Hinchingbrooke, Lord Peterborough, Sir Charles Harbord, young Sidney Montagu and Sir William Godolphin as his guests. There were six or eight dishes, brought up one after another, as noble as any man could need to have, with variety of excellent wines, and all in such good order that his guests were mightily pleased and himself almost bursting with content. After dinner, the Lords sat down to cards, while Samuel showed the commoners his furniture, books and pictures and his wife's drawings. They kept it up all afternoon till seven at night, when they took their leave and rolled away in their coaches through the dark rainy night, leaving their host gloating over all this splendid hospitality—"the best of its kind and the fullest of honour and content to me that ever I had in my life". Afterwards he got his wife to cut his hair and look over his shirt, whence it appeared that he had been entertaining other guests, for "when all come to all she finds that I am lousy having found in my head and body above twenty lice little and great, which I wonder at, being more than I have had I believe these twenty years. I did think I might have got them from the boy," he explained, "but they did presently look over him and found none. So how they come I know not, but presently did shift myself, and so shall be rid of them and cut my hair close to my head. And so with much content to bed".

Yet had his noble guests seen their smiling, courtly little host in certain other situations in his finely furnished home about that time, they would doubtless have been much surprised. Lying weeping to himself, for instance, as he had done two days before, because his wife was angry with him for letting his eyes stray round the playhouse, or waking in the night to see that tyrant bending over him with a pair of red-hot tongs to pinch him because she declared (a sheer invention on her part) that he had been seen that day in a coach with Deb. For as Pepys himself justly recorded at its close, the month had many different days of sadness and mirth.[8]

Yet Mrs Pepys had done a notable service to England's Navy when she surprised her husband with Deb. Deprived of his low pleasures, the Clerk of the Acts applied himself with double ardour to his work. And that January his new labours began to bear fruit. For though his efforts to have Mennes removed ended in nothing but some courteous words of Wren that it would be a pity to occasion any public disparagement to so old and faithful a servant of the King, in other directions things were happening of good augury to England's Navy. On the day after the episode with the tongs, Pepys drafted a long and detailed report on the savings that might be effected by conducting "petty emptions" henceforward on a cash basis, "since nothing can be bought on this or any other terms but for ready money"; such a reform would save, he showed, from £50 to £300 on every £100 expended on such small commodities as double spring-locks, door handles, scuttle hinges, screws, sail needles, hasps and staples, fire shovels, tongs (this item must have given him a tremor), hatchets, spits, charcoal, glue, spades, cottons and kerseys. Five days later he was advocating, with his usual clarity and care, a far greater reform for "reviving the ancient practice of acting by estimates...instead of borrowing from one service to forward another, and sacrificing our own content and good names by the ruining of private men to provide dear, insufficient, and (for the most part) untimely supplies of stores". Thereafter, at great length, he discussed how far it would be possible to reduce the annual charge of the Fleet to the £200,000 within which it was now proposed to confine it; with care £100,000 would suffice to keep the Navy in harbour and another £100,000 to maintain a winter guard of ten ships and a summer fleet of twenty-four—disposed, he modestly explained, as follows: two at Jamaica, six at Tangier and in the Mediterranean, three off Ireland, two at Greenland, one at Iceland, two at Newfoundland, two at Land's End, five in the Downs, and one on the Baltic trade routes. But this was on the basis of ready money being available for all payments, nor did it allow anything for repairs or emergencies.[9]

For the first time since the beginning of 1667 there were definite signs that the government was thinking of setting out a Fleet. On Sunday, January 24th, Pepys was called before the King and Council at Essex House to answer enquiries as to how soon the big ships could be repaired: the Surveyor answered two years, but he, more optimistic, declared that with money they could be made ready by the summer of 1670. Two days later he was called again before the same august company: relations with the Algerines in the Mediterranean were strained and the King had resolved to strengthen Sir Thomas Allin's little squadron at Tangier. "I see", Pepys noted, "that on all these occasions they seem to rely most on me."

They were wise to do so, for in all things naval Pepys was showing a remarkable activity, almost as though he had some premonition of that new Dutch war which, unknown to himself and his fellow subjects, their inscrutable monarch was already planning. He wrote long letters to his fellow reformer Deane about the pros and cons of wet docks, of the qualities of English oak in withstanding shot, of the methods of distinguishing the rates of his Majesty's ships. And he was at great pains to remind his fellow officers (in writing) of the ill-consequences that must follow their prolonged failure to supply answers to the queries of the Commission of Accounts, and himself drew up the requisite memoranda.[10]

Yet his greatest naval work that winter was his defence of the old constitution of the Navy Office against those who were using its defects, which it possessed in common with all other human institutions, to dismiss its present Officers and job themselves and their friends into their salaries. It was a task for which by now Pepys was incomparably fitted. With real pleasure he spent long days and nights searching for old records of the Navy—in his own Office, at the Rolls, at the Crown Office in the Temple—questioning aged officials in the Yards about practices long since discarded or interviewing Hewer's uncle Blackburne, the former Commonwealth Secretary to the Navy, at the "Ship" tavern. On the whole he was well satisfied with the result of his researches: "I do find", he noted, "that the late times" (by which he meant the now vaunted days of Puritan efficiency) "in all their management were not more husbandly than we".

While he prepared his formal defences, Pepys took the steps usual with him to enter the enemies' lines on his own account. Clifford having suggested a talk, he availed himself of the opportunity to inform that ardent reformer of his own integrity and zeal; bore him his accounts to view (in the doing of which he was much embarrassed by being seen by the Duke of York) and did all within his power to make friends with the mammon of unrighteousness. Yet he refused to yield an inch on essentials; when Clifford discovered his thoughts that Sir John Mennes and Colonel Middleton were too old and that Lord Brouncker minded his mathematics too much, Pepys, to use his own words, did not give much encouragement to that of finding fault with his fellow officers, but did stand up for the constitution. He could not have chosen a better defence; for of all the things which Clifford loved, courage was the first.

For a time it looked as though Pepys' defence of the Navy Office, for all its skill, might avail him nothing. Though no one could find a sound reason for removing him, there were some who had motives for doing so which were none the less powerful because they were unjust. "They do think that I know too much", wrote Pepys, "and shall impose upon whoever shall come next." Throughout March his future seemed to hang in the balance. He awaited the result with philosophy, for his eyes were growing steadily worse and he would probably have to retire in any case; if he did so, he could live in the country, "with comfort though not with abundance". Yet still he fought stubbornly, and even got Creed to discover what the Duke of Buckingham and his faction intended towards him and to "instill good words concerning me...for I have not a mind indeed at this time to be put out of my office if I can make any shift that is honourable to keep it". Nor, he added, would he save himself by deserting the Duke of York.

He remained. The truth was, as Coventry remarked to the Lord Keeper, that it would cost the King £10,000 before he could train such another as the Clerk of the Acts. For all his occasional peccadilloes and petty corruptions, Pepys in nine years by his industry, persistence and very real capacity had made himself too useful a man to be discarded. And so, while Penn took his seat at the familiar Navy Board for the last time on March 30th, 1669, Pepys stayed. He was now the only survivor of the original Principal Officers of 1660.[11]

Change was everywhere. In March Coventry, who a little while before had carried all before him, was flung into the Tower for sending a challenge to the royal favourite, Buckingham. Buckingham, whose many tastes included play-writing, had proposed to depict his rival sitting in the middle of a round hole in a somewhat absurd table which he had invented for disposing of his books and papers; and to stop him Coventry had threatened to slit the nose of any actor who took the part and had challenged the ducal author. The person who came best out of the affair was Pepys. He at once visited his old patron in the Tower and offered him his service. For this defiance of the prudent laws of self-interest he was rewarded. For as he paced the stones of Lord North's walk, Coventry spoke to him of the inner history of Clarendon's fall in which he had played so great a part, so that Pepys was "mighty proud to be privy to this great transaction". And if his temerity ran him the risk of enraging certain great men, at least one, the Duke of York, who hated Buckingham and all his gang, was glad of it and was particularly gracious to him when, after Coventry's arrest, he paid his court to him at Deptford. Here the Duchess and all the great ladies of her court were sitting upon a carpet on the ground playing at "I love my love with an A because he is so and so, and I hate him with an A because of this and that"—Lady Castlemaine, who was there, Pepys thought particularly witty. Cheered by this inspiring spectacle he "slunk out" (his own expressive phrase) to Bagwell's, where he found not only his old flame but his former maid, Nell, who, so loved was his company, cried for joy to see him. Yet, though he had a mind to stay, he could not, for his wife was waiting for him and he had to hurry home, where he found her mighty angry for his absence and full of unworthy questions about Pierce and Knepp.[12]

None the less Pepys was beginning to hold up his head at home again as the spring of a new year approached and the nightmare of the wintry day on which he had been surprised with Deb receded into the past. In March he seized the chance of a naval court martial at Chatham to take a brief holiday from Seething Lane—at that moment in a state of considerable upheaval through the marriage of his boy Tom Edwards and his maid Jane Birch, an event on which Elizabeth was expending all her talent for romance and which Samuel himself had done his best to hasten, even to settling £40 on the happy pair. And as he rumbled in the coach down the Kent road with his colleague Middleton, he was happy himself, though the wind blew cold and the last wisp of winter's snow was in the air.

He made the best of his time. On the day after his arrival he took a trip to Maidstone, a place he had long had a mind to see and beheld with great joy the Medway winding up and down, the Friary at Aylesford, the old man whom he discovered beating flax in a barn by the way. But the best sight of the day was his old love, Mrs Jowles, the Becky Allen of that first joyous visit to Chatham of eight years back, whom he spied that morning through her father's window and, after being trimmed, returned in the evening to visit. He found her as expansive as ever. And in his own inimitable way he described the evening's party, "while Mrs Jowles and I to talk and there had all our old stories up, and there I had the liberty to salute her often and pull off her glove, where her hand mighty moist, and she mighty free in kindness to me, and je do not at all doubt but I might have had that that I would have desired de elle had I had time to have carried her to Cobham as she, upon my proposing it, was willing to go, for elle is a whore, that is certain, but a very brave and comely one". Then with a lanthorn he walked over the midnight fields to Chatham, as dark as pitch and mighty cold.

He was in magnificent form at the court martial aboard

the *Charles* next day. He had been made a captain for the occasion—which had caused him a good deal of mirth and the hope of a little extra money—and now before the assembled Captains of the Fleet, he laid open the law and rattled the Muster Masters out of their wits almost. Then while the Court considered its verdict, he and Middleton withdrew and dined off hot salt beef, brought them by the ship's boatswain in a kettle, brown bread and brandy, "so good as I never would desire to eat better meat while I live, only I would have cleaner dishes". For Pepys on holiday had *in excelsis* the gift of being pleased; even the grim Middleton melted to his mood, revealing himself unexpectedly as "a strange good companion and droll upon the road, more than ever I could have thought to have been in him".[13]

Elizabeth as well as Samuel felt the mood of returning summer. Among her husband's acquaintances was one Henry Shere, a young engineer serving at Tangier, "a good ingenious man, but do talk a little too much of his travels". He was something of a poet, and Elizabeth, who had all a woman's longing for aspiring talk with the opposite sex, fell upon him with delight. She was always speaking of him and loved to be in his company. Samuel spied the literary pair (chaperoned by the invaluable Hewer) sitting in the pit at the Duke's playhouse, at which he was somewhat troubled, as also at the pains which Elizabeth took to entertain Shere at dinner; "but yet", he added, "I see no reason to be troubled at it, he being a very civil and worthy man, I think; but only it do seem to imply some little neglect of me".[14]

But at least it gave him some excuse for indulging his own less platonic fancies as the mood of spring dictated. So he took occasion to make a step to Mrs Martin's, to visit likewise her sister, to meet Mrs Bagwell by appointment in a Moorfields tavern and steal a last exciting rendezvous with

Deb, met by chance passing the Conduit on Holborn Hill. And after that we know no more.[15]

For those bright watchful eyes which for close on a decade had noted every changing mood of the world they surveyed seemed at last to be flickering into darkness. The light in the Office window, which for eight years Pepys had faced sitting with his back to the fire at Navy Board meetings, he could bear no longer and he shifted to the other side of the table; so also did the bright flame of the candles at the playhouse almost kill him with pain. And worse, when he bent over his beloved journal, peering at those tiny crowded hieroglyphics through the long tube that was fixed to his eye, he knew that he must close for ever a record which had grown to be almost as dear to him as life itself.[16]

That May, Pepys went about the world much as before, noting and secretly hoarding all cherished experience, though it was pain to do so. We see him on May Day, sitting in his coach with his wife in her flowered tabby gown beside him, driving through the town to Hyde Park, "with our new liveries of serge, and the horses' manes and tails tied with red ribbons, and the standards there gilt with varnish, and all clean, and green reins" and all the people looking upon him; seated at the Office drawing up new instructions for the commanders; or taking the cool air of an evening amid the Hackney marshes. He was pleased when his place grew more secure, sullen when his wife kept him waiting as she dressed herself, merry when he rode up the river as high as Fulham, talking and singing and playing the rogue with the western bargemen. All the while his eyes grew worse. On the 19th of the month he formally petitioned the Duke of York for leave to go abroad during the Parliamentary recess—to Holland, he explained, to study the Dutch Navy, though he and Elizabeth had privately resolved to visit France if such a chance came to them. "The restless exercises of his eyes requisite to the seasonable dispatching of the work of his place during the late war", he explained, had reduced him to this pass. Readily the leave was granted, the Duke assuring him that the King would be a good master to him, and the latter himself expressing his sense of his faithful servant's misfortune and bidding him rest.[17]

On the last day of the month Pepys spent the morning making up his accounts, neglected now for nearly two years, called in at little Mrs Michell's, whose husband, he had found out, was away, kissed her and drove in the evening in the Park. At the "World's End" by Knightsbridge he drank and was merry. Then he returned home and took out his diary for the last time. "And thus ends"—the pen ran haltingly in the guttering candlelight—"all that I doubt I shall ever be able to do with my own eyes in the keeping of my journal, I being not able to do it any longer, having done now so long as to undo my eyes almost every time that I take a pen in my hand and, therefore, whatever comes of it, I must forbear: and, therefore, resolve, from this time forward, to have it kept by my people in long-hand, and must therefore be contented to set down no more than is fit for them and all the world to know; or, if there be anything (which cannot be much, now my amours to Deb are past, and my eyes hindering me in almost all other pleasures), I must endeavour to keep a margin in my book open, to add, here and there, a note in short-hand with my own hand".

"And so I betake myself to that course, which is almost as much as to see myself go into my grave: for which, and all the discomforts that will accompany my being blind, the good God prepare me!" This he dated and initialed, as though he half-guessed the greatness of his achievement. Then he passed into June—and silence.

Epilogue

Pepys did not leave for his holiday the moment he closed his journal. Nearly all that summer he was kept busy in England. The Navy Board's answers to the Commissioners of Accounts were still outstanding, and he was too proud of the good name of the Office to leave it undefended. Moreover he had business of his own with the Commissioners, who were prying into all private sales made by members of the Navy Office to the service. Five years before, at the outset of the Dutch war, he had supplied some six or seven hundred pounds' worth of calico flags which were urgently needed by the Fleet, notwithstanding the Duke's General Instructions which forbade any officer to trade in naval stores. He now explained at great length and most convincingly, that the satisfaction of having done his Majesty a service was the only advantage he ever received from this action: he did not add that he had written in his Diary of October 1664: "This job was greatly to my content".[1]

During the waiting months of the summer, Pepys continued his efforts to remove Mennes: attended the Duke of York in the King's bedchamber, proposed expedients for performing his neglected work and wrote significantly of a "fair salary for an able deputy". Yet somehow he seemed a little aloof from it all, ending a letter to the Clerk of the Ropeyard at Woolwich with the superscription—"until the necessity of the poor and the debauchery of the rich may be equally courted, with money for rewarding their good deeds and a halter to recompense their bad ones, I am your very affectionate friend". As years and power and wealth came to him, he began to put by the passionate self-interest of earlier days as a man lays aside an old suit which he has outworn.[2]

Conscious of his triumph of the previous year he now sought to enter Parliament. In June one of the seats for the coastal Borough of Aldeburgh in Suffolk fell vacant through the untimely death by drowning of Sir Robert Brooke, and Pepys put himself forward as a candidate. He spared no pains to advance his claims on the burgesses, pointed out that his election would engage not only himself but the entire Navy Board to the interests of Aldeburgh, and got the Duke of York, Lord Sandwich, Coventry, Thomas Povy and Mr Wren to write letters on his behalf. And he was careful to promise to reimburse his supporters' expenses, for he was a man of the world and understood the institutions of his country. But it availed him nothing, for the honest burgesses declined to elect one who was a stranger to them and whom they had never even seen. Indeed all Pepys got for his pains was the accusation of being a Papist, which, with other "scandals fouly and grossly dispersed", his opponents studiously invented and scattered about.[3]

Meanwhile his eyes remained as they were—"the ill state of which I must confess", he told Coventry, "cuts off most of the comfort of my life, having nothing in view to hope for relief from but the indulgence of my friends". Coventry, living now in retirement at his country home in Oxfordshire, replied kindly, wishing his skill equal to his affection that he might effect a cure of his old friend's illness. But it was left to his long-awaited holiday to do this.[4]

At the end of July Pepys was still at work, urging his colleagues of the Navy Office to bestir themselves, writing long minutes to the Commissioners of Accounts and sitting among the great at the Tangier Committee. Then in August he made up his accounts, put his papers in order and obtained copious instructions from his cultured and travelled friend, John Evelyn, as to what to see while in France. "Pray forget not", wrote the latter, "to visit the Taille douce shops and make collection of what they have excellent, especially the draughts of their palaces, churches and gardens;...they will greatly refresh you in your study, and by the fireside, when you are many years returned." Before the end of the month, with Elizabeth and her brother Balty as travelling companions, Pepys crossed the Channel.[5]

The holiday, which lasted two months, was a wonderful success—a voyage "full of health and content", and one which left, as he wrote in old age, "a degree of satisfaction and solid usefulness that has stuck by me through the whole course of my life". Armed with introductions from Evelyn and Sir Samuel Tuke, author of the farcical *Adventures of Five Hours*, which in earlier days he had so much admired, he travelled through Holland and Flanders to Paris, where in his best and most irresistible mood he completely conquered the hearts of his new French acquaintances, as did also his "deare and vertuous lady". Deeply refreshed he left on October 6th for Brussels, taking a leisurely route that he might view—he was careful to arrange for this—all the most beautiful towns on the way.[6]

Before he left Brussels Elizabeth was taken ill. She was, however, able to travel, and at the beginning of the last week of October the little party returned to England, where an important summons from the Treasury Commissioners was awaiting Samuel. It was not obeyed. For on the day on which he reached London, Elizabeth went down with a high fever. Neither her youth nor his prayers availed. On November 10th she died, leaving Pepys at the age of thirty-six shaken and alone, with the world to begin anew.[7]

NOTE ON THE DIARY

Pepys' *Diary* contains some 1,300,000 words, covers over 3000 quarto pages and is contained in six volumes of slightly varying size. During his lifetime Pepys had these bound in leather, stamped in gold, with his arms, crest and motto, and placed on the shelves of his library, although, unlike his other books, they were not arranged in strict order of size but were kept together.

The *Diary* is written in Thomas Shelton's system of shorthand. Proper names and occasional words are written in longhand, and certain "roguish" passages in a curious intermixture of French, Spanish, Latin, Greek and English dialect words. These naturally add to the difficulty of transcription from the shorthand, which otherwise presents no great problem. As Shelton's shorthand was known to many of Pepys' contemporaries, and was not a secret cipher—as is sometimes erroneously supposed—it has of late years been argued that Pepys' sole motive in using it was to save time. But others, including Mr W. Matthews—our foremost expert on seventeenth-century shorthand—challenge this view on the grounds that the distinction between code and shorthand was for many years very slender, the same word "characterie" being used for both, and that English travellers of the period frequently carried MS. shorthand bibles when visiting Catholic countries abroad in order to escape the attentions of the Inquisition. It seems probable that, although the facility it afforded of writing quickly was a primary motive for the use of shorthand, Pepys was not uninfluenced by the knowledge that it would not be understood by those whom he had most reason to wish not to read it. The final sentences of the *Diary* lend support to this view.

On Pepys' death in 1703, the *Diary* with his other books passed for life to his nephew John Jackson, and on the latter's demise in

1724, by Pepys' wish to his old College at Cambridge, Magdalene. Though noticed by Peter Leicester on his visit to Cambridge in 1728, it was not transcribed till 1819, when, following the successful publication of Evelyn's *Diary*, Lord Braybrooke, the Visitor of Magdalene College, entrusted the task to a young Bachelor of Arts named John Smith. Smith's labours, which were performed with exceptional accuracy, took him three years and covered 9325 quarto pages in 56 volumes of longhand manuscript. A part of this only—amounting to little over a quarter of the whole—Lord Braybrooke subsequently published with far less accuracy in 1825 under the title of *Memoirs of Samuel Pepys*. Subsequent editions with additional matter were published in 1828, 1848–51, 1854 and 1858.

In 1875, the Rev. Mynors Bright, after retranscribing a part of the *Diary* on an interleaved copy of Lord Braybrooke's 1854 edition, published about 70 per cent. of the whole. The complete diary, omitting only a number of short passages, whose indelicate nature was thought such as to preclude publication, was first printed from Mynors Bright's MS. transcription under the editorship of Mr H. B. Wheatley between 1893 and 1899. Though a monument of labour, the text of this, the fullest edition, abounds in minor errors. For this reason, Mr F. McD. C. Turner, the present Pepysian Librarian, is preparing a new edition of the *Diary* from John Smith's transcript checked from the shorthand original. Messrs George Bell and Sons will publish this edition for the Master and Fellows of Magdalene College.

AUTHORITIES

Note on Authorities cited

The chief authorities for the earlier part of Pepys' life are the *Diary*; the private and official letters printed by Dr J. R. Tanner in *The Further Correspondence of Samuel Pepys*, by Mr Edwin Chappell in *Shorthand Letters of Samuel Pepys*, by Mr R. G. Howarth in *Letters and the Second Diary of Samuel Pepys* (several of which had been previously published by Lord Braybrooke in *The Memoirs of Samuel Pepys* and by John Smith in the *Life, Journals and Correspondence of Samuel Pepys*); the naval collections at Magdalene College, Cambridge, calendared in Volume 1 of Dr J. R. Tanner's *Catalogue of the Naval Manuscripts in the Pepysian Library*; the *Calendar of State Papers, Domestic Series*, from 1658 to 1669; the *Reports of the Historical Manuscripts Commission* and in particular those on the MSS. in the possession of Mr J. E. Hodgkin and of Magdalene College, Cambridge; the residue of unprinted letters in the volume of Pepys' official correspondence recently purchased from the Pepys-Cockerell family by the Trustees of the National Maritime Museum and referred to in these pages as the *Greenwich MS.*; and the vast accumulation of unpublished correspondence and memoranda contained in Volumes A, 62, 170, 171, 174, 178, 182, 185, 187, 191 and 195 of the *Rawlinson MSS.* in the Bodleian Library. There are also some early letters and other matter in Volumes 73–75, 77 and 83 of the *Carte MSS.* (removed in the eighteenth century from Hinchingbrooke, where there is still a certain amount of Pepysian matter in the *Sandwich MSS.*), but the more important of these have been printed by Mr R. G. Howarth. To this list should be added the MS. collection of Pepysian commentary made by the late Mr H. B.

Wheatley and the late Dr J. R. Tanner and used in the preparation of this book by the author; Mr Wheatley's *Pepysiana*; Mr W. H. Whitear's *More Pepysiana*; the *Occasional Papers read by Members at Meetings of the Samuel Pepys Club*; and Mr Edwin Chappell's admirable and exhaustive lecture delivered to the Society for Nautical Research on February 23rd, 1933, and printed in Volume XIX, No. 2 of *The Mariner's Mirror*. There are, of course, many other authorities which are cited in the "source apparatus" which follows.

A full Bibliography will be printed in the second and concluding volume of this Life.

ABBREVIATIONS USED

Sir F. *Bridge*. Samuel Pepys, Lover of Musique (1903).

*C*alendar of *S*tate *P*apers, *D*omestic series.

Carte MSS. (Manuscripts of Thomas Carte in the Bodleian Library.)

E. *Chappell*. Shorthand Letters of Samuel Pepys (1933).

*C*ommons *J*ournal. Vols. VII, VIII, IX.

J. *Davey*. A Catalogue of Historical Documents and Autographs. No. 31 (1889).

*D*ictionary of *N*ational *B*iography.

Greenwich MS.

F. R. *Harris*. Life of Edward Montagu, First Earl of Sandwich. 2 vols. (1912).

*H*istorical *M*anuscripts *C*ommission *Rep*orts.

J. *Hollond*. Two Discourses of the Navy (1896).

R. G. *Howarth*. Letters and the Second Diary of Samuel Pepys (1932).

A. T. *Mahan*. The Influence of Sea-power upon History (1896).
M. *Oppenheim*. A History of the Administration of the Royal Navy (1896).
G. *Penn*. Memorials of Sir William Penn. 2 vols. (1833).
Samuel Pepys. *Diary*.
Naval Minutes (1926).
Pepys Club, *Occasional Papers* read by Members of the, Vol. I (1917); Vol. II (1925).
Pepysian MSS. at Magdalene College, Cambridge (see Tanner, Catalogue of Naval Manuscripts).
Rawlinson MSS. (Manuscripts of Richard Rawlinson in the Bodleian Library.)
E. M. G. *Routh*. Tangier, England's Lost Atlantic Outpost (1912).
Sandwich, Edward Montagu, 1st Earl of. *Journal* (1929).
Sandwich MSS. at Hinchingbrooke.
John *Smith*. The Life, Journals and Correspondence of Samuel Pepys. Vol. I (1841).
J. R. *Tanner*. Further Correspondence of Samuel Pepys (1929).
J. R. Tanner. A Descriptive *Catalogue* of the *Naval Manuscripts* in the Pepysian Library. Vol. I (1903).
A. W. *Tedder*. The Navy of the Restoration (1916).
J. *Thurloe*. Collection of the State Papers of, Vol. VII (1742).
H. B. Wheatley. *Pepysiana* (1899).
W. H. *Whitear*. More Pepysiana (1927).

BIBLIOGRAPHICAL NOTES

CHAPTER I. THE INFANT SAMUEL

1 *Miller and Skertchley, Fenland*; *W. C. Pepys, Genealogy of the Pepys Family*; *Ely Episcopal Records*; *Whitear* 33–42, 97–8, 100–3 et passim; *Pepysiana* 3–13 et passim; *D.* 1 April; 31 May 61; 13 June 66; 12, 16 June 67; Wheatley and Tanner MS. notes; Notes communicated by Miss F. M. Page.

2 *Athenaeum* 6 *June* 1914 (*Notes by W. H. Whitear*); *D.* 17 March; 31 Dec. 64.

3 *D.* 17 Aug.; 3 Sept. 63.

4 *D.* 26 Feb.; 8 July; 2, 14 Oct.; 26 Nov. 60; 21 March; 7 April; 6 Aug.; 11 Nov. 61; 17 Feb.; 17 Aug.; 10 Sept. 62; 9 Aug.; 7 Sept. 63; 25 Aug. 64; 18 Jan. 66.

5 *Whitear* 38, 142–3, 161 et passim; *Rawl. MSS. A.* 178, f. 195; *D.* 20 July; 12 Aug. 60; 22 Aug.; 12, 15 Sept.; 27 Oct. 61; 24 Nov. 62; 30 May 63.

6 *D.* 23 March; 12, 23 May; 13 June 61; 12 April; 4 Sept. 63; 21 Jan.; 27 March 64; 15 Aug. 65; 14 Aug. 66; 30 May 68.

7 *Whitear* 40–1; *Rawl. MSS. A.* 182, ff. 329, 340; *D.* 24 Jan.; 8 Feb.; 21 June; 12 Nov. 60; 4 July; 21 Oct. 62; 18 March; 12 April 64; 23 Dec. 68.

8 *Whitear* 29–33 et passim; *D.* 2 Aug.; 1 Sept. 62; 25, 26 July 63; 14 July 67; 30 Jan.; 3 Dec. 68.

9 *Whitear* 36; *Rawl. MSS. A.* 185, ff. 206–13; 4 Jan. 60; 25 April 64; 12 May; 16 Aug. 67.

10 *Athenaeum* 6 *June* 1914 (*Notes by W. H. Whitear*).

11 *Whitear* 26, 29, 51–2, 135–6; *D.* 15 March 60; 15 July 61; 10 Oct. 62.

12 *Whitear* 13–14, 46–7, 50, 57–8, 166–7; *D.* 15 March 60.

13 *Whitear* 46, 135–6; *Carte MSS.* 73, ff. 49, 170, 585; *Harris* I, 10 et seq.; *D.N.B.*; *Carlyle, Cromwell's Letters* xii–xiv, xviii; *H.M.C. Rep.* v, 91; VIII, Pt II, 59, 63; *D.* 8, 13, 20, 22 July; 6 Aug. 61; 13 Oct. 62; 19 Sept. 63; 11 Oct. 67; 24, 25 May 68.

14 *Robt. Seymour, Survey of London* I, 160–5; *McDonnell, St Paul's School*, passim; *Gardiner, Register of St Paul's School*, *Pepysiana* 32, 99–103; *D.N.B.*; *D.* 15, 24 Jan.; 28 March; 16, 31 May; 7, 13 Oct.; 1 Nov. 60; 18 June; 29 Nov.; 23 Dec. 61; 13 June; 21 July; 17 Sept.; 10 Oct.; 23 Nov. 62; 4 Feb.; 13 Oct. 63; 4 Feb.; 25 July; 25 Dec. 64; 9 March; 3 July 65; 22 Feb. 66; 23 Oct. 67.

CHAPTER II. FIRST MANHOOD

[1] *McDonnell, St Paul's School*; *Pepysiana* 13–15; *Athenaeum* 6 *June* 1914; *D.* 22 Jan. 61.

[2] *Mullinger, University of Cambridge* III, 549–50; *Academy* 29 April 1893; *Times Lit. Suppl.* 1 March 1928; *Walker, Sufferings of Clergy* II, 151; *D.N.B.*; *H.M.C. Rep.* IV, 418; V, 482–3; *D.* 31 Dec. 64.

[3] *Whitear* 108; *Rawl. MSS. A.* 170, f. 124; *D.* 8, 16 Feb.; 6 March; 11, 18, 30 April; 14, 17 May; 22 July; 6 Sept.; 18 Oct.; 5 Nov.; 6, 10, 14 Dec. 60; 6, 10, 26 Jan.; 5, 13 Feb.; 7 April; 8 Sept.; 3, 11, 18 Nov. 61; 21 June; 11, 12 July; 6, 9, 11 Aug. 63; 28 March 64; 2 Jan. 65; 4 Jan.; 8 Feb.; 21 April 69.

[4] *H.M.C. Rep.* V, 482–3; *Grey, Debates* II, 42–6; *Pepysiana* 33, 58–9; *Wheatley, Diary* I, 45 n.; *D.N.B.*; *D.* 8, 25, 26 Feb.; 17 March; 19 May; 15 July; 14 Aug. 60; 10 March 61; 26 June 62; 24 July; 13 Aug. 63; 3 Feb.; 16 March; 14 July; 21 Sept.; 25 Nov. 64; 23 April 65; 10 Feb.; 18 March; 5 April; 6 Dec. 67; 7 Feb.; 25 May 68.

[5] *Rawl. MSS. A.* 185, ff. 260–3; *D.* 4 Nov. 60; 27 Jan. 63; *Pepysiana* 48.

[6] *H.M.C. Rep.* V, 482; *Rawl. MSS. A.* 185, f. 260; *D.* 25 Feb. 60; 8 Oct. 67; 23 May 68.

[7] *D.* 7 Aug. 60; 11 Nov. 61; 2 Jan.; 27 June; 19 July; 27 Nov. 65; 7 Oct. 67.

[8] *D.* 17 Jan.; 11 Feb.; 28 March 60; 26 June; 9 Sept. 62; 7, 8 Aug.; 4, 5, 17 Nov.; 4, 8, 22, 31 Dec. 63; 19 Jan. 65; 3, 19 Nov. 67; *Whitear* 135; *H.M.C. Rep.* V, 484.

[9] *Grey, Debates* II, 426; *D.* 11 March 68.

[10] *D.* 7, 11 Nov. 60; 25 Nov. 61; 26 July 63; 30 Jan. 64.

[11] *Atlantic Monthly* 1891; *Smith* I, 148; *Pepysiana* 17–23; Monument in St Olave's Church; *Wheatley, Diary* I, xix–xx; *D.* 13 Dec. 61; 9 Jan.; 5 June 63; 17 Feb.; 28 March 64; 4 Feb. 65; 3 March 66; 29 March 67; 27 Feb. 68.

[12] *Howarth* 44–7; *Smith* I, 147–8; *D.* 23 Oct.; 2 Nov. 60; 30 Aug. 61; 22 Sept. 63; 3 Feb. 64; 28 Jan. 68.

[13] *D.* 3 Sept. 60; 10 Oct. 61; 5 July 63; 10 Feb.; 10 Oct. 64; 11 Oct.; 25 Dec. 65; 10 Oct. 66; *Notes and Queries* 1 July 1933 (Notes by Mr Edwin Chappell); *Times Lit. Suppl.* 7, 21 April 1932 (Letters by R. G. Howarth and E. S. de Beer).

[14] *Wheatley, Diary* I, xxi; *D.* 18 June; 7 Nov. 60; 9 Jan. 63; 4 Jan.; 3 Feb. 64; 6 Sept. 65.

[15] *D.* 3 April; 31 May; 18 June; 10 July; 19 Aug.; 13 Oct. 60; 11 Jan.; 22 Dec. 61; 12 May; 24 Oct. 62.

Chapter II. First Manhood (*cont.*)

[16] *D.* 13 Aug.; 22, 29 Dec. 61; 6 Jan. 62; 27 May; 4 July; 15 Aug. 63; 4 July 64; 2 Jan. 65.

[17] *D.* 2, 5 Aug.; 15, 21, 31 Oct. 60; 12 May; 24 June; 18 Sept. 61; 16 Nov. 63; 14 Nov. 68.

[18] *D.* 1 Jan. 60; 24 Oct. 62; 9 Jan. 63; 28 March; 12 June; 26 July 64; 11, 13 Sept. 65; 25 Feb. 67.

[19] *Pepysiana* 16; *Rawl. MSS. A.* 187, f. 456; *Harris* I, 80.

[20] *Thurloe* IV, 338, 443, 545, 614; *Harris* I, 80–90; *Carte MSS.* 223, f. 170; *D.* 18 Feb.; 3 Sept. 60; 25 Feb. 67; *Howarth* 1.

[21] *A Deep Sigh breath'd through the lodgings at Whitehall* 1642; *Thurloe* II, 21; III, 194.

[22] *Carte MSS.* 73, ff. 7, 57, 61, 170; *Howarth* 1 et seq.; *L.C.C. Survey* XIII, 30; *D.* 21 Jan. 60; 29 June 64.

[23] *Carte MSS.* 73, ff. 28–35, 49, 57, 59, 61, 175, 177; 74, f. 452; 223, f. 174; *Howarth* 1–9; *Thurloe* V, 433; *Clarke Papers* III, 81–2; *Harris* I, 96–100; *D.N.B.*; *Walker, Sufferings of the Clergy* I, 91; *Rawl. MSS. A.* 62, f. 1; *D.* 11 Feb. 60; 14 July 68.

[24] *Carte MSS.* 73, ff. 170, 175, 187, 190; *Howarth* 9; *Whitear* 13; *D.* 2 Jan.; 16, 17 Feb. 60; 13 Sept. 61; 4 Jan. 62; 25 May 63

[25] *Carte MSS.* 73, ff. 170, 187, 190; *Howarth* 9–11.

[26] *D.* 15 June 60; 4 Sept. 61; 7 Sept.; 7 Nov. 62.

[27] *Carte MSS.* 73, ff. 187, 190; *Howarth* 10–11.

[28] *Carte MSS.* 73, ff. 49, 170, 641; *Howarth* 2; *Whitear* 136; *Harris* I, 226; *D.* 28 Feb.; 1 March; 30 May 60; 2 Jan.; 22 June; 21 Sept. 61; 30 May; 4 July 62; 23 Dec. 64; 5, 9 July 66; 8 March 69.

[29] *Harris* I, 123; *Pepysiana* 106; *D.* 10, 13, 26 March; 2, 6, 17, 23, 30 April 60; 12 May 61; 24 May 62; 18 Jan.; 12 April; 9 June; 28 Aug. 64; 23 April 65; 20 June 68.

[30] *Carte MSS.* 73, ff. 7, 49, 61, 170, 175, 177, 187; *Howarth* 5–10.

[31] *Carte MSS.* 73, ff. 77, 173, 175; *Howarth* 5–10; *D.N.B.*; *D.* 2, 11, 16, 17, 18 Jan.; 7 Feb.; 21 April 60; 22 Oct. 62; 17 Jan. 66; 1 Jan. 68.

[32] *Carte MSS.* 73, f. 59; *D.* 11 Jan.; 17, 18 Feb.; 6, 18 March; 6 July 60; 25 Feb. 67.

[33] *Thurloe* II, 670; *D.* 10, 28 Jan.; 12 Feb.; 7 March; 1 June; 23 Oct.; 21 Dec. 60; 21 March 61; 24 Oct. 62; 10 Aug. 63; 10 March 64; 13 July 65.

[34] *D.* 6, 13, 30 Jan.; 3, 11, 17, 21 Feb.; 14 March; 10, 18, 23 April; 14 May 60; 4 July 62.

[35] *D.* 7 Jan.; 11, 17, 21, 28 Feb.; 5 March; 17, 21 Oct. 60; 30 April 65; 19 Dec. 66; *Carte MSS.* 73, f. 61; *Howarth* 4–5; *Pepysiana* 143–4.

[36] *Rawl. MSS. A.* 185, ff. 206–13; *D.* 26 March; 14 May 64; *Evelyn, Diary* Jan. 1658.

Chapter II. First Manhood (*cont.*)

37 *Rawl. MSS. A.* 182, f. 329; 185, ff. 206–13; *Pepys Club Occ. Papers* I, 59–62; *Whitear* 61; *D.* 7 Jan.; 26 March 60; 26 March; 29 April; 8 Nov. 61; 16, 27 Feb.; 4 May 62; 19 Dec. 63; 27 Jan.; 13 March 69; *Sir D'Arcy Power, An Historical Lithotomy.*

38 *Sloane MSS.* 1536, f. 63; *Pepys Club Occ. Papers* I, 59–61; *D.* 26 March 60; 26 March 62; 30 May 63; 26 March 64.

39 *Pepys Club Occ. Papers* I, 61; *Sloane MSS.* 1536, f. 64; *John Ward, Diary*; *Evelyn, Diary* 10 June 69; *Pepysiana* 48; *D.* 18 Nov. 63; 28 Feb.; 23 Dec. 67; 31 March; 15 July 68; *Carte MSS.* 73, f. 325.

40 *D.* 26 March 60; 26 March 61; 23 Feb.; 26 March 62; 26 March 63; 26 March 64; 26 March 69.

CHAPTER III. A MEAN CLERK

1 *D.* 1 May 60; 26 Aug. 61.

2 *Hall, Antiquities of the Exchequer* 108; *Thomas, The Ancient Exchequer*; *Ackerman, Microcosm of London* I, 207; *Chamberlayne, Angliae Notitia* 118–30.

3 *Harris* I, 110; *Haydn, Book of Dignities*; *D.* 19, 28, 30, 31 Jan.; 9 March; 13 April; 28 June 60; 7 May 63.

4 *Beresford, Godfather of Downing Street*; *Burton, Diary* II, 122; *Thurloe* VII, 6–7; *D.* 26 Jan. 60.

5 *D.* 7, 16, 19, 21, 25, 27 Jan.; 14, 20 Feb.; 28 June 60; 12 March 62; *Thurloe* VII, 9, 360.

6 *D.* 3, 5, 6, 7, 9, 10, 23, 24, 26, 28, 30, 31 Jan.; 2, 5 Feb. 60.

7 *D.* 2, 4, 23, 31 Jan.; 26 July; 13 Nov.; 21 Dec. 60; 21, 30 Dec. 61; 9 Jan. 63; 5 July 65; 19 Nov. 66.

8 *Thurloe* VII, 265; *D.* 4, 6 Jan.; 7 Feb.; 10, 12, 16 March; 4 July; 21 Oct.; 7 Nov.; 12 Dec. 60; 3 June 61; 15 April; 24 July; 14 Nov.; 31 Dec. 62; 21 Sept. 65; *W. H. Ward and K. S. Block, A History of the Manor and Parish of Iver* 165–6.

9 *L.C.C. Survey* XIII, 98; *D.* 20 Feb.; 14, 20 March; 14 Sept.; 6 Dec. 60; 21 Jan. 61; 1 March 62; 29 Dec. 63; 8 Jan. 64; 13 May 66.

10 *H.M.C. Rep.* 9, App. II, 447; *Evelyn, Diary* 27 Nov. 55; *Pepysiana* 114–19; *D.N.B.*; *D.* 23 Jan.; 20 Feb.; 20, 22 March; 1 Aug.; 3 Nov.; 6 Dec. 60; 8, 23, 25 Feb.; 29 June; 16 Nov.; 12 Dec. 61; 5 Dec. 62; 29 Jan. 64.

11 *Thurloe* VII, 489; *D.* 1, 4 Jan.; 4, 8, 17, 19 Feb.; 16, 17 March; 14, 19 Sept. 60.

Chapter III. A Mean Clerk (*cont.*)

12 *D.* 1, 15, 26, 29 Jan.; 2, 9, 17, 21 Feb.; 20 March; 29 April 60; 27 March 61.

13 *D.* 23 Jan.; 4 Feb.; 4, 12 March; 14, 29 Aug.; 23 Sept.; 1, 12, 27 Dec. 60; 26 Aug. 61; 26 March; 14 Sept.; 5 Nov. 62.

14 *Thurloe* VII, 336, 360; *D.* 4, 13 Jan.; 1, 9, 10, 21 Feb.; 17, 19, 22 March; 1 July; 5 Aug.; 2 Sept.; 3 Oct. 60; 12 March 61; 2 May 62; 6 April; 26 July 66.

15 *D.* 28 Feb. 68.

16 *D.* 17, 20–23 Jan.; 18 Feb.; 7 April; 22 June; 9 Aug.; 4 Sept. 60; 20, 28 May; 24 Sept. 62; 18 July 66.

17 *Carte MSS.* 77, f. 170; *D.* 2, 17 Jan.; 10, 14, 19 Feb.; 22 March; 8, 30 Oct. 60; 31 Aug. 61; *Harris* I, 226; *Howarth* 8.

18 *D.* 5, 13, 18, 19, 24, 25, 27 Jan.; 8, 15, 16, 17, 19 Feb.; 4, 6, 19, 22 March; 3 April; 22 May; 4, 14 July; 4, 12, 25 Aug.; 22 Sept.; 23 Oct.; 3 Nov.; 8 Dec. 60; 5, 22 Jan.; 9 June 61; 15, 17 Aug.; 29 Dec. 62; 24 July 63; 4 July 64; 8 Aug. 65; 3 March 66; *Whitear* 112.

19 *D.* 2, 3, 4, 5, 9, 10, 12, 13, 15, 16, 17, 19, 20, 21, 23, 24, 27 Jan.; 1, 3, 5, 8, 11, 12, 15, 17, 18 Feb.; 22 Oct.; 9, 20, 21 Nov.; 3 Dec. 60; 1 Jan.; 6 Nov. 61.

20 *D.* 4, 5, 10, 24 Jan.; 8 March; 22 June 60; 25 March; 10 Sept. 61.

21 *Whitear* 139; *D.* 1, 8, 22, 26, 29 Jan.; 5, 12, 19 Feb.; 1 June; 20 July 60; 4 Jan.; 27 Feb.; 1, 28 April; 31 May; 3, 5 Sept. 61; 23 Jan.; 8 April 62; 31 March; 13 Dec. 63; 4 April; 14, 15 Aug. 64; 22 Sept. 66; 19 March 68.

22 *D.* 1, 6, 22, 29 Jan.; 5, 12 Feb. 60; 7 Jan.; 19 Nov. 61; 26 April 64; 9 March 69; *Pepysiana* 22.

23 *North, Lives* III, 20.

24 *D.* 4, 30 March; 5 Feb.; 8 April; 15 May; 8, 22 July; 16, 23 Sept. 60; 2 April; 11 May 62; 8 May; 2, 9 Aug. 63; 20 Jan. 67; 8 May 68.

25 *Evelyn, Diary* Dec. 57; *Walker, Sufferings of the Clergy*; *D.* 1, 8, 22, 29 Jan.; 17, 19 Feb.; 18 March 60; 30 Nov. 67.

26 *Firth, Last Days of the Protectorate*; *Thurloe* VII passim; *J. G. Muddiman, Henry Muddiman* 16 et seq.

27 *Harris* I, 123; *Sandwich, Journal* 3; *Clarke Papers* IV, 129; *C.J.* VII, 23 Feb. 1658.

28 *Carte MSS.* 73, f. 201.

29 *Sandwich, Journal* 33–4; *D.* 27 Sept. 61.

30 *Clarendon MSS.* 60, f. 436; 61, ff. 172, 291, 303, 335; *Clarendon State Papers* III, 493; *C.S.P.D.* 13, 29 July 1659; *D.* 15 May; 7 Nov. 60; 8 March 63; 22 Sept.; 7 Nov. 65.

31 *D.* 30 Jan.; 17 Feb.; 6, 7 March; 19 July 60; *Harris* I, 138, 148–55; *Sandwich, Journal* 45–7; *Clarendon MSS.* 61, f. 172; *C.J.* 16 Sept. 59.

Chapter III. A Mean Clerk (*cont.*)

32a *Sandwich, Journal* 47–67; *Carte MSS.* 73 passim.

33 *Thurloe* VII, 772–3; *Carte MSS.* 73, ff. 320, 322, 325, 328, 329, 333, 339; *Howarth* 11–18.

34 *D.* 2, 3, 11, 13, 17, 31 Jan.; 8 Feb.; 31 May; 28 Oct. 60; 10 June 61; 20 Jan.; 15 June 64; 19 Feb. 69; *Carte MSS.* 73, ff. 177, 339; *Howarth* 18.

35 *Whitear* IV; *Thomason Tracts* E. 974 (3); *Carte MSS.* 73, ff. 322, 329, 333; *Howarth* 12–13; *D.* 18, 21, 23, 31 Jan.; 1, 3, 4, 6, 22 Feb.; 10, 20 March; 30 June 60.

36 *Carte MSS.* 73, ff. 320, 322, 325, 328, 333, 339; *Howarth* 14–19; *Verney Memoirs* (1925 ed.) II, 150; *Muddiman* 92; *Rugge, Diurnal*; *D.* 8 Jan. 64.

CHAPTER IV. THE CURTAIN RISES

Main Source: *Diary*, 1 January to 17 March, 1660

1 *D.* 4 Sept. 62; 13 June 64; 24 Nov. 65; 17 Aug. 67; *Tanner* 206.

2 *Pepysiana* 270–5; Communication by W. Matthews, Esq.; *D.* 17 Nov. 66; *Shelton, Tachygraphy.*

3 *Carte MSS.* 73, f. 212; *Howarth* 19.

4 *D.N.B.*; *Aubrey*, Bodleian Letters II, pt 2, 371.

CHAPTER V. THE FORTUNATE VOYAGE

Main Source: *Diary*, 17 March to 9 June, 1660

1 *P. M. Barnard, Catalogue* 92 (June 1914), Item 154.

2 *C.S.P.D.* 1660/1 35.

3 *D.* 4 Nov. 65.

CHAPTER VI. CLERK OF THE ACTS

Main Source: *Diary*, 9 June to 31 August, 1660

1 *Harris* I, 191.

2 *Oppenheim* 190; *Pepysiana* 150–7; *Rawl. MSS. A.* 192, ff. 179–83; *Cat. Naval Manuscripts* I, 6–9.

3 *Cat. Naval Manuscripts* I, 9–11; *Tedder* 42–4; *D.N.B.*; *Penn, Memorials* II, 243–5, 589–92; *Hoskins, Charles II in the Channel Islands*; *Pepysiana* 162–75; *Geoffrey Callender, The Portrait of Peter Pett* 1930.

Chapter VI. Clerk of the Acts (*cont.*)

[4] *C.S.P.D.* 1660/1 110.

[5] *C.S.P.D.* 1660/1 139; *Rawl. MSS. A.* 216, f. 29.

[6] *Rawl. MSS. A.* 174, ff. 327, 329.

[7] *Rawl. MSS. A.* 174, ff. 315, 319; 289, f. 18.

[8] *D.* 30 June; 4, 17, 23 July; 28, 29, 30 Aug.; 5, 21, 22 Sept. 60.

[9] *Pepysiana* 287; *D.* 17, 18, 26, 27, 30 July; 1, 2, 11, 20, 21, 25 Aug.; 26 Sept.; 29 Nov. 60; 16, 31 March; 19 April; 10 May; 24 July 61.

[10] *L.J.* 26 July 1660.

[11] *C.S.P.D.* 1660/1 110, 125, 131, 196, 199, 253; *Penn* II, 591; *D.* 30, 31 July; 1, 4, 6, 13, 16, 19, 20, 21, 24–7, 31 Aug. 60.

CHAPTER VII. THE HAPPY PLACEMAN

Main Source: *Diary*, 1 September, 1660, to 16 June, 1661

[1] *D.N.B.*; *Penn*; *D.* 8, 9 Sept.; 9 Oct. 60.

[2] *D.* 21 Aug.; 11, 14 Nov.; 4 Dec. 60.

[3] *D.* 9 March; 30 April; 14, 17 May; 11, 20 Sept.; 12 Nov.; 10 Dec. 60.

[4] *D.* 10, 21, 22 Sept.; 1, 2, 6, 28 Dec. 60; 14 May 61.

[5] *D.* 1, 18, 26 Nov.; 22 Dec. 60; 30 Jan.; 4 Feb.; 18 April; 29 May 61.

[6] *D.* 15 Nov. 60; 14, 18, 22, 26 Feb.; 27 March 61.

[7] *D.* 6, 24 Sept.; 14 Oct.; 11 Nov. 60; 12, 22 Jan.; 6 Feb.; 8 March 61.

[8] *Hollond* 100.

[9] *D.* 15–18, 25 Sept.; 5, 6, 8, 10, 19, 29, 30 Nov. 60; 21 Jan.; 1, 2, 4, 7, 12, 27, 28 Feb. 61.

[10] *D.* 29 Sept. 60; *Rawl. MSS. A.* 174, f. 308.

[11] *D.* 4 Oct.; 30 Nov. 60; 25 Jan.; 17 Feb.; 14, 16 March; 6 June 61.

[12] *D.* 3, 4 Dec. 60; 15 Jan. 61.

[13] *Hollond* lxx–lxxxi.

[14] *D.* 12, 26 Nov.; 9, 10, 14 Dec. 60; 22 Jan.; 28 May 61; *Rawl. MSS. A.* 174, f. 310; *Hollond* lxxx–lxxxii, 327–59.

[15] *Hollond* 343.

[16] *D.* 19, 30 July; 4, 11, 25, 26, 30 Sept.; 1, 5, 22 Oct. 60; *C.S.P.D.* 1661/2 17.

[17] *D.* 11, 12, 18, 26–28 Sept.; 3–5, 9 Oct.; 22–3 Nov.; 13, 17, 20, 22 Dec. 60; 26–29 March; 8, 11, 12, 17, 21, 25, 27 April 61.

[18] *D.* 20, 24, 25 Oct.; 6, 27 Nov. 60.

[19] *D.* 29–31 Oct. 60; 18 March 61.

Chapter VII. The Happy Placeman (*cont.*)

[20] *D.* 26 July; 10 Aug.; 1, 2, 8–10, 19, 26 Oct. 60.

[21] *D.* 3, 12, 14 Oct.; 15, 20, 22, 27 Nov. 60.

[22] *D.* 15, 21, 26 Feb.; 1, 5, 18, 27–28, 30 March; 22 April 61; *Pepysiana* 11; *Rawl. MSS. A.* 174, f. 434; *Notes and Queries* 13 May 1933 (Note by Mr Edwin Chappell).

[23] *D.* 28 March; 10, 11, 24 May 61; *Rawl. MSS. A.* 174, ff. 317, 322

[24] *D.* 13, 29 Oct.; 6, 31 Dec. 60; 23 Jan.; 10 Feb.; 10 March 61.

[25] *D.* 20, 26, 27, 30 May 61.

[26] *D.* 14 April; 1, 3, 12–16 June 61; *Carte MSS.* 73, ff. 523, 525, 538

CHAPTER VIII. A MAN OF PROPERTY

Main Source: *Diary*, 1 April, 1661, to 31 January, 1662

[1] *D.* 2 Oct. 60; 1, 2, 28 April; 8, 31 May 61.

[2] *D.* 8 May; 8, 19, 21, 27 June 61.

[3] *D.* 7, 24 July 61; *Whitear* 145–8.

[4] *D.* 8–13, 16–22 July 61; *Whitear* 46–8, 146–7.

[5] *D.* 23–25, 27, 29, 31 July; 31 Aug. 61.

[6] *Whitear* 159; *D.* 13, 25, 26, 29, 31 Aug.; 3–5 Sept.; 7, 31 Oct. 61.

[7] *D.* 29 July; 21, 26, 29, 31 Aug. 61.

[8] *D.* 16, 19, 22 Aug.; 5, 6, 13 Sept.; 2, 31 Oct.; 7 Nov.; 11 Dec. 61; 19, 23 Jan. 62.

[9] *Carte MSS.* 73, f. 585; *Howarth* 20–1; *D.* 12–15, 26, 27, 31 Aug.; 3 Sept. 61.

[10] *D.* 23, 26, 28 Aug.; 11, 12, 16 Sept.; 3, 7, 12, 14, 31 Oct.; 18 Nov. 61; *Whitear* 48–9, 159–60.

[11] *Whitear* 49–50, 152–9; *D.* 6–8, 11, 14, 16, 19–22, 30 Nov.; 8, 9, 31 Dec. 61; 10, 18, 22 Jan.; 21 Feb.; 17, 19 May; 3 June 62; 27 Oct. 63.

[12] *D.* 26 July; 15, 31 Aug.; 6, 7, 9, 11, 25, 26, 28, 29 Sept.; 3, 8–10, 19, 21–3, 25, 26, 28 Oct.; 1, 4, 5, 10, 12, 13, 15, 18, 25, 27, 30 Nov.; 4, 5, 16 Dec. 61.

[13] *D.* 29 Oct.; 1, 2, 8 Nov. 61.

[14] *D.* 1, 25 Aug. 61.

[15] *D.* 6, 21 Dec. 61; 5 Jan. 62.

[16] *C.S.P.D.* 1658/9 307; *D.* 12, 13, 29 Nov. 61.

[17] *D.* 29 Nov.; 3, 4, 7, 15, 17, 20–3, 31 Dec. 61; 5, 8–10, 17 Jan. 62; *Naval Minutes* passim; *Pepysiana* 182–3.

CHAPTER IX. BUCKLING TO

Main Source: *Diary*, 4 February to 31 December, 1662

[1] *D.* 4, 5 Feb. 62; *Pepysian MSS.* No. 2867, 356–98, 2242; *Cat. Naval Manuscripts* I, 20–3; *Penn* II, 265.

[2] *D.* 12, 20, 28 Feb.; 6, 7, 13, 14, 17–20 March; 8 April 62.

[3] *D.* 25 Feb.; 4, 5, 12 March; 16 April 62.

[4] *D.* 8, 13, 15, 16 Feb.; 9, 16, 22, 25 March 62.

[5] *D.* 24 March; 28 Feb.; 18 April 62.

[6] *D.* 1, 13–15, 17, 20–3, 28, 29 Jan.; 3, 6, 9–12, 18–20, 24, 26, 27 Feb.; 14 March 62; *Evelyn* 3 Aug. 64; *Pepysiana* 139–41; *Bridge* 9, 99.

[7] *D.* 30 March; 15 April; 6, 19, 20–3, 26, 31 May 62.

[8] *D.* 25 May; 1, 19, 28 June; 4, 5, 20 July; 10 Aug. 62.

[9] *D.* 1, 2, 11 July; 4, 13, 15, 25 Aug. 62; *C.S.P.D.* 1661/2 332, 334, 413, 421–2, 442, 444, 446, 453, 457, 459, 461–4.

[10] *D.* 4, 5, 25 June; 3, 21, 24, 30, 31 July; 13 Aug. 62; *C.S.P.D.* 1661/2 398, 408, 422, 439.

[11] *D.* 19, 30 March; 12 April; 1 May; 3, 29 June; 5, 9, 25, 29 July; 5, 6, 12, 19 Aug.; 4 Sept. 62; *Tanner* 1.

[12] *D.* 18 March; 5, 12 April; 8, 10, 15 May; 12, 13 June 62; *C.S.P.D.* 1661/2 356.

[13] *D.N.B.*; *Feiling, Tory Party* 117; *Pepysiana* 171–2; *D.* 7, 10 June; 2, 11, 22, 31 July; 8, 9, 23 Aug.; 3, 14, 31 Sept. 62; *C.S.P.D.* 1661/2 485.

[14] *D.* 6, 9, 20 June; 4, 5, 7–12, 14, 15, 18, 19, 21, 28, 29, 30 July; 1, 7, 9, 11 Aug. 62; 7 Aug. 63.

[15] *D.* 12, 18 Aug. 62; 6 June 63.

[16] *C.S.P.D.* 1661/2 103, 132, 331, 400; 1662/3 232, 270; *D.* 8 Feb.; 19 April 61; 23 June; 4 July 62; 27 June 63; *R. G. Albion, Forests and Sea Power* 49–52.

[17] *Oppenheim* 145, 192, 245–7, 323–4; *Tanner* 156–7, 188; *Greenwich MS.* 106; *D.* 3 July; 6, 20, 25 Aug.; 19, 24 Sept.; 13 Nov.; 3, 18 Dec. 62; 13 April; 19 Oct. 64; 26 March; 4 Aug. 65; 4 April 68; *Rawl. MSS.* 171, f. 344.

[18] *Greenwich MS.* 9; *D.* 30 June; 9, 25 July 62.

[19] *D.* 24, 29 June; 17, 31 July; 19, 25 Aug.; 19 Sept.; 8 Oct.; 1, 16, 23 Dec. 62; *C.S.P.D.* 1661/2 440.

[20] *Davey* Item 2902; *D.* 15 Feb.; 16, 23, 30 March; 7, 20 April; 4, 9 May; 17, 19, 20 Aug.; 27 Oct.; 1, 6, 7 Dec. 62; *Routh* 31.

[21] *D.* 4, 25 Jan.; 4, 8 Feb.; 5 April; 30 June; 12–16, 19, 20 July 62.

Chapter IX. Buckling To (*cont.*)

[22] *D.* 19, 20, 28, 31 July; 1, 21, 24 Aug.; 7 Sept.; 6 Dec. 62.

[23] *Rawl. MSS. A.* 174, ff. 327, 329; *D.* 12, 14 Sept.; 21 Oct.; 10 Nov. 62.

[24] *D.* 27 Sept.; 16, 26, 31 Oct.; 2, 3, 15, 16, 22, 30 Nov. 62.

CHAPTER X. POTS AND PANS

Main Source: *Diary*, 1 October, 1662, to 31 December, 1663

[1] *D.* 4, 18 Oct.; 22, 28 Nov. 61; 18 June; 6 July; 1, 28 Sept.; 5 Oct.; 14, 22 Nov.; 2, 5, 16, 23 Dec. 62; 6 Jan. 63.

[2] *D.* 18 May; 13 Nov. 62.

[3] *Pepysiana* 28–9; *D.* 17, 22, 29 Nov.; 5–9, 19 Dec. 62; 28 May 63.

[4] *Pepysiana* 29; *D.* 22 Nov.; 2, 5, 10, 16, 27, 31 Dec. 62.

[5] *D.* 30, 31 Oct. 62; 1, 3, 7, 27 Nov. 62; 19 Dec. 62; *Whitear* 118.

[6] *D.* 6, 24 Jan.; 13 Feb.; 1, 6, 19 March; 30 Sept.; 3, 11–15 Oct. 62.

[7] *D.* 2, 3, 11, 20–22 Sept.; 18, 19, 21, 22, 25, 26 Oct.; 4, 5, 31 Dec. 62; 15, 19 Jan. 63.

[8] *D.* 4 Feb.; 13 April; 24 June; 21 Oct.; 20 Nov.; 13 Dec. 62.

[9] *D.* 21, 23 Feb.; 17 March; 23 May; 3, 22 June; 13 Oct.; 11 Dec. 63; *Tanner* 3–5; *C.S.P.D.* 1663/4 162, 176.

[10] *D.* 19, 20 Jan.; 8, 9, 10, 11, 12 Feb.; 5 March; 1, 6 April; 13 May; 23, 27 June 63.

[11] *D.* 27 Feb.; 3, 5, 6, 16 March 63.

[12] *Greenwich MS.* 46, 50, 52; *C.S.P.D.* 1661/2 468; *D.* 6, 21–24 March 63.

[13] *D.* 23, 24 March; 2 April 63.

[14] *D.* 1, 20, 23 April; 1, 8 May 63; *Rawl. MSS. A.* 191, ff. 224, 226.

[15] *D.* 29 June; 31 Aug.; 30 Sept.; 31 Dec. 62; 28 Feb.; 1 June 63.

[16] *D.* 28 Feb.; 29 March; 26 April; 31 May 63; *C.S.P.D.* 1663/4 68, 77, 84, 91, 123, 196.

[17] *D.* 14 May 62; 22, 24, 27 Jan.; 2, 10 Feb.; 25 March; 3 April; 1 May 63; *Rawl. MSS. A.* 174 passim; *C.S.P.D.* 1663/4 269.

[18] *D.* 4, 9 Jan.; 14 May 63.

[19] *D.* 17, 22 Jan.; 1, 2, 3, 11, 26 Feb.; 12, 14, 15, 26 March; 1 April 63; *Pepysiana* 29–30.

[20] *D.* 15 Feb.; 15, 18 March; 5, 18, 20, 21, 23–6 April; 1, 8 May 63.

[21] *D.* 27 April; 2, 25 May 63.

Chapter X. Pots and Pans (*cont.*)

[22] *D.* 12, 15, 16 May 63.

[23] *D.* 30 Aug.; 2, 5–8 Sept.; 19 Nov.; 21, 29 Dec. 61; 6 Jan. 62; 19 May 63.

[24] *D.* 3, 24, 31 May; 4, 6–8, 11, 14 June 63.

[25] *D.* 11, 13, 22, 23, 30 June; 4, 6, 7, 12, 19, 23, 31 July; 1, 2, 4, 7, 10, 13, 26, 27 Aug. 63; *C.S.P.D.* 1663/4 181, 186, 190, 235, 249.

[26] *D.* 11, 13, 24, 29 July; 10, 28 Aug. 63.

[27] *D.* 23 July; 27 Aug.; 7 Sept. 61; 21 May; 16 July; 20 Oct. 62; 23 Feb.; 1 March 63.

[28] *D.* 29 June 63.

[29] *D.* 9, 12, 15, 24 July; 4 Aug.; 7 Nov.; 12 Dec. 63.

[30] *D.* 9, 17, 18 July; 7 Aug. 63.

[31] *D.* 4, 5 Aug. 63.

[32] *D.* 2 July; 4, 10, 12, 14 Aug.; 13 Dec. 63.

33 *D.* 17–19, 21 Aug. 63; *Whitear* 83–4.

34 *D.* 14, 16, 19, 25, 27, 30 Aug.; 10 Sept. 63.

35 *D.* 13, 14, 23, 24, 26 Sept.; 2, 5 Oct. 63.

36 *Whitear* 50, 160; *D.* 23, 26, 27, 31 Oct.; 5 Nov. 63.

37 *Harris* I, 243–7; *D.* 29 April; 14, 15 May; 22 July; 4, 10, 24 Aug. 63.

38 *D.* 19 Aug.; 7, 9 Sept. 63.

39 *D.* 24, 27 Sept.; 12, 14–18 Nov. 63.

40 *D.* 22, 28, 29 Nov.; 7, 8, 14, 15, 21–3 Dec. 63.

41 *D.* 31 July; 30 Sept.; 14, 15, 21, 30 Oct.; 6, 27 Nov.; 1, 5, 6, 27, 31 Dec. 63.

CHAPTER XI. THE ARMING OF MARS

Main Source: *Diary*, 1 December, 1663, to 21 November, 1664

[1] *D.* 2 Oct. 63.

[2] *Tanner, Pepys and the Navy* 27–38; *Tedder* 4, 40–1; *Calendar of Treasury Books* I, Introduction.

3 *D.* 31 Aug.; 30 Sept. 61; 28 June 62; 18 Feb.; 21 March; 14 April; 23 May 63.

4 *D.* 3 Dec. 63.

5 *Hollond* 100; *Sloane MSS.* No. 3232; *D.* 8 July 63; 14 March 64; 24 Feb. 65; *C.S.P.D.* 1662/3 13, 21, 66, 87, 173–6, 269.

6 *D.* 16, 17 July; 9, 10 Sept. 63; *C.S.P.D.* 1662/3 214, 270.

Chapter XI. The Arming of Mars (*cont.*)

7 *D.* 21 Sept.; 6 Oct.; 13, 14 Nov.; 14, 15 Dec. 63; *Greenwich MS.* 76, 89; *Tanner* 6–10.

8 *D.* 23 April 63; 1, 8 Jan.; 1, 6, 17, 18, 21–3 Feb.; 1, 6 March; 8, 13–16, 27 April; 26 May; 14, 17 June; 1 Aug. 64; *Greenwich MS.* 93–4; *Rawl. MSS. A.* 174, ff. 2, 44; *Tanner* 10–14; *H.M.C. Rep.* v (*Malet* 314b); *C.S.P.D.* 1663/4 447, 464, 467, 472, 476, 498, 508, 513, 530, 537, 578, 581, 638, 653, 672, 676.

9 *D.* 2 Feb. 64.

10 *D.* 11, 23 Feb.; 16 March; 27 May; 8 Nov. 64.

11 *D.* 31 Dec. 62; 3, 10–13, 22, 25 June; 8, 12 July; 25, 27, 31 Aug.; 21, 22, 24 Sept.; 8 Oct.; 25 Nov.; 4, 9 Dec. 64; *C.S.P.D.* 1663/4 603.

12 *D.* 5, 14, 16, 18, 19, 21, 25, 27, 28, 30 July; 7 Aug.; 6, 10, 16, 26 Sept.; 19 Oct. 64; *Rawl. MSS. A.* 174, f. 89 et seq.

13 *D.* 11 July; 12, 21 Sept. 64.

14 *C.S.P.D.* 1663/4 549; *D.* 20 Jan.; 9, 23, 26 Feb.; 4, 14, 24 March; 21 April 64.

15 *D.* 12, 15, 21, 26 Jan.; 21, 22, 26 Feb.; 11 May 64.

16 *D.* 22 Aug.; 3 Sept. 63; 20 Jan.; 6 Feb.; 13, 14 March 64; *Rawl. MSS. A.* 182, f. 342.

17 *D.* 25 March; 6 April; 4, 13, 20, 25, 27, 31 May; 28 July; 22, 25 Aug. 64; 19 Jan. 65; 21 March 66; *Rawl. MSS. A.* 182, ff. 300–12, 316, 329, 340.

18 *D.* 15 July, 23 Oct. 63; 14–17, 27, 29 May; 1 June 64.

19 *Rawl. MSS. A.* 174, f. 329; *D.* 28 June; 1 July; 14, 21 Aug. 64.

20 *Feiling, British Foreign Policy* 83–138; *Tedder* 102; *Mahan* 96 et seq.; *C.J.* VIII, 548; *C.S.P.D.* 1663/4 562; *D.* 29 Jan.; 2, 9, 15 Feb.; 18, 19, 21, 23, 25 April; 12, 18, 21, 23, 26 May 64.

21 *D.* 15 Feb.; 30 April 64.

22 *D.* 15, 29 Feb.; 12, 31 March; 2, 13, 24, 27, 28, 30 April; 4, 5, 23, 28 May; 1, 17, 18 June; 3, 10 Oct. 64; *Tanner* 26–7; *C.S.P.D.* 1663/4 660.

23 *D.* 27, 30 April; 12 Aug. 64; *Rawl. MSS. A.* 174, f. 66; *C.S.P.D.* 1663/4 606, 619, 623, 638, 665, 667–8, 672.

24 *D.* 14, 20 July 64; *C.S.P.D.* 1664/5 12; *Pepysiana* 89–92.

25 *D.* 13 June 62; 31 Jan.; 1, 22 Feb.; 3, 7 March; 25 April; 30 June 64.

26 *D.* 4, 16 Jan.; 1, 8, 29 Feb.; 5 April; 20, 21, 23 July 64.

27 *D.* 21, 26, 28, 31 Oct.; 1–4, 6, 8, 9, 28 Nov. 63; 18 July; 3, 6, 11, 12, 18, 19 Sept.; 3 Oct.; 9 Dec. 64.

28 *D.* 27 Feb.; 3, 20 Oct.; 3, 8 Nov. 64.

29 *D.* 5, 10, 11, 18, 28 Jan.; 25 Feb.; 14, 27 March; 5, 17 April; 4, 14 July 64; *Francis Osborne, Advice to a Son* (6th ed.) 53.

30 *D.* 21 Feb.; 30 April; 27 June; 28 July; 1, 5, 27, 29, 31 Aug.; 2, 4, 7–9, 14 Sept.; 5 Oct. 64; *Pepysiana* 30; *Whitear* 86.

Chapter XI. The Arming of Mars (*cont.*)

31 *D.* 24, 25 April; 21, 23 June; 18 July; 19, 20, 23, 24, 29, 31 Aug.; 7 Sept. 64; *C.S.P.D.* 1664/5 59, 64.

32 *D.* 3, 5, 10, 18, 25 Oct.; 3, 4, 7–12, 14, 15, 21 Nov. 64; *Tanner* 28–30; *Greenwich MS.* 117; *C.S.P.D.* 1664/5 10, 26–30, 36–8, 42, 45–6, 48–9, 55, 59, 67, 68, 71, 83, 87, 90, 92–4, 99; *Rawl. MSS. A.* 174 passim.

CHAPTER XII. FIRST BLOOD

Main Source: *Diary*, 1 November, 1664, to 30 June, 1665

1 *D.* 4, 11, 24, 26, 28, 29 Nov.; 1–3, 8, 10, 13 Dec. 64; *C.S.P.D.* 1664/5 102–6, 108–10, 113, 116–17, 119, 121–3, 125, 127; *Chappell*, Letters VIII, IX; *Rawl. MSS. A.* 174, ff. 58 et seq.

2 *D.* 10, 17, 20 Nov.; 19, 31 Dec. 64; 4 Jan. 65.

3 *D.* 6, 7, 15, 16, 19, 20 Dec. 64; 2, 8, 9, 20, 23, 27 Jan.; 20, 21 Feb. 65; 18 April 66.

4 *Tanner* 31–2, 37–8, 43–4; *Chappell*, Letters III, IV, XII, XIX, XXV; *Rawl. MSS. A.* 174, ff. 10, 29; *Greenwich MS.* 161, 168; *H.M.C. Rep.* V (*Malet* 315); *National Review* Dec. 1928 (*Canon A. Deane*, "*Sir Anthony Deane*"); *D.* 13, 24 Feb.; 10 May 65; 19 May 66; *C.S.P.D.* 1663/4 595; 1664/5 30, 38, 87, 100, 158, 160–8, 170–4, 176, 177, 179, 181, 185, 188–92, 195–8, 200–4, 206, 209–13, 216, 221, 223–4, 232–3, 236, 237, 239–40, 245, 248, 250–2, 254–5, 257–9 et seq.

5 *D.* 10 June 63; 4, 18 Nov.; 19 Dec. 64; *Chappell*, Letters VII, XVII, XX, XXIV; *Tanner* 28–30, 38–9; *Greenwich MS.* 151; *Cat. Naval Manuscripts* I, 15 n.; *C.S.P.D.* 1664/5 68, 76.

6 *Chappell*, Letters V, XII, XVI, XVII, XXVI; *C.S.P.D.* 1664/5 passim; *Tanner* 41–2.

7 *Chappell*, Letters III, IV; *D.* 5, 16 Dec. 64; *Rawl. MSS. A.* 174, f. 58 et seq.

8 *D.* 30 Nov.; 31 Dec. 64; 9 Jan.; 6, 17 Feb.; 6, 10 April; 19 May; 4, 18 July; 5 Aug.; 13, 23 Oct.; 14, 24 Dec. 65.

9 *D.* 27 Nov. 64; 28 Jan.; 10, 16, 17, 21 March; 10, 17, 19 April; 12, 13, 28 May; 7 Aug.; 30 Sept. 65.

10 *D.* 24, 26 Sept.; 8 Oct.; 25, 28, 29 Nov.; 2, 4–6, 9, 12, 17 Dec. 64; 9, 13, 16, 31 Jan.; 1, 2, 6, 8, 16, 20 Feb.; 16 March 65; *Tanner* 31.

11 *D.* 17–20, 29, 31 March; 10, 26, 30 April; 12, 19, 22, 26 May; 4, 5, 8, 24, 26 June; 2, 7 July 65; *Routh* 34; *Rawl. MSS. A.* 174, ff. 102, 163.

Chapter XII. First Blood (*cont.*)

[12] *Rawl. MSS. A.* 174, ff. 93, 95; *Birch, History of the Royal Society* II, 13; *D.* 17 Jan.; 9 Feb.; 1, 5, 22 March; 18 April; 3 May 65.

[13] *Harris* I, 274; *Tanner* 33, 38–45; *Chappell*, Letters VIII, XVII; *D.* 22, 25 Nov. 64; 10 Feb.; 1, 7, 12 April 65; *C.S.P.D.* 1664/5 passim.

[14] *Tedder* 106–8; *Rawl. MSS. A.* 187, f. 3; *Chappell*, Letter XIX; *Greenwich MS.* 161; *C.S.P.D.* 1664/5 198, 202, 205, 209, 212, 214, 216; *D.* 15 Jan.; 24 Feb.; 3, 10 March 65.

[15] *Tedder* 113; *C.S.P.D.* 1664/5 10; *D.* 28 March 65; *Tanner* 41, 46.

[16] *Chappell*, Letters XI, XXI–XXIII; *D.* 2 Feb.; 2, 17, 25 March; 6, 17, 24, 28 April; 4, 6, 8–10, 14, 15, 18, 20 May 65; *Tanner* 39–40, 43.

[17] *Tedder* 114–15, 117; *Harris* I, 286; *Sandwich, Journal* 198; *Tanner* 43; *Rawl. MSS. A.* 174, f. 458.

[18] *D.* 20–9 May 65; *Tedder* 117–19; *Tanner* 45–6.

[19] *Tanner* 45.

[20] *Dryden, Essay of Dramatic Poesy*; *Tedder* 121–5; *Sandwich, Journal* 223–30.

[21] *D.* 3–5 June 65; *Tanner* 43.

[22] *Smith* I, 85–94; *Tedder* 121–6; *Harris* I, 298–313; *Sandwich, Journal* 223–30; *D.* 8, 9 June 65.

[23] *D.* 12 Aug. 63; *Chappell*, Letter XXVII.

CHAPTER XIII. MR GREATHEART

Main Source: *Diary*, 10 June, 1665, to 31 August, 1666

[1] *D.* 3, 8, 9, 11, 13, 18–22 July; 7 Aug. 65.

[2] *D.* 23–25, 28, 30 June; 2, 4–6, 24 July 65; *Harris* I, 320; *Carte MSS.* 75, f. 350.

3 *D.* 20, 23, 24, 26, 27, 30, 31 July; 1, 3, 4 Aug. 65; *Carte MSS.* 75, f. 327; *Smith* I, 95–100; *Howarth* 21–3.

4 *D.* 6, 8, 10–12, 15, 22, 23 Aug.; 2 Sept. 65.

5 *D.* 7 May; 14, 22, 28, 29 Aug.; 6, 8, 30 Sept.; 29 Oct. 65.

[6] *D.* 3, 12, 14, 16, 19, 22, 30, 31 Aug.; 4, 14, 20 Sept. 65; *C.S.P.D.* 1664/5 518, 526, 560; *Tanner* 49, 53; *Howarth* 24–5.

7 *Chappell*, Letter XXVIII; *Harris* I, 315, 317–19, 322–36; *Sandwich, Journal* 236–67; *Tedder* 128–40; *C.S.P.D.* 1664/5 526–8; *D.* 4–6, 14, 22, 31 July; 5, 8, 19, 23 Aug. 65.

[8] *Tedder* 140; *Harris* I, 337–40; *D.* 28, 31 Aug. 65; *Howarth* 23–4.

Chapter XIII. Mr Greatheart (*cont.*)

9 *Penn* II, 364; *Harris* I, 341; *Howarth* 24; *Chappell*, Letter XXX.

10 *D.* 14 Sept. 65; *Harris* I, 341–4; *Sandwich, Journal* 277–82; *Carte MSS.* 73, f. 247; *Rawl. MSS. A.* 468; *Smith* I, 102–4.

11 *Harris* II, 1–7; *D.* 23 Sept. 65.

12 *Harris* II, 4–6; *D.* 24 Sept.; 12 Oct. 65; *Carte MSS.* 75, ff. 361, 367.

13 *D.* 17–20, 22–5, 27–8 Sept.; 1, 2, 4, 7, 9–12, 14 Oct. 65; *Chappell*, Letters XXXII, XXXIV, XXXV; *Rawl. MSS. A.* 174, ff. 299, 305; *Smith* I, 104–8.

14 *D.* 1, 6 July; 3, 5, 30 Sept.; 7, 15, 31 Oct.; 4 Nov. 65; *C.S.P.D.* 1664/5 453, 499, 518; 1665/6 12, 13 et seq.; *Chappell*, Letters XXVIII, XXXII, XXXIII, XXXVIII; *Tanner* 73–6.

15 *C.S.P.D.* 1665/6 23 et passim; *Chappell*, Letters XXXII, XXXIII, XXXVII; *D.* 15 Oct. 65; *Tanner* 58–9.

16 *D.* 7–10 Oct. 65; *Carte MSS.* 74, f. 234; *Harris* II, 13–15; *Sandwich MSS. Letters* I, 59; *Chappell*, Letter XXXIV.

17 *Harris* II, 14–17, "*The Intelligencer*" 18 Sept. 65; *D.* 16 Oct.; 6 Nov. 65.

18 *C.J.* VIII, 615–19; *D.* 27 Sept.; 5, 16, 27, 31 Oct.; 6 Nov. 65.

19 *Harris* II, 23–32; *D.* 13, 14, 22 Oct.; 13, 29 Nov.; 4, 13, 14, 31 Dec. 65; 6 Jan. 66; *Howarth* 23; *Rawl. MSS. A.* 174, ff. 299, 301.

20 *D.* 2 July; 2, 13, 23, 30 Aug.; 3, 4, 23, 27 Oct.; 23 Nov.; 8, 11, 13, 30, 31 Dec. 65.

21 *Tedder* 113, 141–2; *D.* 22 May; 18 Sept. 65.

22 *Tanner* 52, 56; *Tedder* 113–14; *C.S.P.D.* 1664/5 541; 1665/6 55, 67.

23 *Tanner* 51–3; *C.S.P.D.* 1665/6 7; *Rawl. MSS. A.* 174, f. 231; *Naval Minutes* 250.

24 *C.S.P.D.* 1664/5 556–60; *Tedder* 147; *D.* 12 Dec. 63; 5–7 Oct. 65; *Tanner* 55; *Chappell*, Letter XXXIII.

25 *Tanner* 54–7; *Chappell*, Letter XXXIII; *D.* 7 Oct.; 8 Dec. 65.

26 *Tanner* 57; *D.* 5 Oct. 65.

27 *Chappell*, Letters XXXVI, XXXVIII; *Tanner* 68; *D.* 14, 19, 24, 27, 31 Oct.; 8 Nov. 65; *Cat. Naval MSS.* I, 153.

28 *Chappell*, Letter XXXIII; *D.* 7, 8, 15, 23, 31 Oct. 65; *Tanner* 59, 66, 70–2, 76–9.

29 *D.* 6, 21 Nov. 65; 19 Feb. 66; *Greenwich MS.* 294–303; *Tanner* 76, 78–9.

30 *C.J.* VIII, 619; *C.S.P.D.* 1665/6 129–30, 193, 197, 201–2, 213, 228, 240–1, 243–4, 294, 304, 368, 392, 412, 422, 437, 461, 476–7, 482–3; *Tanner* 70–2; *Greenwich MS.* 310; *Chappell*, Letter XL.

Chapter XIII. Mr Greatheart (*cont.*)

31 *D.* 8, 11, 25, 26, 31 Oct.; 13, 23, 26 Nov.; 1, 3, 4, 17, 18, 20 Dec. 65.

32 *Rawl. MSS. A.* 174, ff. 233, 272; *Tanner* 59–62, 68, 83–4, 86, 92; *H.M.C. Rep.* v, 295; *D.* 22 Nov.; 2, 7, 8, 11 Dec. 65; *C.S.P.D.* 1665/6 passim; *Tanner, Samuel Pepys and the Royal Navy.*

33 *D.* 29 Aug.; 12 Sept. 62; 22 Nov. 65.

34 *D.* 22 Nov.; 1, 2, 7, 11, 15, 31 Dec. 65; *Tanner* 87–8, 92–9; *Rawl. MSS. A.* 174, f. 263.

35 *D.* 1 Jan. 66; *Rawl. MSS. C.* 302, ff. 46–63; *Tanner* 93–111; *B.M. Harleian MSS.* 6287.

36 *D.* 10 Sept.; 15, 29–31 Oct.; 6, 8–10 Dec. 65; 2, 3, 6 Jan.; 23 Feb. 66; *Pepysiana* 139–41; *Bridge* 99–102.

37 *C.S.P.D.* 1665/6 passim; *D.* 2, 3, 6, 10, 14, 19, 20 Feb.; 2, 14 March 66; *Tanner* 120–2; *Rawl. MSS. A.* 195, f. 251; *Howarth* 26–7.

38 *Tanner* 118–19, 122–4.

39 *D.* 20, 28 Feb.; 9, 10 March 66.

40 *D.* 2 March; 17, 21–3 April; 6, 7, 12, 13, 21, 25, 29, 31 May 66; *Tanner* 126–30, 133–6; *Rawl. MSS. A.* 174, f. 233.

41 *D.* 24–26 Feb.; 3 June 66; *Harris* II, 22–4; *Carte MSS.* 34, f. 488; *Penn* II, 516.

42 *Tedder* 151 et seq.; *B.M. Add. MSS.* 32,094, ff. 196–204; *Admiralty Library MS.* 24 (Duke of York's Letter 30 May 1666); *C.S.P.D.* 1665/6 XIX–XXIV; *Duke of Albemarle's Account* (from a MS. in possession of S. Bruce Ingram, Esq.); *Rawl. MSS. A.* 174, f. 209; *Tanner* 130–1; *D.* 31 May–7 June 66.

43 *D.* 7–11, 16, 18, 19, 24, 26, 27 June; 1, 13, 23 July 66; *C.S.P.D.* 1665/6 437, 440, 444 et seq.; *Chappell*, Letters XLV, XLVI, XLVII, XLVIII; *Tanner* 137; *Rawl. MSS. A.* 174, f. 222.

44 *Chappell*, Letter XLVI; *C.S.P.D.* 1665/6 452–4, 458, 462, 468–9; *Rawl. MSS. A.* 195, ff. 287–9; *D.* 30 June; 1, 2, 6, 13 July 66.

45 *D.* 19, 23–31 July; 14, 15 Aug. 66; *Rawl. MSS. A.* 195, f. 202; *C.S.P.D.* 1666/7 21, 27; *Tedder* 176; *Pepysiana* 281.

46 *D.* 24, 26, 27–30 July 66; *Tanner* 141; *Chappell*, Letter XLIX; *C.S.P.D.* 1666/7 71; *Tedder* 177; *Rawl. MSS. A.* 174, ff. 207, 211–13; 187, f. 336.

47 *D.* 31 Dec. 65; 25 Jan.; 1 Feb.; 5, 30 March; 2, 3 April; 12 May; 15 June; 23, 31 July; 12, 18, 20, 22, 27 Aug. 66; *Rawl. MSS. A.* 174, f. 436.

CHAPTER XIV. THE MASTER CHRONICLER

Main Sources: *Diary*, 1–6 September, 1666
W. G. Bell, The Great Fire of London (1920)

1 *Greenwich MS.* 406.
2 *D.* 5 Sept. 66; *Evelyn, Diary* 7 Sept. 66.
3 *D.* 6, 8, 10, 11, 13, 15, 19, 20, 21, 22, 23, 27, 28 Sept. 66.
4 *D.* 12, 17 Sept. 66; 13 Feb. 67; *Evelyn, Diary* 7 Sept. 66; *Bell, Great Fire* 178–80.
5 *D.* 7, 8, 15, 27 Sept. 66; 28 Feb. 67; *Bell, Great Fire* 211.

CHAPTER XV. ENGLAND UNARMS

Main Source: *Diary*, 8 September, 1666, to 12 June, 1667

1 *Tedder* 177–81; *D.* 8 Sept. 66; *C.S.P.D.* 1666/7 89–93.
2 *D.* 3, 8, 16, 21 Aug. 66.
3 *C.S.P.D.* 1666/7 passim; *Tanner* 144; *D.* 8, 14, 19, 20, 28, 29, 31 Oct.; 5, 20 Nov. 66.
4 *Tanner* 146–54; *D.* 20 Oct.; 18–20, 28 Nov. 66; 4, 11 Jan. 67.
5 *D.* 6 Aug.; 25, 27 Oct.; 13 Nov. 66; 2, 15, 22, 24 Jan.; 12 Feb.; 7 March 67; *Pepysiana* 147; *Bridge* 102–6.
6 *D.* 20, 21 Dec. 65; 15 June; 11, 12 July; 8 Aug.; 12, 21, 23, 26, 28 Oct.; 1, 5, 7, 20, 22, 26, 30 Nov.; 3, 14, 18, 21 Dec. 66; 2, 10, 15 Jan.; 1, 16, 18 Feb.; 6, 8, 20, 24, 31 March; 9 April; 23, 31 May; 23 June 67.
7 *D.* 2, 21 Dec. 66; 29 Jan.; 23 May 67.
8 "*Lancet*", 1 June 1895 (Sir D'Arcy Power, Medical History of Mr and Mrs Samuel Pepys); *Pepysiana* 48–50; *Pepys Club Transactions*, Vol. 1; *D.* 5, 10, 14, 23 Oct.; 11 Nov.; 2, 18, 23 Dec. 66; 20 Jan.; 6 Feb. 67.
9 *D.* 6, 13, 27 Jan.; 5, 6, 11 Feb.; 3, 8, 20, 31 March; 9 April; 20 May; 3 July; 14, 31 Oct. 67.
10 *D.* 19–21 March 64; 22 Jan. 65; 21 Feb.; 28 April; 17 June; 8, 9, 22, 27 Sept.; 6, 7, 16, 19, 29 Oct. 66; 7 Feb.; 18, 20, 21, 25, 27 March; 6 April; 10 Oct. 67.
11 *D.* 12 April 64; 14, 25 Jan.; 11, 16, 18 Feb.; 15, 19, 23, 24, 31 March; 2, 4–6, 19 April; 21 May; 8, 13, 17, 20, 23 June; 16 July; 2 Aug.; 20 Sept.; 11, 15 Oct.; 21, 29 Nov.; 12 Dec. 66; 16 Jan.; 1, 2, 3, 18, 24, 26–29 March; 4, 10, 12, 13 April; 16, 23, 26 May; 28 Oct. 67.

Chapter XV. England Unarms (*cont.*)

12 *D.* 30 Oct. 66; 1, 6, 22 March; 11, 12 May 67.

13 *C.S.P.D.* 1666/7 passim; *Chappell*, Letter LI; *D.* 4, 5 April; 25 May; 6 June; 7, 8, 10 Nov.; 13, 15, 16 Dec. 66; 1, 15 Jan.; 5 Feb. 67.

14 *D.* 31 Oct. 66; 26, 31 Jan.; 4, 28 Feb.; *Rawl. MSS. A.* 174, f. 411; *A.* 185, ff. 17–23.

15 *D.* 13, 14, 23, 24, 28 Feb.; 6 March 67; *Tanner* 155–6, 158–61.

16 *Tanner* 193; *Chappell*, Letter L; *Davey*, Items 2898, 2899a; *C.S.P.D.* 1666/7 117, 288, 308, 316, 339, 373, 548; 1667/8 24; *Rawl. MSS. A.* 174, ff. 291–7; *D.* 26 Sept.; 3, 9, 23 Oct.; 8 Nov.; 22, 29 Dec. 66; 1, 7, 16, 21 Jan.; 7, 14, 21, 26, 27 March; 10 April; 22 May; 31 July; 14 Aug.; 17, 18 Sept.; 6, 12–14, 27 Oct. 67.

17 *Victoria History of Kent*, Vol. II (M. Oppenheim, Maritime History) 325; *Tedder* 181–2; *C.S.P.D.* 1666/7 255, 267; *Tanner* 169–73; *Admiralty Library MSS.* 24 (Duke of York's Letters); *D.* 12 March 67.

18 *D.* 16, 20, 28 May; 4 June 67; *Tanner* 173–4.

19 *D.* 21, 22 May; 1, 2, 6 June 67.

20 *Victoria History of Kent* II, 326–7; *D.* 3, 8–12 June 67; *Rawl. MSS. A.* 195, ff. 118, 128.

CHAPTER XVI. AFTERMATH

Main Source: *Diary*, 12 June, 1667, to 12 March, 1668

1 *C.S.P.D.* 1667 passim; *D.* 12–14, 19 June 67.

2 *D.* 19, 25–27 June 67.

3 *Tedder* 187–90; *Victoria History of Kent* II, 328–9; *D.* 21, 23, 26, 27, 29 June; 2, 5, 6, 9, 12, 13, 19, 24, 27, 29 July; 24 Aug. 67.

4 *D.* 7, 21 July; 12–17, 19, 20, 22, 28 Aug.; 25 Sept. 67.

5 *D.* 14 July 67.

6 *D.* 16–18, 20, 22, 26 June; 3, 6 July; 18 Aug.; 1, 3, 6, 17, 30 Dec. 67.

7 *D.* 24 June; 12 July; 2 Aug.; 23 Dec. 67.

8 *Pepysiana* 31; *D.* 24, 27–30 Sept.; 3, 12, 15 Oct.; 7, 22 Dec. 67; 11, 26 Jan.; 10 Feb.; 16, 31 March; 1 April 68.

9 *Tanner* 178–9; *D.* 28, 29 July; 5, 12, 20, 21 Aug.; 23 Oct. 67.

10 *C.J.* IX, Oct. 1667; *D.* 14, 20, 21, 23 Oct. 67.

11 *D.* 25 Oct. 66; 13–16 Feb.; 3, 7, 12–14 March; 15 May; 14, 15, 17, 23 Aug.; 22, 27–30 Oct.; 9, 13, 19, 20, 23, 24, 30 Nov. 67; *Penn* II, 507; *C.S.P.D.* 1666/7 340, 426; 1667/8 9; *Tanner* 142, 184–5; *Chappell*, Letter LI; *Rawl. MSS. A.* 191, ff. 229, 231, 233, 237, 242, 245.

Chapter XVI. Aftermath (*cont.*)

12 *Tanner* 184–5; *D.* 21–3, 25 Oct.; 3, 8, 9, 19 Dec. 67; 5, 31 Jan. 68.

13 *D.* 28 June; 1, 9, 21 July; 2, 3, 10 Sept.; 3, 4, 5, 12, 17 Oct.; 13, 18, 23 Dec. 67; 14, 16 March 68.

14 *D.* 10, 11, 31 Oct.; 1, 26, 27 Nov.; 15 Dec. 67; *Tanner* 182–3, 191.

15 *Greenwich MS.* 526; *C.S.P.D.* 1667/8 211, 214–15, 253; *C.J.* IX; *D.* 3, 5, 11, 12, 14, 18, 19, 21–3, 29 Feb. 68.

16 *D.* 5 March 68; *Rawl. MSS. A.* 191, ff. 182–93, 229, 233.

17 *D.* 6, 8–13 March 68.

CHAPTER XVII. THE HEEL OF ACHILLES

Main Source: *Diary*, 13 March to 25 October, 1668

1 *C.J.* IX; *Rawl. MSS. A.* 174, ff. 299, 301; *Smith* I, 104–8; *D.* 3, 12, 14–16, 20–2, 27, 29, 31 April; 9 May 68.

2 *D.* 9, 13, 14, 18 Dec. 67; 8, 10, 17, 24, 27 May 68; *Rawl. MSS. A.* 174, ff. 430, 432.

3 *D.* 1, 22, 25 Sept.; 4, 14, 17, 18, 29 Oct. 67; 27 Feb.; 18, 20, 23, 27–9 March; 4, 10, 16, 24 April 68; *Bridge* 38 et seq.

4 *D.* 1–3, 7, 8, 13–15, 17, 18, 21, 23–5, 28–30 April; 1–7, 9, 11, 12, 14–16, 18, 20–2, 30 May; 1, 2 June; 27 July 68.

5 *C.S.P.D.* 1667/8 179; *Whitear* 23, 44, 77–8; *D.* 17 June; 12 Dec. 66; 16 Jan.; 12 June; 10 Oct.; 19 Nov.; 21 Dec. 67; 5, 9–11, 21, 24, 30 Jan.; 24 May 68; *Rawl. MSS. A.* 191, f. 227.

6 *D.* 20, 23, 29–30 June; 3, 5, 11–13, 21, 23, 28, 29, 31 July; 1, 2, 5, 11, 12, 21, 23 Aug.; 24 Oct. 68; *Greenwich MS.* 535; *Howarth* 33–4; *Philosophical Transactions* (*Hutton's Abridgement*) I, 266; *Pepysiana* 49–50; *British Journal of Physiological Optics* Vol. II (W. B. Barker, The Blindness of Samuel Pepys); *Sir D'Arcy Power, An Address on why Samuel Pepys discontinued his Diary.*

7 *Rawl. MSS. A.* 195, f. 64; *D.* 19 May; 1, 4, 7, 9, 14, 16, 17, 22–4 July; 12, 14, 16–25, 28–30 Aug.; 8, 11, 13, 21 Sept. 68; *Harleian MSS.* 6003; *Cat. Naval MSS.* I, 28–33; *Pepysian MSS.* 2242, 2867 (Naval Precedents 484–509).

8 *D.* 2, 3, 7, 9, 10, 21, 24–8 Sept. 68; *C.S.P.D.* 1667/8 604.

9 *D.* 27, 28 Sept. 68; *Howarth* 33–4; *Rawl. MSS. A.* 174, f. 339.

10 *D.* 1, 15–17, 20, 22, 26 Sept. 68.

11 *D.* 18 Aug.; 15, 29 Sept.; 11, 23 Oct. 68; *Harris* II, 161; *Tanner* 195.

12 *D.* 6, 10 July; 23 Aug.; 13, 15, 16, 19–25 Oct. 68.

CHAPTER XVIII. ATONEMENT

Main Source: *Diary*, 25 October, 1668, to 31 May, 1669

1 *D.* 25–31 Oct.; 1–10 Nov. 68.
2 *D.* 11–21 Nov. 68.
3 *D.* 1–5, 12, 13, 20, 25, 28, 30 Nov. 68.
4 *D.* 4, 6, 15, 23 Dec. 68; *Tanner* 199–202.
5 *D.* 8, 10–18, 23 Dec. 68; *Tanner* 202–3.
6 *D.* 5, 6, 9, 18, 31 Dec. 68.
7 *D.* 21 April; 8, 11 May; 4, 25 June; 14 July 67; 28 Jan.; 31 July; 20, 23, 24, 30 Oct.; 1, 2, 5, 25, 28–30 Nov.; 3, 4, 11, 12, 23, 30 Dec. 68; 6 Feb.; 10 May 69.
8 3, 6, 9, 12, 17, 18, 21, 23, 29, 31 Jan. 69.
9 *D.* 4 Jan. 69; *Tanner* 204–5, 207–19.
10 *D.* 24, 26 Jan.; 16 Feb. 69; *C.S.P.D.* 1668/9 passim; *Tanner* 220–4.
11 *D.* 8, 10, 12–17, 19 Feb.; 16, 19, 20, 30–1 March; 5, 8, 20 April 69.
12 *D.N.B.*; *C.S.P.D.* 1668/9 222; *D.* 4–7, 9, 13, 16, 20–2, 31 March 69.
13 *Pepysiana* 76–7; *D.* 7, 13, 14, 16, 19, 23–7 March 69.
14 *D.N.B.*; *Routh* 346, 349; *D.* 22 Sept. 67; 31 March; 5, 12, 16, 23, 24 April 69.
15 *D.* 9, 15, 19 April 69.
16 *D.* 14, 28 March; 2, 11, 17, 24, 30 April; 6, 8, 12 May 69; *Sir D'Arcy Power, An Address on why Samuel Pepys discontinued his Diary.*
17 *D.* 14 Dec. 68; 1 March; 1, 7–10, 12, 14–16, 19, 24 May 69; *Tanner* 237–9.

EPILOGUE

1 *D.* 5, 6, 8, 26 Oct. 64; 24 May 69; *C.S.P.D.* 1664/5 137; *H.M.C. Rep.* VIII (*House of Lords* 133); *Tanner* 253–6.
2 *Tanner* 236, 239–41.
3 *Tanner* 243–7, 249, 252, 257–8, 260–1; *Howarth* 38.
4 *Tanner* 245; *Rawl. MSS. A.* 174, f. 227.
5 *C.S.P.D.* 1668/9 412, 413, 418, 427, 429, 454, 462; *Tanner* 250–1, 253–6; *Sandwich MSS.* Appendix f. 53 (28 July 1669); *Rawl. MSS. A.* 174, f. 423; *Howarth* 35–6.
6 *Tanner, Private Correspondence of Samuel Pepys* II, 242; *Howarth* 35–7; *Rawl. MSS. A.* 174, ff. 331, 333, 335, 338, 339, 341, 343.
7 *C.S.P.D.* 1668/9 555, 558; *Howarth* 37; *Rawl. MSS. A.* 174, ff. 331, 333; Monument in St Olave's Church.

INDEX